PORTUGAL

THE ROUGH GUIDE

KU-260-073

THE ROUGH GUIDES

OTHER AVAILABLE ROUGH GUIDES
**SPAIN, PARIS, MEXICO, PERU, GREECE,
CHINA, BRITTANY & NORMANDY, SCANDINAVIA,
ITALY, WEST GERMANY, HUNGARY, CALIFORNIA,
NEW YORK, KENYA, TUNISIA, ISRAEL, CRETE,
EASTERN EUROPE, YUGOSLAVIA, SICILY, FRANCE,
MOROCCO, AMSTERDAM, VENICE and IRELAND**
FORTHCOMING TITLES INCLUDE
**BRAZIL, GUATEMALA & BELIZE, HOLLAND,
BELGIUM & LUXEMBOURG, PROVENCE and THE PYRENEES**

ROUGH GUIDE CREDITS

Series Editor: Mark Ellingham
Editorial: Martin Dunford, John Fisher, Jack Holland, Jonathan Buckley,
  Greg Ward, Richard Trillo, Jules Brown
Production: Susanne Hillen, Kate Berens, Andy Hilliard, Gail Jammy
Typesetting: Greg Ward

Special thanks on this edition are due to Rob Jones, Greg Ward and Jonathan Buckley for their editing and, on the production front, to Greg Ward, Susanne Hillen and Andy Hilliard. For their contributions toward the research in Portugal, particular thanks to Luís, Fernanda, and Jorge; and to Felipa Pedrosa, Maria Ernestina Pires de Silva, Zé-Carlos and Maria-José Menezes, Zé-Manuel and Joana Pedrosa, Maria dos Prazeres, Iréna and Dr. Francisco, Jean and John Martin, Zé-Victor, Santos, Jules Brown, Greg Ward, Zita and Pensão Estoril, Charlie Millar, Gail Jammy and David Evans. Thanks also to all those who have contributed to appeals to Help us Update from past editions: their roll of honour appears at the back of this book, on p.324.

Illustrations: Parts One and Three by Ed Briant; *Basics* by Andrew Harris; *Contexts* by Helen Manning.
This 1990 edition published by Harrap-Columbus,
26 Market Square, Bromley, Kent BR1 1NA.
Reprinted in 1991.

Originally published in 1983 by Routledge & Kegan Paul.

Typeset in Linotron Univers and Century Old Style to an original design by Andrew Oliver.
Printed in the United Kingdom by Cox & Wyman Ltd (Reading)

336p
Includes index.

British Library Cataloguing in Publication Data

The Rough Guide to Portugal – 4th ed. (The Rough Guides).
Ellingham, Mark

1. Portugal – Visitors' guides.
I Title. II. Fisher, John, 1958- . III. Kenyon, Graham. IV. Martin, Alice. Rough Guide to Portugal.
914.69'0444

ISBN 0-7471-0253-8

PORTUGAL
THE ROUGH GUIDE

WRITTEN AND RESEARCHED BY

**MARK ELLINGHAM, JOHN FISHER,
GRAHAM KENYON** and **ALICE MARTIN**

with additional accounts by
Luís Miguel da Costa, Fernanda Valente,
Jorge Bochechas, Phil Lee, Dave Robson
and Manuel Dominguez.

HARRAP-COLUMBUS ■ LONDON

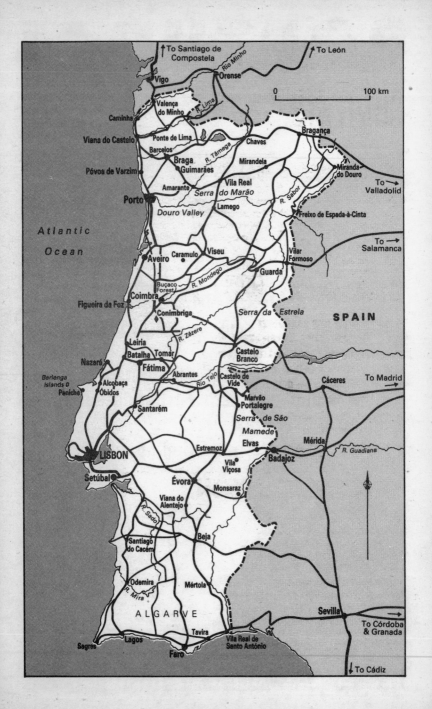

CONTENTS

Introduction vi

INTRODUCTION

P ortugal is an astonishingly beautiful country. Especially if you've come from the arid plains of central Spain, the rivers, forests and lush valleys are so total a contrast that it's hard, at first, to take in. Suddenly the landscape is infinitely softer and greener, with flowers and trees everywhere. Life also seems easier-paced, and the people more courteous; the Portuguese themselves talk of their nation as a land of *brandos costumes* – gentle ways.

For so small a country, Portugal has tremendous variety both in landscape and in its ways of life and traditions. Along the coast around Lisbon, and on the now well-developed Algarve in the south, there are highly sophisticated resorts, while Lisbon itself, in its idiosyncratic, rather old-fashioned way, has enough diversions to please most city devotees. But in its rural areas – the southern Alentejo, the mountainous Beiras, or northern Trás-os-Montes – this is still a conspicuously underdeveloped country, 'the Third World of Europe' as its inhabitants put it. Tourism is changing many areas but for anyone wanting to get off the beaten track, there are limitless opportunities to experience smaller towns and countryside areas that have changed little in the past century.

In terms of population, and of customs, differences between the **north and south** are particularly striking. Above a roughly sketched line, more or less corresponding with the course of the river Tagus, the people are of predominantly Celtic and Germanic stock. It was here, at Guimarães, that the 'Lusitanian' nation was born, in the wake of the Christian reconquest from the North African Moors. South of the Tagus, where the Moorish, and Roman, civilisations were most established, people tend to be darker-skinned (*moreno*) and of a perhaps more 'Mediterranean' mentality (though the Portuguese coastline is, in fact, entirely Atlantic). **Agriculture** reflects this divide as well, with oranges, figs and cork in the south, maize and potatoes in the north – where the system of farming dates back to pre-Christian days, amid a mass of tiny plots divided and subdivided over the generations.

More recent events are woven into the pattern. The 1974 **revolution** came from the south – an area of vast estates, rich landowners and a dependent workforce – while the conservative backlash of the 1980s came from the north, with its powerful religious authorities and individual smallholders wary of change. Two-thirds of the support for the PCP, the largest Communist party outside of the Eastern Bloc, derives from the Alentejo. More profoundly even than the Revolution, **emigration** has altered attitudes and the appearance of the countryside. After Lisbon the largest Portuguese community is in Paris, and there are migrant workers spread throughout France and Germany. Returning, these emigrants have brought in modern ideas and challenged many traditional rural values.

The greatest of all Portuguese influences, however, is **the sea**. The Atlantic seems to dominate the land not only physically, producing the consistently temperate climate, but mentally and historically. The Portuguese are very conscious of themselves as a seafaring race; mariners like Vasco da Gama led the way in the discovery of the New World, and until little over a decade ago Portugal remained a colonial power, albeit by then in deep crisis. On the positive side, the colonies have lent African and South American strands to the country's culture: in the distinctive music of *fado*, blues-like songs heard in Lisbon and Coimbra, for example, or in the Moorish-influenced *Manuelino*, Baroque 'Discovery' architecture that abounds in coastal towns like Belém and Viana do Castelo.

This 'glorious' history has also led to the peculiarly national characteristic of *saudade*: a slightly resigned, nostalgic air, and a feeling that the past will always overshadow the possibilities of the future. The 48 years of isolation under the dictator Salazar, which ended with the 1974 revolution and return to democracy, reinforced such feelings, as the ruling elite spurned 'contamination' by the rest of Europe. Only now, with Portugal's entry into the European Community, are things beginning to change. A belated industrial revolution is finally underway, and the population becoming increasingly geared toward Lisbon and the cities. For those who remain in the countryside, however, life remains disarmingly traditional, and social mores stuck in the past. Women wear black if husbands are absent – as many are, working in France, or Germany, or at sea.

Where To Go and When

Since Portugal is so compact, it's easy to take in something of each of its elements – northern river valleys, southern coast, and mountains – even on a brief visit. Distances are small and easily covered, whether you rent a car or make your own way by public transport.

Scenically, the most interesting parts of the country are in the north: the **Minho**, green, damp, and often startling in its rural customs; the sensational gorge and valley of the **Douro**, followed along its course by the railway, off which antiquated branch lines veer into remote **Trás-os-Montes**; and the wild, mountainous *serras* of **Beira Alta**. For contemporary interest, spend at least some time in both **Lisbon** and **Porto**, the only two cities of real size. And if it's monuments you're after, the whole centre of the country – above all **Coimbra**, **Évora**, and the **Estremadura** – retains a faded grandeur dating from the Age of the Discoveries in the sixteenth century and from the later gold and diamond wealth of colonial Brazil.

The **coast** is virtually continuous beach – some eight hundred kilometres of it – and only on the **Algarve** (and there, only the western half) and a few pockets around Lisbon and Porto has there been more than casual tourist development. Elsewhere, resorts remain small-scale and thoroughly Portuguese, with great stretches of deserted sands between them. Perhaps the loveliest are along the northern **Costa Verde**, around Viana do Castelo, or for isolation the wild beaches of **southern Alentejo**. It must be added, however, that this *is* the Atlantic and it can often be windswept and exposed. If you like your swimming warm, the only area where the water approaches

Mediterranean temperatures is the **eastern Algarve** where a series of sand-bank islands, the still unexploited *ilhas*, protect the shore.

Apart from swimming, **when you go** seems to matter little. The entire country is warm from **April to October**, if slightly erratically so in the rainy north, while the Algarve is amazingly mild throughout the year – it hardly has a winter. (The **Serra de Estrêla**, in contrast, does; with snow for skiers and plenty of chilly winds.) Escaping the crowds is little problem outside the Algarve and Lisbon, and anywhere else you should find rooms without difficulty throughout the year. Even in the Algarve, and even in season (when private houses rent out rooms), there is usually something vacant.

Average Daytime Temperatures (°F)						
	JAN.	MAR.	MAY	JULY	SEPT.	NOV.
LISBON	53	57	63	70	70	59
PORTO (Costa Verde)	49	53	59	67	65	53
COIMBRA (Costa da Prata)	50	56	60	67	67	56
FARO (Algarve)	54	57	65	75	72	60

PART ONE

THE
BASICS

I am very happy here, because I loves oranges, and talks bad Latin to the Monks, who understand it as it is like their own. And I goes into society (with my pocket pistols) and I swims in the Tagus all across at once, and I rides on an ass or a mule and swears Portuguese, and I have got a diarrhoea, and bites from the mosquitoes. But what of that? Comfort must not be expected by folks that go a-pleasuring.

— Byron in Portugal, July 1809.

GETTING THERE

You need a full couple of days to go overland from Britain to Portugal, so for most visitors flying is the most viable option. There are direct flights year-round from London to Lisbon, Porto and Faro (in the Algarve), and from Manchester to Lisbon (with connections to Porto and Faro. In summer, numerous package companies sell charter flights from a variety of British regional airports – most of them to Faro. And you can also, of course, approach Portugal overland from Spain, to which there are many more (and often cheaper) charter deals.

Road or rail alternatives are worth considering if you plan to visit Portugal as part of an extended trip through Europe. There is at present no direct ferry from Britain to Portugal (a line between Plymouth and Viana do Castelo is rumoured for the future), but drivers can knock off much of the journey by travelling from Plymouth to Santander in northern Spain.

Irish travellers will generally need to route via Britain. *TAP*, the Portuguese national airline, have connecting flights from Dublin to Manchester, and have an arrangement with *British Airways* for add-on flights from Belfast.

There are no direct flights to Portugal from Australia or New Zealand. As usual with European destinations, it is almost always cheapest to transit via London, picking up flights or rail tickets on from there.

FLIGHTS

Most of the cheaper flights to Portugal are **charter** deals, sold either with a package holiday or, through 'consolidators', as a flight-only option. They have fixed and unchangeable outward and return dates, and a maximum stay of one month. For longer stays or more flexibility, or simply if you're travelling out of season (when few charters are available), you'll need a **scheduled** flight. As with charters, these are offered under a wide variety of fares, and are again often sold off at discount by consolidators.

CHARTERS

Travel agents throughout Britain sell **discount charter flights** to Portugal. Even the high street chains frequently promote 'flight-only' deals, or heavily discount all-inclusive holidays, when their parent companies have chartered too many airline seats. The greatest variety of flights, however, tends to be from the **London** airports to Faro; Lisbon and Porto are less on the package trail. Flying from **elsewhere in Britain**, you'll often find flights have a connection or stop in London or Manchester.

In Britain as a whole, the best **sources** of flights are the classified advertising sections in *The Sunday Times*, the Saturday travel section of *The Independent*, and local evening papers. In London, scour the back pages of *Time Out*, the *Evening Standard* and the various free magazines distributed for London-resident Australasians. Obviously the more flexible you can be on dates the better your chances of a rock-bottom deal; if you're prepared to take a 'leaving tomorrow at 2am from Luton Airport' flight, you can often pick up a real bargain. Whatever, phone around at least half a dozen agents for a range of offers. **Portuguese specialists** in London are detailed in the box overpage.

Student Deals

Student/youth charters are also sporadically available to Lisbon – and more frequently and cheaper to Madrid (trains to Lisbon) or Malaga (trains to the Algarve). The main operators are *USIT/Campus Travel*, who have offices throughout Britain and Ireland. Again, see box overpage.

SCHEDULED FLIGHTS

The advantages of scheduled flights are that they can be pre-booked well in advance and remain valid for three months – sometimes longer.

As with charters, deals on scheduled flights are available from most high street travel **agents**, as well as from a number of specialist flight and student/youth agencies (same sources of flights as for charters). And again, you will usually do well to phone around a number of outlets to compare prices.

TAP (Air Portugal) fly from London (Heathrow) to Lisbon, Porto and Faro, and from Manchester to Lisbon, with connections to Porto and Faro. **British Airways** handle all three destinations from London (Gatwick). *TAP* and *BA* work in conjunction with each other, so you can book a flight to Portugal from any airline in Britain, with a low-cost add-on fare for the routing through London or Manchester. There are, as ever, a bewildering variety of fare structures, ranging from around £99 to £400 return, depending on class, ticket status and season. For a summer flight to any of the three Portuguese airports, you should reckon on £120–160 return from London; a little more from elsewhere.

FLIGHTS FROM IRELAND

Comments above on charters and scheduled flights apply equally to Ireland as a starting point. Costs, however, are generally higher. Reckon on £140–180 for a return flight in summer.

The cheaper flights, including most of the youth/student offers, are often via London or Manchester, with a tag-on fare from Ireland for the connection. As ever, it's worth spending the time to shop around.

The two most useful agencies are *USIT* and *Joe Walsh Tours* (see box below for addresses).

FLIGHTS FROM AUSTRALIA AND NEW ZEALAND

You're unlikely to find any special deals from Australia or New Zealand direct to Portugal; it makes more sense to fly another European route and then make your own arrangements. **STA Travel**, who have offices throughout Australia and New Zealand, are usually a good bet for discount (and youth/student) flights to London, and they can arrange connections on to Portugal if you want.

Their head office addresses are:

Australia

STA , 1a Lee St, Sydney 2000 (☎212/1255).

New Zealand

STA, 10 O'Connel St, Auckland (☎399/191).

TRAINS

Travelling to Portugal by train can be a very good deal if you're under 26 and if you plan to visit other countries en route. If not, then a return flight is likely to work out a fair bit cheaper, as well as a lot more relaxing.

AGENCIES AND AIRLINES

AIRLINES

TAP, 19 Regent St, London SW1 (☎01/839-1031); or Room 25, level 7, Manchester International Airport (☎061/499-2161).

British Airways, 75 Regent St, London W1 (☎01/897-4000).

DISCOUNT FLIGHT AGENCIES

Abreu, 109 Westbourne Grove, London W2, (☎01/229-9905/6/7).

Elair, 1 Wardour Street, London W1 (☎01/734-4070).

Goldair, 321-322 Linen Hall, 162-168 Regent St, London W1 (☎01/287-1003). Specialist in connecting Athens to Turkey/Israel/Egypt.

Springways Travel, 71 Oxford St, London W1 (☎01/734-0393).

STUDENT/YOUTH AGENCIES

CampusTravel, 52 Grosvenor Gdns, London SW1 (☎01/730-3402). London branch of USIT.

STA Travel, 86 Old Brompton Rd, London SW7 (☎01/937-9921).

Both STA and USIT (useful for non-students, too) have agencies throughout Britain.

IRELAND

USIT, 7 Angelsea St, Dublin (☎0001/778-117). Student/youth specialists with good charter deals.

Joe Walsh Tours, 8-11 Lower Baggot St, Dublin (☎0001/789-555). General budget fares agent.

Aer Lingus, 59 Dawson St, Dublin (☎0001/795-030).

YOUTH DEALS

The cheapest return train ticket to Portugal from London is an **InterRail** pass (£145 from British Rail or any travel agent). This is available to anyone resident in Europe and is valid for a month's free travel on all European railways. The only extra you pay is half the price of travel in the country of issue (and, coming from Britain, on the Channel ferries). If you plan to cross over to Morocco from Spain the pass will also secure reduced rate tickets on certain ferry crossings.

In Portugal itself you can get a fair amount of travel from the pass, as the railway network covers most of the country and works pretty well.

An alternative, slightly cheaper, though without the European-wide flexibility is a *Eurotrain* or "*BIJ*" ticket (again available to anyone under 26) from Britain to any Portuguese destination. This allows unlimited stopovers on the pre-specified route, and you can stay for longer; *BIJ* tickets have two months' validity, or can be purchased as one-ways. The price you pay also includes all ferry crossings en route.

Details and tickets are available from *USIT/ Eurotrain* and *Transalpino* (see box below), or any student/youth agency.

REGULAR TICKETS

The *Eurotrain* tickets represent a saving of around 30 percent on the cost of a standard rail ticket. If you're over 26 and determined to travel by train, you'll pay around £250 return (£130 one way) from London to Lisbon. Even in peak season, it would be hard to pay more than this for a scheduled flight.

Details from *British Rail*, see below.

ROUTES

There are two **main routes** into Portugal:

● **From Paris** via Irun–San Sebastian, Vilar Fomoso, Guarda and Pampilhosa to Porto or to Coimbra and Lisbon.

● **From Madrid** via Cáceres, Marvao-Beira, Abrantes and Entroncamento to Lisbon or to Coimbra and Porto.

For other crossings see our rail map (p.11) and the "Travel Details" at the end of each section.

(p.11)

COACHES

Supabus, part of the *National Bus Company*, and *Eurolines* operate twice-weekly services from London to Lisbon (via Coimbra) and to the Algarve. Fares are from about £65 one-way, £110 return.

These currently leave Victoria Coach Station at 9pm on Saturday and Tuesday (for Lisbon), the same time on Wednesday and Sunday for the Algarve: 44 hours to Lisbon, 46 to Faro. You have to change in Paris from the London terminus at Place Stalingrad to the southbound one at Porte de Charenton – there should be a transfer bus, but it's an easy enough journey on the metro (Line 4: *Direction Creteil*).

Tickets are available in Britain from any *National Bus* or *Eurolines* agent, or from Victoria Coach Station: ☎01/730-3453 for details.

Alternatively there are coaches six days a week (not Monday) from Paris to Lisbon, and very frequent services to most other towns in Portugal. **Coming back**, providing you've booked in advance, you can join these coaches at any stage, and it's easy enough to pick up a coach for the last leg back from Paris.

Return bookings can be made in Portugal at *Intercentro* in Lisbon (Avda. Casal Ribeiro 18), *Internorte* in Porto (Praça da Galiza 96), and elsewhere at larger travel agencies and *Rodoviária Nacional* terminals.

BY CAR

There's been talk for a while of a direct ferry service starting up from England to Viana do Castelo, which at present is a cargo route. Failing that, it remains a good three day's driving from Britain to Portugal, and only really wothwhile if you intend to take it in fairly relaxed stages through Spain and France.

Your route obviously depends on what you want to see along the way, but its quickest to take the **coast road** through France via Nantes and Bordeaux, entering Spain at Irun. This can be followed from the standard channel ports or, further west, off the **ferries** from Portsmouth–Cherbourg (4hr 30min; *P&O*), Poole–Cherbourg

(4hr.: *Brittany Ferries*),Weymouth–Cherbourg (4hr.; March–Oct only; *Sealink*), Portsmouth–Caen (5hr. 45min.; *Brittany Ferries*), Portsmouth–St Malo (9hr.; *Brittany Ferries*) or Plymouth–Roscoff (6hr.; *Brittany Ferries*).

Ferry costs vary enormously and depend on the size of car, number of passengers and, especially, the season – from October to March there are very good deals on all the longer crossings. Full details can be obtained from travel agents or from *Sealink* (☎01/828-4142), *P&O* (☎01/734-4431) and *Brittany Ferries* (☎0752/21321).

THE SANTANDER FERRY

You can cut out a lot of driving by taking the ferry from **Plymouth to Santander** in northern Spain. The journey takes 24 hours and the boat runs twice weekly for most of the year (once a week in January, and with a 3-week gap around Christmas) carrying cars and passengers. Seat prices for a one-way trip range from around £60 according to the season, cars from £60–130. Details and tickets, again, from most agents or direct from *Brittany Ferries*, Plymouth (☎0752/21321).

Easy too, but very expensive, is the *Motorail Service* from Boulogne–Biarritz – details from Victoria Station (☎01/834-2345). There are also *Motorail* services across Spain.

HITCHING

If you're **hitching** the best plan is to get as far south into France as you can afford by some other means. Hitching out of the channel ports is a nightmare, as is Paris and the 100km or so around the capital. Try taking the coach as far as Tours or train to Chartres. From there it's not too far to Irun, and once in Spain local buses and trains are cheap fallbacks if necessary.

For anyone planning to spend some time in Paris en route, one possible alternative is to join *Allostop*, the French hitch-hiking association. For the princely sum of 35F they will enrol you for a single journey and put you in touch with a driver going your way (to whom you contribute petrol costs). The Paris *Allostop* office is at 84 Passage Brady (☎42 46 00 66: open Mon.–Fri.9am–1pm and 2–6pm).

Flying to Madrid may well work out cheaper than to Portugal. Connections west are routine and there are some rewarding stops en route.

TRAINS

Trains from **Madrid** (Estacion Atocha) to **Lisbon** (Estação Santa Apolónia) take between six and ten hours. The fastest route is **via Badajoz**, long held to be the 'gateway to Portugal' and a close neighbour of the star-shaped fortress town of Elvas (see the *Alentejo* chapter), the first stop the train makes in Portugal. There are other places to visit along this line, such as the lofty towns of Portalegre and Abrantes (see the *Alentejo* and *Ribatejo* chapters) making it the recommended route through the country. Departures from Madrid are at 7.40am, 2.25pm, or 6pm.

Another attractive route goes **through Valencia de Alcantara**, reaching Lisbon in nine to ten hours. Trains depart at 10.10am and 10.55pm, stopping only at the border – so you'll probably want food provisions for the trip.

Alternatively, if you're working your way around Spain first, you can cross from Old Castile at **Fuentes de Onoro** (1.22am, 3.48am, or 4.31am: 1hr., to Guarda, 6 hr. to Lisbon) or, at more sociable hours, from **Vigo** in Galicia (7.10am, 1.50pm, or 8.25pm; 3 hr. to Porto).

The journey times given allow for the difference of one hour between Spain and Portugal, but give yourself plenty of time in any case, if only to buy tickets.

BY BUS

Buses from **Madrid to Lisbon** run from the international depot, **Estacion sur de Autobuses** (calle Canarias 17; metro Palos de Moguer), a short way south of the Atocha train station.

It's a somewhat less comfortable way to travel, but the advantage of taking a bus lies in the shorter length of the journey (fewer delays than with the trains] and in the choice of times of departure. You'll have to go to the station to see what company is operating at what time – timetables are often unavailable or inaccurate – but you're sure to find something to suit your needs.

RED TAPE AND VISAS

For **longer stays** you can either get a special visa before you leave – from a Portuguese Consulate – or apply for an extension once you're in the country. These are issued by the nearest District Police headquarters or the Foreigner's Registration Service (Av. Antonio Augusto de Aguilar 18, Lisbon; ☎554047) which has branch offices – *Serviço de Estrangeiros* – in most major tourist centres. You should apply at least a week before your time runs out and be prepared to prove that you can support yourself without working (for example by keeping your bank exchange forms every time you change money).

The traditional way to get round this is simply to leave the country for a couple of days and get a new two-month period stamped in your passport. This is not strictly legal but very widely practised.

Visas or extended stay visas are available through any **Portuguese Consulate** abroad. The address in Britain is: 83 Brompton Road, London SW3 (☎01/235-6216).

British, Australian and EC nationals need only a valid passport for entry to Portugal, and can stay on an ordinary stamp for up to three months. American and Canadian citizens can stay up to two months in Portugal; New Zealanders must, for some reason, obtain a visa, allowing a three month stay.

COSTS, MONEY AND BANKS

Portuguese inflation is high – around nine percent – but it has remained stable since entry into the EC in 1986, and as a tourist, you're unlikely to feel the pinch. Costs for accommodation, transport, food and drink are all way lower than in northern Europe, and a fair bit less than in Spain. Even in the relatively upmarket Algarve you'll find prices very reasonable.

SOME BASIC COSTS

Portugal is not a big consumer society. Once you've paid for a room or a campsite, it is only really food and transport that will make dents in budgets. At the bottom line, if you use campsites and buy picnic lunches, you could get by on as little as £8 a day; staying in rooms and eating most of your meals in budget restaurants, £10–12 should be ample; and if you're travelling in a pair, £30 a day between two will deny few pleasures.

Rooms start at about £8–12 a double (£6–10 for a single) in the cheaper pensions or in private houses, rising to around £15 a double in a two- or three-star pension or one- or two-star hotel. **Campsites** are very much cheaper – £2 a night each, sometimes less.

Meals are even more of a bargain. Though prices can rise in the resorts, more or less anywhere else you should be able to get a substantial basic meal for around £3.50. **Drink** too is more than reasonable – a decent bottle of wine costs little more than £2, while a glass of the local stuff in a bar can be less than ten pence.

Transport isn't going to break the bank either. Distances are small and fares on **trains** (especially) and local **buses** are among Europe's lowest. From Porto to Lisbon or Lisbon to the Algarve – the longest single journeys you might want to take – will cost around £10 by either means. **Car hire**, if booked abroad, in conjunction with a flight, can be as low as £60 a week; on the spot in Portugal, it's often not a lot more.

To some extent all these prices will depend on where and when you're there – the cities and developed tourist areas are invariably the most expensive, and costs in the Algarve, in particular, are noticeably higher. And as always, if you're travelling alone you'll spend considerably more than you would in a group of two or more people – sharing rooms and food saves enormously.

STUDENT CARDS

It's worth getting an **International Student Identity Card (ISIC)** if you can, for free or reduced admission to many museums and sights, and occasional other discounts. Almost as good, and available to anyone under 26, is a **Federation of International Youth Travel Organisation (FIYTO)** youth card. They can be obtained from student travel specialists – see addresses under "Getting There".

MONEY

The Portuguese currency is the **escudo**, abbreviated as **$** or **esc**. The $ sign follows the amount of escudos, with divisions after it: ie 100$00 is 100esc, 20$50 is 20½ esc. The current **rate** is around 260 esc to the pound sterling.

You can buy escudos in advance at most British or overseas banks. There seems no longer to be any maximum limit on these transactions.

CARRYING MONEY

Travellers' cheques – sold at most British banks (even if you don't have an account), or from offices of *Thomas Cook* – are probably the safest and easiest way to carry money: accepted by all Portuguese banks and by exchange bureaux (*cambios*) at airports and major railway stations.

Eurocheques (order them from your bank) are widely accepted, and the cards work in many cash dispenser machines. You can also get cash advances on *Access* and *Visa* **credit cards**. These possibilities, however, often involve lengthy queues, much paperwork, and possibly a trek to find the right bank. In Lisbon, Faro and even Porto you may find a branch of your British bank (e.g. *Lloyds*, *Barclays*), to cash up to £50.

All banks charge fairly hefty **commissions** on transactions – often 500esc for each exchange – so it is worth changing a reasonable amount of money at a time. There are much lower commissions (generally 200esc) on foreign currency exchanges at *caixas* – savings banks or building societies – some of which also change cheques.

You'll find a **bank** and/or *caixa* in all but the smallest towns. Standard **opening hours** are Monday to Friday 8.30am to 3pm. In Lisbon and in some of the Algarve resorts they may open in the evening to change money, and in Lisbon some of the banks are also installing automatic exchange machines for – they take £10 and £20 notes and the rates are very fair.

INFORMATION AND MAPS

This book includes plans of all Portugal's major towns and of other places where we think you'll need one. You can pick up a wide range of free pamphlets, and some additional maps, from the Portuguese Tourist Organisation. Though some of their descriptions are best read with a pinch of salt, it is well worth calling in (or writing) for information before you set out.

MAPS

Large-scale **maps** (*planta*, *carta*, or *mapa*) of the country are best bought in Portugal (from bookshops) where they'll be cheaper and more up to

PORTUGUESE TOURIST OFFICES

ABROAD

Portuguese National Tourist Offices are to be found in most European capitals. They include:

LONDON 1–5 New Bond Street (1st floor), W1 (☎01/493-3873).

DUBLIN c/o Portuguese Embassy, Knock Sinna House, Fox Rock, Dublin 18 (☎0001/893-569).

DEN HAAG Javastraat 96, 2 (☎070/639358).

STOCKHOLM Linnegatan 2S (☎60265408).

MADRID Gran Villa 27 (1st floor), Madrid 13 (☎341/522-4408).

IN PORTUGAL

In Portugal itself you'll find a tourist office, or *Turismo*, in Lisbon's central Praça dos Restauradores and in almost every town of any size. Most are detailed in the guide and, aside from the help they can give you in finding a room, they often have local maps and leaflets that you won't find in the national offices.

Their hours are generally Monday to Saturday 9am to 6pm (sometimes later).

---

date than those you can find on sale abroad. The *Automóvel Clube de Portugal* (Avda. Rosa Araújo 49A, Lisbon) produce a very useful **roadmap**, as do the Spanish company *Plaza y Janes*.

More detailed army-produced **ordnance survey** type maps for walkers can be obtained in Lisbon at the *Servicos Cartográficos do Exécito* (Avda. Dr. Alfredo Bensaúde, Olivais Norte), or in Porto at *Porta Editora* (Rua da Fábrica). At either outlet, however, you will need to get a Portuguese national to make the purchase for you. Overseas, the London map shop *McCarta* (122 Kings Cross Road, WC1, ☎01/278-8278) usually has a few sheets in stock. Many of these maps are disastrously out of date, but they're the best you'll get.

HEALTH AND INSURANCE

As an EC country, Portugal has free reciprocal health agreements with other member states. To take advantage you'll need form E111, available, officially with two weeks' notice, from regional DHSS offices. No inoculations are required, unless you plan to continue to North Africa in which case you should have a cholera-typhoid jab and an up-to-date polio booster. Water is drinkable from the tap anywhere in Portugal, and from most freshwater sources, too. Be wary, however, of pools and streams in the south of the country.

TRAVEL INSURANCE

Reassuring as the EC health agreements may sound, some form of **travel insurance** is still all but essential. Local doctors may not be too impressed with the E111, and in many parts of Portugal public health care still lags behind much of northern Europe. With insurance you'll still have to pay, but will be able to claim back the cost of any drugs prescribed by pharmacies, providing you've kept the bills.

Your **baggage and tickets** will also be covered should they be stolen, though be sure to register any theft with the police within 24 hours. Travel insurance schemes (from around £20 a month) are sold by all travel agents: *ISIS* policies, available from most student/youth specialists, though useable by anyone, are good value. Also well worth considering is the special student/youth policy issued by *Campus Travel* (see "Getting There").

CHEMISTS AND HOSPITALS

For minor complaints people generally go to a *farmácia* (chemist), which you'll find in almost any village; in larger towns there's usually one where English is spoken. Pharmacists are highly trained and can dispense many drugs that would be available only with a prescription in Britain. **Tampons** are also available at *farmácias* (ask for them by brand name), as are most forms of contraception, including (on prescription) the pill. **Condoms** – *preservativos* – are rarely on display,

but always available; ask, and the pharmacist will set out an array on the counter, in the best formal Portuguese manner.

In the case of serious illness, you can get the address of an **English-speaking doctor** from a Consular Office or, with luck, from the local police or tourist office. There's a **British Hospital** in Lisbon at Rua Saraiva de Carvalho 49 (☎60/2020).

In **emergencies** dial ☎115 (free) for the National Ambulance Service.

GETTING AROUND

You can get almost everywhere in Portugal easily and efficiently by either train or bus. Trains are a bit cheaper, and some lines highly scenic, though train stations are often some way from the main town; buses are almost always fast and efficient, running to a central terminal. Car hire is also worth considering, for at least a part of your stay, with costs, currently, the lowest (by some way) in Europe.

TRAINS

CP, the Portuguese railway company, operate all trains. About 90 percent are designated *Regional*, stop at most stations en route, and have first- and second-class carriages. For these there are standard charges and if you're travelling on InterRail your pass will be valid. The next range up, *Intercidades*, are twice as fast and twice as expensive, and you should reserve your seat if using them. The fastest, most luxurious, and priciest of all are the *Rápidos* (known as 'Alfa'), which speed between Lisbon and Porto – sometimes with only first-class seats. Both these latter classes involve supplements for rail pass holders.

Always turn up at the station with time to spare; long queues often form at the ticket window and on certain trains, even with a rail card, you'll need to queue for seat bookings too. *CP* sells its own **rail passes** (valid on any train and in first class) for around £45 a week, £70 for a fortnight, and £95 for three weeks – only worthwhile if you plan extensive rail travel. Over 65s can get half-price travel if they buy a *Cartão Dourado* (for next to nothing), valid on most trains except suburban ones during rush hour.

Times and frequencies of journeys are given in the "Travel Details" for each chapter, and local peculiarities are also pointed out in the text. If you need more detail, complete **train timetables** are available in England from *Thomas Cook Travel Publications* in Peterborough, or from *BAS Publications* (48/50 Sheen Lane, London SW14), and in Portugal from station information desks.

BUSES

The majority of buses are run by the state-owned *Rodoviária Nacional* (*RN*) and nearly all of these will leave from a town's central terminal. On a number of routes though – particularly Lisbon–Algarve, Lisbon–Porto and along the Porto coast – other private companies run **express services**. Sometimes, as with **coaches** from Lisbon to the Algarve, they can knock hours off the standard multiple-stop bus journeys; other times, as in the Porto area (there are 63 individual bus companies in the north alone, so you can imagine what connections are like), you'll have no choice but to use them.

The most useful bus routes are detailed in the text – along with the addresses of their individual terminals and departure points.

PORTUGAL: TRAINS

To Tuy & Vigo
Monção
Valença
Caminha
Viana do Castelo
Braga
Barcelos
Guimarães
Póvoa de Varzim
Lousado
Porto
Espinho
Arco de Baúlhe
Chaves
Bragança
Mirandela
Vila Real
Amarante
Régua
Tua
Pocinho
Sernada
Vouzela
Viseu
Nelas
Vilar Formoso
Aveiro
Sta. Comba Dão
Guarda
To Salamanca & Paris
Cantanede
Pampilhosa
Coimbra
Covilhã
Figueira da Foz
Lousã
Fundão
Pombal
Leiria
Castelo Branco
Tomar
Abrantes
SPAIN
Caldas da Rainha
Entroncamento
Marvão
To Madrid
Torres Vedras
Santarém
Setil
Portalegre
Sintra
Mora
Cascais
LISBON
Vendas Novas
Estremoz
Elvas
To Sevilla
Setúbal
Évora
Vila Viçosa
Badajoz
Casa Branca
Alcaçer do Sal
Reguengos de Monsaraz
Moura
Beja

1. Tâmega Line
2. Corgo Line
3. Tua Line
4. Douro Line
5. Vouga Line

Sines
Atlantic Ocean
0   100 km
Lagos
Silves
Tunes
Tavira
Portimão
Faro
Vila Real de Sto. António
To Huelva & Sevilla

DRIVING AND CAR HIRE

Obviously you have far more freedom to visit out-of-the-way places if you've got your own car, but even if it's full you'll probably end up paying more than on public transport – petrol (*super*) prices are higher than in Britain, although diesel (*gasóleo*) is much cheaper.

To drive in the country, you'll need a **Green Card** from your insurers, and it's worth taking out a bail bond or extra cover for legal costs. Portugal has one of the highest **accident** rates in Europe, most of them happening on the infamous Lisbon–Porto and Lisbon–Algarve highways and on the Cascais coast road. Avoid these – the motorways have high tolls, in any case – and stick to the smaller roads which have potholes but less traffic.

Portuguese driving can, certainly, be crazy. No one recognises the same set of rules and you'll find people driving at night without dipping their headlights at all, or coasting down the middle of the road and never observing a right-of-way. August is especially lethal, with Portuguese emigrant workers (especially in the north) returning home in fast cars to show off to relatives.

CAR HIRE

Car-hire companies can be found in all the major towns and at the airports in Lisbon, Porto and Faro. Local firms usually charge less than the big three – *Hertz, Avis, and Eurocar* – and we've listed addresses for some of them in the Lisbon and Porto chapters; tourist offices can give details of others.

It often makes sense to **book in advance in Britain**: try *Cars Abroad* (01/287-3402) *Holiday Autos* (☎01/491-1087) *SunDrive* (☎01/734-4747), *Suncars* (☎0444/456446) or *Harkland* (☎0800/282787), or see if you can find a deal when you buy your ticket. Expect to pay £60–90 a week.

Make sure you check such important details as brakes and insurance coverage and keep receipts for damages – you may be able to get some back from the company. Officially, you must be aged 23 years or more to hire a car in Portugal.

BREAKDOWNS

If you **break down** you can get assistance from the *Automóvel Clube de Portugal* who have reciprocal arrangements with the *AA* and most other automobile clubs.

In the north, phone their Porto service at ☎02/29271 or ☎02/29272; in the south, phone Lisbon ☎01/775475 or ☎01/775402. Both operate 24 hours a day.

HITCHING

Hitching is variable. It can take hours to get out of Lisbon or Porto because there's nowhere good to stand – and quite often competition from Portuguese national servicemen. But most other towns are very small, their centres within easy reach of the main highways, and present no problems.

The Portuguese are a kind, strikingly generous people and the main difficulty – in a predominantly rural, village-orientated country – is that they tend not to be driving very far. If you have time this hardly matters.

BIKES

Bicycles are not a bad way of seeing the country, though everywhere north of Lisbon is hilly and you'll find it hard work in mountainous Beira Alta or across the burnt plains of southern Alentejo. They are generally carried free by airlines, or alternatively can be rented in Lisbon from *TIP Tours*, Avda. Costa Pinto 91A (☎01/2865150).

It's inexpensive to transport bikes on trains (about 150esc a journey), but the procedure can require some patience. You should arrive at the baggage office a good hour and a half before your train, and be prepared to pester someone into opening up in the eventuality of finding the office shut. On long-distance trains (from England for example) allow three days for the bike to arrive.

SLEEPING

In almost any Portuguese town you should be able to find a double room for around £8 to £12 a night, a single for £6 to £10. Unlike Spain, you'll very rarely find anything much cheaper than this – but then you're unlikely to have to pay much more either.

We've detailed budget places to stay in most of the destinations listed in the guide, and even in mid-season you shouldn't have much problem finding a bed. The main exceptions are Lisbon, the Algarve, and a few major resorts such as **Nazaré and Figueira da Foz** – but if you have problems in any of these the local tourist offices can usually help out.

ROOMS, PENSIONS AND HOTELS

In seaside resorts there are invariably **rooms** (*quartos* or *dormidas*) to let in private houses, in addition to pensions and hotels. These are either advertised or just hawked by women who descend on you at bus and train stations. They're slightly cheaper than pensions – especially if you haggle, as is sometimes expected – and again local tourist offices have full lists.

Usually, though, you'll stay in a **pension** – *pensão* – which are graded from 1 to 3 stars. Most serve meals, often in bargain all-in packages, but they rarely insist you take them. Similar to *pensoes* (the plural form) are *hospedarias* and *casa de hóspedes* – boarding houses – though you don't see very many of these.

A 3-star *pensão* is usually about the same price as a 1-star *hotel*; the latter can even be cheaper. 2-star hotels (and up) rise in price pretty fast, from £20 a double room to international rates for the 4- or 5-star places. Additional hotel categories include the state-run *pousadas*, similar to the Spanish *paradores*. These are expensive, charging at least 4-star hotel prices, but are often converted from old monasteries or castles and can be worth a look (or a drink) in themselves. The most interesting are those at Évora, Estremoz and Óbidos. *Estalagens* and *albergarias* are both equivalent to 4- or 5-star hotels.

STAR RATINGS

Quirks abound in the official municipal **grading/ pricing systems** and you can often pay less in a really luxurious 3-star *pensão* than in a 1-star pit. Similarly, some 1-star pensions are far nicer than those with 2 or 3. Wherever you arrive ask to see the room before you take it.

If you want a cheaper room – especially if you're travelling alone, in which case you'll frequently have to pay most of the price of a double – be persistent. '*Tem um quarto mais barato*?' is the relevant phrase.

YOUTH HOSTELS

There are only fifteen **youth hostels** (*Pousadas de Juventude*) in Portugal but in contrast to Spain they do tend to stay open all year.

The price for a dormitory bed is around £4 a night, a little extra if you need to rent sheets and blankets. Most operate a curfew (usually 11pm or midnight) and all demand a valid IYHF card – £6.50 (under 21, £3) available in Britain from the YHA (14 Southampton Street, London WC2; ☎01/ 836 8541), or in Portugal from the *Associação Portuguesa de Pousadas de Juventude*, Rua Andrade Corvo 46, Lisbon (Mon.–Fri. 1–8pm, Sat. 9.30am–12.30pm; ☎01/571054).

All of the hostels are detailed in the guide. Among the best are those at **Lindoso** (in the Gerês National Park), **Penhas da Saúde** (in the Serra da Estrêla – skiing country), **Sagres** (on the site of 'Henry the Navigator's Fortress'), **São Martinho do Porto, Areia Branca, Oeiras** (on the seafront near Lisbon), **Coimbra** (the most recently established), **Portalegre** (in a monastery) and **Leiria** (good atmosphere in general).

CAMPSITES

Portugal has over a hundred authorised **campsites**, most of them small, low-key and attractively located – and all of them remarkably cheap. Charges are per person and per tent, with showers, parking, and so on extra; even so, it's rare that you'll end up paying more than £2 a person.

The most useful are again detailed in the text but you can get a fairly complete map and list from any Portuguese tourist office, or a detailed booklet called *Roteiro Campista* (with prices, exact locations, facilities, etc.) from Portuguese bookshops or large news-kiosks.

Camping outside official sites is legal, but with certain restrictions. You're not allowed to camp 'in urban zones, in zones of protection for water sources, or less than 1km from camping parks, beaches, or other places frequented by the public'. This last stipulation sounds unreasonably heavy – what it means in practice is that you can't camp on beaches (above all in the Algarve, where "freelance camping" is impossible), though you can, discreetly, nearby. With a little sensitivity you can pitch a tent for a short period almost anywhere in the countryside.

Campsite thefts are, sadly, a regular occurrence in the Algarve; you are doubtless most at risk from fellow campers. In the rest of the country problems are rare, the locals extremely honest, and you can leave equipment without worrying.

EATING AND DRINKING

Portuguese food is excellent, cheap and served in quantity. Virtually any café, whatever its appearance, will serve you a basic meal, or at least a snack, for under £3, and for a few pounds more you have the run of most of the country's restaurants. Even on the luxury level, there are only a handful of Portuguese restaurants which will cause a crisis for a credit card.

CAFÉS AND SNACKS

If a **café** cooks in a big way you'll probably see blackboard lists of dishes or maybe just a sign reading *Comidas* (meals) or *Sandes* (sandwiches). All cafés also serve alcohol as well as coffee and soft drinks – and they're much cheaper places to drink than bars, which tend to have slightly cosmopolitan pretensions and prices.

Often you'll find a whole range of dishes served at a café (see the lists below) but the classic Portuguese **snacks** are *prego* (steak roll) usually served with a fried egg (*prego no prato*), *rissóis* (deep-fried rissoles, often wonderful), *pastéis de bacalhau* (cod fishcakes), and *sandes* (sandwiches).

Among the latter are *sandes de queijo* (cheese), *de fiambre* (ham), *de presunto* (smoked ham), *de chouriço* (smoked sausage), and *sandes mista* (usually ham and cheese).

Sometimes, too, you'll see food displayed on café-counters, particularly shellfish – if you fancy anything, just ask for '*uma dose*' (a portion). '*Uma coisa destas*' (one of those) can also be a useful phrase.

Markets (often held in indoor covered sites, *mercados*) are also good hunting grounds for snacks and many have stalls serving complete meals. In the north, especially, try *broa* (corn/rye bread) with local cheese and *membrillo* (hard quince jelly).

RESTAURANT MEALS

Even if your money's fairly tight, you won't need to depend exclusively on snacks and market picnics. *Restaurantes* are rarely too expensive – and since servings are so large, you can often have a substantial meal by ordering a '*meia dose*' (half portion), or '*uma dose*' between two. This is normal practice; you don't need to be a child.

Regional differences and specialities aren't as great as in Spain, but it's always worth taking stock of the *prato do dia* (plate of the day) and, if you're on the coast, going for fish and seafood. If you've had enough rich food, any restaurant will fix a *salada mista* (a mixed salad), which usually has tomatoes, onions and olives as a base, and you can ask for it *sem molho* (without oil). Meat is not the greatest feature of Portuguese cooking – except for pork, above all *porco á alentejana* (with clams) – and smoked hams.

Soups, everywhere, are extraordinarily cheap, and the thick vegetable soup often known as *caldo verde*, sometimes boosted with pieces of smoked sausage and black pudding, can be almost a meal in itself; it's served mainly in the north. (Strictly speaking, *caldo verde* is diced green cabbage.) *Canja de galinha* (chicken broth) is available nationwide. Don't be fooled by Porto's exotic-looking *tripa* (tripe) dishes, though – the beans and spice can taste good but stomach-lining is always as disgusting as you'd expect.

Many of the cheaper *restaurantes* offer a good value, three-course **menu of the day** (*menú do dia*) – a soup and fish or meat dish, nearly always followed by the ubiquitous *pudim flan* (creme caramel) or *arroz doce* (rice pudding). Often **pensões** will also serve meals of this kind and, especially in the more trendy tourist resorts, they can be the cheapest places to eat.

In larger towns you'll come across *cervejar-ias* (beer houses – often with good snacks and full meals, too) and *marisqueiras* (specialist seafood bars).

CAKES

Lastly a word about **cakes** – *bolos* or *pastéis* – which are often at their best in *casas de chá* (teahouses), though you'll also find them in *cafés* and in *pastelarias* (cake shops).

These are serious business in Portugal and enthusiasts won't be disappointed. Among the best are the Sintra cheesecakes (*queijadas de Sintra*), *palha de ovos* (egg straw) from Abrantes, *Bolo de Anjo* (angel cake), and the full range of marzipan cakes from the Algarve. The incredibly sweet egg-based *doces de ovos* – most infamously from Aveiro – are completely over the top.

WINES AND OTHER DRINKS

Portuguese **wines** (*tinto* red, *branco* white) are dramatically inexpensive and of an amazing overall quality – even the standard *Vinho da casa* that you get in the humblest of cafés.

The fortified **port** (*vinho do Porto*) and **madeira** (*vinho da Madeira*) wines are much the best known, and you should certainly sample both. The port trade is still quite largely under the control of the long-established British-owned companies. The wines are produced in the valley of the Douro and brought downriver by barge to be stored in the great wine lodges at Vila Nova de Gaia, a riverside suburb of Porto: you can visit them for tours and free tasting. Alternatively, for reasonable prices you can try any of 300 types and vintages of port at the *Instituto do Vinho do Porto* (Port Wine Institute) bars in Lisbon and Porto. But even if your quest for port isn't serious enough to do either, be sure to have a glass or two of the dry white ports, still more or less unknown in Britain.

Among **table wines** the best reds are from the **Dão** region, a roughly triangular area between Coimbra, Viseu and Guarda around the Rio Dão. Tasting a little like Burgundy, and produced mainly by local co-operatives, they're available throughout the country.

The light, slightly sparkling **Vinhos Verdes** – 'green wines', in age not colour – are again produced in quantity, this time in the Minho. They're drunk early and don't mature or improve with age, but are great with meals, especially shellfish. There are red and rosé as well as white *vinhos verdes*; all are excellent and the reds are unavailable outside Portugal, so savour the opportunity.

Among smaller regions offering interesting wines are **Colares** near Sintra (a very long-established vine, producing deep, dry, dark reds), **Bucelas** in the Estremadura (crisp, dry whites), **Reguengos** in Alentejo, **Bairrada** in the Beiras, and **Lagoa** in the Algarve.

SPIRITS AND FIREWATERS

Portuguese **brandy** and champagne are also produced, but both are outflanked by their Spanish rivals – sold almost everywhere, and very cheaply. Portuguese **gin** is weaker than international brands but ridiculously cheap; if you're asking for this or any other spirits at a bar always specify you want '*gin nacional*', '*vodka nacional*', etc. – it'll save you a fortune.

Local **firewaters** are more impressive in their own right. They include *Bagaço* (the fieriest), *Aguardente*, *Ginginha* (made from cherries), and the very wonderful *Licor Beirão* (a kind of cognac with herbs).

BEER

The most common of the local lager-type **beers** (*cerveja*) is *Sagres* but there are dozens of other varieties – if you're curious, they can all be tasted at the Silves Beer Festival held in the town's castle for a week every June. When drinking draught beer order *um fino* or *uma imperial* if you want a small glass; *uma caneca* will get you a pint.

COFFEE AND SOFT DRINKS

Coffee (*café*) comes either black, small and expresso-strong (*uma bica*, or simply *um café*), small and milky (*um garoto*, or, in the north, *um pingo*), or large and milky (*um galão*).

Tea (*chá*) is usually black; *com leite* is with milk, *com limão* with lemon, but *um chá de limão* is hot water with a lemon rind. *Chá* is a big drink in Portugal (which originally exported tea-drinking to England) and you'll find wonderfully elegant *casas de chá* dotted around the country.

All the standard **soft drinks** are available. The best is arguably the native *Sumol*, which is extremely fruity and appetising. You can also get mineral water (*água mineral*) almost anywhere. Fresh orange juice is *sumo de laranja*.

A LIST OF FOODS AND DISHES

Basics

Pão	Bread	*Pimenta*	Pepper
Carne	Meat	*Queijo*	Cheese
Peixe	Fish	*Salada*	Salad
Manteiga	Butter	*Ovos*	Eggs
Legumes	Vegetables	*Água*	Water
Mariscos	Shellfish	*Pequeno almoço*	Breakfast
Acepipes	Hors d'oeuvres	*Almoço*	Lunch
Sal	Salt	*Jantar*	Dinner

Soups

Açorda (de Marisco)	Bread soup (with shellfish)	*Sopa á alentejana*	Garlic/bread soup with poached egg on top
Caldo verde	Vegetable broth		
Canja de galinha	Chicken soup with rice and boiled yolks	*Sopa de grão*	Chickpea soup
		Sopa de hortaliça	Vegetable soup
Gaspacho	Chilled vegetable soup (only served in the south)	*Sopa de mariscos*	Shellfish soup
		Sopa de peixe	Fish soup

Fish and Shellfish

Ameijoas	Clams	*Espadarte*	A large kind of swordfish
Arroz de marisco	Seafood paella		
Atum	Tuna	*Gambas*	Prawns
Bacalhau	Dried salted cod, the standard Portuguese fish: 365 ways of cooking include *com batatas e grão* (with boiled potatoes and chickpeas), *á Brás* (with eggs and fried potatoes), *na brasa* (roasted on coals), *á Gomes de Sá* (sliced, with boiled eggs and potatoes) and *á minhota* (with chips)	*Garoupa*	(Like) Bream
		Lampreia	Lamprey (similar to eel)
		Lagosta	Crayfish (pricey)
		Linguado	Sole
		Lula or *Chocos*	Squid
		Mexilhões	Mussels
		Peixe espada	Swordfish
		Pescada	Hake
		Polvo	Octopus
Caldeirada	Fish stew	*Robalo*	Sea bass
Camarões	Shrimps	*Salmão*	Salmon
Carapaus	Mackerel	*Salmonetes*	Mullet
Cataplana	Pressure-cooked clams with bacon, sausages and peppers, only served in the Algarve	*Sarda*	Mackerel
		Sardinhas	Sardines
		Truta	Trout

Meat and Poultry

Almondegas	Meatballs	*Coelho*	Rabbit
Bife á Portuguesa	Beefsteak in mustard sauce, usually topped with a fried egg; a cheap standard	*Cordorniz*	Quail
		Costeleta	Chop
		Cozido á Portuguesa	Boiled casserole of chicken, lamb, pork, beef, sausages, beans, etc. Served with rice.
Borrego	Lamb		
Cabrito	Kid		
Carne de porco	Pork (*lombo*, loin; *á alentejana*, with clams)		
Carneiro	Mutton	*Dobrada*	Tripe (*tripas à moda do Porto*, a kind of tripe curry with beans and vegetables!)
Chanfana, Ensopado, Sarapatel	Lamb and/or goat stews		

Meat and Poultry (continued)

		Terms	
Fígado	Liver		
Frango	Chicken	*Assado*	Roasted
Iscas	Pork liver	*Cozido*	Boiled/stewed
Leitão	Suckling pig	*Frito*	Fried
Perú	Turkey	*Grelhado*	Grilled
Salsicha	Sausage	*Molho*	Sauce
Vitela	Veal	*No forno*	Baked

Vegetables and Fruits

Alface	Lettuce	*Laranja*	Orange
Alho	Garlic	*Limão*	Lemon
Ameixas	Plums	*Maça*	Apple
Arroz	Rice	*Melão*	Melon
Batatas	Potatoes	*Morangos*	Strawberries
Cerejas	Cherries	*Pimento*	Pepper
Favas	Broad beans	*Salada*	Salad
Feijão	Beans	*Uvas*	Grapes
Figos	Figs		

Cheeses

The best of the cheeses is the *Queijo da Serra* (from the Serra da Estrêla). *Cabreiro* or *Queijo de cabra* is a feta-like goats' cheese. Also worth trying are the soft cheeses of *Tomar* and *Azeitão*.

COMMUNICATIONS: POST, PHONES AND THE MEDIA

POST OFFICES

Post Offices (*Correios*) normally open Mon.–Fri. 9am–6pm, larger ones sometimes on Saturday mornings too. The main Lisbon and Porto branches operate a limited 24-hour service.

Portuguese **postal services** are reasonably efficient, letters and cards to Britain and Europe taking under a week. To buy **stamps**, queue up at the counter marked *selos*.

POSTA RESTANTE

You can have mail sent to you at any post office in the country. To receive mail '**posta restante**', look for a counter marked *encomendas*.

Letters should be marked clearly, and your name, ideally, should be written in capitals and underlined. If you are expecting mail, take your passport and ask them to check under your christian name and any other initials (including Ms., etc.) as well as your surname – filing can be erratic. There is a fee for collecting post equivalent to the cost of a domestic letter (currently 27esc).

PHONES

You can make **international calls** direct from almost any kiosk in the country, but you'll need a good stock of 25esc pieces and a great deal of patience with the international lines (always blocked or cutting you off in mid-speech). Cafés also have phones with a digit system, but they work out to be quite pricey. So the best bet is still to go to the old-fashioned **post offices**. The only trouble with these is that most are closed in the evenings, which can be inconvenient, though no more expensive as there is no cheap-rate period for international calls.

To make a call, dial 00 for the European exchange and 097 for the international one, then the country code (UK 44, Ireland 353, USA & Canada 1, West Germany 49, Netherlands 31, Denmark 45, Sweden 46, Finland 358), the city code (minus its first 0), and finally the number.

MEDIA

For entertainment, mainly in Lisbon or Porto, check **listings** in *SE7E* and *Sabado*, and for a more artistic view of the country's culture, if you can read Portuguese, see *JL* (*Journal das Letras*).

English-language magazines include the old and staid *Anglo-Portuguese News*, the *Algarve News* and *Algarve Magazine*; the first two can be useful for finding work, none are especially informative. **British newspapers** can be bought in Lisbon, Porto and other major towns, and quite widely in the Algarve resorts.

If you have a short wave radio, you can pick up the **BBC World Service**, with hourly news on 648 KHz Medium Wave and 15.07 MHz Short Wave. **Portuguese radio** puts out an English-language programme for tourists at 8.30am or 10am (between 558 and 720 KHz/87.9 and 95.7FM depending on where you are).

FESTIVALS AND OTHER ENTERTAINMENTS

Rural and traditional, Portugal maintains a remarkable number of folk customs which find their expression in local carnivals (*festas*) and traditional pilgrimages (*romarias*). Some of these have developed into wild celebrations lasting days or even weeks and have become tourist events in themselves; others have barely strayed from their roots. Every region is different, but in the north especially there are dozens of village festivals, everyone taking the day off to celebrate the local saint's day or the harvest – performing ancient songs and dances in traditional dress for no one's benefit but their own.

EASTER AND ST JOHN'S EVE

Although festivals take place throughout the year – and it is often the obscure and unexpected

event that turns out to be the most fun – there are certain occasions that stand out. **Easter Week** and **St. John's Eve** (June 23-24) are celebrated everywhere with religious processions.

The former is particularly magnificent in **Braga**, full of ceremonial pomp, while the latter tends to be a more joyous affair – in **Porto**, where it's the highlight of a week of celebration, everyone dances through the streets all night, hitting each other over the head with leeks.

LOCAL FESTIVALS AND MARKETS

The festival list is potentially endless. Check with the local tourist office for details of what's going on around you, or buy the yearly *Borda d'Água* (30esc from newsstands), an information leaflet detailing saints' days, star signs, gardening tips and, most importantly, all the country's annual fairs.

Among the biggest and best known of the local **popular festivals** are:

Queima das Fitas, celebrating the end of the academic year in **Coimbra** (mid-May).

Santarém's Fair (last Sun. in May for two weeks).

Festa de São Gonçalo in **Amarante** (1st weekend in June).

Lisbon's Popular Saints, especially St. Anthony (throughout June).

Festa do Colete Encarnado in **Vila Franca de Xira**, with Pamplona-style running of bulls through the streets (first week in July and again at the *Festas Bravas*, first week in Oct.).

Vila Viçosa's horse fair (mid-Aug.).

Festa da Nossa Senhora da Agonia in Viana do Castelo (third weekend in Aug.).

Lamego's celebrations around the *Romaria de Nossa Senhora dos Remédios* (last week in Aug. to mid-Sept.).

On a more strictly religious note are the great **pilgrimages to Fátima**, May 13 and October 13 and, to a lesser extent, on the 13th of every month in between.

Look out too for the great *feiras*, especially at Barcelos – originally markets, as often as not nowadays you'll find a combination of agricultural show, folk festival and funfair.

BULLFIGHTS

The Portuguese **bullfight** is neither as commonplace nor as famous as its Spanish counterpart and as a spectacle it's marginally preferable. In Portugal the bull isn't killed, but instead wrestled to the ground in a genuinely elegant colourful, and skilled display. However, the bull is usually injured and it is always slaughtered later in any case. If you choose to go – and we would urge visitors not to support the events put on simply for tourist benefit on the Algarve – these are the basics.

A *Tourada* opens with the bull, its horns padded, facing a mounted *toureiro* in elaborate eighteenth-century costume. His job is to provoke and exhaust the bull and to plant the dart-like *farpas* in its back while avoiding the charge – a demonstration of incredible riding prowess. Once the beast is tired, the *moços-de-forcado* or simply *forcados* move in, an eight-man team who try finally to immobilise it. It appears a totally suicidal task – they line up behind each other across the ring from the bull and persuade it to charge them, the front man leaping between the horns while the rest grab hold and try to subdue it.

The great Portuguese bullfight centre is **Ribatejo**, where the animals are bred. If you want to see a fight, best to witness it here, amid the local aficionados. The season lasts from around April to October, with the most prestigious events taking place as part of the festivals in Vila Franca de Xira and Santarém, and at the Campo Pequeno in **Lisbon**. Strictly tourist events are also held in the larger towns of the Algarve.

MUSIC

Portugal's rich musical traditions – and current performers – are covered in some depth in the "Contexts" section of this guide. Suffice to state here that there is much on offer, and much that should be experienced – from the strange laments of *fado* to the African bands from former Portuguese colonies who have settled in Lisbon – and to point out a few of the main annual events. The best source for information on these (and most cultural activities in Portugal) are the weekly magazines *SE7E* and *Sabado*.

The **rock music** scene is almost exclusively centred on Lisbon, and tends to follow British influences. To catch the more interesting bands, especially those from the former African colonies, keep your eyes open for bills advertising festivals, and check listings in *SE7E* for Lisbon, Porto and (in summer) Vila Real de Santo António.

Jazz is active in a small way, too, and there's an excellent international **Jazz Festival** run by the Fundação Gulbenkian during the summer, with Cascais hosting a much smaller one around the same time. Vilar de Mouros, near Caminha, sporadically hosts an August jazz/rock week, too.

More **classical** tastes are catered to by the summer **Estoril Festival** and events in Lisbon and elsewhere sponsored by the Fundação Gulbenkian. Tourist offices have complete schedules.

CINEMA AND TV

Cinemas in Portugal are extremely cheap, and **films** often shown in English with Portuguese subtitles. Listings can be found in the local newspaper or on placards, invariably placed somewhere in the central square of every small town.

Portuguese **television**, too, imports many British and American shows – most bars have one on in a corner somewhere. You also get televised bullfights and, above all, *telenovelas* – **soap operas** somewhere between *Eastenders* and *Dallas*. These are often from Brazil, though Portugal has now produced three or four. Look out for the locally-produced *Passerelle*, about the fashion world, and the amazing *Roque Santeiro*, the story of a man who returns to his village to find he has been made a saint in his absence. Even if you don't understand a word, they all make totally compulsive viewing.

FOOTBALL

Football is the Portuguese national sport, with a long and often glorious tradition of international and club teams. The leading clubs, inevitably, hail from Lisbon (*Benfica* and *Sporting*) and Porto (*FC Porto*). Just about every Portuguese supports one of these three teams, paying scant attention to the lesser, local teams. *FC Porto* are current heroes, still resting on the laurels of their European Cup victory in 1987 – an event that was greeted with nationwide celebration.

If you want to see a league match, the season runs from September to May. Tickets are inexpensive, and matches given due prominence in the press. You may also be lucky enough to catch one of the big three teams, or even the national side, in European action. The spectacle of a packed capacity soccer stadium somewhat puts bullfights in the shade.

FINDING WORK

Portugal has employment problems of its own, and without a special skill you're unlikely to have much luck finding any kind of long-term work. The most realistic option is teaching English.

PERMANENT JOBS

For **teaching English** in Portugal a TEFL diploma is a distinct advantage, though not absolutely essential.

Work is best arranged before you leave – check the education supplement in *The Guardian* – as this avoids work-permit hassles. If you're already in Portugal you could just apply to individual schools (try the British Council, Rua Luis Fernando 1–3, Lisbon) or advertise your services privately.

Au-pair work is also a possibility. Again there are ads in British newspapers (*The Times* above all) or once in Portugal you could try advertising in the *Anglo-Portuguese News* (Av. de São Pedro 14D, Monte Estoril).

TEMPORARY JOBS

As far as temporary jobs go, the only opportunities are in tourist-related work on the **Algarve**; foreigners are not normally employed on the harvests. The Algarve, however, does offer quite a range of ways of getting money, all of them dependent to some extent on your self-confidence and/or lack of scruples.

Most obvious, if perhaps least rewarding, is **bar work**. This is not easy to find – you'll stand the best chance approaching one of the many British-owned places – and even when you do, it often brings in barely enough money to live on, after very long hours. Better, at least in terms of time involved, is to try your hand **giving out disco invitations** to holidaymakers. This work is available in Albufeira, Lagos, Praia da Oura, etc. It's paid solely on commission but it does leave you free during the day – and much of the night – to seek your own entertainment.

Which leads nicely into the biggest scam in the country – perhaps in Europe – of **selling time shares**. Here possibilities exist for making really big money, though not everyone of course strikes lucky. The work again involves walking the streets in the major resorts (add Quarteira, Vilamoura, and Monte Gordo to the above), this time inviting British holidaymakers to view time-share resorts and villas. It is extremely tiring, soul-destroying and, at its most successful, pretty disreputable work. But earnings are on a commission basis and this can add up to hundreds of pounds.

To find time share work, just ask the people who are already doing the job on the street what to do. They'll tell you who to contact and how depressing it all is.

One last outlet is to head for the huge new **yacht marina** at Vilamoura. Only half-built, it already holds around a thousand craft, slowly being surrounded by trendy bars, boutiques and cafés. You could try some of these, but it's even better to approach the yachties themselves. Almost all boat owners have hundreds of little tasks that need doing and, given the opportunity, will pay a few thousand escudos to anyone presenting themselves as a handyman/woman. Mostly it's **painting** or **scrubbing down** decks – hardly skilled labour – but if you can convince someone you know what you're doing the quality of work you'll be given may improve.

Between late September and early November there's even the possibility of long-distance **crewing** to the Canaries, Caribbean, etc.; for this sort of angle try *Wellies Bar* (sic) as well as word of mouth. For the more menial odd-jobs you just need persistence and a thick skin: spend a couple of days asking around and something should turn up.

If you do decide to stay on in the Algarve to work, you can **extend** your sixty days unofficially by crossing the border at Vila Real de Santo António (the easiest way). The official way is to go to one of the *Serviço de Estrangeiros* offices in Portimão, Albufeira, or Faro.

TROUBLE AND SEXUAL HARASSMENT

Portugal is a remarkably crime-free country, though there's the usual petty crime in larger tourist resorts. Hire cars are always prey to thieves – leave them looking as empty as possible – and campsites in the Algarve are less reliable than elsewhere.

For your own part, **drug offences** (and marijuana has not been decriminalised here as it has in Spain) carry heavy sentences and you'd be foolish to try to bring anything in. **Nude bathing**, still rare and theoretically an arrestable offence, could bring a fine; even going topless may provoke a warning. Portuguese **police**, though, are far more human than their Spanish counterparts and don't look for trouble.

SEXUAL HARASSMENT

Portugal is not technically a Mediterranean country, but the machismo is as overt and ingrained as in any other Latin state. Though male attention is marginally less hot-blooded and flamboyant than in, say, Spain or Italy, it is no less persistent and wearing.

Walking past pavement cafés – in Lisbon, above all – is like stepping on a bed of snakes, as men hiss their approval; they don't really expect you to notice and after a while it blends into the background, as hooting horns and wolf-whistles might elsewhere. Likewise you can, with effort, acclimatise to the constant staring – if it's all too much, escape somewhere really civilised like the Gulbenkian Museum or the *Instituto do Vinho do Porto* in Lisbon or the *Museu de Arte Moderna* in Porto, where you will be ignored completely, for a change!

With the exception of certain areas in Lisbon (particularly the Cais do Sodré and parts of the Bairro Alto by night) and parts of the Algarve, Portugal is, however, one of the least dangerous countries in Europe. Of course you may come across more aggressive sexual harassment in red-light areas (often around train stations) in the larger towns such as Porto and Coimbra, but on the whole it's a rural country, intensely traditional and formal to the point of prudishness.

People may initially wonder why you're travelling on your own – especially inland and in the mountains, where Portuguese women never travel unaccompanied – but once they have accepted that you are a crazy foreigner you're likely to be welcomed, adopted and offered food and lodging in their homes.

Hitching is extremely easy and not dangerous so long as you are two or more. You'll be surprised how 'informal' men become if you're alone – not recommended. One man in your party and the lifts take longer to come, but if you're walking the streets together you'll find that the sound effects disappear.

Remember that the Portuguese invariably look cross and talk very loudly even when they are being kind and helpful. Often it's simply a language barrier which makes situations that at home would be routine assume real menace. Get around at night by taxi – very cheap anyway; by day public transport is good and quite safe. Coaches have a cosier feel than trains, and you should avoid the latter on a Friday afternoon and evening when the whole army seems to be on leave for the weekend.

THE WOMEN'S MOVEMENT

There are relatively few **women's organisations** in Portugal. The best contact points are the *IDM* centre and the feminist bookshop *Editora das Mulheres*, both in Lisbon (see that chapter for addresses).

Also of interest is the *Comissão da Condição Feminina* (Av. da Republica 32-2° esq., Lisbon), which researches and maintains a watching brief on all aspects of women's lives in Portugal; members organise conferences and meetings, are very active in areas of social and legal reform, and are linked with feminists throughout the country.

DIRECTORY

ADDRESSES Most addresses in Portugal consist of a street name and number followed by a storey number, e.g., Rua da Afonso Henriques 34-3°. This means you need to go up to the third floor of no. 34. An 'esq'. or 'E' (standing for *esquerda*) after a floor number means you should go to the left; 'dir'. or 'D'. (for *direita*) indicates that the apartment or office you're looking for is on the right.

AIRPORT TAX None.

BAGGAGE You can often leave it at a station for a very small sum while you look for rooms. On the whole the Portuguese are highly trustworthy, and even shopkeepers and café owners will keep an eye on your belongings for you.

BEACHES Beware of the heavy undertow on many of Portugal's western Atlantic beaches and don't swim if you see a red or yellow flag. The sea is warmest on the eastern Algarve – at beaches past Faro.

CAMERAS/FILMS Not cheap by Portuguese standards and the price seems shocking compared with food, drink and other national products. It's best to buy them at home.

CONSULATES AND EMBASSIES See listings for Lisbon and Porto.

CONTRACEPTIVES Durex are available from *farmácias* – so too is the pill, but you'll need a prescription and pay through the nose.

EMERGENCIES ☎115 for ambulance service (no coin required).

FARMÁCIAS (chemists) Open Mon.–Fri. 9am–1pm and 3–7pm. When closed all display a notice on the door with the address of the nearest one open – or look in the local paper, especially in Lisbon, Porto and the Algarve.

GAY LIFE Not especially prominent, or at least commercialised, though there are a couple of clubs, and a gay beach, part of Caparica, near Lisbon (see Lisbon chapter). Attitudes in the capital are fairly tolerant; elsewhere a gay consciousness has yet to make much impact.

LAUNDRY There are few self-service launderettes, but loads of *lavandarias*, where you can get your clothes washed, mended and ironed (overnight) at a fairly low cost.

MUSEUMS, CHURCHES AND MONUMENTS The important ones stay open all day from around 10am–6pm; the smaller ones close for lunch from 12:30pm–2. Almost all museums and monuments close for the day on Monday. Churches often require 'modest dress' (which usually just means not shorts).

NATIONAL PARKS The head office in Lisbon (Rua Ferreira Lapa 29-1°) has details on all Portugal's parks and reserves, but in general neither head nor district offices have much time for foreign visitors, concentrating as they do on awakening a spirit of conservation and protection of wildlife in their compatriots.

OPENING HOURS Like Spain, Portugal has held onto the institution of the siesta. Most shops and businesses, plus smaller museums and post offices, close for a good lunchtime break – usually from 12.30 to 2.30 or 3pm. **Shops** generally open around 9am, and after re-opening keep going until 7pm. Except in the larger cities, they tend to close for the weekend at Saturday lunchtime. **Banking hours** are Mon.–Fri. 8.30am–3pm.

PUBLIC HOLIDAYS The main public holidays, when almost everything will be shut and transport services reduced are: Jan. 1; April 25 (commemorating the 1974 Revolution); Good Friday; May 1; Corpus Christi (usually early June); June 10 (*Dia de Camões e das Communidades* – Camões day, the 'community' bit was added after the Revolution); Aug. 15; Oct. 5 (Day of the Republic, dating back to 1910); Nov. 1; Dec. 1 (celebrating independence from Spain in 1640); Dec 8 and Dec 25. There are in addition local holidays: in Lisbon and Porto, June 13 and June 24 respectively.

PUBLIC TOILETS 'Ladies' often charge and are clean, 'Gentlemen' may look more aesthetic (lots of ironwork) and are free, but usually pretty unattractive inside. A sign that says *Retretes* will head you in the right direction, then it's *senhores* for men and *senhoras* for women; the doors will generally have the usual block figure wearing a skirt or trousers.

SWIMMING POOLS Every sizeable town has one, usually outdoors.

TAMPONS From any *Farmácia* – ask for them by brand name.

TIME Portugal keeps Greenwich Mean Time – one hour behind Spain and Britain. Daylight Saving goes into effect on the last Sunday in March (Spring ahead) and ends on the last Sunday in September (Autumn back).

WATER You can drink the water pretty much everywhere (except from streams in the south), but it often tastes better out of a bottle, either sparkling (*com gás*) or still (*sem gás*).

METRIC WEIGHTS AND MEASURES

1 ounce = 28.3 grammes	1 inch = 2.54 centimeters (cm)
1 pound = 454 grammes	1 foot = 0.3 metres (m)
2.2 pounds = 1 kilogramme	1 yard = 0.91 metres
1 pint = 0.57 litres	1.09 yards = 1m
1 quart = 1.14 litres	1 mile = 1.61 kilometres (km)
1 gallon = 4.5 litres	0.62 miles = 1km

PART TWO

THE
GUIDE

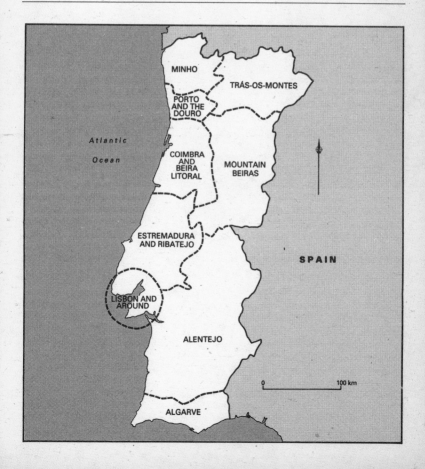

- MINHO
- TRÁS-OS-MONTES
- PORTO AND THE DOURO
- COIMBRA AND BEIRA LITORAL
- MOUNTAIN BEIRAS
- ESTREMADURA AND RIBATEJO
- LISBON AND AROUND
- ALENTEJO
- ALGARVE

Atlantic Ocean

SPAIN

0   100 km

CHAPTER ONE

LISBON AND AROUND

There are few more immediately likeable capitals than **Lisbon**. A lively and varied place, it remains in some ways curiously provincial, rooted as much in the 1920s as the 1980s. Wooden trams from before the First World War clank up outrageous gradients, past mosaic pavements and art-nouveau cafés, and the medieval village-like quarter of Alfama hangs below the city's castle.

Yet as you explore the city these first impressions merge into a half-truth. Modern Lisbon has kept an easygoing, human pace and scale, with little of the underlying violence of most cities (and all ports) of its size. But in other

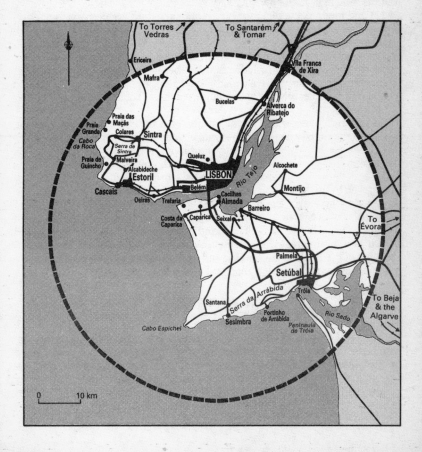

respects it's been changing – inevitably so, for its population has doubled over the present century to nearly a million, a tenth of all Portuguese. The 1974 Revolution originated here, and its effects have brought considerable freedoms, particularly for the capital's once-regimented youth. Vital, too, has been the vast influx of **refugees** – *retournados* – from Portugal's former colonies of Angola, Cabo Verde, São Tomé e Principe, Guinea Bissau, and Mozambique. The *retournados* imposed a heavy burden on an already strained economy, and on the severe housing shortage in the city, but their overall integration is one of the chief triumphs of modern Portugal.

It has certainly brought a significant **cultural** legacy. Alongside the traditional *fado* clubs of its Bairro Alto quarter, Lisbon now has jazz bands, free open-air concerts, and regular festivals of African music. The city has a real sense of involvement in **politics**, too, despite the current, moribund state of the major parties. Everywhere you go, graffiti artists seem to have got to the walls first, and in working class parts of the city, like Alcántara, some superb murals remain from the revolutionary years.

Art and monuments of a more conventional nature are perhaps thinner on the ground, largely as a result of the 1755 Earthquake. But there is one building from Portugal's Golden Age – the **Jerónimos Monastery** at Belém – that is the equal of any monument in the country (and most in Spain). And more modern developments include the **Gulbenkian Foundation** museum complex, with its superb collections of ancient and modern art, and some adventurous contemporary architecture, such as Tómas Taveira's amazing post-modernist shopping centre at **Amoreiras**.

All of which, along with a grand location on a switchback of hills above the broad Tagus estuary, makes for a stimulating and very beautiful city, demanding at least a few days of anyone's Portuguese itinerary. It could, equally, form a base for a week or two's holiday, with day escapes and excursions easy and rewarding to make. The sea is close by, half an hour's journey taking you to the beach suburb of **Cascais**, or to the miles of dunes along the **Costa da Caparica**. Slightly further afield lie the lush wooded heights and royal palaces of **Sintra**, the 'glorious Eden' that Byron considered 'the most beautiful . . . in the world' until he found its claims surpassed by Albania. And if you become interested in Portuguese architecture, there are the Rococo delights of the **Palácio de Queluz** and its gardens en route, or the extraordinary monastery of **Mafra** – a good first step into Estremadura.

LISBON (LISBOA)

Physically, **LISBON** is an eighteenth-century city: elegant, open to the sea, and carefully planned. The description does not cover its modern expanse, of course – there are suburbs here as poor and inadequate as any in Europe – but is accurate within the old central boundaries of a triangle of hills. This 'lower city', the **Baixa**, was the product of a single phase of building, carried out in under a decade by the dictatorial minister, the Marquês de Pombal, in the wake of the **Great Earthquake** of 1755.

The Earthquake, History and Monuments

The quake – which was felt as far away as Scotland and Jamaica – struck Lisbon at 9.30am on November 1, All Saints' Day, when most of the city's population were at mass. Within the space of ten minutes there were three major tremors – the epicentre was in the sea just off Lisbon – and fires, spread by the candles of a hundred church altars, raged throughout the capital. A vast tidal wave swept the seafront, where refugees sought shelter: in all, 40,000 of a 270,000 population were killed.

The destruction of the city shocked the continent, with Voltaire, who wrote an account of it in his novel *Candide*, leading an intense debate with Rousseau on the operation of providence. For Portugal, and for the capital, it was a disaster that in retrospect seems to seal an age. Eighteenth-century Lisbon was arguably the most active port in Europe, and it had been a central and prosperous city since **Roman**, perhaps even Phoenician, times. In the Middle Ages, as **Moorish** *Lishbuna*, it thrived on its wide links with the Arab world, and on the rich territories of the south, Alentejo and Algarve. Its reconquest by the Christians, including a ramshackle force of British mercenaries, was an early and cloudy triumph of the Crusades, its one positive aspect the appearance of a first true Portuguese monarch in **Afonso Henriques**.

Over the centuries following, however, Lisbon was twice at the forefront of European development and trade, on a scale that is hard to envisage today. The first phase came with the great Portuguese **discoveries** of the **late-fifteenth and sixteenth centuries**, such as Vasco da Gama's opening of the sea route to India. The second was in the opening decades of the **eighteenth century**, when a colonised Brazil was found to yield both gold and diamonds. Each of these ages produced a brilliant and extravagant patron. The sixteenth century is dominated by the figure of **Dom Manuel I**, under whom the flamboyant national style known as Manueline developed. Lisbon takes its principal monuments, the tower and monastery at Belém, from this era. The eighteenth century, more extravagant though with less brilliant effect, produced **Dom João V**, best known as the obsessive builder of Mafra, which he created as a response to Philip II's El Escorial in Spain.

Survivals: the City Structure

Eighteenth-century prints show a pre-quake Lisbon of tremendous opulence and mystique, its skyline characterised by towers, palaces and convents. There are glimpses of this still – the **Belém** suburb survived the destruction, as did the old Moorish hillside of **Alfama** – but these are isolated neighbourhoods and monuments.

It is instead **Pombal's** perfect, neoclassical grid that covers the centre. Given orders, following the earthquake, to 'Bury the dead, feed the living and close the ports', the king's minister followed his success in restoring order to the city in its rebuilding. The **Baixa**, still the heart of the modern city, adheres to his strict ideals of simplicity and economy. Individual streets were assigned to each craft and trade and the whole was shaped by public buildings and squares. Only the **Rossio**, the main square since medieval times, remained in its original place, slightly off-centre in the symmetrical design.

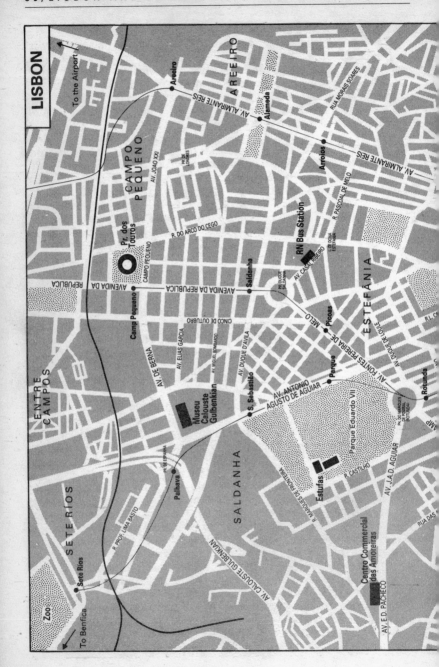

LISBON

To the Airport

To Benfica

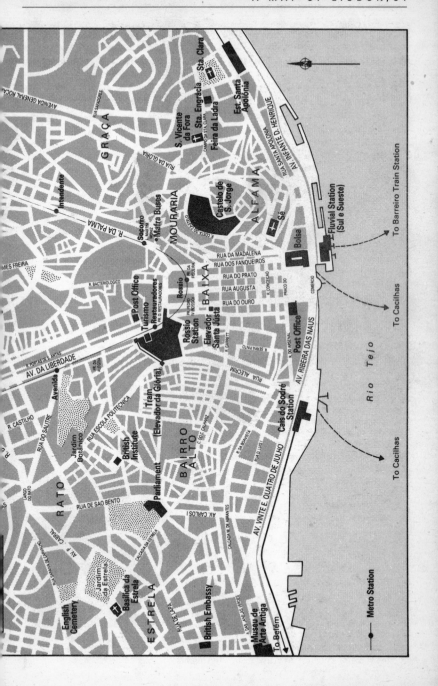

Sta. Clara

Est. Santa
Apolónia

S. Vicente
da Fora

Feira da Ladra

AVENIDA GENERAL ROÇA

RUA SAPADORES

GRAÇA

RUA DA GLÓRIA

To Barreiro Train Station

RUA SANTA POLÓNIA

AV. INFANTE D. HENRIQUE

Intendente

Castelo de
S. Jorge

ALFAMA

Fluvial Station
(Sul e Sueste)

Matra Buses

MOURARIA

Sé

To Cacilhas

R. DA PALMA

MES FREIRA

Socorro

RUA DA MADALENA

Bolsa

RUA DOS FANQUEIROS

R. BACTERIOLÓGICO

Post Office

RUA DO PRATO

Rossio

RUA AUGUSTA

BAIXA

Turismo

RUA DO OURO

Restauradores

PR. D. RESTAURADORES

PRAÇA DO
COMÉRCIO

Rossio
Station

Elevador de
Santa Justa

R. GARRETT

R. CASTILHO

AV. DA LIBERDADE

Post Office

R. PORTAS DE S. ANTÃO

Avenida

Train
(Elevador da Glória)

RUA ALECRIM

AV. RIBEIRA DAS NAUS

Rio Tejo

RUA DO SALITRE

RUA ESCOLA POLITÉCNICA

Jardim
Botânico

British
Institute

BARRO
ALTO

Cais do Sodré
Station

To Cacilhas

RATO

Parliament

LARGO
DO RATO

RUA DE SAO BENTO

AV. CARLOS I

Jardim
da Estrela

ESTRELA

Basílica da
Estrela

AV. VINTE E QUATRO DE JULHO

English
Cemetery

British Embassy

Museu de
Arte Antiga

To Belém

● Metro Station

Getting around and finding a place to stay

It could hardly be easier to get your bearings in the **Baixa**, Pombal's central city grid. At one end, opening on to the River Tagus, is the broad, arcaded **Praço do Comércio** (or Terreiro do Paço), with its ferry stations for crossing the river, tram terminals for Belém, and grand triumphal arch. At the other – linked by almost any street you care to take – stands the **Rossio**, more three squares than one, merging with the **Praça da Figueira** and **Praça dos Restauradores**.

These squares, filled with cafés, occasional street musicians, lost-looking tourists and streetwise dealers, form the hub of Lisbon's daily activity. At night the focus shifts to the **Bairro Alto**, high above and to the left of the Baixa, and best reached by funicular (*Elevador da Glória*) or the great street 'elevador' (*Santa Justa*) built for the city by Eiffel.

East of the Baixa, the **Castelo de São Jorge**, a brooding landmark, holds a still taller hill, with the **Alfama** district – the oldest, most fascinating part of the city – sprawled below.

Points of arrival

The place to head for on arrival is the **Rossio**. Most of the city's pensions are within walking distance of the square and in the adjoining Praça dos Restauradores the **Turismo** will provide you with accommodation lists and a large-scale **map** of the city – useful in that it outlines Belém and other places of interest outside the area of our own plan.

Trains

Long distance trains – from Coimbra, Porto, and the north (and from Badajoz, Madrid and France) – use the **Santa Apolónia station**. This is about fifteen minutes' walk from the Praça do Comércio, or a short ride on buses #9 or #46 to the Rossio. At the station there's a small information office (often run by boy scouts) and an 8am to 8pm money exchange. A useful bus from here is #90, which runs past the Fluvial station (see below), Rossio, the youth hostel, Saldanha and the airport (7am–9pm), but costs 190esc.

Local trains – from Sintra or anywhere else in Estremadura – emerge right at the heart of the city in the **Rossio Station**. This is a strange mock-Manueline complex with the trains an improbable escalator-ride above the street-level entrances. It is complete with all facilities – shops, exchange, etc.

Trains from the Algarve and south. A slightly more involved but also more scenic approach. The railway lines from the south terminate at the suburb of **Barreiro**, on the far bank of the river, where you catch a ferry (included in the price of the train ticket) to the **Fluvial** (or *Sul e Sueste*) station next to the Praça do Comércio. Buses #1, #2, #9, #32, #39, #44 and #45 run up from the Fluvial to the Rossio.

Buses

The various bus terminals are scattered about the city, but all are positioned near a metro station. Leaving Lisbon, you can usually buy tickets if you turn up half an hour in advance – though for the summer expresses to the Algarve you need to book at least 24hr in advance.

Rodoviária Nacional (referred to as *RN*), the national company, has three main terminals: Avenida Casal Ribeiro (very near metro *Saldanha*) for destinations north of Lisbon; Praça de Espanha (metro *Palhavã*) or Avda. Cinco de Outubro 75 (bus #1 or #21 from Praça dos

Restauradores) for anywhere south. Leaving Lisbon, it's best to ask at Turismo for times and information on which buses leave from which terminal, as there's no strict system.

Other **private bus companies** operate from the following terminals:

Campo Pequeno: *AVIC* serve the northwest coast, and *SOLEXPRESSO* the Alentejo and Algarve. Also long-distance buses to the rest of Europe.

Campo das Cebolas, near Praça do Comércio: destinations in the Minho.

Largo Martim Moniz, north-east of the Rossio: *Empresa Mafrense* services for Mafra and Ericeira (hourly).

Algarve departures. In season several companies run fast, excellent value express buses between Lisbon and the Algarve. Among the companies are *Resende*, whose buses use a terminal on Rua dos Bacalheiros, near the river. Travel agents or the Turismo have details of others.

The Airport

From the **airport**, just twenty minutes from the centre, buses #44 and #45 (6am–1am) run past the youth hostel to the Praça dos Restauradores and on to the Cais do Sodré (for Cascais). The *Linha Verde* bus (every 15 min. from 7.30am–1.30am, double the price at 200esc) goes to the Rossio, Praça do Comércio or Santa Apolónia.

Alternatively, there are taxis – very reasonable, at around 600esc.

Getting around

Getting around Lisbon presents few problems. Most places of interest are within easy walking distance – and transport connections are detailed in the text for those that aren't. The bus network operates from around 6am to 9.30pm; the trams keep going until midnight, and the metro until 1am. Taxis are among the cheapest in Europe, and are a useful complement at all hours.

If you're staying for more than a few days, the **tourist pass** (*Passe Turístico*; 1245esc for seven days, 850esc for four) might be worth considering; it is available, on production of a passport, at the booth by the Elevador Santa Justa and (sometimes) at other transport terminals. For longer stays, there is the *Passe Social*, renewable each calendar month at 2070esc (you'll need a photograph); again easiest obtained at the Elevador. Both of these cover all public city transport.

Note that although one of the safer cities in Europe, Lisbon has its share of pickpockets. Take special care on buses and around the main squares.

Trams

At the slightest excuse you should ride one of the city's **trams** (*eléctricos*). Ascending some of the steepest gradients of any city in the world, many are worth taking for the pleasure of the ride alone, for example:

● **#12** São Tomé in the Alfama to the Largo Martim Moniz, near Praça da Figueira.

● **#28** A great ride from São Vicente to the Estrela gardens, passing through Rua da Conceição in the Baixa.

● **Elevador da Bica** A funicular-like ride down from Rua do Loreto/Rua Luz Soriano in Bairro Alto to Rua de São Paulo near the river.

Most of the trams run every ten to fifteen minutes throughout the day, from around 6.30am to midnight. Look up for the tram-stop (*paragem*) signs, suspended from the cable.

Ticket prices are currently 30–77.5esc for a journey.

The Metro

The *Metropolitano* covers a few useful routes – to the Gulbenkian museum, or the zoo, for example – though as a visitor to the city you're unlikely to make extensive use of it. The most central stations are at Praça dos Restauradores and in the Rossio.

Tickets are 45esc a journey; or a bit cheaper bought in blocks (*módulos*) of ten. Modulos, like passes, are most easily obtained at the Elevador Santa Justa.

Buses

City buses (*carris*) run just about everywhere in the Lisbon area and can prove valuable for getting to and from the rather far-flung bus terminals – and the football stadiums.

Tickets are comparatively expensive, at 100esc, and some journeys may require two tickets. If you are staying any length of time, it is well worth buying *módulos* (430esc for 20); these are available from kiosks near main bus stops, above Pombal for example.

Taxis

Lisbon's taxis are excellent value, so long as your journey is within the city limits. All journeys are metered and drivers almost always switch them on; you should rarely pay more than 200–300esc for a trip.

The only problem is persuading one to stop. Taxis can be found quite easily by day, especially around the main squares, where there are ranks in the Rossio and at the near end of Avenida da Liberdade. But at night it's a different matter. If you're going home from a bar or club it's usually best to get someone to phone.

The *Rádio Taxis* number is ☎825061 (or 825062/3/4/5/6/7/8/9).

Trains

There is a local line **west along the coast** through Belém, to Estoril and Cascais, departing from the Cais do Sodré station. Tickets, as on all Portuguese trains, are inexpensive.

Ferries

Ferries cross the Tagus at various points. Prices are from 60 to 160esc one way.

Praça do Comércio (*Sul e Sueste*) to: Barreiro, Cacilhas and Montijo (the latter only in the bullfighting season).

Cais do Sodré to Cacilhas (buses run to Caparica and most southern bank destinations).

Belém to Trafaria (buses to Caparica).

Accommodation

Lisbon has scores of small, cheap **pensions** (*pensões*), often grouped one on top of the other in tall tenement blocks. Most of the year you should have little difficulty in finding a room – from around 1000 to 1500esc single, 2000 to 2500esc double – within a few minutes' walk of the Rossio. Anything cheaper is usually in the business of 'thirty-minute rooms' as the Portuguese put it, but most are safe enough. In midsummer, however, things are different, with possibilities often stretched to the limit and most single rooms 'converted' to doubles. At this time you should be prepared to take anything vacant, and look around next day, if need be, for somewhere better.

If you have money for the more expensive categories of **hotels** (4000esc and up) it can save a lot of walking to use the **reservation service** at the Praça dos Restauradores **Turismo**. The service operates during normal tourist office hours (Mon.–Sat. 9am–7.30pm, Sun. 10am–6pm); there is no commission charge.

Looking around on your own, however, especially for the cheaper options, pick from one of the pensions below, most of which are 2-star or 1-star rated. These are not exhaustive listings – you should come across other pensions in the streets and regions given – but they do cover all of the main concentrations in the central areas. When doing the rounds, be warned that the pensions tend to occupy upper storeys (leaving one person with all your bags is a good idea) and that those within the same building are generally independent of each other, so try all of them for space. Also, front-facing rooms are pretty noisy in Lisbon.

Addresses – written as 53-3°, etc. – specify the street number followed by the storey number.

Around the Rossio

Rossio (Praça D. Pedro V): *Santo Tirso* (18-3°); *Évora* and *do Sul* (both at 59-2°).

Praça da Figueira: *Coimbra e Madrid* (3-3°/4°); *Beira Minho* (6-2°; fair); *Ibérica* (10-2°); *Sonso* (10-3°).

Praça dos Restauradores: *Pensão Restauradores* (13-4°); *Imperial* (79).

Avenida da Liberdade: The Avenida extends beyond Restauradores to the formal Parque Eduardo VII. Pensions, generally a bit more expensive than those above, include: *Pemba* (11-3°); *Residencial Mucaba* (53-2°); *Lis* (180); *Dom Sancho I* (202-3° & 5°); *Casa de São João* (240-3°); *Ritz* (240-4°).

Off the Avenida da Liberdade

Less obvious than the area above – and thus more likely to have space – are a group of pensions on either side off the Avenida da Liberdade.

Rua das Portas de Santo Antão (parallel to the east of Av. da Liberdade): *Modelo* (12; good); *Flor da Baixa* (81-2°; cheap and good); *Florescente* (99; huge, 4-storey pension, reasonably priced and almost always with space); *Portuense* (expensive).

Rua da Gloria (west of the Avenida, behind Rossio station): a noisy street by night but a fair location. Try: *Iris* (2a–2°; clean and cheap); *Monumental* (21); *Virginia* (72-2° & 3°).

Rua da Alegria (extension of Rua da Gloria): *Milanesa* (25-2°).

Praça da Alegria: A good base, with the *Sevilha* (11-2° & 3°; inexpensive); *Alegria* (12-1°); *Solar* (12-2°).

The Baixa

Many of the smaller Baixa streets have pensions, particularly on the **east side** of the grid.

Rua dos Douradores: *Bom Conforto* (83-3°); *Norte* (159-1° & 2°); *Santiago* (222-3°; a good bet).

Rua da Prata: *Prata* (71-3°; cheap and recommended).

Other, cheaper options, on the **west of the Baixa**, include:

Rua dos Sapateiros: *Rossio* (173-2°); *Arco Bandeira* (at the top end).

Rua do Crucifixo:*Galiza* (50-5°).

Or, climbing up towards Bairro Alto:

Calçada do Carmo (behind Rossio station): *Pensão Estação Central* (17-21°); *Pensão Henriques* (37-11°). These two are handy but distinctly unthrilling choices.

Calçada do Duque (by the church of San Roque): *Pensão do Duque* (53; clean and very reasonably priced).

Travessa da Poco da Cidade: Pensão Camoes (very pleasant, though a fair bit pricier).

Rua dom Pedro V: *Londres* (53-1°; ☎365523).

Around the Castle

Oddly enough, there are no pensions in the Alfama district, but there are a few attractive places on the periphery – climbing up towards the castle.

Rua São João da Praca: *Pensão São João da Praça* (☎862591; good inexpensive choice in a quiet area above Alfama).

Costa do Castelo: *Pensão Ninho das Aguias* (74; ☎862151; more expensive, at around 3000esc a double, and rather surly, but beautifully sited in its own garden on the street looping around the castle).

Bairro Alto and the Outskirts

Bairro Alto is perhaps the most lively and atmospheric part of the city to stay in. To get up there, either take a taxi or the funicular-tram from beyond the Turismo in Praça dos Restauradores.

Rua da Barocca: This street has a basic pension and there are a couple of others halfway down in the Travessa do Poço da Cidade.

Rua do Teixeira (just behind the Port Wine Institute building): *Pensão Globo* (37)

Rua da Atalaia: *Pensão Atalaia* (past the *Frágil* nightclub; probably the cheapest – and noisiest – pension in town).

Calçada do Duque (near São Roque): *Pensão Duque* (just outside the nightclub zone but atmospheric).

If these pensions are all full they may be able to direct you to cheap rooms nearby. (See "Bairro Alto" for a detailed map of this area).

Further afield, you might also try:

Calçada Marquês de Abrantes (trams #18, 25 or 26 from Praça da Figueira or Praça do Comércio to *Conde Barão*): *Residencial Beiratejo* (43-2°) and *Mané* (97; cheap and dingy).

Youth Hostels

Youth Hostel (*Pousada de Juventude*), Rua Andrade Corvo 46 (☎532696; closed 2–6pm). Lisbon's main hostel; not a bad location but a rather large, soulless place with a midnight curfew. It's very near the Parque Eduardo VII – one block below the *Picoas* metro stop, or take buses #1, 44 or 45 from Restauradores, Rossio or Cais do Sodré, or #90, 44 or 45 direct from the airport.

Oeiras Youth Hostel (Forte do Catalazete, ☎2430638; also closed 2–6pm). The second Lisbon hostel is 20km outside the city, overlooking the beach at Oeiras. Take a slow train from the Cais do Sodré and follow signs from Oeiras station under the coast road (*Estrada Marginal*) and through the park – around 1km. It's small, so phone before setting out.

Campsites

Parque Nacional de Turismo e Campismo. The city campsite is located in the Parque Florestal Monsanto, on the edge of the city. It is a pleasant enough site, with a swimming pool and shops, though lousy service at the café, and a highly inconvenient location for anyone without transport. The entrance is on the *Estrada da Circunvalação*. If you are travelling by public transport, take bus #14 from Praça da Figueira (or close to the *Sul e Sueste* station) or even a train, more reliable in the rush hour, from the Cais do Sodré to Algés, then bus #50 to the campsite. To return to Praça da Figueira take the #43. The Monsanto park itself is an attractive picnic area by day, though less cosy at night.

Costa da Caparica. An alternative to Monsanto is to camp at one of the beaches along the Costa da Caparica. There are several small and lively campsites here, 30–50 minutes away by bus (see "The Beaches").

The City Quarters

Lisbon's interest lies as much in the everyday aspects of the city as in any specific sights. The cafés, markets, trams, ferries across the Tagus: all these are sufficient stimulation for random wanderings. The most rewarding areas, as you'd expect, are the oldest: the upper and lower towns of **Baixa** and **Bairro Alto**, and the winding lanes and anarchic stairways of **Alfama**.

The two sections following this detail, respectively, the city's museums and the neighbourhood of Belém, along the seafront to the west.

Around the Baixa

The lower town – **the Baixa** – is very much the heart of the capital, housing many of the country's administrative departments, banks and business offices. Yet it is also a speedy introduction to the contradictions of the city. Although it appears on first impressions an imposing quarter – Europe's first great example of neoclassical design and urban planning – it's not long before you realise that the uniform streets, even in the chic shopping districts, are not quite all they seem. For all Lisbon's cosmopolitan air, this is the nearest a Western European capital gets to the Third World. Begging, lottery-ticket selling and shoe-shining are all growth industries.

Streets and Markets

The positive side of this – at least for outsiders – is the survival of tradition. Many of the **streets in the Baixa** maintain their crafts and businesses as Pombal devised: Rua da Prata (Silversmiths' Street), Rua dos Sapateiros (Cobblers' Street), Rua do Ouro (Goldsmiths' Street), Rua do Comércio. And they are, along with the mosaic pavemented squares, a visual delight – the buildings, full of Art Deco advertising survivals, along with the occasional Communist street mural from the 1974 Revolution.

The markets around Baixa are particularly wonderful. The **fish market**, which takes place from dawn behind the **Cais do Sodré** station, is a good case in point: you can still see *varinas*, fishwives from Alfama who were joined a few years ago by groups from Cabo Verde, bargaining and carting off great baskets of wares on their heads. Take a look inside the market, too. Even if you're not tempted by the arrays of food, the flower displays on the upper storey are a visual delight. Rua da Arsenal, just behind the market, is packed with stalls selling fresh fish and dried cod, and grocers stocked with everything – including unbelievably cheap wines and spirits.

Chiado and the Rossio

Architecturally, and as points towards which to gravitate, the most interesting places in the Baixa are the squares – the **Rossio** and **Praça do Comércio** – and, on the periphery, the lanes leading east to the **Sé** (Cathedral) and west up **towards Bairro Alto**. This latter area, known as **Chiado**, suffered much damage from a fire that swept across the Baixa in August 1988, destroying the *Grandella* department store and many old shops in Rua do Crucifixio.

Chiado, however, remains the city's most affluent quarter, focused on the fashionable shops and – fortunately spared from the fire – the beautiful old café-tearooms of the **Rua Garrett**.

Of these cafés, *Brasileira*, at Rua Garrett 120, is the most famous, having been frequented by generations of Lisbon's literary and intellectual leaders – the very readable Eça de Quieroz and Portugal's greatest twentieth-century poet, Fernando Pessoa, among them. It's not an especially expensive place to sit, at least for coffee, although if you're seriously into pastry shops (and

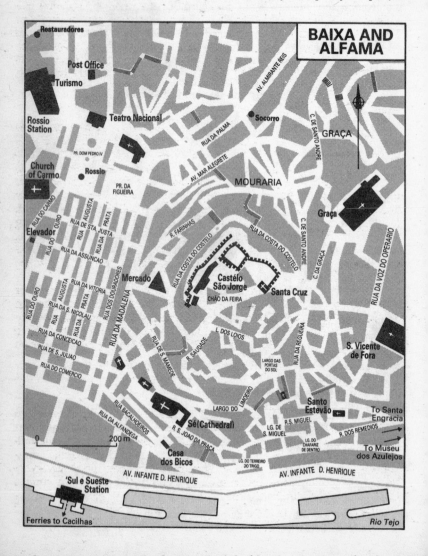

BAIXA AND ALFAMA

Lisbon has a wide range) the best eats are at the *Pastelaria Suíça*, on the Rossio.

The Rossio – which itself is more or less encircled by cafés – is modest in appearance, but very much a focus for the city. Its single concession to grandeur is the **Teatro Nacional**, built along the north side in the 1840s and said to have dreadful acoustics. Here, prior to the earthquake, stood the Inquisitional Palace; bullfights, public hangings and autos-da-fé (ritual burnings of heretics) used to take place in the square. The nineteenth-century statue above the fountains is of Dom Pedro IV (after whom the square is officially named), though curiously it's a bargain adaptation: cast originally as Maximilian of Mexico, it just happened to be in Lisbon en route from France when news came through of his assassination. The church beyond the square, **São Domingos**, was where the Inquisition actually read out its sentences; though blackened and gutted by a fire in the 1950s, the building is still in religious use.

Praça do Comércio

At the waterfront end of the Baixa, the **Praça do Comércio** was intended as the climax to Pombal's design, at its centre an exuberant bronze of Dom José, monarch during the 'quake and the capital's rebuilding. Seen from the river – the Fluvial terminal, where ferries across to Barreiro and Cacilhas dock, is just off the square – the design is graceful and impressive, with the streets of the Baixa extending into the distance beyond. Close up, however, it seems less substantial, and less glamorous, having been requisitioned as a car park for the government employees working in its classical buildings. The town planners are working on projects to bring it back into the hub of city life, specifically by making the area pedestrian and opening more cafés, but the only sign of life is still at the dimly-lit, old-world café-restaurant of *Martinho da Arcada*, one of the poet Pessoa's haunts.

Like the Rossio, the square has a popular name – *Terreiro do Paço*, after the old royal palace which stood here (and whose steps still lead up from the Tagus) – and it too has played an important part in the country's history. In 1908, alongside the Central Post Office, King Carlos I and his eldest son were shot and killed, opening the way to the declaration of the Republic two years later.

The Cathedral and around

A couple of blocks east of the Praça do Comércio is the church of **Conceição Velha**, severely damaged by the earthquake but retaining its flamboyant Manueline doorway, an early example of this style and hinting at the brilliance that emerged at Belém. It once formed part of the Misericórdia (almshouse) – you'll find one of these impressive structures in almost every Portuguese town or city. Nearby, at Campo das Cebolas, stands the curious **Casa dos Bicos**, set with diamond-shaped stones and again offering an image of the richness of pre-1755 Lisbon; the building is not routinely open, though it sees fairly regular use for cultural exhibitions.

The Sé

The Cathedral – or **Sé**, as they're called in Portugal – stands very stolidly above. Founded in 1150 to commemorate the city's reconquest from the Moors, it has a suitably fortress-like appearance, similar to that of Coimbra, and in fact occupies the site of the principal mosque of Moorish *Lishbuna*. Like so many of the country's cathedrals, it is Romanesque – and extraordinarily restrained in both size and decoration. The great rose window and twin towers form a simple and effective façade, but inside there's nothing very exciting: the building was once splendidly embellished by Dom João V, but his Rococo whims were swept away by the earthquake and subsequent restorers. All that remains is a group of Gothic tombs behind the high altar and the decaying thirteenth-century cloisters.

For admission to these you must buy a (nominally priced) ticket, which also covers the Baroque *Sacristia* (9am–1pm and 2–6pm) with its small museum of treasures – including the relics of Saint Vincent, brought to Lisbon in 1173 by Afonso Henriques in a boat piloted by ravens (see "Sagres", in the *Algarve* chapter). For centuries the descendants of these birds were shown to visitors but the last specimen, despite great care from the sacristan, died in 1978. Nevertheless, ravens are still one of the city's symbols.

The Castle

From the Sé, the Rua das Cruzes da Sé leads directly into the heart of the **Alfama**. Rua do Limoeiro winds upward towards the **Castelo**, past sparse ruins of a Roman theatre, the well-positioned **Miradouro de Santa Luzia**, and the *Espirito Santo Foundation*, home of the **Museum of Decorative Art** (see "Museums", following).

The **conquest of Lisbon from the Moors** – and the siege of the Castelo de São Jorge – are depicted in *azulejos* on the walls of **Santa Luzia**. An important victory, leading to Muslim surrender at Sintra and throughout the surrounding district, this was not, however, the most Christian or glorious of Portuguese exploits. A full account survives, written by one Osbern of Bawdsley, an English priest and crusader, and its details, despite the author's judgmental tone, direct one's sympathies to the enemy.

The attack, in the summer of 1147, came through the opportunism and skilful management of Afonso Henriques, already established as 'King' at Porto, who persuaded a large force of French and British Crusaders to delay their progress to Jerusalem for more immediate goals. The Crusaders – scarcely more than pirates – came to terms and in June the siege began. Osbern records the Archbishop of Braga's demand for the Moors to return to 'the land whence you came' and, more revealingly, the weary and contemptuous response of the Muslim spokesman: 'How many times have you come hither with pilgrims and barbarians to drive us hence? It is not want of possessions but only ambition of the mind that drives you on'. For seventeen weeks the castle and inner city stood firm but in October its walls were breached and the citizens – including a Christian community coexisting with the Muslims – were forced to surrender.

The pilgrims and barbarians, flaunting the diplomacy and guarantees of Afonso Henriques, stormed into the city, cut the throat of the local bishop, and sacked, pillaged and murdered Christian and Muslim alike. In 1190 a later band of English Crusaders stopped at Lisbon and, no doubt confused by the continuing presence of Moors, sacked the city a second time.

Castelo de São Jorge
A triumphant statue of Afonso Henriques – who alone emerges from the account with honour – stands at the entrance to the **Castelo** (9am–9pm; free). Beyond stretch gardens and terraces, walkways and pools, enclosed within the old Moorish walls.

At first the Portuguese kings had taken up residence within the *castelo* – in the *Alcáçova*, the Muslim palace – but by the time of Manuel I this had been superseded by the new royal palace on Terreiro do Paço. Of the Alcáçova only a much-restored shell remains, in which a small, rather insignificant museum (Roman and Islamic tombstones, etc.) has been installed. But the castle as a whole is an enjoyable place to spend a couple of hours, wandering amid the ramparts and towers to look down upon the city.

Crammed within the castle's outer walls is the tiny medieval quarter of **Santa Cruz**, once very much a village in itself, while to the north sprawls the old **Mouraria**, to which the Moors were relegated on their loss of the town. This, despite a few grand old houses, is largely in decay and at present being substantially redeveloped. Of the Moorish-Medieval town, only the Alfama quarter, stumbling from the walls of the *castelo* to the banks of the Tagus, has survived and adapted over the years.

Alfama

The oldest part of Lisbon, **Alfama** was buttressed against significant damage in the 1755 earthquake by the steep, rocky mass on which it's built. Although none of its houses dates from before the Christian conquest, many are of Moorish design and the Kasbah-like layout is much as Osbern described it, with 'steep defiles instead of ordinary streets . . . and buildings so closely packed together that, except in the merchants' quarter, hardly a street could be found more than eight foot wide'.

In Arab times Alfama was the grandest part of the city but with subsequent earthquakes – Lisbon averages one every 200 years – the new Christian nobility moved out, leaving it to the fishing community so evident today. Today, it is undergoing some commercialisation, with its cobbled lanes and 'character', but although the antique shops and restaurants may be moving in, they are far from taking over. The quarter retains a largely traditional life of its own; you can eat at local prices in the cafés; the flea market engulfs the periphery of the area twice a week; and this is very much the place to be during the great June festivals of the 'Popular Saints', when makeshift tavernas appear at every corner.

The steep defiles, alleys, and passageways are known as *becos* and *travessas* rather than *ruas*, and it would be impossible (as well as futile) to try and follow any set route. At some point in your wanderings around the quarter, though, head for the **Rua de São Miguel** – off which are some of the most interesting *becos* – and for the (lower) parallel **Rua de São Pedro**, the main market street leading to the lively **Largo do Chafariz de Dentro**. The most promising areas for café-restaurants are Rua da Regueira, above the Largo do Chafariz, and Rua de Santo Estevão.

The Flea Market and Around

The **Feira da Ladra**, Lisbon's rambling and ragged **flea market**, fills the Campo de Santa Clara, at the edge of Alfama, on Tuesday morning and all day Saturday. Though it's certainly not the world's greatest – 'you will find stalls with shabby ready-made clothes' says the cautious Turismo pamphlet – it does turn up some interesting things: oddities from the former African colonies, old prints of the country, and some good Portuguese army-surplus gear. Out-and-out junk is spread on the ground above Santa Engrácia, half-genuine antiques at the top end of the *feira*. (Tram #28 runs from Rua da Conceição in the Baixa to São Vicente, and bus #12 runs between Santa Apolónia station and the Praça Marquês de Pombal.)

While at the flea market, take a look inside **Santa Engrácia**, the loftiest and most tortuously-built church in the city. Begun in 1682 and once a synonym for unfinished work, its vast dome was finally completed in 1966. If you ask nicely, you may be allowed to take the lift to the dome – looking down on the empty church and out over the flea market, port and city.

More interesting, architecturally, is nearby **São Vicente de Fora**, whose name – 'of the outside' – is a reminder of the extent of the sixteenth-century city. It is also where Afonso Henriques pitched camp during the siege and the conquest of Lisbon. Built during the years of Spanish rule by Philip II's Italian architect, Felipe Terzi, its severe geometric façade was an important Renaissance innovation. Through the cloisters, tiled with *azulejos*, you can visit the old monastic refectory, since 1855 the pantheon of the Bragança dynasty. Here, in more or less complete (though unexciting) sequence, are the bodies of all Portuguese kings from João IV, who restored the monarchy, to Manuel II who lost it and died in exile in England in 1932; included is Catherine of Bragança, the widow of Charles II and (as the local guide points out) 'the one who took the habit of the fifth o'clock tea to that country'.

Bairro Alto

Bairro Alto, the upper town, is the natural place to wind up at night – in the *fado* houses, bars, excellent restaurants or even the refined and somewhat dauntingly named Port Wine Institute. For details on all this see "The Facts".

By day, the quarter's narrow seventeenth-century streets have a very different character, with children playing in the streets, the old sitting in doorways, and nightlife venues seemingly as much concealed as closed. It is well worth a morning or afternoon's exploration, with two of the most interesting churches in Lisbon – Carmo and São Roque – on the fringes, and a couple of approaches to the quarter that are a treat in themselves.

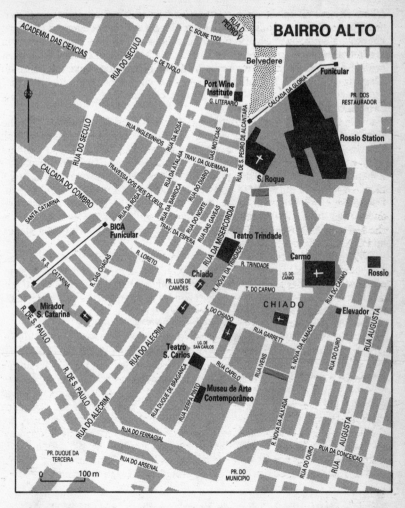

Eiffel's **Elevador Santa Justa**, just off the top end of Rua do Ouro on Rua de Santa Justa, is the most obvious: one of the city's most extraordinary and eccentric structures. A lift whisks you up through Eiffel's metal latticework, depositing you on a platform from where there are views over the Baixa below. Alternatives, and hardly more conventional feats of engineering, are the two **funicular-like trams**. One, *Elevador da Glória*, links the quarter directly with the Praça dos Restauradores, taking off just behind the tourist office on the left; the other, *Elevador da Bica*, climbs up to Rua do Loreto (west of the Praça de Camões) from Rua de São Paulo/Rua da Moeda, northwest of Cais do Sodré. Both funiculars and the lift currently cost 22.5esc one-way.

The ruined Gothic arches of the **Convento do Carmo** hang almost directly above the exit of Eiffel's *elevador*. Once the largest church in the city, this was half-destroyed by the earthquake but is perhaps even more beautiful as a result. In the nineteenth century its shell was adapted as a chemical factory. These days it houses a small 'archaeological museum' (10am–6pm; closed Mon.) with a very miscellaneous collection of medieval tombs and *azulejos*; admission, as so often, is a nominal charge. At night in summer free classical concerts are often held here.

São Roque

The church of **São Roque**, over towards the Chiado in the Largo Trindade Coelho, looks from the outside like the plainest in the city, its bleak Renaissance façade (by Filipo Terzi, architect of São Vicente) having been further simplified by the earthquake. Nor does it seem impressive when you walk inside. But hang around in the gloom and the sacristan will come and escort you around, turning on lights to an incredible succession of side chapels, each lavishly crafted with *azulejos* (some emulating reliefs), multicoloured marble, or Baroque painted ceilings. The climax – to which you're proudly directed – is the **Capela de São João Baptista**, last on the left.

This chapel, for its size, is estimated to be the most expensive ever constructed and was certainly one of the most bizarre commissions of its age. It was ordered from Rome in 1742 by Dom João V to honour his patron saint and, more dubiously, to requite the pope, whom he had persuaded to confer a patriarchate upon Lisbon. Designed by the papal architect, Vanvitelli, and using the most costly materials available (including ivory, agate, porphyry and lapis lazuli), it was actually erected at the Vatican for the pope to celebrate mass before being dismantled and shipped to Lisbon. The cost, then, was about a quarter of a million pounds, which is perhaps its chief curiosity. But there are other eccentricities. Take a close look at the four 'oil paintings' of John the Baptist's life and you'll find that they are in fact mosaics, intricately worked over what must have been years rather than months.

The site of the Crusader camp during the Siege of Lisbon is occupied by the **Igreja dos Mártires**, in nearby Rua Garrett. This was also, as the name suggests, a burial ground, particularly for the English contingent of the besieging army.

Estrela

A fourth church, the **Basílica da Estrela** on the far side of Bairro Alto, is also worth the half-hour walk (or take tram #28 from Chiado). Not so much for the building itself – a vast monument to late-eighteenth-century Baroque – as for the view across the city from its dome, and for the **public gardens** below. Lisbon takes its gardens seriously, even the small patches amid squares and avenues, and these are among the most enjoyable, a quiet refuge often graced with an afternoon brass band.

Through the park and on the Rua de São Jorge is the gate to the **English Cemetery** (post-Crusader; ring loudly for entry) where among the cypresses lies Henry Fielding, author of *Tom Jones*, whose imminent demise may have influenced his verdict on Lisbon as 'the nastiest city in the world'.

Further out: Parque Edourado VII, Amoreiras, and the Zoo

North of the Praça dos Restauradores are the city's principal gardens – the **Parque Eduardo VII**. The easiest approach is by metro (to *Parque*), though you could walk up (energetically) in about twenty minutes along the Avenida da Liberdade or take any bus going to the Rotunda.

The park's big attractions are the **Estufas**, huge and wonderful glasshouses, filled with subtropical plants, flamingo pools, and endless varieties of palms and cacti. They're near the top end of the park, open 9am to 6pm (erratically closed at lunchtime), and once again admission charges are low enough to allow casual visiting.

There are some excellent cafés close by, and a student mensa and bar at the top end of the park, to while away an hour or two more of the evening. At the Estufa Fria itself, rock and classical concerts and an antiques fair are occasionally held.

Several useful **bus links** from the park are: at the bottom end of the Rotunda #31, #41 and #46, which run north a few blocks to the Gulbenkian museum (ten minutes' walk; see below), and #27 and #49, which run west to the Monastery of Jerónimos at Belém; and from the top of the park near the Estufa Fria #51 direct to Belém.

Amoreiras

In the daytime, a **free bus** ferries shoppers from the Rotunda to Lisbon's new post-modernist shopping centre, **Amoreiras** (Avda. Duarte Pacheco), visible on the city skyline from almost any approach. The complex, designed by Tomás Taveira, is Portugal's most adventurous – and most entertaining – modern building: a wild lego fantasy of pink and blue, sheltering 10 cinemas, 60 restaurants, 370 shops and a hotel. Most of the shops stay open until 11pm, seven days a week.

Buses #11 (from Rossio; last bus back at 8pm) and #23 go past Amoreiras and also past the **Aqueduto das Águas Livres**, opened in 1748, just behind. A Jack-the-Ripper figure was supposed to have thrown victims off the aqueduct in the eighteenth century – they would have had a drop of 65m from the central arch. You'll have a pretty good view of the aqueduct from the road if you take the Praça de Espanha bus to Caparica.

The Zoo and Fronteira Palace

The **Jardim Zoológico** is not the most inspiring of European zoos – it has the standard unhappy captives in poor housing – but it is really as much a rambling garden as anything else. In this, and in the peculiarly Portuguese eruptions of kitsch (an extraordinary dog's cemetery), it's enjoyable enough; opening hours are 9am to 7pm daily.

Opportunists might like to ring for the housekeeper at the gate of the **Palácio dos Marqueses da Fronteira** (private, but you can look around the gardens), which is five minutes away. After the bland surroundings of the housing development on the Rua de São Domingo and after crossing the little-used railway line, the fantastic gardens of this small, pink country house feel like an oasis. Have a look at the tiled conversation piece that the

Marquês built for messing around in boats. The allegorical panels on the lower level, taken from Camões' tale of the *Doze da Inglaterra*, mark a historic moment in the history of *azulejos* when, in the mid-seventeenth century, the Portuguese dropped the formal Moorish methods of design (as in the upper level) and turned to painting straight on to tiles.

Buses #31, #41 and #46 (or the metro, to *Sete Rios*), link the Rotunda with the Jardim Zoologico.

The Museums

Visitors will need to remember that all Lisbon's museums – except for the Arte Popular at Belém – together with a number of churches and public gardens close for the whole day on **Monday** and on **public holidays**. Admission charges vary, the Gulbenkian is very cheap, others tend to range from 200–400esc; in many cases an ISIC card will get you in free.

At the Gulbenkian and Arte Antiga there are very good, inexpensive café-restaurants; the former also has very pleasant gardens if you prefer to take a picnic, and free concerts (starting around 1pm) most Sundays.

Museu Calouste Gulbenkian

July–Oct. open Tues., Thurs., Fri., Sun. 10am–5pm, Sat. & Wed. 2–7.30pm; Nov.–June open Tues.–Sun. 10am–5pm; closed Mon. all year. Avda. de Berna – bus #31, #41 or #46 from the Rossio, or metro to Palhavã or, better still and close to the Modern Art section, São Sebastião. 40esc admission; free on Sun.

Like some kind of crystallisation of the British Museum and the Courtauld Gallery, the **Museu Calouste Gulbenkian** is *the* great museum of Portugal. It is housed in a superb complex, set in its own park, and its extraordinary collections seem to take in virtually every great phase of Eastern and Western art – from Ancient Egyptian scarabs to Art Nouveau jewellery, Islamic textiles to French Impressionists. In a new, separate building, across the park, a **Centro de Arte Moderna** has also just been opened – its excitingly displayed works, exclusively Portuguese, touch on most styles of twentieth-century art.

Astonishingly, all were acquired by just one man, the Armenian oil magnate, Calouste Gulbenkian (1869–1955), whose legendary art-market coups included buying works from the Leningrad Hermitage after the Russian Revolution. In a yet stranger deal made during the last war, Gulbenkian literally auctioned himself and his collections to the European nations: Portugal bid security, an aristocratic palace home (a Marquês was asked to move out) and tax-exemption to acquire one of the most important cultural patrons of the century.

Today the Gulbenkian Foundation runs an orchestra, three concert halls and two galleries for temporary exhibitions in the capital alone. It also finances work in all spheres of Portuguese cultural life – there are Gulbenkian museums and libraries in the smallest towns – and makes charitable grants to a vast range of projects both in Portugal and in Britain, where Gulbenkian once lived. A schedule of current Gulbenkian activities in Portugal is available at the admissions desk of the museum.

The Main Museum
The **Museu Gulbenkian** is the public showplace of the foundation. It is divided into two complete and distinct halves – the first devoted to Egyptian, Greco-Roman, Islamic and Oriental arts, the second to European – and ideally you'll want to take them in on separate visits. The collections aren't immense in numbers but each contains pieces of such individual interest and beauty that you need frequent unwinding sessions – well provided for by the basement café-bar and gardens. Expert explanatory notes in English are usually available in every section; if you want to work out what to see in advance, ask for a complete set at the entrance.

It seems arbitrary to hint at highlights, but they must include the entire contents of the **Egyptian room**, which covers almost every period of importance from the Old Kingdom (2700 B.C.) to the Roman period. Particularly striking are a carved ivory spoon from the time of Amenophis III, and an extraordinarily lifelike *Head of a Priest* from the penultimate, Ptolomaic period. **Mesopotamia** produced the earliest forms of writing, and two cylinder seals, one from before 2500 B.C., are on display here, along with architectural sculpture from the Assyrian civilisation.

Fine statues, silver and glass from the **Romans** and intricate gold jewellery from ancient **Greece** come soon after, followed by remarkable illuminated manuscripts and ceramics from **Armenia**, porcelain from **China** and beautiful **Japanese** prints and lacquer-work. Islamic arts are magnificently represented by ornamented texts, opulently woven carpets, glassware (such as the fourteenth-century mosque lamps from **Syria**), and precious bindings from **Persia** and **India** (mostly fifteenth-century).

In the **European section** don't miss a group of French medieval **ivory diptychs** (particularly six scenes depicting the Life of the Virgin) and a thirteenth-century copy of Saint John's prophetic **Apocalypse**, produced in Kent and touched up in Italy under Pope Clement IX.

In the **painting** section you'll find work from all the major schools: from fifteenth-century Flanders, there's a pair of panels by **Van der Weyden**; from the same period in Italy comes **Ghirlandaio's** *Portrait of a Young Woman*; from the seventeenth century, there are two exceptional portraits – **Rubens'** of his second wife, *Helena Fourment*, and **Rembrandt's** *Figure of an Old Man* – plus works by van Dyck, Frans Hals, and Ruisdael; **Fragonard** is the best represented of the eighteenth-century artists, whose company includes Gainsborough, Sir Thomas Lawrence and Francesco Guardi; and finally Corot, Manet, Monet, and Renoir supply a good showing from nineteenth- to twentieth-century France.

Sculpture is poorly represented on the whole, though a French sixteenth-century religious statue of *Mary Magdalene*, a fifteenth-century medallion of *Faith* by Luca della Robbia, a 1780 marble *Diana* by Jean-Antoine Houdon, and a couple of Rodins stand out. Otherwise **ceramics** from Spain and Italy;

furniture from Louis XV to Louis XVI; eighteenth-century works from **French goldsmiths;** fifteenth-century **medals** (especially by Pisanello); tapestries and textiles; and, above all, an Art Nouveau collection with its 169 pieces of fantasy jewellery by **René Lalique** are the best of the tail-end of this great collection.

The Modern Art Centre

To reach the **Centro de Arte Moderna**, cross the gardens with their specially commissioned sculptures. This museum keeps the same hours as the main section (charging a further 40esc), and is also highly recommended.

Big names on the twentieth-century Portuguese scene include Almada Negreiros, the founder of *modernismo* (his portrait of Fernando Pessoa in the *Museu da Cidade* is particularly well known), Amadeu de Sousa Cardoso and Guilherme Santa-Rita (both of Futurist inclinations), Vieira da Silva (a criss-cross of lines), and Paula Rego (who paints creepy kids).

Museu de Arte Antiga

Tues., Wed., Fri., Sat, 9am–5pm, Thurs. & Sun. 9am–7pm. Rua das Janelas Verdes 95 – by tram #19 from the Praça do Comércio (10 min.), by bus #40 from Rua do Comércio, and bus #27 or #49 from Belém.

The **Ancient Art Museum** – Portugal's national collection – is the one other gallery that stands up to Gulbenkian standards. It doesn't have the same eclecticism, of course, nor the familiarity of international highlights, but the core of the museum – fifteenth- and sixteenth-century Portuguese works by such artists as Nuno Gonçalves – is excellent, and well displayed in a beautiful converted palace of the period.

Gonçalves and his fellow painters of the so-called 'Portuguese school' span that indeterminate and exciting period when Gothic art was giving way to the Renaissance. Their works, exclusively religious in concept, are particularly interesting in their emphasis on portraiture – transforming any theme, even a martyrdom, into a vivid observation of local contemporary life. Stylistically, the most significant influences upon them were those of the Flemish, 'Northern Renaissance' painters: Jan van Eyck, who came to Portugal in 1428, Memling and Mabuse (both well represented here), and Roger van der Weyden.

The acknowledged masterpiece, however, is Gonçalves's *Panéis de São Vicente* (Saint Vincent Altarpiece), a brilliantly marshalled canvas depicting the saint, Lisbon's patron, receiving homage from all ranks of its citizens. On the two left-hand panels are Cistercian monks, fishermen and pilots; on the opposite side the Duke of Bragança and his family, a helmeted Moorish knight, a Jew (with book), a beggar, and a priest holding St. Vincent's own relics (a piece of his skull, still possessed by the cathedral). In the epic central panels the moustachioed Henry the Navigator, his nephew Afonso V (in green), and the youthful (future) Dom João II pay tribute to the saint. Among the frieze of portraits behind them, that on the far left is reputed to be Gonçalves himself; the other central panel shows the Archbishop of Lisbon.

Later Portuguese painters – from the sixteenth to the eighteenth century – are displayed too, along with good collections of **ceramics** (showing the influence of Indian and Oriental designs from the new trading links). But after Gonçalves and his contemporaries (notably Gregorio Lopes and Frei Carlos), the most interesting works are by the **Flemish and Germans** (Cranach, Bosch – a fabulous *Temptation of St. Anthony* – and Dürer), and miscellaneous gems by Raphael, Zurbarán and, rather oddly, Rodin.

Other Museums in Central Lisbon

Museum of Azulejos (*Museu dos Azulejos*).

11am–1pm and 3–5pm; Rua Madre de Deus 4; tram #3 or #16 from the Praça do Comércio, or walk along the road above Santa Apolónia station.

This is installed in the church and cloisters of Madre de Deus, whose own eighteenth-century tiled scenes of the life of St. Anthony form its centrepiece. Portugal's longest *azulejo* – the wonderfully detailed 120-foot Panorama of Lisbon – is now on display. All highly recommended.

City of Lisbon Museum (*Museu da Cidade*).

2–6pm; Palácio Pimenta, top left Campo Grande; buses #1 and #36 from the Rossio and #7 from Praça da Figueira.

Set in an old palace at the far end of the Campo Grande, the main interests of this new and imaginative collection are prints and models of pre-1755 Lisbon and Almada Negreiros' portrait of Fernando Pessoa.

Costume Museum (*Museu do Trajo*).

10am–1pm and 2.30–5pm; Palácio do Monteiro-Mor, Largo São João Baptista 4; bus #36 from Rossio, almost to the end of its route, or buses #7 from Praça da Figueira and #7B from Sete Rios.

Another recent museum, again in an eighteenth-century palace (with gardens and restaurant). The collections are extensive and well above specialist interest.

Science Museum (*Museu da Academia de Ciencias*).

9am–noon and 2–5.30pm, closed Saturday afternoon and Sunday; Rua da Academia de Ciencias.

A real old-fashioned science museum, with dinosaur bones to trip over and rows of fossils laid out in wooden cases. A charmer – and free.

Military Museum (*Museu Militar*).

10am–4pm; opposite Santa Apolónia station.

Another very traditional museum – old weapons in old cases – which, unfortunately, lacks the dinosaur appeal.

Overseas Museum (*Museu Ultramarino e Etnográfico*).

11am–1pm and 3–5pm, closed weekends; Rua das Portas de Santo Antão 100, parallel to the Avda. da Liberdade.

Ethnic displays from the former colonies.

Contemporary Art Museum (_Museu de Arte Contemporânea_).

10am–12.30pm and 2–5pm; Rua Serpa Pinto 6, close to Chiado and Rua Garrett.

About as un-contemporary as you could imagine – nineteenth- and even eighteenth-century portraits. For genuinely contemporary Portuguese art check the Gulbenkian's recently opened permanent collection.

Museum of Decorative Arts (_Museu das Artes Decorativas Portuguesas da Fundação Espírito Santo_).

10am–5pm; Largo das Portas do Sol, on the way up to the castle.

Guided tours only (and in Portuguese only) through this restored seventeenth-century mansion. Furnishings are rich and some pieces interesting but _everything_ is pointed out ('traditional Portuguese, Indian, Brazil', etc.). An endurance test.

The five Belém museums are detailed in the section below.

The Monastery of Jerónimos and Belém

Even before the Great Earthquake, the Monastery of Jerónimos (closed Mondays and lunchtimes) at **Belém** was Lisbon's finest monument: since then, it has stood quite without comparison.

The suburb is easily reached by tram – #15, #16 and #17 run from the Praça do Comércio, taking about twenty minutes.

The Monastery

It was from Belém in 1497 that Vasco da Gama set sail for India, and it was here too that he was welcomed home by Dom Manuel 'the Fortunate' (_O Venturoso_). Da Gama brought with him a small cargo of pepper, enough to pay for his voyage sixty times over. The **Monastery of Jerónimos** stands as a testament to his triumphant discovery of a sea route to the Orient, which amounted to the declaration of a 'golden age'. It was built in honour of a vow Dom Manuel made to the Virgin in return for a successful voyage, on the site of the old _Ermida do Restelo_ or _Capela de São Jerónimo_, a hermitage founded by Henry the Navigator, where Vasco da Gama and his companions had spent their last night ashore in prayer. Its funding also was a levy on the fruits of his discovery – a five percent tax on all spices other than pepper, cinnamon and cloves, whose import had become the sole preserve of the crown.

Begun in 1502 and substantially complete when its funding was withdrawn by João III in 1551, the monastery is the most ambitious and successful achievement of Manueline architecture. It is less flamboyantly exotic than either Tomar or Batalha – the great culminations of the style in Estremadura – but, despite a succession of master-builders, it has more daring and confidence in its overall design. This is largely the achievement of two outstanding figures, **Diogo de Boitaca**, perhaps the originator of the Manueline style with his Church of Jesus at Setúbal, and **João de Castilho**, a Spaniard who took over construction from around 1517.

The Church and Cloister

It was Castilho who designed the **main entrance** to the church, a complex, shrine-like hierarchy of figures centred around Henry the Navigator (on a pedestal above the arch). In its intricate and almost flat ornamentation, it shows the influence of the then-current Spanish style, Plateresque (literally, the art of the silversmith). Yet it also has distinctive Manueline features – the use of rounded forms, the naturalistic motifs in the bands around the windows – and these seem to create both its harmony and individuality. They are also unmistakably outward-looking, evoking the new forms discovered in the east, a characteristic that makes each Manueline building so new and so interesting – and so much a product of its particular and expansionary age.

This is immediately and spectacularly true of **the church** itself, whose breathtaking sense of space alone would place it among the great triumphs of European Gothic. Here, though, Manueline developments add two extraordinary fresh dimensions. There are tensions, deliberately created and carefully restrained, between the grand spatial design and the areas of intensely detailed ornamentation. And, still more striking, there's a naturalism in the forms of this ornamentation that seems to extend into the actual structure of the church. Once you've made the analogy, it's difficult to see the six central columns as anything other than palm trunks, growing both into and from the branches of the delicate rib-vaulting.

Another peculiarity of Manueline buildings is the way in which they can adapt, enliven or encompass any number of different styles. Here, the basic structure is thoroughly Gothic, though Castilho's ornamentation on the columns is much more Renaissance in spirit. So too is the semicircular apse (around the altar), added in 1572, beyond which is the entrance to the remarkable double cloister.

Vaulted throughout and fantastically embellished, the cloister (9am–6pm; 400esc) is one of the most original and beautiful pieces of architecture in the country. Again it holds in balance Gothic forms and Renaissance ornamentation and again its exuberance has created innovations – in the rounded corner canopies and delicate twisting divisions within each of the arches. These lend a wavelike, rhythmic motion to the whole structure, a conceit extended by the typically Manueline motifs drawn from ropes, anchors and the sea. In this – as in all aspects – it would be hard to imagine an art more directly reflecting the achievements and preoccupations of an age.

Museums

In the wings of the monastery are two **museums**. The enormous **Museu da Marinha** (10am–12.30pm and 2–5pm; free, closed Mon.), in the west wing, is more interesting than most of its kind; packed with models of ships, naval uniforms, and a surprising display of artifacts from Portugal's oriental trade and colonies.

In contrast, the **Museu de Arqueologia** (same hours), in the east wing, seems sparse and, apart from some fine Roman mosaics unearthed in the Algarve, thoroughly unexceptional. A third museum, **Museu Agrícola do Ultramar** – agriculture from overseas – is close to the eastern corner of the monastery and the Jardim Colonial, and speaks for itself.

Around Belém

The Tagus at Belém has receded with the centuries, for when the Monastery of Jerónimos was built it stood almost on the beach, within sight of caravels moored for the expeditions to India and Brazil and of the **Torre de Belém**, guarding the entrance to the port.

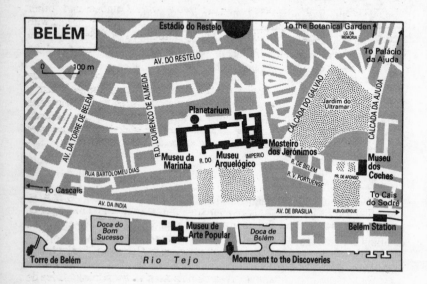

Torre de Belém

The tower, still washed on three sides by the sea, is just a couple of hundred metres down from the monastery. Whimsical, multi-turreted, and with a real hat-in-the-air exuberance, it was built over the last five years of Dom Manuel's reign (1515–20). As such, it is the one completely Manueline building in Portugal, the rest having been adaptations of earlier structures or completed in later years.

Its architect, Francisco de Arruda, had previously worked on Portuguese fortifications in Morocco, and a Moorish influence is very strong in the delicately arched windows and balconies. Prominent also in the decoration are two great symbols of the age: Manuel's personal badge of an armillary sphere (representing the globe), and the cross of the military Order of Christ, once the Templars, who took a major role in all the Portuguese conquests.

The tower's interior (10am–5pm) is unremarkable except for a 'whispering gallery'; it was used into the nineteenth century as a prison, notoriously by Dom Miguel (1828–34), who kept political enemies in the waterlogged dungeons.

Museums and the Monument to the Discoveries

Close by are a number of museums. The best – if it has re-opened after reconstruction work – is the **Museu de Arte Popular** (9am–12.30pm and 2–6pm), a province-by-province display of Portugal's still very diverse folk arts, housed in a shed-like building on the waterfront.

Almost adjacent is the vast concrete **Monument to the Discoveries**, erected in 1960 to commemorate the 500th anniversary of the death of Henry the Navigator. Henry appears on the prow with Camões and other Portuguese heroes. Within the monument is a small exhibition space, with interesting and changing exhibits on the city's history. For 180esc, you can climb right up to the top, from where you get fine views of the Tagus and the Belem Tower.

At the corner of Belém's other main square – Praça Afonso de Abuquerque, a few minutes' walk from the monastery along Rua de Belém – there's the **Museu dos Coches**, said to be the most visited and certainly the most tedious attraction in Lisbon. It consists of an interminable line of mainly eighteenth-century royal coaches – Baroque, heavily gilded, and sometimes beautifully painted. If you're curious, go at weekends, when it's free: the hours are 10am to 6.30pm (closed Mon.).

Ferries and Cakes

If you feel like escaping to a **beach** you can get a **ferry** across the Tagus from Belém to TRAFARIA – only three kilometres by bus from Costa da Caparica (see below); boats run on the hour and half hour (6.30am–12.30am) from a terminal right by the electric railway station. Alternatively, trains from here continue to Cascais (see below), with a connection at Oeiras, in 35 minutes.

Finally, before leaving Belem, it's worth taking a tour of the **coffeeshops** – especially the one by the tram stop, which bills itself as the 'Unica fabrica de pasteis de Belem' – delicious flaky tartlets filled with custard-like cream.

The Facts

The best source for all things going on in Lisbon is the weekly paper *Se7e* (*sete* meaning seven in Portuguese), available from any city newsagent and including fairly comprehensive, easily decipherable **listings**; the *Turismo* staff are usually willing to translate or fill you in on transport details.

Restaurants

Lisbon has some of the best value bars and restaurants of any European city – in fact picking a place at random, outside the city centre, it's hard to go far wrong. **By day**, choices could extend through the lunchtime workers' cafés around Alfama, the fish restaurants across the Tagus at Cacilahas, or down-coast at Cascais, or the multitude of set meals on offer for office employees in the Baixa. **By night** the obvious place to be is Bairro Alto, with the city's most adventurous restaurants, and, to a lesser extent, Alfama.

Bairro Alto

In summer Bairro Alto often has a festival atmosphere, with a rock band – occasionally a folk or *fado* act – playing on the **Jardim do São Pedro** terrace, near the top of the *Elevador da Glória*. Spread around the terrace, when anything's going on, are a dozen or so foodstalls, and if you're happy to eat standing up you can do so for next to nothing.

Close by are a series of small, inexpensive restaurants. A personal favourite is *O Tacão Pequeno*, almost opposite the Jardim at Travessa da Cara 3A – just half a dozen tables, so book or go early. Dozens of other good possibilities are to be found along and around the **Rua da Atalaia**, a couple of blocks in and the liveliest street of the neighbourhood. On Atalaia itself, try *O Bichano* (no. 78; go early, it's always crowded), *Atalaia* (no. 35–37), or, upmarket but excellent, *Papaçorda* (no. 57–59).

Rua da Baroca, parallel, has more places, *Fidalgo* (no. 27; cheap and a trendy hangout) and *Ideal da Barocca* (no. 14; fish specialties) among them; so does the **Travessa da Queimada**, a few blocks down, including one of the best deals in the quarter, *O Barriga* (no. 31), and the attractive Praça das Flores (try *Casa de Pasto Flores* at no. 40). Slightly **further afield**, but exceptional, is *Casa Faz Frio* (Rua Dom Pedro V 96), a beautiful and very traditional restaurant – not expensive if you share the vast portions.

For **late-night** snacks there's *Cervejaria da Trindade* (Rua Nova da Trindade 200; open until 2am, last entrance 1.30am), another aesthetic experience, covered in *azulejos*. Nearby, on the Largo da Trindade, you might also check out *Os Anarquistas* (no. 14) or further out on the Rua do Loreto, the crowded but very cheap *Casa da India*.

Alfama

Across the city centre, **Alfama** is less commercialised. Restaurants here, with only a handful of exceptions, are more often workers' cafés, good for soups and grilled sardines. **Rua da Regueria**, above the Largo do Chafariz de Dentro, has a heavy concentration.

Túnel de Alfama, on Rua de Santo Estevão, is more of a conventional restaurant – but cheap and very substantial – or try the pricier *Casa do Leão* near the castle. For a change, *Wong*, near the Mouraria market at Calçada da Mouraria 8, offers well-priced Chinese food. There's a profusion of back-alley bars in this quarter, most unnamed and unadvertised, except by the figures of old men playing cards out on the pavement.

Baixa

In the **Baixa** you need to be selective – particularly on **Rua das Portas de Santo Antão**, where several of the famed seafood restaurants have geared standards (and prices) very firmly to tourists. **Rua dos Douradores**, towards the right-hand side of the grid, is more rewarding and **Rua dos Correiros** has a number of unpretentious places where you can buy perfectly good food in rather unexciting surroundings – *Restaurante Lagosta* is one of the more enjoyable. *Bom Jardim*, known locally as 'O Rei dos Frangos', on the alleyway connecting Restauradores with the Rua das Portas de Santo Antão, is *the* place for chicken.

Cacilhas

Cacilhas, a port suburb across the Tagus, is just a ten-minute ferry trip from the Fluvial stations at Praça do Comércio (*Sul e Sueste*) or at the Cais do Sodré, and has a whole string of **fish tavernas** along its waterfront. *Floresta*, a huge canteen at no. 7 on the main Rua do Ginjal, is impressive.

Belém

At Belém, there are four or five excellent places on and around the Rua Vieira Portuense, parallel to the main Rua de Belém. The *Restaurante Montenegro* (no. 44; closed Sat.) is recommended. Somewhere to go for broke on seafood is the *Associação Regional de Vela do Centro* (a sailing club on the Doca de Belém), where you can eat above the boathouse overlooking the river and the Monument to the Discoveries.

Vegetarian

Specifically **vegetarian options** include the *Restaurante do Sol* (workers' co-op restaurant; open weekdays only, closes early) and *Café Maquina* (ultimate fruit juices!), both up the steps behind the Rossio station at Calçada do Duque 21–23; and *A Colmeira*, a macrobiotic restaurant at Rua da Emenda 110 (a continuation of Rua da Atalaia, heading towards the river, near Largo de Camões; Mon.–Fri. noon–3pm & 7–8.30pm, Sat. noon–3pm). Another vegetarian restaurant, with an adjacent health food supermarket, is at Rua 1 Dezembro 47.

Markets and Mensas

For **rock-bottom** eating, there are stalls in the **mercado** behind Cais do Sodré station, in addition to the picnic foods on sale.

Alternatively, if you're a student, the city has some of the cheapest **cantinas** (student canteens) anywhere in Europe – with full meals well under 200esc a shot. Lunch hour begins at noon and the evening meal begins at 6pm – there is always a queue and you have to show your student card (almost anything goes) before purchasing a ticket; after that watch what everyone else does.

These are located: at the junction of Rua Gomes Fereira/Rua Escola de Medicina Veterinária (metro to *Picoas* and then follow Rua Tomás Ribeiro for a couple of blocks); at Cidade Universitária in the centre of the dusty student campus, with macrobiotic dishes (metro to *Cidade Universitária*); and at the Cantina Nova (Avda. das Forças Armadas; *Entrecampos* metro and walk up a couple of blocks, or bus #32 from Rossio).

Bars, Clubs and Discos

Although there are exciting places scattered all over the city, **bars** – and almost anything else that stays open after 10pm – are mostly located in **Bairro Alto**. In the 1930s Bairro Alto became a centre for late-night meeting places, known as *tartúlias*, where political activists, but above all poets and artists, met to discuss hot topics. There is still something of this feel about the area, with its clubs and bars, but you do not need an introduction to most clubs; just keep your eyes open as you wander the streets at night. Be aware, too, that the area is the city's sex centre – though most people up in the quarter are there just to eat, drink or listen to music.

Bairro Alto Clubs and Bars

Most of the livelier and more esoteric places are concentrated on and around the **Rua da Atalaia**. The trendiest, for the last few years, has been Fragil at no. 126: one of the few clubs in the country that maintains a door policy of admitting only its own kind – it is in part a gay club. The area's regular drinking bars are perhaps just as much fun, or if you want Brazilian music, try the club *A Gafieira* (Calçada do Tijolo, on the right as you approach from Rua da Atalaia; ring to enter) where you can drink exquisite *caiparinhas*.

Over **towards the river end of Bairro Alto**, the rougher side of town around Cais do Sodré station, are the *Jamaica*, which provides a reggae/hard rock backdrop, and *Tokyo*, with a younger scene and more modern sounds; both are on Rua N. Carvalho. Further over still, in the **Santos** district (in the general direction of the *Museu de Arte Antiga*), three lively places are *O Xafarix* (Largo Vitorino Damásio), *O Berro* (Rua da Esperança 158), and *O Calçada* close by – all are near the Avenida Dom Carlos I.

A good, if odd, place to precede more serious drinking is the **Port Wine Institute Bar** (Rua São Pedro de Alcantara 45; Mon.–Sat. 10am–10pm), too refined for its own good (though this may be welcome for women on their own – no hissing and staring!) but offering the chance to sample over 300 types and vintages of port, from 65esc up.

Baixa and Alfama

Wandering around the **Baixa** towards midnight you would imagine that the city had closed up and gone to bed; a single exception is the bar *Bora-Bora* at Rua da Madalena 201. In **Alfama** the action is to be found pretty well exclusively in the *fado* clubs, detailed with all other music places in the next section. Again, though, there is one exception: *Sua Excelência O Marquês*, a very trendy bar on the Largo Marquês do Lavradio, behind the Sé.

Discos

Currently, the city's trendiest discos are in the outlying area of **Alcântara** (take a taxi), near the *Pingo-Doce* supermarket. These are *Banana-Power* (Rua de Cascais 51– 53), the most exclusive in a Taveira designed complex with a bar and restaurant attached, and *Alcântara-Mar* (Travessa da Cozinha Económica). More regular Portuguese are to be found in the again far-flung *Loucuras* (Avda. Álvares Cabral 37, up from Largo do Rato) and *Spring-Fellow* (Rua Óscar Monteiro Torres, close to Campo Pequeno).

In **Bairro Alto**, there are a couple of discos out towards the Jardim Botânico: *Trumps* (Rua da Imprensa Nacional) – the city's Hippodrome equivalent – and *Bric-a-Bar* (Rua Cecilio de Sousa 84), which is smaller and predominantly gay. A less attractive gay alternative, exclusive and obnoxiously cruisy, is *Xeque-Mate*, nearby at Rua de São Marcal 170.

Music and Entertainment

Tourist brochures tend to suggest that Lisbon entertainment begins and ends with **fado**, the city's traditional 'blues' music, offered in thirty or so night-clubs in the Bairro Alto and elsewhere. There's no reason – except perhaps ever-rising admission prices – not to sample some *fado*, but don't miss out on other possibilities. Portuguese **jazz** can be good, **rock** an occasional surprise, and if you check out *Se7e* and the posters around Restauradores there's a good chance of catching **African music** from the former colonies of Cabo Verde, Guinea Bissau and Angola. And of course there's more conventional, or daytime, entertainment: over seventy **cinemas**, two above-average **football** teams and, depending on your personal politics, **bullfights**.

Fado

Imagine an Afghani humming along to a Billie Holliday record and you're halfway to grasping the spirit of **fado**, the weirdest, most melancholic music in Europe. It's thought to have originated, via the Congo, in Alfama, as a kind of working-class blues, and Lisbon is still the best place to hear it, either at *Casas de Fado* or *Adegas Típicas* (traditional bars). There's no real distinction between these places: all are small, all serve food (though you don't usually have to eat), and all begin around 9 to 10pm, get going towards midnight and stay open until maybe 3 or 4am. Their drawbacks are inflated minimum charges – rarely, these days, below 1000–1500esc – and, in the more popular and accessible places, extreme tackiness. Uniformed doormen are fast becoming the norm, as are warm-up singers crooning Beatles songs and photographers snapping the happy tourist couples. Beware.

The following are among the more prominent clubs in **Bairro Alto**:

Mil e Cem (Travessa da Espera 38). Not, on the whole, the best music nor the oldest surroundings, but a good atmosphere and one of the cheaper minimum charges in the city.

Viela (Rua das Taipas 14). Less touristy than most.

A Severa (Rua das Gáveas 55), *Adega Machado* (Rua do Norte 91), and *Painel do Fado* (Rua São Pedro de Alcântara 65). The big three with the big names – and prices.

Elsewhere in the city you might also try:

Parreirinha d'Alfama (Beco do Espirito Santo 1: just off Largo do Chafariz de Dentro, Alfama). Reasonable music – used to be a cheap option in Alfama but now normal prices.

Fado Menor (Rua das Praças 18) – 1000esc cover charge and good music, *Patio das Cantigas* (Rua de São Caetano 27), and *Senhor Vinho* (Rua do Meio). Renowned *fado* houses in Santos/Estrela, the area just beyond Bairro Alto.

A Cesária (Rua Gilberto Rola 20) and *Timpanas* (Rua Gilberto Rola 16). A cab ride away, beyond Estrela in Alcântara, and said to be the real McCoy.

Ask Turismo to check **opening nights** before setting out.

African Music, Rock and Jazz

The best place to hear **African music** – if you're there at the right time – is a summer festival, when the city's bands are sometimes promoted alongside international West African acts. But there are regular gigs through the year, and three more or less stable **clubs**: *Lontra* (Rua de São Bento, Bairro Alto), and *Monte Cara* (Rua do Sol ao Rato: off Largo do Rato, northwest of Bairro Alto), both featuring mainly Cabo Verde bands, and with an 800esc cover that includes a couple of drinks; and *Bom Tom* (Rua São João da Praça, Alfama) featuring occasional Angolan bands.

Rock music is a chancier business, though there are a handful of established, interesting bands, among them: GNR, Rádio Maçau, Xutos e Pontapés, Mler Ife Dada, Rui Veloso and Heróis do Mar. Look out, too, for visiting **Brazilian singers** – the wonderful Milton Nascimento, Maria Bethânia, Gilberto Gil, Ney Matogrosso and Chico Buarque de Holanda are some examples – who, like mainstream British or American bands on tour, tend to play **stadium gigs** at the Coliseu dos Recreios (Rua das Portas de Santo Antão), Pavilhão do Restelo (belonging to the *Belenenses*, Belém's soccer team, in Restelo) or Pavilhão de Cascais. Otherwise, these are the main outlets:

Rock Rendez-Vous (Rua da Beneficência 175, near the Gulbenkian). Where all the promising Portuguese groups play and folkies hang out – in spite of the name. For 300–400esc you get admission and a drink. Open Tues.–Sat. from around 8pm, with bands most nights.

99 da Barroca (Rua da Barroca 99, Bairro Alto) and *Cocote Club* (Rua da Trombeta 4). Rock 'clubs' with occasional live bands.

Chafarica (Calçada do São Vicente 81, Alfama). Brazilian bar with regular live music – a good place anyway to wind up an evening.

There's just one regular **jazz venue**, the *Hot Clube de Portugal*, a tiny basement club with local and visiting artists (Praça da Alegria, off Avda. da Liberdade; open Thurs.– Sat. 10pm–2am, 500esc cover and pricier drinks). In addition to jazz bands, the *Hot Clube* (and other places – see *Se7e*) sometimes hosts **folk** singers, products of the new 'political music' that emerged with the 1974 Revolution. Names to watch out for include Sérgio Godinho, Vitorino Fausto, and the band Trovante.

Classical Music, Theatre and Dance
Most serious **cultural events**, including just about every classical music concert in the city, are sponsored by the **Gulbenkian Foundation**. If you're interested, it's worth picking up a schedule of events from them as soon as you arrive – or checking possibilities with the tourist office. Concerts are held at the **Carmo** church in Bairro Alto (often sponsoring free concerts in summer – go for the atmosphere, as aircraft, bats and mad beggars often interrupt the music), the **Sé** (Cathedral) and the **Basílica da Estrela** (Estrela church), and of course the Gulbenkian's own three concert halls.

There are also performances of Portuguese and foreign **plays** at the Teatro Nacional de Dona Maria II (in the Rossio) and an **opera** season (Sept.–June) at the Teatro Nacional de São Carlos on Rua Serpa Pinto.

Cinemas
An unsung glory of staying in Lisbon. The city and its environs have some 75 **cinemas**, virtually all of them showing **original language** films with Portuguese subtitles. You'll find, on any one night, a selection of American, British, French and African movies. Ticket prices are low (around 300esc; usually 200esc on Monday), and some of the theatres are beautiful in them-

selves – Art Nouveau and Deco palaces, often with original period bars. There is, incidentally, no censorship of films in Portugal.

The capital's national film theatre is the *Institut de Cinemateca Portuguesa* (Rua Barata Salgueiro 39, not far from Rotunda and the Avda. da Liberdade). Shows are at 6.30pm and 9.30pm every day and the films might be Portuguese (look out for Jorge da Sena among others) or anything from Truffaut to Valentino. Another place for film buffs to check is the new shopping centre at **Amoreiras** (Av. Duarte Pacheco), which features no less than ten screens. At the corner of Restauradores near the Post Office is a stand with details of what's on at all Lisbon's cinemas.

Football

Benfica – Lisbon's most famous soccer team – have fallen off since the days of Eusébio but still seem to have the most international success and are fun to watch. Bus #41 from Rossio, Rotunda or Praça da Espanha runs nearby their *Estadio da Luz*, one of the largest stadiums in Europe. **Sporting Lisboa**, their traditional rivals, play at the *Estádio José Alvalade* – bus #1 or #36 – and the Porto team are worth looking out for.

Details of matches are printed in all daily papers. Tickets are available from the *ABEP* ticket kiosk in Praça dos Restauradores, or from the grounds.

Bullfights

Bullfights take place most Thursdays and Sundays at the principal Campo Pequeno bullring (metro *Campo Pequeno*), at Montijo across the Tagus and less frequently at Cascais. Just over 30km outside the city, at Vila Franca de Xira, the centre of Portuguese bull breeding, a Pamplona-style **running of the bulls** takes place during the *Festa do Colete Encarnado* (first weekend of July; see "Ribatejo" in Chapter Two for details).

Other Festivals and Events

The main **Lisbon popular festivals** are in June, with fireworks, rides and partying to celebrate the *Santos Populares* – St. Anthony (the largest, taking over Alfama on June 12–13), St. John (23–24; highly recommended) and St. Peter (28–29).

On the cultural front, there is a big annual **International Jazz Festival** at the Gulbenkian in the summer and various events in Cascais, mostly held in the Parque Palmela. And through July and August the **Estoril Festival** takes place, putting on internationally known orchestras, musicians and dance groups – sometimes quite adventurously.

Again at Estoril, and a lot better than it sounds, is the state-run **Handicrafts Fair**. Crafts of all kinds are displayed from every region of the country along Avenida Amaral: if you buy anything, haggle at length – it's expected of the *Lisboetas*. The fair runs through July and August, from around 5pm until midnight, and is supplemented with foodstalls.

From May to September there's also a permanent fairground, the **Feira Popular**, opposite the *Entrecampos* metro station. Cheap eats, cheap rides and a thoroughly Portuguese night out (until 1am, when the metro too closes down).

Directory

Airline Offices Most are along Avenida de Liberdade – *British Airways* are at no. 36-2° (☎365444), *Air France* at 224A, *Air Maroc* at 225A, and *TWA* at 258A. *TAP* (Air Portugal) and *KLM* are in the Praça Marquês de Pombal, at the end of the Avenida, and *Pan Am* is at Praça dos Restauradores 46.

Airport Information ☎721101, 802060, or 889181 (*TAP*). Airport bus services are detailed under "Points of Arrival".

Anti-Nuclear/Peace Groups Contact always helps – among the many groups are *Comité Anti-Nuclear* (Rua São Bento 672: ☎689553), *Colectivo de Anti-Militaristas* (Avda. Dom Carlos 1130) and a local branch of *Pax Christi* (Avda. Eva 14-7°), the Catholic peace organisation.

Antiques and Junk The *Feira da Ladra* flea market is held on Tuesday morning and all day Saturday (see p.42). Cheapish antique/junk shops are concentrated on Rua de São Bento at the far end of the Bairro Alto. If you're interested in **Portuguese tiles** – *azulejos* – check out the factory-shops of *Fábrica Santana* (Rua do Alecrim: 100m down from the Chiado/Largo do Carmo) or *Fábrica Viúva Lamego* (Largo do Intendente; metro *Intendente*), both of whom sell copies of traditional designs.

Banks Most head offices are in the Baixa and surrounding streets; hours Mon.–Fri. 8.30–11.45am and 1–2.45pm. *Banco Borges & Irmão* (Avda. da Liberdade 9A) is open 8.30–11.45am and 3–7pm Mon.–Fri. There's an **8am-until-8pm currency exchange** at Santa Apolónia railway station. *American Express* is operated by *STAR Travel*: main office at Avda. Sidónio Pais 4A; a smaller one at Praça dos Restauradores 14 will phone to see if you have mail. **British banks** include *Lloyds*, at the top right of the Avenida da Liberdade.

Bookshops *Livraria Bertrand* (Rua Garrett 75) and *Livraria Buchholz* (Rua Duque de Palmela 4) are good for English novels and the former also has a range of British magazines which you can browse through. *Livraria Britanica* (Rua São Marcal, opp. the Jardim Botânico) is pricey but well stocked. A good Portuguese bookshop (which stocks *Rough Guides*) is next to the *Elevador Santa Justa*.

Bus information *Rodoviaria Nacional* (☎7265807); or contact Turismo.

Car Hire *Avis*, *Budget* and *Europcar* all have desks at the airport, though there are far less queues (and often lower prices) at smaller agencies like *Dollar* and *Budget*. *Avis* is also at Praça dos Restauradores 47, *InterRent* at Avda. da Liberdade 12. And many more – Turismo have full lists.

Embassies UK (Rua S. Domingos á Lapa 37, ☎661191 – take bus #27 from Rua Brancamp near Rotunda); **Ireland** (Rua da Imprensa á Estrela 1-4°, ☎661569); **Australia** (Avda. da Liberdade 244-4°, ☎523350); **Canada** (Rua Rosé Araújo 2-6°, ☎563821; **USA** (Avda. das Forças Armadas, ☎726600); **Netherlands** (Rua do Sacramento á Lapa 4-1°, ☎661163); **Sweden** (Rua Miguel Lupi 12-2°, ☎606097).

Emergencies Phone ☎115. Red Cross point: Praça do Comércio. Fire: ☎322222. Police: ☎366141.

Hospitals British Hospital, Rua Saraiva de Carvalho 49 (☎602020; night emergency ☎603785; daily clinics 10am–1pm and 6–8pm).

Late-night shopping, films and restaurants at *Centro Comercial das Amoreiras* (Avda. Duarte Pacheco) until 11pm. Bus #11 from Rossio or #23 from Rotunda (after 9.30pm catch any bus to Rotunda, then take a taxi or walk).

Launderette at Rua Saraiva de Carvalho 171. Bus #9 from Rossio.

Lost/Stolen Credit Cards American Express and Visa (☎545650).

Maps for walkers Topographic maps (between 400–600esc each) of the whole country from the Army, *Serviços Cartográficos do Exército*, Avda. Dr. Alfredo Bensaúde, Olivais Norte; open 9–11.30am and 1–4.30pm; bus #25 from Praça do Comércio to *Laboratória Química Militar*.

Money Exchange There are two **'automatic exchange'** machines which take £10 and £20 notes. One is just between Rossio and Restauradores, the other at the river end of Rua Augusta. Both break down with infuriating regularity.

Newspapers English language **newspapers** are sold in the Rossio and at the *International Press Centre*, by the Turismo, on the west side of Praça dos Restauradores.

Phones Long-distance phones at the corner of the Rossio (no. 65: 8am–11pm) or from any telephone booth – but the lines are often blocked and 25esc does not last very long. Much cheaper, the Restauradores post office (8am–11pm, but telephones only until 9pm) runs an excellent service – take a ticket for a place in queue.

Police If you need help, or have something stolen, the office to go to is on Rua Capels, west of the Baixa near the Teatro San Carlos.

Post Offices The main post office is on the Praça do Comércio (Mon.–Fri. 9am–7pm), though its **Posta Restante** section has a separate entrance at Rua do Arsenal 27 (closes at 2pm). Posta Restante also goes on occasion to the post office in Praça dos Restauradores. At both ask them to check for letters under your surname and first name – and all other initials if possible. **Airmail** leaves from a special box in the Restauradores post office (open until 11pm). It's the fastest service available – sometimes just two days to the UK (as opposed to the usual five or six by regular post).

Student Information *Centro Nacional de Informação Juvenil* (Avda. da Liberdade 194); open 9.30am–7pm; offers practical advice and a library.

Swimming Pools The easiest to reach is *Piscina Areeiro* (Avda. do Roma, metro *Areeiro* or *Roma*); 9am–1pm and 3–7.30pm. *Piscina dos Olivais* is further afield but preferable – bus #31 from Rossio (45 min.) or #10 from Areeiro (20 min.).

Theft Go directly to the 24-hr. Tourism Police in Chiado (Rua Capelo 13, ☎366141) and report any incident within 24 hours in order to reclaim travel insurance – in most cases travellers' cheques can be replaced at the bank or agent recommended by the company. See also "Lost/Stolen Credit Cards", above.

Tourist Information Phone the Turismo in Praça dos Restauradores on ☎363314.

Trains See "Points of Arrival" for details of station terminals for the different destinations. Full timetables are available at the Rossio information office. Information ☎876025.

Travel Firms Student/youth firms include *Transalpino* (Avda. Guerra Junqueiro, near Praça de Londres; metro *Alameda* or buses #7 or #40 from Praça da Figueira/Cais do Sodré), *Wasteels* (near Santa Apolónia station), *Tagus Juvenil* (Praça de Londres 9B; ☎884957), and *Turicoop* (Rua Pascoal de Melo 15; ☎531804); the main international bus agents are *Intercentro* (Avda. Casal de Ribeiro 18B: ☎571745). Other travel firms can be found along Avenida da Liberdade, including the charter agents *Abreu* at no. 160 (☎371341).

Women's Movement The best contact points are the *Editora das Mulheres* bookshop, right in the centre of the Baixa at Rua da Conceição 17, and *IDM* (*Informação e Documentacuão das Mulheres*) at Rua Filipe de Mata 115A (about ½km north of the Gulbenkian; metro *Palhavã* or bus #31 from Rossio or Praça da Espanha). *IDM* is a women's centre incorporating a small library and the sole women-only café in Lisbon. Run by a collective, they are very eager to welcome foreign travellers and publicise the centre's activities. English spoken.

PHONE CODES

All numbers in the Greater Lisbon area are prefixed ☎01.

AROUND LISBON

Transport around the capital is reliable, and basing yourself in Lisbon you could take in a fair part of Estremadura and Alentejo on day trips. A good idea, however, since even **Sintra** (just fifty minutes by train from the Rossio station) demands a longer look, is to stay overnight. For quick escapes from the city, it's better to stick to the **beaches** – Costa da Caparica, Cascais or Guincho – or to such architectural attractions as **Queluz** or, if you're keen, **Mafra**.

Both Sintra and Mafra are well situated for travel **on to Estremadura**, with the seaside resort of **Ericeira** a good next move. If you are planning a **day trip** note that most of the Sintra palaces are closed on Monday, those of Queluz and Mafra on Tuesday.

Beaches: Caparica, Cascais and Guincho

Lisbon has four beaches within easy reach: at **Estoril** and **Cascais** (down the coast from Belém), at **Guincho** (to the north), and along the **Costa da Caparica**, a thirty-kilometre expanse of dunes just south of the capital across the Tagus.

If you want to **stay by the sea** both Cascais and Caparica can offer reasonably priced pensions, while Guincho has one good campsite and Caparica a whole string. Obviously it's as easy to commute into Lisbon as out from it.

Costa da Caparica

It takes a little over an hour (outside of rush hour) to reach **Costa da Caparica** from the capital, and it's here that most locals come if they want to swim or laze around on the sand. There are foreign tourists, too, but they're in a minority: this is a thoroughly Portuguese resort, lively, crammed with restaurants and beach cafés, and fun. It is also – as far as sea and sand go – more or less limitless. A mini-railway runs along 8km or so of dunes (in season only) and if you're into solitude you need only take this to the end of the line and walk. En route to Caparica, and perhaps more fun if you have kids to entertain, is a new 'Wave Park', **Parque Onda**. For 600esc admission, you can career down all manner of slides into huge pools.

Access

The most enjoyable approach is to take a **ferry from the Fluvial station** (by Praça do Comércio) to **Cacilhas**, and then pick up the connecting bus which leaves right in front of the dock where the boats come in. The ferries run every ten minutes, the last returning at 9.35pm (9.10pm at weekends); the crossing takes ten minutes. If you miss the last one you can still get back to the capital by taking a boat to the **Cais do Sodré** terminus; this runs through the night.

Alternatively, and much speedier, you can take a **bus** from the centre of town direct to Caparica over the swaying *Ponte 25 Abril*. Buses leave from the main Praça de Espanha terminal (metro *Palhavã*: go for the *Via Rapida*) and from Areeiro and Campo Pequeno every twenty to thirty minutes. Either of these routes will give wonderful views of the city and take you past the **statue of Christ** – a smaller version of the Rio landmark. This itself is worth a halt: a lift shuttles you up the plinth and to a (highly dramatic) viewing platform. On a good day, Lisbon stretches like a map below you, and you can catch the glistening roof of the Pena Palace at Sintra in the distance.

Caparica: Practicalities and the Beaches

At **CAPARICA** all buses stop in a dusty depot close to the beginning of the sands. If you walk along the beach to the left you come to the main square, where there's a **tourist office**, market, cinema and banks. There aren't very many hotels in Caparica but the tourist office will find you a **room** in a guest house. A particularly attractive place to stay, if there's space, is the *Hotel-Restaurante Pátio Alentejano*, Rua Professor Salazar de Sousa 17 – just off the beach at the western end of town. **Campsites**, which range along the first few kilometres of the beach, are on the whole overcrowded and overpriced, and you may well decide to pick your own spot, (though beware of thieves) close to one of the mini-train stops. A recommended **restaurant**, among dozens of fish and seafood places along the main street, Rua dos Pescadores, is the *Casa dos Churros* at no. 13.

The beaches, which take in coves and lagoons as they spread southward, speak for themselves. It's useful to know, though, that each of the twenty **mini-train stops**, based around one or two beach-tavernas, has a very particular scene or feel. Earlier stops tend to be family oriented, often with a campsite and pool nearby. Later ones are on the whole younger and more trendy, with nudity (though officially illegal) more or less obligatory – stop no. 17 in particular. Stop no. 9 has become established as gay. Be warned that there are crowds on most beaches near Lisbon in August.

Oeiras, Estoril, Cascais and Guincho

Quirks of the Tagus currents have spared Caparica from the pollution of Lisbon and its shipping: the **Estoril coast** has suffered badly. Even at Cascais you'd be wise to keep your head above water – and many Portuguese have forbidden their children to swim along this whole stretch.

The main place en route, after Belém is **OEIRAS**, where the Tagus officially turns into the sea. Accommodation here is limited to a youth hostel (nicely sited, overlooking the sea) and a tiny **campsite**, right in the centre of town. Both have a good turnover, so you'll probably find a place if you arrive early. The **Turismo** here, across from the fire station in the centre of town, is very helpful and there are numerous restaurants.

If there's not much going on at the **Palácio do Marquês de Pombal** (an adult education centre near the campsite), the guard might be able to take you around the magnificent **gardens**, anyway, or just peer over the walls to see its massive grotto.

Estoril

The attractions of the first large resort along this coast are fairly dubious. Long the haunt of exiled royalty, **ESTORIL** has pretensions of being a 'Portuguese Riviera'. It is crowded with grandiose expatriate villas and the luxury hotels of the idle rich – who remain, as Mary McCarthy described them in 1955, 'silent, like sharks, endlessly masticating, with their medicines before them'. Unless you're curious about such clientèle, it's probably better to stay on the **electric train** (which runs every 15 min. from Cais do Sodré) a few more kilometres to Cascais.

Cascais

Although **CASCAIS**, too, is now a major resort, it has a much younger, less exclusive feel and even retains a few elements of its previous existence as a fishing village. There's a lively Wednesday market and Sunday evening bull-fights (not just for the tourists). At weekends, crowds gather around the **Boca do Inferno** (the Mouth of Hell, a few kilometres further), where great waves crash against caves in the cliff face.

Through the summer, accommodation is at a premium in Cascais, and pensions in any case are sparse. However, with persistence you should be able to find a **private room**. For eating, try *Dom Pedro I* opposite the man's statue in Praça 5 de Outubro (closed Sun.; cash only).

Guincho

GUINCHO (6km from Cascais – and unpolluted) is a great sweeping field of beach with a body-crashing surf of white Atlantic rollers. It's a superb place to windsurf – the 1989 World Championships were held here – but also a dangerous one. The undertow here is notoriously strong and people are drowned every year: be careful, even if you're a confident swimmer.

The beach is little developed, fronted by just a couple of (expensive) hotels. With a little discretion, it's possible to camp nearby. For food, try *O Camponês* at Malveira da Serra, towards Colares, or, if you can afford a blow-out, *A Muchaxo*, acclaimed as the best seafood restaurant in the Lisbon area.

Sintra

Summer residence of the kings of Portugal, and of the Moorish lords of Lisbon before them, **SINTRA**'s verdant charms have long been celebrated. British travellers of the eighteenth to nineteenth century found a new Arcadia in its cool, wooded heights, recording with satisfaction the old Spanish prov-erb: 'To see the world and leave out Sintra is to go blind about'.

Byron stayed here in 1809 and began *Childe Harold*, his great mock-epic travel poem, in which the 'horrid crags' of 'Cintra's glorious Eden' form a first location. Writing home, in a letter to his mother, he proclaimed the village

> *perhaps in every aspect the most delightful in Europe; it contains beauties of every description natural and artificial. Palaces and gardens rising in the midst of rocks, cataracts and precipices; convents on stupendous heights, a distant view of the sea and the Tagus . . . it unites in itself all the wildness of the Western Highlands with the verdure of the South of France.*

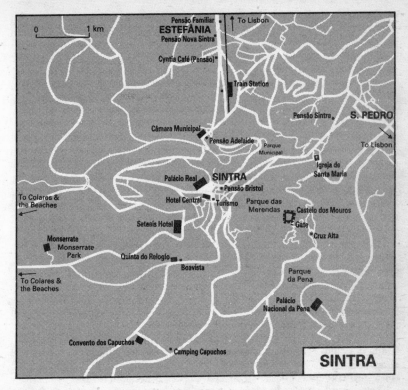

That the young Byron had seen neither of these is irrelevant: his description of Sintra's romantic appeal is exact – and still telling two centuries later. Move mountains and give yourself the best part of two full days.

Orientation and Practicalities

Sintra loops around a series of green and wooded ravines, a confusing place to get your **bearings**, consisting of three distinct and separate villages: ESTEFÂNIA (around the railway station), SINTRA-VILA (the main town) and, two kilometres to the east, SÃO PEDRO DE SINTRA. The centre of Sintra-Vila is gathered about the extraordinary National Palace, distinguished by a vast pair of conical chimneys. This is the most obvious landmark to head for, about ten minutes' walk from the station.

Rooms

Finding a room at Sintra in summer can be a problem, though if you arrive early in the day you should end up with something. There are a fair number of **pensions**: best value is probably the *Adelaide*, midway between the train station and Sintra village, or *Pensão Economica* is cheaper. Alternatively, some well-priced **private rooms** are touted at the station or, perhaps better, bookable through the extremely helpful **Turismo** in the centre. If you feel like **staying in style**, try *Hotel Central*, a nineteenth-century place right in the centre, or, considerably more upmarket, ask the tourist office to book you bed and breakfast in a local *quinta*, or manorhouse. *Quinta San Jose* (☎01/927-8582) offers macrobiotic meals.

The nearest **campsites** are well out of town: at the Capuchos convent (a 9km climb – and no buses) and, more convenient, at the local **beach-villages** of PRAIA DAS MAÇAS and AZENHAS DO MAR (see below).

Bars and Food

Bars and restaurants are generally poor value, relying too heavily on the coach trips. *Restaurant Tulhas*, near the tourist office, is one of the best – though not cheap. Much better are the *Bar Brazil* on São Pedro and the two *Adega do Saloio* grillhouses, at the far end of the street: take Rua 1 de Dezembro almost to the end, then the left fork Travessa de Chão de Meninos. Also worth some attention is the **cake and pastry** place on the left hand side of the road heading from the centre of town towards the station.

There is little on the entertainment front, though *Bar Topico*, close by the *Pensão Adelaide*, is worth checking out, with **live music** on Friday and Saturday nights in summer.

Tours and transport

If your time is limited, the Turismo runs excellent **half-day tours** taking in the Capuchos convent, Seteais and Montserrate; much easier and cheaper than taking taxis. There is also a twice-daily local bus to Pena. Walking, though, is most satisfying, and you should be able to hitch back from any of the main sights. Whatever mode of transport you choose take a **picnic**: the only refreshments out of town are cold drinks from a stall below Pena park.

You could also take in **Mafra** (see below) from Sintra – there's a 10.30am bus from Sintra station and another back at 1.30pm. And by train it's an easy matter to go down to **Queluz** or, equally, Lisbon itself (50 min.): trains run in either direction well after 1am. Heading for the coast, there are regular, direct buses to **Ericeira**.

São Pedro and its Fair

At São Pedro, on the second and last Sunday of each month, there's a country **fair**, with food, crafts and antiques/junk. In its wake, the village has become something of an antiques centre, with numerous stores, all year round.

There is a full-blown *festa* over the feast of St. Peter (June 28–29).

The Paço

The **Palácio Nacional** – or **Paço Real** as it's also known – was probably in existence under the Moors. It takes its present form, however, from the rebuilding and enlargements of Dom João I (1385–1433) and his fortunate successor, Dom Manuel, heir to Vasco da Gama's inspired explorations. Its style, as you might expect, is an amalgam of the Gothic – with impressive roofline battlements – and the latter king's 'Manueline' additions, with their characteristically extravagant twisted and animate forms. Inside, the Gothic-Manueline modes are tempered by a good deal of Moorish influence, adapted over the centuries by a succession of royal summer occupants. The last royal to live here, in the 1880s, was Maria Pia, grandmother of the country's last reigning monarch – Manuel II, 'The Unfortunate'.

Today the Paço is run as a museum, with guided **tours** every twenty minutes from 10am to 5pm daily (closed Wed.). The tours are frankly a pain – unless you go very early before the buses arrive – but the palace does have four or five rooms that are well worth seeing. On the upper floor, where you're taken first, after the kitchens, is the Manueline **Sala das Armas**, its domed and coffered ceiling emblazoned with the arms of 72 noble families – originally 74 until the Távoras and Aveiros were erased for their eighteenth-century intrigues against the crown. Nearby is the **Palace Chapel** and next to it a chamber, its floor worn by incessant pacing, where the half-mad Afonso VI was confined for six years by his brother Pedro II. Afonso eventually died here in 1683, listening to mass through a grid in the wall; Pedro had seized his throne, his liberty and his queen.

Highlights on the lower floor are the Manueline **Sala dos Cisnes**, so-called for the swans on its ceiling, and the **Sala das Pegas**. This last takes its name from the flock of magpies (pegas) painted on the frieze and ceiling, holding in their beaks the legend *por bem* ('in honour') – said to have been the response of João I, caught by his Queen Philippa (of Lancaster) in the act of kissing a lady-in-waiting. He is reputed to have had the room decorated with as many magpies as there were women at court in order to halt and satirise their gossip – a story told almost identically of one of the Loire châteaux.

The Castle and Pena Palace

The charms of Sintra lie less in its palace buildings than in exploring the many **walks and paths**. One of the best leads up from the town, past the church of Santa Maria to the ruined ramparts of a **Moorish Castle** (open daily). Taken with the aid of Scandinavian crusaders by Afonso Henriques, its fortifications span two rocky pinnacles, with the remains of a mosque spread about halfway between them. Views from here are extraordinary, casting south beyond Lisbon's bridge to the Serra de Arrábida, west to Cascais and Cabo da Roca (the westernmost point of Europe), and north to Peniche and the Berlenga islands.

Pena Palace

Beyond the *castelo* – a good sixty- to ninety-minute walk up from town – is the lower entrance to the immense **Pena Park** (free admission 10am–6pm), at the top end of which (20 minutes' climb) rears the fabulous **Palácio de Pena.**

The Palace (10am–5pm; closed Mon.; 400esc) is a wild fantasy of domes, towers, ramparts and walkways, approached through mock-Manueline gateways and a drawbridge that does not draw. A compelling riot of kitsch and madness, it was built in the 1840s to the specifications of Ferdinand of Saxe-Coburg-Gotha, husband of Queen Maria II, and it bears comparison with the mock-medieval castles of Ludwig of Bavaria. The architect, the German

Baron Eschwege, has immortalised himself in the guise of a warrior-knight on a huge statue that guards the palace from a neighbouring crag.

Inside, Pena is no less bizarre, for it has been preserved exactly as left by the royal family on their flight from Portugal in 1910. The result is fascinating: rooms of concrete decorated to look like wood, turbanned Moors nonchalantly holding electric chandeliers – it's all here. Of an original convent, founded to celebrate the first sight of Vasco da Gama's returning fleet, a chapel and genuine Manueline cloister have been retained.

Above Pena, past the statue of Eschwege, a marked footpath climbs to the **Cruz Alta**, highest point of the Serra de Sintra. Another footpath (unmarked) winds down to the left from Pena, coming out near Seteais (see below).

Seteais, Monserrate and Beyond

After the ludicrous follies of Pena, a visit to Seteais and Monserrate – the other obvious goals of a Sintra walk – comes as something of a relief. **Seteais** (open daily), just right of the Colares road (15 minutes' walk from the town), is one of the most elegant palaces in Portugal, completed in the last years of the eighteenth century and entered through a majestic classical arch; it is now an intensely luxurious hotel and restaurant, though wonderful for huge high-teas if you've got money to blow.

Beyond, the road leads past a series of beautiful private *quintas* (manors or estates) until you come upon **Monserrate** – about an hour's walk. The road forks just once: take the lower (right-hand) branch.

It's difficult to do justice to the beauty of Monserrate, whose vast **gardens** (open daily), filled with endless varieties of exotic trees and subtropical shrubs and plants, extend as far as the eye can see in every direction. William Beckford, author of the Gothic novel *Vathek* and perhaps the wealthiest Englishman of his age, rented the *quinta* from 1793 to 1799, having been forced to flee Britain through homosexual scandal (buggery then being a hangable offence). He found it 'a beautiful Claude-like place', improved its landscaping, imported a flock of sheep from his estate at Fonthill, and posted 'bevys of delicate warblers and musicians' around the grounds while he wrote in summer pavilions. In the 1850s the gardens were further enriched under the direction of the head gardener from Kew.

The gardens are now owned by the state and in the process of renovation. Entrance is officially 9am to 5pm daily, though the gates are rarely locked.

Colares and the Convento dos Capuchos

About forty minutes' walk beyond Monserrate is **COLARES**, a quiet and beautiful village famed for its wines (ask for them in Sintra). A more interesting walk, however, is to the **Convento dos Capuchos** (9am–6pm; closed Tues.), an extraordinary hermitage with tiny, dwarf-like cells cut from the rock and lined with cork. Philip II, King of Spain and Portugal, pronounced it the poorest convent of his kingdom; Byron, visiting a cave where one monk had spent 36 years in seclusion, mocked:

> *Deep in yon cave Honorius long did dwell,*
> *In hope to merit Heaven by making earth a Hell.*

IGREJA DE SANTA CRUZ

Situada na parte baixa da cidade de Coimbra, foi construída em 1131.

A sua reconstrução teve lugar no séc. XVI, em estilo Manuelino.

Fazia parte do Mosteiro de Santa Cruz, da ordem dos Cónegos Regrantes de Santo Agostinho, fundada por D. Telo e da qual foi Primeiro prior São Teotónio, Primeiro Santo Português.

São dignos de visita, para além da Igreja, o Claustro do Silêncio, a Sala do Capítulo, a Sacristia e o Coro Alto.

— Na Igreja apreciamos o Púlpito, maravilhosa obra Renascentista de Nicolau Chanterene, os Túmulos Reais dos primeiro e segundo Reis de Portugal, respectivamente D. Afonso Henriques e D. Sancho I.

— Na granciosa Sacristia (1622), belos quadros de pintores portugueses (séc. XVI) e os azulejos que revestem totalmente as paredes.

— Na Sala do Capítulo, a Capela de São Teotónio.

— No Claustro (1517), as abóbadas Manuelinas.

— No Coro Alto, a preciosa talha dourada do Cadeiral (Séc. XVI).

Eglise de Sainte Croix

Située au centre de la ville de Coimbra, elle a été construite en 1131.

Sa reconstruction a été effectuée pendant le XVIè siécle et elle rappelle le style Manuélin.

L'Église Sainte-Croix faisait partie du Monastère de Sainte-Croix qui appartenait à l'Ordre des Chanoines réguliers de Saint-Augustin.

Il a été fondé par D. Telo et Saint Teotónio, le premier Saint Portugais, fut le Premier Curé à le diriger.

Outre l'Église, le Cloître du Silence, la Salle du Chapitre, la Sacristie et le Haut Choeur valent la peine d'être visités.

À l'intérieur de l'«Église, nous pouvons apprécier la Cahire, merveilleuse oeuvre de la Renaissance de Nicolau Chanterenne, les tombeaux Royaux des premier et deuxième Rois du Portugal, D. Afonso Henriques et D. Sancho I.

La grandiose Sacristie (1622) est embellie par de magnifiques tableaux de peintres portugais (XVIè siécle) et par des faiences qui revêtent entièrement les murs.

A l'intérieur de le Salle du Chapitre, on trouve la Chapelle de Saint Teotónio.

Le Cloître (1517), lui, nous présente des voûtes illustrant bien le style Manuélin.

Et finalement, le Haut Choeur offre à nos regards les si Èges sculptés à l'or fin.

№ 11700

The convent is most easily approached by the ridge road from Pena (9km), but there is also an indistinct path through the woods from Monserrate, starting above the fountain opposite the entrance to the town.

Down to the Sea: The Beaches and Cabo da Roca

Continuing west from Colares, the road winds round through the hills to the beach villages of **PRAIA DAS MAÇAS** and **AZENHAS DO MAR**. In season there are buses from Sintra (every half hour from the train station) and in high season a tram from Colares to Maças. Both villages have campsites and a scattering of rooms. They are easy daytrips.

A little harder to reach, unless you take the tour offered at Sintra tourist office, is **CABO DA ROCA**, 14km to the south-west of Colares. The cape is little more than a lighthouse and a couple of stalls, where you can buy a certificate recording that you've visited "the westernmost point of Europe" – which indeed you have. It's an enjoyable drive.

Mafra

Connected by regular buses from Sintra (leaving from the railway station; 1hr.) and from Lisbon (1hr. 30 min.), **MAFRA** makes an interesting approach to Estremadura. It is distinguished – and utterly dominated – by just one building: the vast **Palace-Convent** built in emulation of Madrid's Escorial by João V, the wealthiest and most extravagant of all Portuguese monarchs. It is open from 10am to 5pm daily, except Tuesday.

The Palace-Convent

Begun in 1717 to honour a vow made on the birth of a royal heir, **Mafra convent** was initially intended for just thirteen Franciscan friars. But as wealth poured in from the gold and diamonds of Brazil, João and his German court architect, Frederico Ludovice, amplified their plans to build a massive basilica, two royal wings and monastic quarters for 300 monks and 150 novices. The result – completed in thirteen years at a cost, crippling to the state, of over £4 million – is quite extraordinary and, on its own grandiose terms, extremely impressive.

In style it is a mix of Baroque and Italianate neoclassicism, but it is the sheer magnitude and logisitics that stand out. In the last stages of construction over 45,000 labourers were employed, while throughout the years of building there was a daily average of nearly 15,000; there are 5200 doorways, 2500 windows, and two immense belltowers each containing over 50 bells. An apocryphal story records the astonishment of the Flemish bellmakers at the size of this order: on their querying it, and asking payment in advance, Dom João retorted by doubling their price and his original requirement.

Parts of the convent are now used by the military but an ingenious cadre of guides can still march you around a sizeable portion in about an hour. Many of the **royal apartments** are tedious though a few are remarkable: the *Sala das Trophas*, for example, with its furniture (even chandeliers) constructed of antlers and upholstered in deerskin. Beyond them are the **monastic quar-**

ters, which include cells, a pharmacy and a curious infirmary with beds positioned so the ailing monks could see mass performed.

The highlight, however, is the magnificent Rococo **library** – brilliantly lit and rivalling that of Coimbra in both design and grandeur. Byron, shown the 35,000 volumes by one of the monks, was asked if 'the English had any books in their country?' The **basilica** itself, which can be seen outside the tour, is no less imposing, with the multicoloured marble designs of its floor mirrored in the ceiling decoration.

Practicalities

The town of Mafra is dull – and with frequent buses heading on to the lively resort of Ericeira (12km; see following chapter) there seems no point in lingering. If you need to stay, the owner of the *Restaurante Primavera* (facing the palace across the main road) lets out clean and comfortable **rooms** in a house 400m from the town centre; the restaurant itself is good, too.

Queluz

The **Palace of QUELUZ** , just twenty minutes by train from Lisbon's Rossio station (or 30 min. on the way back from Sintra) is as perfect a counterpoint to Mafra as you could imagine. Elegant and restrained, it is the country's finest example of Rococo architecture, with low, pink-washed wings enclosing a series of rambling and beautiful eighteenth-century formal gardens.

The palace was built by Dom Pedro III, husband and regent to his niece Maria I who lived here throughout her 39-year reign (1777–1821), quite mad for the last 24. William Beckford (see p.68) visited when the Queen's wits were dwindling, and ran races in the gardens with the Princess of Brazil's ladies-in-waiting; at other times firework displays were held above the ornamental canal and bullfights in the courtyards. It's all easy to imagine today. On a more mundane note the original kitchen, the **Cozinha Velha**, has been converted to a (fairly) expensive restaurant – a good spot to have tea, at least.

Open daily (except Tues.) from 9am to 1pm and 2 to 5pm, the palace lies about 800m downhill from the station of QUELUZ-BELAS; ask anyone there to direct you towards the 'palácio'.

South of the Tagus: Setúbal and its Coast:

As late as the nineteenth century, the southern bank of the Tagus estuary was an underpopulated area used as a quarantine station for foreign visitors; the village of TRAFARIA here was so lawless that the police only visited when accompanied by a military force. The huge suspension bridge, inaugurated as the 'Salazar Bridge' in 1966 and renamed after the 1974 Revolution, finally ended what remained of this separation between 'town and country'. Since then, Lisbon has spilled over the Tagus in a string of tatty industrial suburbs that spread east of the bridge, while to the west the Costa da Caparica (see p.62–63) has become a major holiday resort.

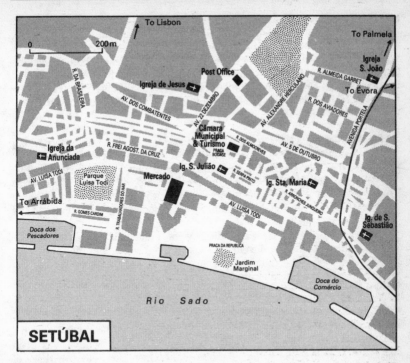

SETÚBAL

Setúbal

Some fifty kilometres from Lisbon, **SETÚBAL** is Portugal's third port and a major industrial centre, once described by Hans Christian Andersen as a 'terrestrial paradise'. Most of its charm is long gone but, if you're heading south and have time to break up the journey, it does have a remarkable church – the **Igreja de Jesus**, designed by Diogo de Boitaca and possibly the first of all Manueline buildings – and some excellent beaches nearby.

The **Igreja** is essentially late Gothic, with a huge, flamboyant doorway but Boitaca transformed its interior design by introducing fantastically twisted pillars to support the vault. The rough granite surfaces of the pillars contrast with the delicacy of the blue-and-white *azulejos* around the high altar, which were added in the seventeenth century. The church stands on the Praça Miguel Bombarda along the main Avenida 5 de Outubro, about 400m from the train station or the centre of town.

Next door to the church, housed in the old monastic quarters, is a small but very fine **municipal museum** (Tues.–Sun. 10am–12.30pm and 2–5pm) with a superb collection of fifteenth- to sixteenth-century Portuguese 'primitive art' as well as sections dedicated to fifteenth- to eighteenth-century jewellery and to local archaeology. You might also climb up to the Castelo São Felipe, to the west of the town. This is now a pousada, but drinks are affordable and there are fine views over the mouth of the Sado and the Troia peninsula.

Considering Setúbal's size, it can be remarkably difficult to find regular **accommodation**. Try along Avenida Luisa Todi, or just off the main square, Praça Bocage, though and you should come up with something. If you're stuck, the **Turismo** (on the Praça; 9am–5pm) runs a helpful accommodation service for places in private homes. Inexpensive seafood restaurants abound in the dock area and around the west end of Avenida Luisa Todi. The best – and reasonably priced – is *Antonio's* on Rua dos Trabalhadores do Mar.

Tróia

Setúbal's traditional **beaches**, reached by frequent car/passenger ferry (long queues in summer) from the town, are on the **Península de Tróia**, a large sand spit that hems in the Sado estuary. The peninsula was first settled by the Phoenicians and subsequently by the Romans, whose town of *Cetobriga* appears to have been overwhelmed by a tidal wave in the fifth century. There are some desultory remains, including tanks for salting fish, opposite the marina on the landward shore.

Once a wilderness of sand and wild flowers, Tróia must have been magnificent, but it's now heavily developed. To avoid the worst, and the crowds, be prepared for twenty minutes or so south along the beach. Following the (much longer) road behind the beach you will eventually reach a **campsite**, past a series of hotels and a golf course.

Palmela

The small town of **PALMELA**, a couple of kilometres to the north, is worth a visit for the views from the **castle**, which, like that of Setúbal, has been restored and extended to include a *pousada*. On a clear day the views of Lisbon, Setúbal, the Sado and Tróia are spectacular.

The Parque Natural da Arrábida

Between Setúbal and Sesimbra lies the **Parque Natural da Arrábida**, whose main feature is the 500m granite ridge known as the Serra de Arrábida, visible for miles around and popular for its wild mountain scenery. The twisted pillars of Setúbal's Igreja de Jesus were hewn from here.

The **bus** from Setúbal to Sesimbra takes the main road well back from the coast through the town of **VILA FRESCA DE AZEITÃO**, where the José Maria Fonseca **wine vaults** can be visited. The free tour is interesting and a good introduction to the local speciality – Setúbal Moscatel.

The area is best appreciated, however, from the twisting coast road (N10-4), which isn't served by public transport. Nestling in the cliffs down this road is the sixteenth-century **Convento de Arrábida,** whose crumbling white buildings with their stunning ocean views are the home of a silent Franciscan order. Nearby is the tiny harbour village of **PORTINHO DE ARRÁBIDA** which has a couple of excellent beaches, wonderful out of season. Next along is **GALAPOS**, arguably the best beach along this whole coast. Camping is strictly forbidden in the Parque Natural; the area's official **campsite**, well signposted, is 6km south at VILA FRESCA DE AZEITÃO.

Sesimbra

Although in the throes of rapid development as a resort, becoming surrounded by a ring of modern apartment buildings, the centre of the little fishing town of **SESIMBRA**, with its steep narrow streets, manages to retain a peaceful and unhurried atmosphere. Indeed, most mornings it's impossible to walk around without tripping over fish baskets, nets being mended, and lines being untangled. A Moorish castle dominates the town from a vantage point 250m above, and there's a thin strip of sandy beach between the town and the fishing quay. The **municipal museum** features archaeological finds from the area and is housed in the same building as the **marine museum** on Avenida da Liberdade, just down from the **bus station**. The fishing port itself, with its brightly painted boats, is extremely photogenic and the fish auctions make an interesting visit.

Sesimbra is packed in July and August and **accommodation** is virtually impossible to find. Even out of season, the few pensions are priced beyond the scope of the budget traveller. However the **Turismo** (9am–6pm; closed 12.30–2pm in winter), on the seafront at Avenida dos Náufragos 17, will put you in touch with rooms in private houses and there's a good, well-located **campsite** at *Forte do Cavalo* just past the fishing port and five hundred metres from town.

Of the dozens of excellent value **fish restaurants**, *Sesimbrense*, on the corner of Largo Município and Rua Jorge Nunes, is especially recommended. In the cafés, sample the local speciality of *Tortilla de Laranja*, a type of orange cake.

Moving on, there are seven fast **buses** a day to and from Lisbon (Praça de Espanha) and nine to Setúbal.

West of Sesimbra

Six buses a day make the eleven-kilometre journey west from Sesimbra to the **Cabo Espichel**, a desolate end-of-the-world plateau where the road winds up at a wide church square. This is enclosed on three sides by ramshackle eighteenth-century pilgrimage lodgings, which are now hardly used. Beyond, wild and windswept cliffs drop almost vertically several hundred feet into the Atlantic.

A few kilometres to the north and up the coast from here is the village of **ALDEIA DO MECO** with four buses a day from Sesimbra, providing easy access to the southern beaches of the **Costa da Caparica** (see p.62–63 for the northern section). Again these are prone to overcrowding in July and August, but they can be almost deserted and extremely warm and pleasant in, say, May or October. Several villages have *quartos* and there is a growing number of official **campsites** – a particularly good one at FETAIS, between Aldeia do Meco and Praia do Penedo. The best strip of beach is that known as LAGOA DE ALBUFEIRA, which is extremely clean, and excellent for windsurfing.

t r a v e l   d e t a i l s

Trains from Lisbon

from Rossio station

Sintra Line Every 16 min. to Queluz (20 min.) and Sintra (50 min.). Last back from Sintra at 1.47am.

Oeste Line 11 daily to Torres Vedras (1½ hr.); 7 to Caldas da Rainha (1¾–2 hr.); 2 to Leiria (2¾ hr.) and 1 to Figueira da Foz (4 hr.). Only slow trains stop at Óbidos – 8 daily (2½ hr.).

from Cais do Sodré station

Cascais Line Every 20 min. to Estoril (28 min.) and Cascais (32 min.). Every other train stops at Belém (7 min.).

from Terreiro do Paço (Fluvial station: via Barreiro, 30 min.)

Algarve Line 2 daily and 1 night train to Alcaçer do Sal (2 hr.), Albufeira (5 hr.), Faro (5¼ hr.), Tavira (6 hr.) and Vila Real de Santo António (6½ hr.), with 3 other fast ones to Albufeira and Faro. Change at Tunes (see *Algarve*) for Lagos and at Faro for Tavira and Vila Real.

Alentejo Line 3 daily via Casa Branca (2hr.) to Évora (3hr.) and Beja (4 hr.). Connections at Évora to Estremoz, Vila Viçosa and at Beja to Moura.

Setúbal Line Hourly to Palmela (1¼ hr.) and Setúbal (1½ hr.).

from Santa Apolónia station

Norte Line 10 daily to Coimbra (2½ hr.), Aveiro (3 hr.) and Porto (4 hr.). Some are faster, more expensive expresses.

Leste Line 4 daily to Abrantes (2½ hr.), Portalegre (4 hr.). Elvas (5 hr.) and Badajoz, Spain (5¾ hr.).

Beira-Baixa Line 5 daily to Abrantes (2½ hr.), Castelo Branco (4½ hr.), Covilha (6 hr.) and Guarda (7 hr.).

Beira-Alta Line 5 daily to Coimbra (3 hr.) and Guarda (7 hr.).

Galiza (Galicia) Line 3 daily to Porto (4 hr.), Valença (7 hr.), Tuy, Spain (7¾hr.) and Vigo (9 hr.).

Madrid Line 1 day, 1 night train to Madrid-Atocha (12 hr.), via Entroncamento (1 hr.), Abrantes (1½ hr.) and Marvão (3 hr.).

Paris Line 1 daily (4pm) express to Paris-Austerlitz (26 hr.) via Coimbra B (2½ hr.) and Guarda (7½ hr.).

Buses from Lisbon

Mafra/Ericeira (10 daily; 1½ hr./1 hr. 50 min.); Torres Vedra (12; 2½ hr.); Peniche (8 in 3 hr., 2 in 1¾ hr.); Nazaré (3; 4 hr.); Tomar (3; 2½ hr.); Évora (6; 3½ hr.).

Daily *Beiras Express* to Leiria (2½ hr.), Coimbra (3½ hr.), Viseu (5¼ hr.), Guarda (7¼ hr.) and Vilar Formoso (8¼ hr.).

Also, in season, **express buses** to the Algarve (Lagos, Faro, Albufeira, etc.) in around 5½–7 hr.: details from travel agents or from the tourist offices.

For details of **bus terminals** see the listings above.

Hitching from Lisbon

Heading **south** (to the Algarve or Madrid), try by the Praça da Espanha bus station or buy a ferry-train ticket to Setúbal, then walk 3km east along N10 to the A2 junction. For the **north**, take the airport bus to the Aeroporto and stand by the A1 (Coimbra/Porto) approach road – or even farther back by the tollgate at the beginning of A1. On Friday the Portuguese National Service troops are always on the move.

CHAPTER TWO

ESTREMADURA AND RIBATEJO

T he **Estremadura** and **Ribatejo** regions have played a crucial role in
each phase of the nation's history – and the monuments are there to
prove it. A comparatively small area, it boasts a quite extraordinary
concentration of vivid architecture and engaging towns. **Alcobaça**,
Batalha and **Tomar** – the most exciting buildings in Portugal – all lie within
ninety minutes' busride of one another. But even without them the regions'
attractions are compelling and immensely varied: ferries sail from Peniche to
the utopian **Berlenga Island**; **Óbidos** is a completely walled medieval
village; spectacular underground caverns can be visited at **Mira d'Aire**, and
tremendous castles at **Porto de Mós**, **Leiria** (itself an elegant town) and on
Almourol, an islet in the middle of the Tagus.

The Estremaduran coast – the lower half of the **Costa de Prata** – provides
an excellent complement to all this, and if you're exclusively after sun and
sand it's no mean alternative to the Algarve. Nazaré and Ericeira are justifia-
bly the most popular resorts but there are scores of totally undeveloped
beaches. If you want to camp in relative isolation try the area around São
Martinho do Porto, or the coastline west of Leiria backed by the fourteenth-
century pine forest of Pinhal de Leiria.

Virtually all of these highlights fall within the boundaries of Estremadura,
which, with its fertile rolling hills, is second in beauty only to Minho. The flat,
bull-breeding lands of **Ribatejo** (literally 'banks-of-the-Tagus') fade into the
dull expanses of northwestern Alentejo and there's no great reason to cross
the river unless you're pushing on to Évora or can catch up with one of the
region's lively traditional **festivals**. The wildest and most unusual of these are
the *Festas do Colete Encarnada* of **Vila Franca de Xira,** with Pamplona-style
bull-running through the streets: for details of this and others see p.99.

Ericeira and Torres Vedras

October 5 1910 marked the end of Portuguese monarchy. Dom Manuel II –
'The Unfortunate' – was woken in his palace at Mafra by reports that an angry
Republican mob was advancing from Lisbon. Terrified, he fled to the harbour
at **ERICEIRA** and sailed into the welcoming arms of the British at Gibraltar,
to live out the rest of his days in a villa at Twickenham. Baedeker's guide-
book, published the same year, described Ericeira as 'a fishing village with

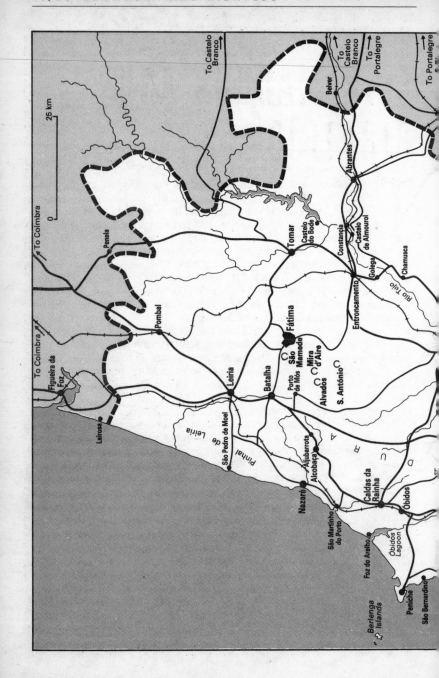

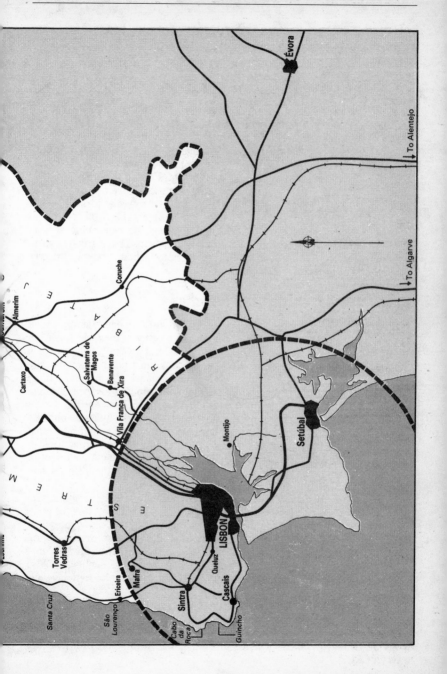

excellent sea bathing' and recent development has done little to change the town's original character. There are one or two large hotels and a few night-clubs and the place is doubtless on the way to resort status – but it hasn't quite happened, yet.

At the centre of town is the Praça da República, a small square busy with sidewalk-cafes, wonderful pastry shops, and a cinema that shows mainly subtitled Hollywood films. Activity, bars and restaurants are all concentrated on Rua Dr. Eduardo Burnay, which leads from a corner of the Praça to the town's main **beach**; a second beach, prettier and much less crowded, lies about 25 minutes' walk past the next headland – there's a small, primitive **campsite** here, but not much else. If you want a roof over your head, try one of three cheap **pensions**: *Fortunato* (Rua Dr. Eduardo Burnay), *Gomes* (Travessa J. Mola – just around the corner from the **Turismo** on Rua Dr. Eduardo Burnay) or *Severa* (Rua Poste do Cabo – one of four parallel streets running from the main Praça to the old fishing quarters). The **bus** north from Ericeira passes a fine series of untouched beaches, the best being at SÃO LOURENÇO, a peaceful hamlet with a sandy campsite. There are also virtually hourly buses to Mafra (see p.69), continuing to Lisbon – making Ericeira a useful first or last stop in Estremadura.

Torres Vedras: Battles and Beaches

TORRES VEDRAS, 15km inland, is well known in European history: it took its name from the Duke of Wellington's famous defence (*Linhas de Torres*) in the **Peninsular War** against Napoleonic France. The line consisted of a chain of 150 hilltop fortresses stretching some 40km from the sea directly west of Torres Vedras to Alhandra, where the Tagus widens out into a huge lake; astonishingly, they were built in a matter of months and without any apparent reaction from the French. Here in 1810 Wellington and his forces retired, comfortably supplied by the sea and completely unassailable; the French, frustrated by impossibly long lines of communication and by British scorching of the land north of the Lines, had eventually to retreat back to Spain in utter despair. Thus from a last line of defence Wellington completely reversed the progress of the campaign – storming after the disconsolate enemy to effect a series of swift and devastating victories.

In view of this historical glory, modern Torres Vedras is somewhat disap-pointing. There are a few ruins of the old fortresses and a couple of good sixteenth-century churches, but all this is swamped by a dull sprawl of recent buildings. Booklets and old maps can be read at the **Turismo** (in the central Praça da República) and directly facing it is the **Museu Municipal** (10am–noon and 2–6pm; closed Mon.) with a room devoted to the Peninsular War. Unless you get hooked on the local wine, there's not much else to delay your progress.

If you need somewhere to stay there's a **pension** facing the Torres Vedras bus station on Avenida 5 de Outubro (the railway station and Turismo lie at opposite ends of this street) but you'd probably be better off taking one of the many buses on to Peniche, Óbidos or the popular local resort of PRAIA DE SANTA CRUZ.

Praia de Santa Cruz and Other Beaches

Most people at **PRAIA DE SANTA CRUZ** are locals from Torres Vedras and this gives the place a friendly feel, as well as some excellent and cheap places to eat. The beach itself is long and wide and there's a campsite just five minutes' walk from the sea. By the side of the station is the *Pensão Miramar* – the one place to stay.

Less crowded – and good for camping outside the official sites, especially if you're prepared to do a bit of walking – are the quieter villages north of here, served by the coastal buses en route to Peniche.

At **CONSOLAÇÃO** (four kilometres off the road, just south of Peniche) and further south at **AREIA BRANCA** (literally 'White Sand'; 21km from Torres Vedras), there are small official campsites (both very cheap), and at the latter an extremely attractive **youth hostel** (☎061/42127), overlooking the sea.

Peniche and Berlenga Island

PENICHE, impressively enclosed by ramparts and one of the most active fishing ports in Portugal, is the embarkation point for the Ilha Berlenga. As late as the twelfth century the town was itself an island but the area has silted up and it is now joined to the mainland by a narrow isthmus with gently sloping beaches on either side and a campsite between them. It's an attractive place for a brief stay, of interest in its own right (above all for the fortress which dominates the south side of town), and with a great market held on the campo on the last Thursday of the month.

If you are camping in season try to arrive early in the day and, if the **campsite** is full, get yourself on the waiting list – vacancies are established at 1.30pm (be there!); the site is a fair walk from the town, or a 250esc taxi ride. Other **accommodation** is pretty limited. Try the *Pensão Aviz* (near the **Turismo**, in gardens by the ramparts) or ask around for rooms in private houses – look for signs saying *quartos* or *dormidas* in windows, especially on Rua Marechal. There are plenty of **restaurants** along the Avenida do Mar but these tend to be pricey; down near the docks it's a bit cheaper and the fish are grilled outside.

The Fortaleza and Cabo Carvoeiro

The sixteenth-century **Fortaleza** of Peniche was one of Salazar's most notorious jails. Greatly expanded in the 1950s and 1960s to accommodate the growing crowds of political prisoners, it later served as a temporary refugee camp for *retornados* from the colonies.

Nowadays it's a museum, with the familiar mix of local archaeology, natural history and craft displays, among which you can still see the old cells (on the top floor), the solitary-confinement pens (*segredos*), and the visitors' grille (*parlatório*): an impressive monument to anti-Fascism. It's open from 3 to 7pm, except on Monday.

If you've got more time to spare there's a beautiful walk beyond the fortress – out to the tip of **Cabo Carvoeiro**, the rugged peninsula beyond

Peniche. Pick up a map of this area (and of the town) from the Turismo: it's about 1½ hours to the lighthouse on the point.

Berlenga Island

The **ILHA BERLENGA**, 10km offshore and just visible from the cape, is all that you could imagine it to be, a dreamlike place like a Scottish isle transported to warmer climes. Just one square mile in extent, it is the largest island of a tiny archipelago, with a jagged coastline cut with grottoes, miniature fjords, and extraordinary rock formations. In summer the sea is calm, crystal clear, and perfect for snorkelling and diving – rare in the Atlantic. The only people who live here are about two dozen fishermen, while the whole island has been declared a **National Bird Reserve**, the home of thousands upon thousands of seagulls and eiders (as in down), perched in every conceivable cranny and clearly plotting to leave their mark on every possible victim. Makeshift paths are marked out with stones, and guardians keep an eye out for visitors straying out of bounds and disturbing the birds.

Human (and rat) life revolves around the main landing dock with its colour-washed fishing boats and small sandy beach. It really can get crowded and noisy down here at the height of the season – it takes very few people to make the place seem packed, especially on the **campsite** (free), which clings to a strictly limited site on the rocky slopes above the harbour. The only buildings are a cluster of huts, a small bar-restaurant and a lighthouse; there's a shop, too, for basic supplies, though you'd be better off stocking up before leaving Peniche. A short walk beyond the lighthouse, on an islet joined by the narrowest of causeways, is the seventeenth-century **Forte de São João Baptista**. Formerly a youth hostel, this became a basic **pension** in 1985; it's a fabulous place to stay, but as these are the only beds on the island it's a good idea to check its current status with the Turismo in Peniche. **Rowing boats** can be hired at the jetty to explore the intricacies of the coastline: don't miss the *Furado Grande*, a fantastic tunnel 75m long which culminates in the aptly named *Cova do Sonho* (Dream Cove) with its precipitous cliffs.

Ferries and Permits

The **ferry service** from Peniche to Berlenga operates from June 1 to September 20 and costs 450esc round trip. Current timetables are: three daily during July and August (9am, 11am and 5pm; return at 10am, 4pm and 6pm); and once a day through June and September (10am; return at 5 or 6pm). In July and August you may have to get up at 6am to secure a boat ticket for the same day. Tickets are 300esc one way, or 500esc day return.

The journey takes one hour and if the weather is difficult, times will change and boats may be cancelled. In any case, be sure to go without breakfast – it's a rough ride, as evidenced by a grim collection of buckets under the seats! If you want to **stay on the island**, you must obtain a **camping permit** from the Turismo in Peniche. In summer, there are often more applicants than permits, so you may have to wait a day or two. If you're organised, you can write to the tourist office and book in advance.

Obidos, Caldas da Rainha and São Martinho do Porto

ÓBIDOS, 'The Wedding City', was the traditional bridal gift of the kings of Portugal to their queens. The custom was begun in 1282 by Dom Dinis and Dona Isabel, and the town can hardly have changed in appearance since then. It is very small and completely enclosed by lofty medieval walls: streets are cobbled, houses whitewashed with bright blue and yellow borders, and at all points steep staircases wind up to the ramparts, where you can gaze across a ludicrously fable-like countryside of windmills and vineyards. It's touristy, of course, but less than you might expect.

One corner of the triangular fortifications is occupied by a splendid, massively towered **Castle** built by Dom Dinis and now converted into a *pousada*. Other hotels in Óbidos also tend to be expensive – the only reasonably-priced one is *Casa de Hóspedes Madeira* (Rua Direita), and your next best bet (with huge rooms and four-poster beds) is *Residencial Martinho de Freitas*, outside the walls on the road to the station. The cheapest option is to consult the list of private houses offering **quartos** which is posted in the **Turismo**, on Rua Direita. It's worth staying since, as so often, the town reverts to its own life when the daytime tourists disperse in the late afternoon. One of the better cheap places to **eat** is the *cafe 1 de Dezembro*, next to the church of São Pedro.

The parish church – **Igreja de Santa Maria**, in the central Praça – was chosen for the wedding of the ten-year-old child king, Afonso V, and his eight-year-old cousin, Isabel, in 1444. It dates mainly from the Renaissance though the interior is lined with seventeenth-century blue *azulejos* in a homely manner typical of Portuguese churches. On the left-hand wall is an elaborate tomb designed by Nicolas Chanterene, an influential French sculptor active in Portugal in the first half of the sixteenth century. The *retablo* in a side chapel opposite was painted by **Josefa de Óbidos**, one of the finest of all Portuguese painters – and one of the few women artists afforded any reputation by art historians. Born at Seville in 1634, Josefa spent most of her life in a convent at Óbidos. She began her career as an etcher and miniaturist and this remarkable handling of detail is carried through into her later full-scale religious works. Another of her paintings, a portrait, can be seen in the adjacent **museum** (10am–1pm and 2–5pm).

Other good reasons to stay in Óbidos include an excellent Saturday morning **market** and, in the second week of October, a long-established **Early Music Festival**, with free evening performances in many of the churches.

Caldas: a Royal Spa

Five kilometres north of Óbidos, **CALDAS DA RAINHA** – Queen's Spa – was put firmly on the map by Dona Leonor. Passing by in her carriage, she was so impressed by the strong sulphuric waters that she founded a hospital here, initiating four centuries of noble and royal patronage. That was in 1484 but the town was to reach the peak of its popularity in the nineteenth century when, all over Europe, spas became as much social as medical institutions. The English Gothic novelist, William Beckford, stopping off on his journey to Batalha and Alcobaça (recorded in *Travels in Spain and Portugal*, one of the best nineteenth-century travel books), found it a lively if depressing place – 'every tenth or twelfth person a rheumatic or palsied invalid, with his limbs all atwist, and his mouth all awry, being conveyed to the baths in a chair'.

Disappointingly little remains of all the royal wealth poured into the spa, though it is still a pleasant brief stop on your way to Nazaré or Alcobaça. There's a good campsite, centrally located in the Parque Rainha D. Leonor, and an excellent fruit market every morning in the central Praça.

From here the spa complex, still very much in use, is a short walk downhill. Protruding from the back of the royal hospital is the striking Manueline belfry of the church of **Nossa Senhora do Pópulo**, while at the back of the adjoining park is the curious **Museu de José Malhoa** (10am–5pm; closed Mon.). It is devoted to sculpture, paintings and ceramics from the turn of the century, including florid and original caricatures by Rafael Bordalo Pinheiro.

Ironically, perhaps, given the intentions of spa visitors, the town's gastronomic speciality is *cavacas*, meringues piled high and dripping with sugar.

São Martinho do Porto

SÃO MARTINHO DO PORTO was until recently one of the most enticing spots on the Portuguese coastline. It still has a vast beach, sweeping right around a virtually landlocked bay to form a wonderful natural swimming pool, and it's still among the warmest places to swim on the west coast, the sands sloping gently down into calm, shallow, solar-heated water. Unfortunately it is also now a very crowded and noisy resort, its campsite and rooms packed, the beach and the water dirty and murky.

Which is probably to say it's no worse than many other Portuguese resorts – just don't come expecting an unspoiled beach paradise. There's a good northern beach if the crowds around the bay get too overwhelming. Accommodation can in any case be difficult to come by, especially in midsummer. Your best bets are the *Pensão Luz* (behind the **Turismo**, also a good area for cafes) or *Pensão Americano*; otherwise you're down to searching out **quartos** or heading around the bay to the **campsite** by the railway lines.

The **youth hostel** listed as being at São Martinho is in fact 6km away, on a hill above ALFEIZERÃO: there are buses to the town (a 20-min. walk away) or to the hostel itself, as usual well equipped and well run. *Tantos* is an excellent and cheap eatery near the hostel.

Nazaré

Unless you actively enjoy crowds, **NAZARÉ** is somewhere to avoid at all costs in the height of summer. After years of advertising itself as the most 'picturesque' seaside village in Portugal, it has finally destroyed itself in the process. Gaily coloured tents running along the beach, trinket stalls, and high prices are the present-day characteristics of a village quite unable to absorb the increasing numbers that flock here every year. It's a pity, as local traditions happily coexisted with the tourists for some time, women weaving barefoot through the town bearing immense trays of fish on their heads, and the fishermen sitting unperturbed on the beach, clad in tartan shirts and woollen hats, mending their nets beside brilliantly painted sardine boats. Nowadays, however, the boats have all but disappeared to a new harbour, 15 minutes' walk from the village, where cranes have replaced the oxen once used to haul in the boats. In Nazaré, meanwhile, the traditional dress worn by women drying sardines on the beach, looks increasingly quaint and phoney.

The Village
The village was originally based on a rock face, 110m above the present sprawl of tower-block holiday flats – the legacy of pirate raids which continued well into the nineteeth century. You can still get to this district of **Sítio** on the funicular, which rumbles up almost continuously from 7.30am to midnight; join the crowds wandering around the *miradouro* and the pilgrimage church of **Nossa Senhora da Nazaré**, built to celebrate the miraculous escape from death of a local mayor whose horse (lost in a thick mist while out hunting) reared up at the very edge of the cliff.

It's not an impressive shrine, despite an icon carved by St. Joseph and painted by St. Luke (a handy partnership active throughout Europe), but it does have a well-attended **Romaria** (Sept. 8–10) with processions, folk dancing and bullfights. Get your elbows out and join the fun. The Sitio ring also stages Saturday night bullfights in summer.

Rooms, Food and Transport
Pensions in Nazaré tend to be fully booked throughout the summer but **quartos** are plentiful and fairly reasonably priced: you'll be accosted at the bus station by their owners, who seem to have fixed minimum prices among themselves. Alternatively, consult one of the two **Turismos**: in the main square in town (where there are a couple of reasonable **restaurants**: try the *Tasquinha* on Rua Adrião Batalha), or down on the seafront. Avenida da República, on the front, also has the friendly *Adega Oceano* (no. 51).

The nearest **railway station** is at VALADO, 6km away, from where you can reach Leiria, Figueira da Foz and Coimbra. There are frequent buses to Nazaré from the main square there.

Beaches
The problem with Nazaré's **beaches** – grand tent-studded sweeps of sand, stretching out to the north beyond the headland of Sitio and south across the narrow Alcoa estuary – is that the swimming is dangerous. The Atlantic can be fierce along the Estremaduran coast, so, for safety's sake, stick to the patrolled main beach where the bathers are packed in as tightly as the sardine boats.

Alternatively, tramp southwards to **GRALHA**, where you'll find a number of small coves and one sheltered beach isolated enough to be a popular spot for nude bathing.

Alcobaça

From the twelfth to the nineteenth centuries, the Cistercian **Abbey of ALCOBAÇA** was among the greatest in the Christian world. Owning vast tracts of farmland, orchards and vineyards, it was immensely rich and held jurisdiction over a dozen towns and three seaports. Its church and cloister are the purest and the most inspired creation of all Portuguese Gothic – and, with Belém and Batalha, they are today the most impressive architectural monuments in the country. In addition, it's the burial place of those romantic figures of Portuguese history, Dom Pedro and Inês de Castro.

The building (daily 8.30am–5.30pm) is the reason for visiting Alcobaça, yet when you arrive it is not the architecture that overwhelms you so much as the spirit of the place. Even in its forlorn emptiness the immense monastery, deserted since its dissolution in 1834, seems to assert power, magnificence and opulence. And it takes little imagination to people it again with the monks, said once to have numbered 999. Mass was celebrated here without interruption, but the residents' legendarily extravagant and aristocratic life-styles were the common ingredients of the awed anecdotes of eighteenth-century travellers. Even William Beckford, no stranger to high living, found their decadence unsettling, growing weary of 'perpetual gormandising . . . the fumes of banquets and incense . . . the fat waddling monks and sleek friars with wanton eyes, twanging away on the Jew's harp'. Another contemporary observer, Richard Twiss, for his part found 'the bottle went as briskly about as ever I saw it do in Scotland' – a tribute indeed.

For all the 'high romps' and luxuriance, though, it has to be added that the monks enjoyed a reputation for hospitality, generosity and charity, while the surrounding countryside is to this day one of the most productive areas in Portugal, thanks to their agricultural expertise.

A Tour of the Abbey

Founded by Dom Afonso Henriques in 1147 to celebrate the liberation of Santarém from the Moors, Alcobaça is a truly vast complex – and its main **Church**, modelled on the famous Cistercian abbey of Citeaux in France, is the largest in Portugal. External impressions are disappointing, as the Gothic façade has been superseded by unexceptional Baroque additions of the seventeenth and eighteenth centuries.

Inside, however, all later adornments have been swept away, restoring the narrow soaring aisles to their original vertical simplicity. The only exception to this magnificent Gothic purity is the frothy Manueline doorway to the sacristy, hidden directly behind the high altar, and, as at Tomar and Batalha, encrusted with intricate, swirling motifs of coral and seaweed.

The Tombs of Pedro and Inês

The Abbey's most precious treasures are the fourteenth-century **tombs of Dom Pedro and Dona Inês de Castro**, each occupying one of the transepts and sculpted with phenomenal wealth of detail. Animals, heraldic emblems, musicians and biblical scenes are all portrayed in an architectural setting of miniature windows, canopies, domes and towers; most graphic of all is a dragon-shaped hell's mouth at Inês's feet, consuming the damned.

The tombs are inscribed with the motto 'Até o Fim do Mundo' (Until the End of the World) and in accordance with Dom Pedro's orders have been placed foot to foot so that on the Day of Judgment the pair may rise and immediately feast their eyes on one another.

Pedro's earthly love for Inês de Castro, the great theme of epic Portuguese poetry, was cruelly stifled by high politics. Inês, as the daughter of a Galician nobleman, was a potential source of Spanish influence over the Portuguese throne and Pedro's father, Afonso V, forbade their marriage. The ceremony took place nevertheless – secretly at Bragança in remote Trás-os-Montes – and eventually Afonso was persuaded to sanction his daughter-in-law's murder. When Pedro succeeded to the throne in 1357 he brought the murderers to justice, personally ripping out their hearts and gorging his love-crazed blood appetite upon them. More poignantly he also exhumed and crowned the corpse of his lover, forcing the entire royal circle to acknowledge her as queen by kissing her decomposing hand (see Coimbra).

The Kitchen

From one highlight to another. Beckford – Romantic dilettante that he was – stood bewildered by the charms of these tombs when 'in came the Grand Priors hand in hand, all three together. "To the *kitchen*", said they in unison, "to the kitchen and that immediately".' They led him past the fourteenth-century Chapter House to a cavernous room in the corner of the cloisters.

This route you can follow. Alcobaça's feasting has already been mentioned but this **kitchen** – with its cellars and gargantuan conical chimney, supported by eight trunk-like iron columns – sets it in real perspective. A stream tapped from the River Alcôa still runs straight through the room: it was used not merely for cooking and washing but also to provide a constant supply of fresh fish, which plopped out into a stone basin! At the centre of the room, on the vast wooden tables, Beckford continued to marvel at

> *pastry in vast abundance which a numerous tribe of lay brothers and their attendants were rolling out and puffing up into a hundred different shapes, singing all the while as blithely as larks in a corn field. 'There', said the Lord Abbot, 'we shall not starve. God's bounties are great, it is fit we should enjoy them'.*

And enjoy them they did, with a majestic feast of 'rarities and delicacies, potted lampreys, strange Brazilian messes, edible birds' nests and sharks' fins dressed after the mode of Macau by a Chinese lay brother'! As a practical test for all this obesity the monks had to file through a narrow door on their way to the **Refectory**; those who failed to make it were forced to fast until they could squeeze through.

The Cloisters

The **Cloisters of Silence**, notable for their traceried stone windows, were built in the reign of Dom Dinis, the 'poet-king' who established an enduring literary and artistic tradition at the abbey. An upper storey of twisted columns and Manueline arches was added in the sixteenth century, along with, in its standard position opposite the refectory, a beautiful hexagonal lavatory.

The **Sala dos Reis** (Kings' Room), off the cloister, displays statues of virtually every King of Portugal down to Dom José, who died in 1777. Blue eighteenth-century *azulejos* depict the siege of Santarém, Dom Afonso's vow and the founding of the monastery. Also on show here is a piece of war booty which must have warmed the souls of the brothers – the huge metal cauldron in which soup was heated up for the Spanish army before the battle of Aljubarrota in 1385 (for more of which, see 'Batalha', below).

The rest of the Abbey, including four cloisters, seven dormitories and endless corridors, is closed to the public. Parts of it are currently occupied by a mental asylum – sad glimpses of which can be caught from some of the windows in the visitable parts. For the best overall view of the abbey, make your way to the ruined hilltop **castle**, about five minutes' walk away.

Staying in Alcobaça

Though Alcobaça is not a hive of activity, it's not a bad place to stay, particularly if you are camping. Get a map at the **Turismo** opposite the Abbey and head for one of the following: the 2-star *pensão* in the same square, the 3-star *pensão* just off the Praça on Rua Frei Antonio Brandão, the cheaper *Quartos Alcôa* on the Praça da República beside the Abbey, or, best of all, *Pensão Mosteiro*, on Rua Frei Estevão Martins. There's also a flourishing **campsite**, two minutes' walk from the bus station; turn left along Avenida Manuel da Silva Carolino.

Restaurante Trindade, on the Praça Afonso Henriques near the Abbey, or Cervejaria Roma, opposite the abbey, should go some way towards satisfying your appetite after the Beckford passages quoted above; both are good value.

Buses leave regularly for Nazaré and for Leiria – the latter a good base also for visiting Fátima and Batalha.

Leiria and the Pinhal do Rei

A striking royal castle hangs almost vertically above the graceful town of **LEIRIA**, a place of cobbled streets, attractive gardens and fine old squares. With regular bus services from the commercial centre of town to the three big sites of northern Estremadura – Alcobaça, Batalha and Fátima – it makes a handy, if also rather dull, centre for excursions. It's not a town where very much goes on.

The Castle and Town

The **Castle** (9am–7pm) incorporates an elegant royal palace with a magnificent balcony high above the River Lis. One of the most important strongholds in Moorish Portugal, it was reconquered by Afonso Henriques as he fought his way south in 1135 – though the actual building you see today dates mostly from the fourteenth and eighteenth centuries. Within its walls stands the church of N. S. da Penha, erected by João I in about 1400 and now reduced to an eerie roofless shell.

At the heart of the old town **Praça Rodrigues Lobo** stands surrounded by beautiful buildings and arcades and dominated by a splendidly pompous statue of the eponymous seventeenth-century local poet. It's a promising area, too, for bars and restaurants, as well as rooms (see below).

Practicalities

The **Turismo** – their map is especially useful for the **campsite**, some distance out of town – and **bus station** are on opposite sides of a park overlooking the river in the modern city centre. The **railway station** is about 4km out of town; there's a bus service, but it doesn't cost much to take a taxi.

For accommodation, make your way to the Praça Rodrigues Lobo and look around the restaurants (sometimes offering rooms) and **pensions** around here and on the narrow side streets: try Rua Mestre Aviz and Rua Miguel Bombarda. Other cheap rooms are to be found in Largo Paio Guerres and Largo Cónego Maia, both near the sixteenth-century cathedral. *Hotel Lis* (Largo Alexandre Herculano 10) is popular but well priced. There's also a fancy **youth hostel** with a good atmosphere (Largo Cândido do Reis 7, ☎044/31868).

As for **restaurants**, a couple of very cheap places can be found if you head off down the Rua Dr. C. Mateus (opposite the Turismo) and past Largo de Santana (try second on the right); seafood is good at *Jardim* (by the Turismo), and real Portuguese cuisine – slightly more expensive, but worth every penny – can be found at *Tromba Rija* (Rua Professores Portelas, ☎044/32072), out of town on the Marrazes road; go under EN1 and take a left after the *Casa da Palmeira*.

The Pine Forest and Beaches

Some of the most idyllic spots on this stretch of coast are in the **Pinhal do Rei** (or *Pinhal de Leiria*), a vast 700-year-old pine forest stretching from São Pedro de Muel to Pedrogão. The coastline of Estremadura has changed drastically over the last few centuries – Peniche was once an island, Nazaré was under the water until the seventeenth century, and in Roman times the sea splashed against the walls of Óbidos. Although there were trees here before, the Royal Pine Forest was planned by Dom Dinis, a king renowned for his agrarian reforms, to protect fertile arable land from the menacing inward march of the sand dunes; it has since grown into an area of great natural beauty, with sunlight filtering through endless miles of trees and air perfumed with the scent of resin.

Official **campsites** are located at PEDROGÃO, VIEIRA DE LEIRIA (on the Lis estuary, famous for its fish restaurants) and, the best one of all, at the popular resort of **SÃO PEDRO DE MUEL**, where your tent's sheltered in the woods from the Atlantic winds. The São Pedro **youth hostel** (☎044/59236) has a marvellous location on the sea, but is seasonal (May 1–Sept. 30); **buses** to Leiria are rather erratic (less so in summer and at weekends; last one back at 6pm) and involve a change at MARINHA GRANDE.

Sadly, the northern part of this coastline – indeed the whole coast north from Praia Velha almost as far as Figueira da Foz (see *"Coimbra and Beira*

Litoral", Chapter 3) – is now **severely polluted**. This is due to the noxious emissions of two paper plants at LEIROSA: a correspondent who walked the coast all the way from Figueira to São Marinho do Porto described seeing the beaches polluted red, the sea foaming red and stinking along the whole stretch, and PEDROGÃO a ghost town inhabited only by protest posters. Even in **PRAIA VELHA**, a delightful local resort with some great restaurants, the sea is rather dubious, which may explain the handy showers on the beach. So stick to the area between Praia Velha and São Pedro de Muel, where there are several charming beach hut settlements populated largely by Portuguese holidaymakers. **South of São Pedro**, too, you can find sheltered stretches of beach – especially around VALE DE PAREDES, an area popular with Portuguese camping outside the established campsites – but here you're no longer in the forest.

Batalha

The **Mosteiro de Santa Maria da Vitória**, better known as the **Abbey of BATALHA** (The Battle Abbey), is the supreme achievement of Portuguese architecture – the dazzling richness and originality of its Manueline decoration rivalled only by the Jerónimos Monastery at Belém (another UNESCO world monument). Beautiful and exuberant, it is a symbol of national pride, built to commemorate the battle that sealed Portugal's independence after decades of Spanish intrigue.

With the death of Dom Fernando in 1383, the royal house of Burgundy died out; in its wake followed a period of feverish factional plotting. Fernando's widow, Leonor Teles, had a Spanish lover even during her husband's lifetime, and when he died she betrothed her daughter, Beatriz, to Juan I of Castile, encouraging his claim to the Portuguese throne. João Aviz, illegitimate stepbrother of Fernando, also claimed the throne. He assassinated Leonor's lover and braced himself for the inevitable invasion from Spain. The two armies clashed on August 14, 1385, at the Battle of Aljubarrota, 15km south of Batalha. Faced with seemingly impossible odds, João struck a deal with the Virgin Mary, promising to build a magnificent abbey in return for her military assistance. It worked: Nuño Álvares Pereira led the Portuguese forces to a memorable victory and the new king duly summoned the finest architects of the day.

The Abbey

The honey-coloured **Abbey** (9am–sunset) was transformed by the uniquely Portuguese Manueline additions of the late fifteenth and early sixteenth centuries, but the bulk of the building was completed between 1388 and 1434, in a profusely ornate version of French Gothic. Pinnacles, parapets, windows and flying buttresses are all lavishly and intricately sculpted. Within this flamboyant framework there are also strong elements of the English perpendicular style. Huge pilasters and prominent vertical decorations divide the main façade; the nave, with its narrow soaring dimensions, is reminiscent of those at Winchester, while the chapter house bears a close resemblance to those at Wells and York.

The Capela do Fundador

Medieval architects were frequently attracted by lucrative foreign commissions, but there is a special explanation for the English influence at Batalha. This is revealed in the **Capela do Fundador** (Founder's Chapel), directly to the right upon entering the church. Beneath the octagonal lantern rests the joint tomb of Dom João I and Philippa of Lancaster, their hands clasped in the ultimate expression of harmonious relations between Portugal and England.

In 1373 Dom Fernando had entered into an alliance with John of Gaunt, Duke of Lancaster, who claimed the Spanish throne by virtue of his marriage to a daughter of Pedro the Cruel, King of Castile. A crack contingent of English longbowmen played a significant role in the victory at Aljubarrota, and in 1386 both countries willingly signed the **Treaty of Windsor**, 'an inviolable, eternal, solid, perpetual, and true league of friendship'. As part of the same political package Dom João married Philippa, John of Gaunt's daughter, and with her came English architects to assist at Batalha. The alliance between the two countries, reconfirmed by the marriage of Charles II to Catherine of Bragança in 1661 and the Methuen Commercial Treaty of 1703, has become the longest-standing international friendship of modern times – it was invoked by the Allies in World War II to establish bases on the Azores, and the facilities of those islands were offered to the British Navy during the 1982 Falklands war.

The four younger sons of João and Philippa are buried along the south wall of the Capela do Fundador in a row of recessed arches. Second from the right is the **Tomb of Prince Henry the Navigator**, who guided the discovery of Madeira, the Azores and the African coast as far as Sierra Leone. Henry himself never ventured further than Tangiers but it was a measure of his personal importance, drive and expertise that the growth of the empire was temporarily shelved after his death in 1460.

Concerted maritime exploration resumed under João II (1481–95) and accelerated with the accession of Manuel I (1495–1521). Vasco da Gama opened up the trade route to India in 1498, Cabral reached Brazil two years later, and Newfoundland was discovered in 1501. The momentous era of burgeoning self-confidence, wealth and widening horizons is reflected in the peculiarly Portuguese style of architecture known (after the king) as Manueline. As befitted the great national shrine, Batalha was adapted to incorporate two masterpieces of the new order: the Royal Cloisters and the so-called Unfinished Chapels.

The Claustro Real

In the **Claustro Real** (Royal Cloister) stone grilles of ineffable beauty and intricacy were added to the original Gothic windows by Diogo de Boitaca, architect of the cloisters at Belém and the prime genius of Manueline art. Crosses of the Order of Christ and armillary spheres – symbols of overseas exploration – are entwined in a living network of lotus blossom, briar branches and exotic vegetable shapes. Off the east side opens the early fifteenth-century **Sala do Capítulo** (Chapter House), remarkable for the audacious unsupported span of its ceiling – so audacious, in fact, that the Church authorities were convinced that the whole chamber would come crashing down and only employed as labourers criminals already condemned to death. The architect, Afonso Domingues, could only finally silence his critics by sleeping in the chamber night after night. Soldiers now stand guard here over Portugal's **Tomb of the Unknown Warriors**, one killed in France during World War I, the other in the country's colonial wars in Africa (see *Contexts*).

The **Refectory**, on the opposite side of the cloisters, houses a Military Museum in their honour. From here a short passage leads into the **Claustro de Dom Afonso V**, built in a conventional Gothic style which provides a handy yardstick against which to measure the Manueline flamboyance of the remodelled Royal Cloisters.

The Capelas Imperfeitas

The **Capelas Imperfeitas** (Unfinished Chapels) form a separate structure tacked on to the east end of the church and accessible only from outside the main complex. Dom Duarte, eldest son of João and Philippa, commissioned them in 1437 as a royal mausoleum but, as with the cloisters, the original design was transformed beyond all recognition by Dom Manuel's architects. The Portal rises to a towering 50 feet and every inch is carved with a honeycomb of mouldings. Florid projections, clover-shaped arches, strange vegetables; there are even stone snails. The place is unique among Christian architecture and evocative of the great shrines of Islam and Hinduism: perhaps it was inspired by the tales of Indian monuments that filtered back along the eastern trade routes. Although conveniently referred to as Manueline, it is really in a class by itself and illustrates the variety and uninhibited excitement of Portuguese art during the Age of Discovery.

The architect of this masterpiece was Mateus Fernandes, whose tomb lies directly outside the entrance to the Capela do Fundador. Within the Portal, a large octagonal space is surrounded by seven hexagonal chapels, two of which contain the sepulchres of Dom Duarte and his queen, Leonor of Aragon. An ambitious upper storey – equal in magnificence to the Portal – was designed by Diogo de Boitaca but the huge buttresses were abandoned after a few years and the Chapels have remained roofless and 'unfinished'.

The Village: Practicalities

The Battle Abbey stands alone, the huddle of cottages that once surrounded it swept away and replaced by a bare concrete expanse. There's not much else here but a sprinkling of tourist shops (with very pushy salespeople), bars and restaurants, which all do brisk business during the Fátima weekend in early October, when the place is packed. *Dormidas* are advertised within a few paces of the bus stop but it's preferable to visit Batalha on a trip from Leiria; eight buses a day depart from there. You can also reach Tomar and Fátima very easily (about 30 min. and 1 hr. 40 min. respectively).

Porto de Mós and the Caves at Mira d'Aire

High above the small, white village of **PORTO DE MÓS**, just 8km south of Batalha but well off the tourist trail, a grandiose thirteenth-century **Castle** of the Knights Templar stands guard (10am–1pm and 2–4pm). Bright green cones crown its turrets and from a noble balcony – added in the fifteenth century and similar to the one at Leiria – one can gaze down over the village. Bars, restaurants and a solitary, ramshackle but cheap and friendly *pensão* are grouped around the bus stop on the main road. More significantly, Porto de Mós is the nearest base from which to visit three of Estremadura's fabulous underground caves. If you're doing this, there's a convenient bus to Mira d'Aire which leaves around 8am (last one back around 5pm); Porto de Mós also has a small, helpful **Turismo**.

Mira d'Aire and other Caves

The largest, most spectacular and most accessible caves in Portugal are **Grutas de MIRA D'AIRE** (9.15am–9pm), ten minutes' walk from the bus stop in the drab textile town from which they take their name. Discovered in 1947 and opened to the public just over a decade ago, they comprise a fantasy land of spaghetti-like stalactites and stalagmites and bizarre rock formations with names like 'Hell's Door', 'Jelly Fish' and 'Church Organ'. Rough steps take you down and the excellent 45-minute guided tour (in French or Portuguese, or even English on occasion) culminates in an extravagant fountain display in a natural lake 110m underground. You might have to wait some time for a group of acceptable size to gather.

Alvados and Santo António

There are similar *grutas* or caves in open country near the hamlets of **ALVADOS** and **SANTO ANTÓNIO** (both 9am–9pm). Three buses a day run between Porto de Mós and Mira d'Aire, passing within 3km of Alvados and 7km of Santo António. Hitching along the main road is not too difficult but there's a good chance you'll have to walk part of the way if you want to visit these more remote sites. All caves are clearly marked and the tourist offices in Leiria, Batalha and Fátima can give you a map of the area showing precise locations.

Grutas da Moeda

The labyrinthine **Grutas da Moeda** (9am–9pm) at **SÃO MAMEDE** are also well worth seeing, not least because one of the chambers has been converted into a unique bar with rock (!) music, subtle lighting and stalactites nose-diving into your glass of beer. They're best visited from Fátima, 6km away, where, with some concerted haggling, you should be able to arrange for a reasonably priced taxi. The whole area, full of old salt mines and pits, forms part of the *Parque Natural das Serras d'Aire e dos Candeeiros*, with a head office in RIO MAIOR (Jardim Marginal).

Fátima

FÁTIMA is the fountainhead of religious devotion in Portugal and one of the most important centres of pilgrimage in the Catholic world. The cult of Fátima is founded on a series of six **Apparitions of the Virgin Mary**. On May 13, 1917, three peasant children from the village were tending their parents' flock when, in a flash of lightning, they were confronted with 'a Lady brighter than the sun' sitting in the branches of a tree.

According to the memoirs of Lúcia, who was the only one who could hear what was said and to survive into her teens, the Lady announced, 'I am from Heaven. I have come to ask you to return here six times, at this same hour, on the thirteenth of every month. Then, in October, I will tell you who I am and what I want'. News of the miracle was greeted with scepticism, and only a few casual onlookers attended the second appearance, but for the July 13 apparition, the crowd had swollen to a few thousand. Although only the three children could see the heavenly visitor, Fátima became a *cause célèbre*, with the anticlerical government accusing the Church of fabricating a miracle to revive its flagging influence and Church authorities afraid to acknowledge what they feared was a hoax. The children were arrested and interrogated but refused to change their story.

By the date of the final appearance, October 13, as many as 70,000 people had converged on Fátima where they witnessed the so-called Miracle of the Sun. Eye-witnesses described the skies clearing and the sun, intensified to a blinding, swirling ball of fire, shooting beams of multicoloured light to earth. Lifelong illnesses, supposedly, were cured; the blind could see again and the dumb speak. It was enough to convince most of the terrified witnesses. Nevertheless the three children remained the only ones actually to see the Virgin, and only Lúcia could communicate with her.

To her only were revealed the three **Secrets of Fátima**. The first was a message of peace (this was during World War I) and a vision of Hell, with anguished, charred souls plunged into an ocean of fire. The second was more prophetic and controversial: 'If you pay heed to my request', the vision declared, 'Russia will be converted and there will be peace. If not, Russia will spread her errors through the world, causing wars and persecution against the Church' – all this just a few weeks before the Bolshevik takeover in St. Petersburg, though not, perhaps, before it could have been predicted. The third secret has never been divulged – it lies in a drawer of the Pope's desk in the Vatican, read by successive popes on their accession but supposedly too horrible to be revealed, though the present incumbent has hinted that the day may not be far off when he will announce its contents.*

The Basílica and the Town

To commemorate the extraordinary events and to accommodate the hordes of pilgrims who flock here, a shrine has been built; it has little to recommend

---

* In 1984 an Irish priest tried to hijack an *Aer Lingus* plane to persuade the Pope to reveal the secret. Unfortunately the crisis was defused with no one any the wiser.

it but its size. The vast white **Basílica** and its gigantic esplanade are capable of holding more than a million devotees. In the church the tombs of Jacinta and Francisco – Lúcia's fellow witnesses, neither of whom survived the European flu epidemic of 1919–20 – are the subject of constant attention in their chapels on either side of the main exit. Long, neoclassical colonnades flank the Basílica and enclose part of the sloping esplanade in front. This huge area, reminiscent of an airport runway, is twice the size of the famous piazza of St. Peter's in Rome. On its left-hand side the original holm oak tree in which the Virgin appeared was long ago consumed by souvenir-hunting pilgrims; the small Chapel of the Apparitions now stands in its place, with a new tree a few yards away.

Whatever your feelings about the place, there is an undeniable (and to some people suffocating) atmosphere of mystery around it, perhaps created by nothing more than the obvious faith of the vast majority of its visitors. Certainly it's intensified at the times of the great **annual pilgrimages** on May 12–13 and the same dates in October. Crowds of up to 100,000 congregate, mostly arriving on foot, some even walking on their knees in penance. Open-air mass is celebrated at 5am and an image of the Virgin is paraded by candlelight as priests move among the pilgrims hearing confessions. The fiftieth anniversary of the apparitions attracted one-and-a-half million worshippers, including Pope Paul VI and Lúcia, who is still alive, a Carmelite nun in the Convent of Santa Teresa near Coimbra. She was again part of the vast crowd that greeted John Paul II here in 1982.

Hospices and small convents have sprung up in the shadow of the Basílica, and inevitably the fame of Fátima has resulted in its commercialisation. As each year goes by, the grotesquely kitsch souvenirs on sale move even further into hitherto unexplored territories of bad taste – look out for the Fátima ballpoint pens, which when tilted reveal the Virgin in glory. Business is particularly brisk on Sunday, when it's fascinating to watch the thousands of local families converging by bus, car, lorry and cart – yet the shrine itself is in no way swamped. You're expected to dress 'respectably' if you venture inside.

There is a pleasant walk up to the place of the **'Apparitions of the Angel'**, outside the village, along which pilgrims follow the Stations of the Cross.

Practicalities

Pensions and **restaurants** abound in Fatima, most of them decked out in tasteful shades of Marian blue. But frankly there's little reason to stay except during the big pilgrimages (when all of them are full up anyway) to witness the midnight processions. At these times people camp all around the back and sides of the Basílica.

Reguengó do Feital

The regular **bus services** to Fatima from Leiria and Tomar make a relaxed day trip easy. Coming from Batalha you'll pass **REGUENGÓ DO FETAL**, an alternative religious site that's host to a torchlit procession (lit by burning oil carried in shells) up to a hilltop sanctuary around October 3.

Tomar

The Convento de Cristo at **TOMAR**, 34km east of Fátima, is an artistic *tour de force* which entwines the most outstanding military, religious and imperial strands in the history of Portugal. The *Ordem dos Templários* (Knights Templar) and their successors, the *Ordem de Cristo* (Order of Christ), established their headquarters here and successive Grand Masters employed experts in Romanesque, Manueline and Renaissance architecture to embellish and expand the convent in a manner worthy of their power, prestige and wealth. In addition, Tomar is an attractive town in its own right – especially during the *Festas dos Tabuleiros*, every third July, when the place goes wild. Aim to spend a couple of days here if you can.

Accommodation and Practicalities

Tomar has a **campsite** and at least four reasonable **pensions**: *Nun' Álvares* (recommended; the restaurant has local dishes and a strong red wine), *Luz* (good value) and *Tomarense* (not as cheap), all near the bus and railway stations, and *Beira Rio* near the post office on Rua Alexandre Herculano. All four double as **restaurants**; you might also try *Restaurante Boa Vista* across the Ponte Velha.

A fine alternative to the campsite, if you have transport, is the **site** at CASTELO DE BODE (13km from Tomar and 7km from the train station at Santa Cita, the stop before Tomar), Lisbon's main water source and a magnificent setting in the pine woods next to the Rio Zêzere. You can hire boats to reach the islands in the reservoir.

The Town

Built on a simple grid plan, Tomar's old quarters preserve all their traditional charm – whitewashed, terraced cottages line narrow cobbled streets. On the central Praça da República stands an elegant seventeenth-century town hall, a ring of houses of the same period, and the Manueline church of **São João Baptista**, remarkable for its octagonal belfry and elaborate doorway. Inside hang six pictures attributed to Gregório Lopes (ca. 1490–1550), one of Portugal's finest artists. Nearby at Rua Joaquim Jacinto 73 you'll find an excellently preserved fourteenth-century **Synagogue**, interesting in a town dominated for so long by crusading Defenders of the Faith; you can get the key at the Turismo. Its stark interior, with plain vaults supported by four slender columns, houses a collection of thirteenth- to fourteenth-century Hebraic inscriptions. In 1496 Dom Manuel followed the example of the *Reyes Católices* (Catholic Kings) of Spain and ordered the expulsion or conversion of all Portuguese Jews. The synagogue at Tomar was one of the very few to survive so far south – there's another at Castelo de Vide in the Alentejo. Many Jews fled northwards, especially to Trás-os-Montes where Inquisitional supervision was less hawk-eyed.

Midway between the town and the Convento de Cristo, it's worth taking the time for a look around the unassumingly beautiful Renaissance church of

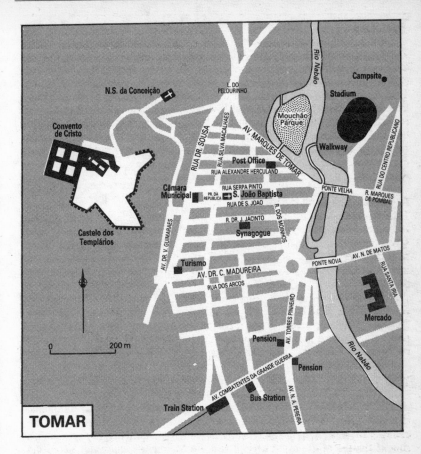

TOMAR

Nossa Senhora da Conceição ('Our Lady of the Immaculate Conception').
It is attributed to Diogo de Torralva, architect of the Convento's Great
Cloisters. The Turismo hold keys for the church.

The Convento de Cristo

The **Convento de Cristo** (9.30am–12.30pm and 2–6pm; closed Mon.; small
fee) is set among pleasant gardens with splendid views, about a quarter of an
hour's walk uphill from the centre of town. Founded in 1162 by Gualdim Pais,
first and grandest Master of the **Knights Templar,** it was, as headquarters of
the Order, both a religious and a military centre.

One of the main objectives of the Templars was to expel the Moors from
Spain and Portugal, a reconquest seen always as a crusade against the Dark
Forces – the defence of Christianity against the Infidel. Spiritual strength was
an integral part of the military effort and, despite magnificent additions, the

sacred heart of the whole complex remains the **Charola**, the twelfth-century temple from which the knights drew their moral conviction. It is a strange place, more suggestive of the occult than of Christianity. At the centre of the sixteen-sided, almost circular, chapel stands the high altar, surrounded by a two-storeyed octagon. Deep alcoves, decorated with sixteenth-century paintings, are cut into the outside walls; the Templars are said to have attended mass on horseback. Like almost every circular church, it is ultimately based on the Church of the Holy Sepulchre in Jerusalem, for whose protection the Knights Templar were originally founded.

The Order of Christ – and Dom Manuel's Additions

By 1249 the Reconquest in Portugal was completed and the Templars reaped enormous rewards for their services. Tracts of land were turned over to them and they controlled a network of castles throughout the Iberian peninsula. But as the Moorish threat receded, the Knights became a powerful political challenge to the stability and authority of European monarchs. Philippe-le-Bel, King of France, took the lead by confiscating all Templar property in his country and there followed a formal papal suppression of the Order in 1314. In Spain this prompted a vicious witch-hunt and many of the Knights sought refuge in Portugal, where Dom Dinis coolly reconstituted them in 1320 under a different title: the **Order of Christ**. They inherited all the Portuguese property of the Templars, including the headquarters at Tomar, but their power was now subject to that of the throne.

In the fifteenth and sixteenth centuries, the Order of Christ played a leading role in extending Portugal's overseas empire and was granted spiritual jurisdiction over all conquests. Prince Henry the Navigator was Grand Master from 1417 to 1460, and the remains of his **Palace** in the Convento de Cristo can be seen immediately to the right upon entering the castle walls. Henry ordered two new cloisters: the **Claustro do Cemitério** and the **Claustro da Lavagem**, both reached via a short corridor from the Charola and attractively lined with *azulejos*.

Dom Manuel succeeded to the Grand Mastership in 1492, three years before he became king. Flush with imperial wealth, he decided to expand the convent by adding a rectangular **nave** to the west side of the Charola. This new structure was divided into two storeys: the lower serving as a chapter house, the upper as a choir. The **Main Doorway**, which leads directly into the nave, was built by João de Castilho in 1515, two years before Dom Manuel appointed him Master of Works at Belém. Far from being concerned with the actual structure of the building, the architect treated the doorway as a surface to be adorned profusely with appliqué decoration. There are strong similarities in this respect with contemporary Isabelline and Plateresque architecture in Spain.

The crowning highlight of Tomar, though, is the sculptural ornamentation which surrounds the windows on the main façade of the **Chapter House**. The richness and self-confidence of Manueline art always suggests the Age of Discovery, but here the connection between the two is crystal clear. A wide range of maritime motifs is jumbled up in two tumultuous window frames which serve as eternal memorials to the sailors who established the

Portuguese Empire. Everything is here: anchors, buoys, sails, coral, seaweed and especially the ropes, knotted over and over again into an escapologist's nightmare. The windows can only be appreciated from the roof of the Claustro de Santa Bárbara adjacent to the Great Cloisters, which unfortunately almost completely obscure a similar window on the south wall of the Chapter House.

A New Style: João III

João III (1521–57) transformed the Convent from the general political headquarters of the Order into a thoroughgoing monastic community, and he endowed it with the necessary conventual buildings: dormitories, kitchens and no less than four new cloisters (making a grand total of seven). Yet another, much more classical, style was introduced into the architectural mélange of Tomar. So meteoric was the rise and fall of Manueline art within the reign of Dom Manuel that, to some extent, it must have reflected his personal tastes. João III on the other hand had an entirely different view of art. He is known to have sent schools of architects and sculptors to study in Italy, and his reign finally marked the much-delayed advent of the Renaissance in Portugal.

The two-tiered **Great Cloisters**, abutting the Chapter House, are one of the purest examples of this new style. Begun in 1557, they present a textbook illustration of the principals of Renaissance neoclassicism. Greek columns, gentle arches and simple rectangular bays produce a wonderfully restrained rhythm. At the southwest corner a balcony looks out on to the skeletal remains of a second Chapter House, begun by João III but never completed.

Santarém

SANTARÉM, capital of the Ribatejo, was built high above the River Tagus and commands a tremendous view over the rich pasturelands to the south and east. It ranks among the most historic cities in Portugal: under Julius Caesar it became an important administrative centre for the Roman province of Lusitania; Moorish Santarém was regarded as impregnable (until Afonso Henriques captured it by enlisting the aid of foreign Crusaders in 1147); and royal *Cortes* (parliaments) were convened here throughout the fourteenth and fifteenth centuries. All evidence of Roman and Moorish occupation, though, has vanished and – with the notable exceptions of two Gothic churches – Santarém has little to show for its impressive history. Even so, a visit is rewarded by the famous view from the *miradouro* known as the Portas do Sol. Best of all, plan your stay to coincide with one of the **Regional Festivals** held here (details below).

Practicalities

The **railway station** lies several hundred feet below the town but local buses are usually ready to ferry passengers to the **bus station** in the centre. Rua Pedro Carnavarro, roughly opposite the bus station across some gardens, leads very quickly to Rua Capelo e Ivens, the main pedestrian street of the old town. Maps and *festa* schedules are available here from the **tourist office** at no. 63, and the staff are extremely helpful in suggesting cheap **accommodation** – the nearest is on Travessa do Frões and there's a **campsite** and more *quartos* near the Mercado and the Câmara Municipal. All restaurants are shown on the free map.

Around the Town

The main square in the old town is Praça Sá da Bandeira, overlooked by the many-windowed Baroque façade of the Jesuit **Seminário** (1676). Rua Serpa Pinto or Rua Capelo e Ivens lead from here towards the signposted Portas do Sol, about fifteen minutes' walk away, and the best of Santarém's churches lie conveniently en route.

At the end of Rua Serpa Pinto the Manueline **Igreja de Marvila** is brightly decorated with seventeenth-century *azulejos* and has a beautiful stone pulpit, comprising eleven miniature Corinthian columns. Rua J. Araújo, at right-angles to the side of the church, descends a few yards to the architectural highlight of Santarém: the early fifteenth-century **Igreja da Graça** (9.30am–1pm and 2.30–5.30pm). A spectacular rose window dominates the church and overlapping 'blind arcades' above the portal are heavily influenced by the vertical decorations on the main facade at Batalha. Pedro Álvares Cabral, discoverer of Brazil in 1500, is buried within but his austere tomb-slab is over-shadowed by the elaborate sarcophagus of Pedro de Menezes (d. 1437), first Governor of Ceuta.

Continuing towards the *miradoura*, a third sidetrack is the twelfth-century church of **São João de Alporão**, now an archaeological museum. Take a look at the Flamboyant Gothic tomb of Duarte de Menezes (d. 1464). So comprehensively was he butchered by the Moors in North Africa that only a single tooth was recovered for burial! Avenida 5 de Outubro eventually finishes at the **Portas do Sol** (Gates of the Sun), a large garden occupying the site of the Moorish citadel. Modern battlements look down on a long stretch of the Tagus with its fertile sandbanks. And beyond, a vast chunk of the Ribatejo disappears into the distance – green, flat and monotonous.

Bulls and Festivals

This thinly populated agricultural plain is the home of Portuguese **bullfighting**. The very best horses and bulls graze in the lush fields under the watchful eyes of *Campinos*, mounted guardians dressed in bright eighteenth-century costume. Agricultural traditions, folk dancing (especially the fandango), and bullfighting all come together in the great annual **Feira Nacional da Agricultura**, held at Santarém for two weeks starting on the fourth Sunday in May, while dishes from every region in Portugal are sampled at the **Festival de Gastronomía** (last week in Oct., first one in Nov.). For a fixed price (low) you can eat as much as you like.

More bullfights are staged here during the **Milagre Fair** (2nd Sun. in Apr. for two weeks; fights on Sat.), the **Piedade Fair** (2nd Sun. in Oct. for two weeks), and throughout the summer, and there are cattle markets on the second and fourth Sunday of every month.

OTHER RIBATEJO FESTIVALS

During August, dozens of small festivals and bullfights take place in the strip of bull-rearing towns down along the other side of the Tagus – the nearest to Santarém are ALMEIRIM (6km) and ALPIARÇA (9km). Posters should advertise such events well in advance and it's not hard to hitch on the day itself from wherever you are in the area. Other towns to keep an eye out for include CHAMUSCA (on the left bank of the Tagus, northeast from Santarém); GOLEGÃ (right bank of the Tagus, near Chamusca – with a **Feira Nacional do Cavalo** in the first week of Nov.); SALVATERRA DE MAGOS (south from Santarém on the left bank of the Tagus); BENAVENTE (to the south of Salvaterra – also headquarters of the *Reserva Natural do Estuário do Tejo*); and MONTÍJO (easily reached by ferry from Lisbon, with plenty of action and few tourists).

Running of the Bulls: Vila Franca de Xira

The true mecca for aficionados of the bullfight is **VILA FRANCA DE XIRA**. A Pamplona-style running of the bulls, with the usual casualties, takes place here on the first and second Sunday in July at the **Festa do Colete Encarnado** ('Red Waistcoat' – a reference to the costume of the *campinos*), and on the first Sunday in October at the Annual Fair. Accommodation on these occasions is difficult to find and it's easier to visit the festivals on a day trip from Lisbon, 32km to the south. When not hosting these events Vila Franca is a dull and drab industrial city; the only reason to visit would be for the major bullfights, staged throughout the season.

Up the Tagus: Almourol and Beyond

As if conjured up by some medieval-minded magician, the **Castle of Almourol** stands deserted on a tiny island in the middle of the River Tagus. Built by the Knights Templar in 1171, it never saw military action – except in sixteenth-century romantic literature – and its double perimeter walls and ten small towers are perfectly preserved. There is a beautiful rural panorama from the tall central keep.

Railway lines hug the banks of the Tagus at this point and there are two convenient stations, Almourol and Tancos, fifteen and thirty minutes' walk respectively from the island. The former is stuck in the middle of nowhere but **TANCOS** is actually a small village with a couple of bars catering to a nearby army barracks. There's no accommodation anywhere but unofficial camping shouldn't be too difficult in such deserted territory, so long as you avoid the rifle range.

To **reach the castle** strike out along the railway tracks: the river banks are an impassable forest of eucalyptus trees, cacti and assorted bushes. For around 200esc per person, one of two old **ferrymen** will row you around the island and deposit you on a miniature beach to explore the castle at leisure. Your day is very much determined by the temper of your ferryman – usually there's no problem about taking picnics over to the island, but it has happened that the self-appointed custodian of the island has objected.

An alternative destination for off-peak travellers is the castle of **Belver** (see the *Alentejo* chapter) farther up the Tagus: a rival both in stature and position, if certainly less romantic.

Upstream to Constância

Constância and Abrantes, 3km and 15km upstream respectively, are ideal places to spend the night after visiting Almourol. **CONSTÂNCIA**, a sleepy whitewashed village arranged like an amphitheatre around the Tagus and the mouth of the Rio Zêzere, is widely publicised as the dwelling place of **Luís de Camões**, Portugal's national poet. In fact he was here for only three years (1547–1550), taking refuge from the court of Dom Sebastião, whom he had managed to offend by the injudicious dedication of a love sonnet to a woman on whom the king himself probably had designs. Costância is said to have remained dear to the poet's heart until the end of his life. In more troubled times, the town served the Duke of Wellington in 1809: he amassed his forces here and prepared for the Battle of Talavera in Spain.

If you stay in Constância, ask for *dormidas* in the central cafes or, if you are **camping**, hitch to the lakeside setting of Castelo de Bode, 9km up the Rio Zêzere and halfway to Tomar in eastern Estremadura. Alternatively, move on to Abrantes, where train connections link up with the lower Beiras and the Alto Alentejo.

Abrantes

ABRANTES occupies a position similar to that of Santarém, perched strategically above the Tagus, but the streets and praças are much prettier and the views more varied and just as extensive. The best vantage point is the **Castle**, dating mainly from the early fourteenth century and very badly damaged. As at Santarém, Romans and Moors established strongholds here and the citadel was sharply contested during the Peninsular War. Santa Maria do Castelo, in the middle of the castle, houses a motley archaeological **museum** (10am–12.30pm and 2–5pm; closed Mon.), the prize exhibits being three tombs of the Almeidas, Counts of Abrantes. From the battlements there's a terrific view of the countryside and the rooftops of Abrantes. Two large, whitewashed churches tower above all else; both were rebuilt in the sixteenth century.

Abrantes has a **tourist office** at the entrance to the town from the Tagus, where Rua do Montepio turns off the main road and climbs to the central Praça Barão da Batalha; the **bus station** is a few yards from here along Rua N. S. da Conceição. There are three reasonable **pensions**: the main praça merges into the small Largo Avelar Machado, and from here Rua Avelar Machado leads almost immediately to the 2-star *Pensão Central* in Praça Raimundo Soares; just off the opposite corner of this praça stands the run-down 1-star *Pensão Abrantes* (Rua Miguel de Almeida 17); and the 1-star *Pensão Aliança* is on Rua Cidade das Caldas, a continuation of Rua Miguel de Almeida. One of the most stylish low-budget restaurants in all Portugal is the *Restaurante Huambo*, on the corner of the main praça and Largo Avelar Machado.

Of the two **railway stations** (neither of which is central), the one at Alferrarede (northeastern side of town) is marginally closer to town and is the first stop on the **Beira Baixa line** to Belver, Castelo Branco and Guarda.

The other, south of the river (2km; second on the right), is the main station and offers the possibilities of the **Leste line** either to Valencia de Alcântara in Spain (via Castelo de Vide and Marvão stations) or to Crato, Portalegre and Badajoz (in Spain), and the **Portalegre line**, which continues on to Estremoz.

travel details

Trains

Oeste Line 11 daily from LISBON to Torres Vedras (1 hr. 30 min.), 7 to Óbidos (1 hr. 50 min.) and Caldas da Rainha (2 hr.), 2 to Leiria (3¾hr.), and 1 to Figueira da Foz (4 hr.; change for Coimbra at Bifurcação de Lares – 15 daily, 2 hr.).

Lisbon–Entroncamento 25 daily in 1½–2 hr., via Vila Franca de Xira (25 min.) and Santarém (1 hr. 10 min.).

From Entroncamento there are trains to Porto, Coimbra, Guarda, Portalegre, etc. – and to Tomar (16 daily; 20–30 min.) and to Almourol/Abrantes (9 daily – not all stop at Almourol; 15/50 min.).

From Abrantes

Beira Baixa Line 7 daily to Belver/Castelo Branco (¾/2 hr.), 6 to Covilha (4 hr.), and 4 to Guarda (5½ hr.).

Leste Line 5 daily to Crato and Portalegre (1 hr. 40 min./2 hr.), 3 to Elvas (2 hr. 50 min.) and Badajoz, Spain (3 hr. 20 min.). Change at Torre das Vargens for Castelo de Vide (2 hr.), Marvão (4 daily; 2½ hr.), and Valencia de Alcântara, Spain (2; 3 hr.).

Portalegre Line 2 daily to Portalegre and Estremoz (9.15am and 7.40pm; 3 hr. 15 min.).

Buses

From Lisbon Mafra/Ericeira (hourly; 1½–1¾ hr.); Torres Vedras/Areia Branca/Peniche (hourly; 1 hr. 40 min./2 hr. 25 min./3 hr.); Vila Franca de Xira/Santarém (½ hourly; 50 min./2 hr.); Leiria (8 daily; 2½ hr.).

From Peniche Consolação/Areia Branca (hourly; 15/35 min.); Óbidos/Caldas da Rainha/São Martinho do Porto (hourly; 40 min./50 min./1 hr. 20 min./1 hr. 50 min.).

From Nazaré Alcobaça (hourly; 20 min.); Leiria (10 daily; 1 hr. 10 min.).

From Leiria Batalha/Alcobaça (8; 20 min./50 min.); Batalha/Fátima/Tomar (4; 20 min./50 min./2 hr.); Porto de Mós /Mira d'Aire/Santarém (4; 30 min./50 min./1 hr. 50 min.); Coimbra (hourly; 1 hr. 40 min.).

Others Ericeira–Sintra (8; 45 min.); Tomar–Abrantes (4; 45 min.); Abrantes–Santarém (6; 1 hr. 25 min.).

CHAPTER THREE

COIMBRA AND BEIRA LITORAL

L ife on the fertile plain of the **Beira Litoral** has been conditioned by the twin threats of floodwaters coming down from Portugal's highest mountains and silting caused by the restless Atlantic: it's an area where drainage channels have to be cut to make cultivation possible and where houses must be built on high ground. On the shore itself a variety of ways of exploiting the richness of the ocean have evolved. At **Aveiro**, situated in the north at the centre of a network of waterways, the production of salt and the harvesting of seaweed have become staples of the local economy, and a peculiar method of sea-fishing has developed which involves the whole community – a remarkable spectacle that alone justifies a detour.

The **Costa de Prata**, stretching south from Aveiro, is one of the least spoiled coastlines in Portugal – an endlessly sandy reach, with small-scale towns and resorts. **Figueira da Foz**, a lovely resort at the mouth of the **Rio Mondego**, is the only real development along its entire length. Trailing upstream from the estuary, you'll see why the Mondego (one of the very few Portuguese rivers whose basin lies wholly within the country) has been celebrated so often in Portuguese poetry as the *Rio das Musas* – River of the Muses.

The highlight of Beira Litoral, however, has to be **Coimbra**, stacked high on the right bank of the Mondego midway. Home of the country's oldest university, this is an elegant and historic city, diverting both in its monuments and in its strong cultural life created by the student population. Just a few kilometres away at **Conimbriga** is Portugal's most extensive Roman site, while less than half an hour to the north, the delightful spa town of **Luso** lies beneath the ancient **forest of Buçaco**.

Coimbra

COIMBRA was Portugal's capital for over a century (1143–1255) and in fame and historic importance it ranks second only to Lisbon and Porto. Its university, founded in 1290 and finally established here in 1537 after a series of moves back and forth to Lisbon, was the only one in Portugal until the beginning of this century. It remains important and prestigious – though Lisbon has far more students nowadays – and provides the greatest of Coimbra's monuments. For a small, provincial university town, though, there are a

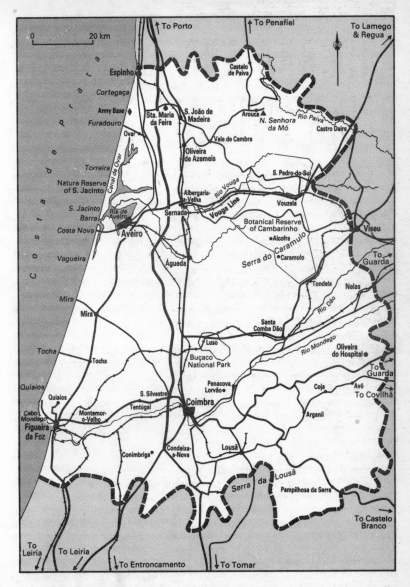

remarkable number of other riches: two cathedrals, many beautiful smaller churches and scores of ancient mansions. Most of these grand houses, in the serpentine streets of the old quarter, are privately-owned, but one hosts the **Museu Machado de Castro**, ranking with the Teixeira Lopes museum in Porto (p.157) as the best collection of sculpture in Portugal.

Coimbra is an enjoyable place to be, too – lively when the students are in town, decidedly sleepy during the holidays. The best time of all to be here is in May, when the students celebrate the end of the academic year in the **Queima das Fitas**, graduates ceremoniously tearing or burning their gowns and faculty ribbons. This is when you're most likely to hear the genuine Coimbra *fado* (though the tourist office organises events throughout the summer), distinguished from the Lisbon version by its mournful pace and romantic or intellectual lyrics.

Getting your bearings – some practical details

Old Coimbra was built on a hill, with the university crowding its summit, on the right bank of the Rio Mondego. Its slopes are a convoluted mass of ancient alleys around which the modern town has spread and most of the interest remains concentrated on the hill or in the commercial centre at its foot. Chances are you'll get lost as soon as you start to climb past the remains of the city walls, but it's no problem – head up to get to the university, down and you can't miss Rua Ferreira Borges (the main shopping street) or the river.

There are two **railway stations**: the one you want to get to is Coimbra A. Mainline and through trains almost all stop at Coimbra B where there'll be a connecting train to take you to the centre in a couple of minutes – just follow everyone else. Coimbra A is right at the heart of things – the **Turismo** (9am–8pm daily; ☎039/23886; good town plans) is straight ahead along the river, opposite the bridge in the triangular Largo da Portagem, and most of the cheapest places to stay and to eat are in the immediate vicinity.

The main **bus station** is on Avenida Fernão de Magalhães, about 15 mins' walk from the centre. Almost all long-distance buses operate from here, as do international services to Spain, France and Germany. The latter tend to originate from Lisbon so it's essential to reserve ahead; the most central **travel agencies** are *Abreu* (Rua da Sota 2) and *Visa* (Avda. Fernão de Magalhães 11).

Tickets for **town buses** (serving the campsite and youth hostel) are sold in *módulos* (blocks) at the Largo da Portagem and the Praça da República.

Accommodation

The Rua da Sota (left and immediately right out of the station) and the little streets off it are pretty sleazy, but the **pensions** aren't on the whole as bad as they look and there are some excellent rock-bottom restaurants.

In Rua da Sota itself try the *Pensão Vitória* (no. 9; ☎039/24049; good restaurant downstairs) – it's slightly better than the *Lorvanense* (no. 27) or *Sota* (no. 41). The Rua do Poço and Rua das Azeiteiras are even cheaper – the *Pensão Flôr de Coimbra* (Rua do Poço 8) serves extremely cheap meals to residents.

If you're prepared to **pay a bit more for comfort** try the *Pensão Rivoli* in the Praça do Comércio (3-star, but worth it), *Residencial Larbelo* in the Largo da Portagem (no. 33; ☎039/29092/3/4; a good deal), or one of the hotels on Avenida Emídio Navarro, which runs alongside the river – there are also a couple of 2-star pensions here, *Jardim* (no. 65; seen better days) and *Parque* (no. 42; recommended). *Pensão Gouveia* (Rua João de Ruão 21) is away from the centre, but quieter and convenient for the bus stations.

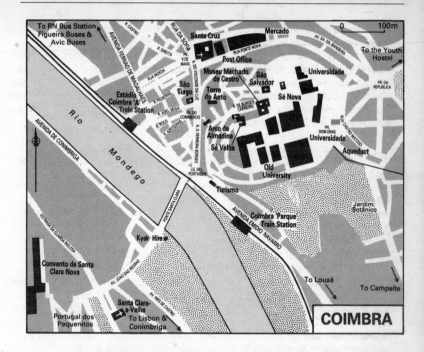

Staying **in the student area** of town, you could try several options near the Praça da República: *Diogo* (no. 18-2°) is an old-fashioned sort of place with views over the square and, beneath the aqueduct, *Antunes* (Rua Castro Matoso 8, ☎039/23048) offers good service – it's best to book.

Alternatively the **youth hostel** (above the park on Rua Henrique Seco 14) is new, friendly and immaculately run. Or there's a reasonable **campsite** (open all year; ☎039/72997) – with a **swimming pool** adjacent – at the municipal sports complex; bus #5 runs there from the centre.

Restaurants

It's not difficult to find somewhere to eat. As well as the Rua da Sota pensions, there are inexpensive places all over the centre.

For really **basic fare** and loads of atmosphere try the little dives on Beco do Forno or Rua dos Gatos, two tiny alleys between the Largo da Portagem and Rua da Sota; or there's *Adega Paço do Conde*, tucked out of the way on the Largo do Paço do Conde (cheap, lively and buzzing with Coimbrans), or the equally noisy *O Funchal* on Rua das Azeiteiras. A good concentration of workers' cafés (lunchtime and early evening meals) are to be found along the Rua Direita, which winds through the old town.

Moving only **a little more upmarket**, there's a very fine chef, and an outdoor grill, at the *Restaurant Pingão*, on the outskirts of the town at Rua Figueira da Foz 166. Good, too, and surprisingly reasonable for somewhere with such a touristic location is the café-restaurant *O Palácio* (closed Sun.), which looks out onto the Old Cathedral (*Sé Velha*) square. Higher up, the *Trovador* with live Coimbra *fado* would be a good place for a splurge.

Try, as well, one of the traditional **coffee houses** along Rua Ferreira Borges and Rua Visconde da Luz – the banks and big shops are all near here and the cafés are filled with businessmen and package-laden shoppers. The Praça da República, across town by the Parque de Santa Cruz, is also surrounded by cafés and **bars**, this time populated with students. The *Associação Académica* (Rua Castro Matoso) stays open lunchtime and late in the evening, and offers excellent value along with a smoky student atmosphere. You can also find pizzas and other international dishes down on the Praça itself.

Finally, there is a **market** in the mornings off Rua Olímpio Nicolau Rui Fernandes, above the post office, while the Torre de Anto, at the bottom of the old town near the Arco de Almedina, now houses a **handicraft co-op** with very reasonable prices.

The City

It's best to start your exploration of Coimbra with the university, not only because of its importance but because it's the easiest place to find and from its balcony the city is laid out below you like a map. Before leaving, set your sights on your next destination and with luck you should be able to find it when you get down.

The Old University

The main buildings of the **Old University** date from the sixteenth century when João III declared its establishment at Coimbra permanent. They're set around a courtyard dominated by the Baroque clocktower nicknamed *A Cabra* – the goat – and a statue of João III looking remarkably like Henry VIII. The elaborate stairway to the right leads into the administrative quarters and the **Sala dos Capelos** – the hall in which degrees are conferred. Hung with portraits of Portugal's kings, it has a fine wood-panelled ceiling with gilded decoration in the Manueline style. The highlight of this part of the building though is the narrow **catwalk** around the outside walls.

The central door off the courtyard leads past the **Chapel**, not the finest of Coimbra's religious foundations but one of the most elaborate – covered with *azulejos* and intricate decoration including twisted, rope-like pillars, a weirdly frescoed ceiling and a gaudy Baroque organ.

To the left is the famous **Library**, a Baroque fantasy presented to the faculty by João V in the early eighteenth century. These rooms telescope into each other, focusing on the founder's portrait in a disconcertingly effective use of trompe l'oeil. The richness of it all – tons of marble and gold leaf, tables inlaid with ebony, rosewood and jacaranda, Chinese-style lacquer work and carefully calculated frescoed ceilings – seems a little out of place in a centre of learning, but it's impressive nevertheless. The most prized valuables, the library's rare and ancient books, are locked away out of sight and, impressive multilingual titles notwithstanding, the volumes on the shelves seem largely chosen for their aesthetic value; no one seems likely to disturb the careful arrangement by actually reading anything.

The university buildings keep erratic opening hours: either from 10am to 2pm and 5 to 7pm, or from 10am to 5pm, depending on the time of year; ring the bell by the door and be prepared to wait. Once inside, there are guides, usually students, for each of the three sections – most appreciate tips.

Museu Machado de Castro

Below the university a good first stop is at the **Museu Machado de Castro** (Tues.–Sun. 10am–1pm and 2.30–5pm), just down from the unprepossessing Sé Nova (New Cathedral). Named after an eighteenth-century sculptor, the museum is housed in the former archbishop's palace – which would be worth visiting in its own right even if it were empty. As it is, it's positively stuffed with treasures: sculpture (especially a little medieval knight, riding home with his mace slung over his shoulder), paintings, furniture and ceramics.

Underneath all this is the Roman **Cryptoportico**, a series of subterranean galleries probably used by the Romans as a granary and subsequently pressed into service for the foundations of the palace.

The Cathedral

The **Sé Velha** squats about halfway down the hill; an unmistakable, heavy, fortress-like bulk. Started in 1162, it's one of the most important Romanesque buildings in Portugal, little altered and seemingly unbowed by the weight of the years; the one significant later addition – the Renaissance *Porta Especiosa* in the north wall – has, in contrast to the main structure, almost entirely crumbled away. Solid and square on the outside, it's also stolid and simple within, the decoration confined to a few giant conch shells holding holy water and some unobtrusive *azulejos* from Seville around the walls. The Gothic tombs of early bishops and the low-arched cloister are equally restrained.

Santa Cruz and Santa Clara

Restraint and simplicity certainly aren't the chief qualities of the **Mosteiro de Santa Cruz** (9am–12.30pm and 2–6pm) at the bottom of the hill past the old city gates. Although it was originally founded by São Teotónio even before the cathedral, nothing remains that has not been substantially remodelled. Its exuberant façade and strange double doorway set the tone. In the early sixteenth century Coimbra was the base of a major sculptural school that included the French artists Nicolas Chanterene and Jean de Rouen (João de Ruão), as well as the two Manueline masters João and Diogo Castilho, all of whom had a hand in rebuilding Santa Cruz.

The new tombs for Portugal's first kings, Afonso Henriques and Sancho I, and the elaborately carved pulpit set into a wall are among their very finest works. The Manueline theme is at its clearest in the airy arches of the Cloister of Silence, its walls decorated with bas-relief scenes from the life of Christ. From here a staircase leads to the raised *coro*, above whose wooden benches is a frieze celebrating the nation's flourish of empire-building.

It was in Santa Cruz that the romantic history of Dom Pedro and Inês de Castro (see "Alcobaça", p.85) came to its ghoulish climax. Pedro, finally proclaimed king, had his lover exhumed and set up on a throne in the church, where his courtiers were forced to pay homage to the decomposing body. Inês had originally lain in the **Convento de Santa Clara-a-Velha** across the river, alongside the convent's founder, the Saint-Queen Isabel.

Isabel, Coimbra's patron saint, was the wife of Dom Dinis, and infuriated him by constantly giving away his wealth to the poor. One of her many miracles was performed when, confronted by her irate husband as she smuggled out yet another cargo of gold, she claimed to be carrying only roses. By the time her bag was opened that was exactly what was in it. The beautifully simple Gothic hall church she built has been almost entirely covered by silt from the Mondego since then and now stands only as a ruin.

The two tombs have long since been moved away, Inês's to Alcobaça and Isabel's to the **Convento de Santa Clara-a-Nova**, higher up the hill and safe from the shifting river. The new (well, 1650) convent doesn't have much of the charm of the old and the fact that the nuns' quarters now house a Portuguese army barracks doesn't help. Its two saving graces, which make the climb worthwhile, are the tomb itself – made of solid silver collected by the citizens of Coimbra – and the vast cloister financed by João V, a king whose devotion to nuns went beyond the normal bounds of spiritual comfort.

Portugal dos Pequeninos and the Botanic Gardens

Between the two convents is **Portugal dos Pequeninos**, a park full of scale models of many of the country's great buildings interspersed with 'typical' farm houses and sections on the overseas territories, heavy with the White Man's Burden. Historically and architecturally accurate it's not, but the place is fun and great for kids who can clamber in and out of the miniature houses. It's open daily from 9am to 7pm in the summer; out of season times vary. A short distance beyond is a somewhat more sombre little park, the **Quinta das Lágrimas** (Garden of Tears), in which, so legend has it, Inês de Castro was finally tracked down and murdered.

If you like gardens though, the most rewarding site in Coimbra is the **Jardim Botânico**, or Botanical Gardens, on the far side of the hill from Portugal dos Pequeninos. Founded in the eighteenth century, they once enjoyed a world-wide reputation and if they've seen better days, it's still very pleasant to stroll among the formally laid out beds of plants from around the world. The gardens are open all day. Nearby are impressive remains of the sixteenth-century **Aqueduct of São Sebastião**.

Along the Mondego: Penacova and Lorvão

The stretch of the **Mondego river** to the northeast of Coimbra is a delight – and its valley, hilly and wooded, is followed by the minor road D110.

Penacova and kayak rides

PENACOVA is a small town high above the river, with a good campsite on the bank, and the superb *Restaurante Panorâmica* (go for the veal stew, its cheapest dish). There is little enough to the place – the appeal is in the river and woods around – though an oddity, as elsewhere in this region, are the highly elaborate cocktail sticks on sale. These are hand-carved by local women and are beautiful artefacts – the more delicate like feathered darts.

More tangible an attraction, perhaps, are the **kayaks** hired out at the campsite in summer. For a not too excessive fee you can take one of these downriver to Coimbra, and the organisers (the university) will take your baggage to meet up with you in the Quinta das Lágrimas (see Coimbra, opposite). You can also organise this trip from the Coimbra end. Alternatively, the road route is covered by numerous buses (4 times daily from Coimbra, with the most convenient leaving at 11.30am).

Lorvão

A strange and sad side trip from Penacova, or Coimbra, could also be made to the **Convento de Lorvão**, at the village of LORVÃO (bus to Rebordosa, then walk the remaining 4km).

This very ancient complex was founded by Benedictines in the ninth century, predating the arrival of the Arabs, and later taken over by Cistercian nuns. (The abbesses are buried horizontally in the graveyard; the lesser sisters are buried vertically, in twos and threes.) Most of what you see now dates from heavy restoration in the eighteenth century. If you ring for admission, you can visit the church, which displays the skull of an Arab king in its treasury, and with luck climb up to the *zimbório* or domed roof, with its splendid views over the village. The building serves as a distressingly old-fashioned mental institution; the inhabitants may lower paper cups down into the courtyard on pieces of string, to receive money or cigarettes.

Lousã

Another popular daytrip, southeast from Coimbra, is to the elegant old village of LOUSÃ, and its surrounding countryside. Trains from Coimbra stop well below Lousã itself; set off uphill and then veer sharp right. You'll find a succession of intricately decorated chapels and *casas brasonadas* along the main street. Watch out for a sign reading '*Castelo & Ermidas*', tucked away between a china shop at no. 2 and a café at no. 13. This path brings you out after 3km at a spot where a tributary of the Mondego curls around a narrow gorge between two splendid wooded hills. On one there sits a miniature castle, on the other is a small hermitage dedicated to Nossa Senhora da Piedade. Pilgrims mingle with swimmers, come to bathe in the chilly river pool between the two; picnickers abound; and there's a café if you haven't brought supplies.

Conimbriga

The ancient city of **CONIMBRIGA**, about 16km southwest of Coimbra, is easily the largest Roman site in Portugal. There was probably a Celtic city on the site even in the Iron Age, but the finest of what survives dates from the latter days of the Roman Empire, from the second to the fourth century A.D., when Conimbriga was a major stopping point on the road from Olisipo (Lisbon) to Bracara Augusta (Braga). By no means the largest town in Roman Portugal, it has survived so well only because its inhabitants abandoned it, apparently for the comparative safety of Coimbra. That the city came to a violent end is clear from the powerful wall thrown up right through its heart – even cutting some houses in two.

It is the wall, with the Roman road leading up to and through it, that first strikes you – little else, indeed, remains above ground level. In its hurried construction anything that came to hand was used and a close inspection reveals pillars, inscribed plaques and bricks thrown in among the rough stonework. Most of what has been excavated is right around the wall – the bulk of the city, only half-excavated, lies in the ground beyond it. What you can see is impressive enough, though. There is a series of houses with excellent mosaic floors, pools whose original fountains and water-ducts have been restored to working order, and a complex series of baths with their elaborate – and beautiful – below-floor heating systems revealed.

You get a free map at the entrance (Tues.–Sun. 9am–1pm and 2–6pm) but if you're at all interested it's worth buying the official guide. In the summer you may find students on site to explain the finer points of the excavations.

The **museum**, opposite the site entrance, displays fascinating finds from the dig, including bronze jewellery and coins, and fragments of statues. Around the back is an excellent **café** with views from its terrace down into the valley, whose steep sides were for many years Conimbriga's main defence.

Getting there: Condeixa

The one daily **bus** from Coimbra to the site leaves from the station at around 9am, but you can get to **CONDEIXA-A-NOVA** at least every hour and from there Conimbriga is less than thirty minutes' walk. If you head to Condeixa, a pleasant town with several bars and cafés around its central square, in the early afternoon, you can spend a leisurely few hours at the site and then either catch the direct bus back to Coimbra or arrange a lift with other tourists.

The Forest of Buçaco

The **Forest of Buçaco** is something of a Portuguese icon. The country's most famous and most revered woods, a monastic domain through the Middle Ages, were the site in the Peninsular War of a battle that saw Napoleon's first significant defeat. They are today a little undertended and overvisited, but remain an enjoyable spot for a day's rambling; from Coimbra it is easy enough to visit as a daytrip, or you could stay in the nearby spa town of Luso. For anyone with money to burn, the forest itself shelters one of the country's most exclusive and expensive hotels – the *Palace*, attached to the old Carmelite monastery.

Benedictine monks established a hermitage in the midst of the forest as early as the sixth century, and the area remained in religious hands right up to the dissolution of the monasteries in 1834. The forest's great fame and beauty, though, came with the Carmelite monks who settled here in the seventeenth century, building the walls which still mark its boundary. In 1643 Pope Urban VIII issued a papal bull threatening anyone who damaged the trees with excommunication – an earlier decree had already protected the monks' virtue by banning women.

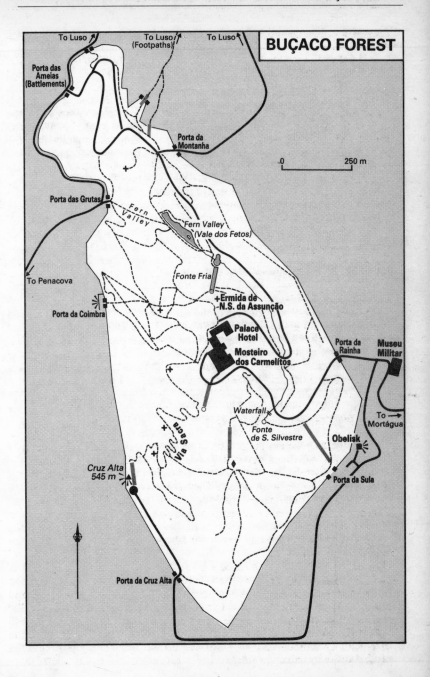

BUÇACO FOREST

To Luso

To Luso
(Footpaths)

To Luso

Porta das
Ameias
(Battlements)

Porta da
Montanha

0   250 m

Porta das Grutas

Fern
Valley

Fern Valley
(Vale dos Fetos)

Fonte Fria

To Penacova

+Ermida de
N.S. da Assunção

Porta da Coimbra

Palace
Hotel

Mosteiro
dos Carmelítos

Porta da
Rainha

Museu
Militar

To
Mortágua

Waterfall

Fonte
de S. Silvestre

Obelisk

Via Sacra

Cruz Alta
545 m

Porta da Sula

Porta da Cruz Alta

The monks, meanwhile, were propagating the forest, introducing varieties new to Portugal from all over the world. Nowadays there are estimated to be over 700 different types of tree, but the most impressive remain some of the earliest – particularly the mighty Mexican Cedars.

Around the Forest

Walks are laid out everywhere in Buçaco: along the **Vale dos Fetos** (Valley of Ferns) to the lake and cascading **Fonte Fria**, for example, or up the **Avenida dos Cedros** to the **Coimbra Gate**. But you can wander freely anywhere in the forest, and in many ways it is at its most attractive when it's wildest, away from the formal pathways.

The **Via Sacra**, a winding track lined with chapels in which terracotta figures depict the stages of the journey to Calvary, leads from the hotel to the Cruz Alta, a giant cross at the summit of the hill. From here, as from the Portas de Coimbra, there are magnificent panoramas of the surrounding country. It's a lovely place, if not always the haven of peace the monks strove to create – at weekends and holidays the woods are packed with picnicking Portuguese.

The Palace Hotel and the Battle of Buçaco

The **Palace Hotel**, in the heart of the forest on the site of the Carmelite monastery, was built as a summer retreat for royalty but since it was only completed in 1907, three years before the declaration of the Republic, it saw little use. An enormous imitation Manueline construction, it's dauntingly plush, but anyone can stroll in, have a drink and admire the Afonso Mucha prints or the *azulejos* depicting the **Battle of Buçaco**.

Fought largely on the ridge just above the forest, this encounter marked the first serious reverse suffered by Napoleon in his campaigns on the Peninsula. The French under Massena launched a frontal assault up the hill on virtually impregnable Anglo-Portuguese positions, sustaining massive losses in what for the Duke of Wellington was little more than a delaying tactic, giving him time to retreat to his lines at Torres Vedras (see p.78).

A small **military museum**, outside the forest near the Portas da Rainha, contains maps, uniforms and weapons from the campaign. Just above it a narrow road climbs to the obelisk raised as a memorial to the battle, with vistas inland right across to the distant Serra da Estrela, from where the **Porta de Sula** leads back into the forest.

Transport

All of the non-express **buses** from Coimbra to Viseu take a short detour from Luso through the forest, stopping at the hotel and again by the Portas da Rainha, so you can easily stay over for a few hours on a trip in this direction, or a day's excursion from Coimbra. Alternatively you could camp out in the forest or spend a leisurely night in the spa town of Luso, an easy walk below.

Luso

LUSO lies on the main road to Viseu and on the Beira Alta rail route to Guarda, some 30km from Coimbra on the northwestern slope of the Serra do

Buçaco. Unexceptional in itself – and mostly frequented by people taking the traditionally curative radioactive waters – the town is well provided with pensions and restaurants and is a pleasant place to rest up for a day or two. You should have no problem finding a **room**, with excellent, inexpensive choices all over the centre. *Pensão Central* and *Pensão Astória* on Rua Emídio Navarro are good bets and the **Turismo** in the central praça can help if there's any difficulty.

Right next to the Turismo is the spa's wonderful nineteenth-century **Salão do Chá** – all white wicker, potted palms and art nouveau. There's also a **swimming pool** (attached to the Grand Hotel), whose rather stiff admission fee is more than recompensed if you feel like a few hours basking.

The Vouga Line and Vouzela

The **Rio Vouga** is one of the most beautiful, somnolent rivers in Portugal, its grey waters followed along the banks by the branch line of the **Vouga Railway**. This is a beautiful ride for its own sake, though for those with transport of their own there's an equally magnificent road along the opposite bank.

The train, like many of the minor northern Portuguese services, has, sadly, become a little erratic in recent years and many of the departures have been replaced by a bus service. These follow the road, but make every possible effort to call in on station stops along the way.

If you are coming from Porto, and the buses rather than trains are operative, it's better to change at ALBERGARIA-A-VELHA rather than SERNADA. This gives you an extra hour for lunch, while the coach doggedly follows the train route to Sernada and then back along the main road past Albergaria, in order to join the north bank road to Vouzela, the main town between Albergaria and Viseu.

Vouzela

VOUZELA is a small provincial town with an almost palpable sense of civic pride. The locals – and the tourist board – boast of the peculiar sweet cakes, or *pasteis de Vouzela* (only for the most sweet-toothed), richly flavoured traditional dishes like *Vitela de Lafões*, and the heady local *vinho verde* (also labelled *Lafões*, after the nearby valley). Vouzela is also proud to possess its own local paper, which for a town with little over two thousand inhabitants is quite a feat.

There are no particular monuments or sights, though Vouzela does serve as a transit point for the thermal spa of São Pedro do Sul, at which Dom Afonso is said to have bathed his wounded leg after the battle at Badajoz.

The Town
The old centre of Vouzela is built around a sluggish stream, the backdrop to the main morning activity – washing clothes. Beneath a low **Romanesque bridge**, garments are spread to dry on the tall grass and soap suds run blue in the clear water. Around the bridge the houses are all of the small town

manor-type, with granite steps and balconies and white-washed plaster-work. Gracefully topping this scene, an elegant viaduct loops its way across the roof tops, whilst the **Serras of Arada** (to the north) and of **Caramulo** (to the south) rise up, dark and green, in every direction.

Back along the lane towards the main through-road, the **Turismo**, in a former prison, makes a good first stop in town. On the floor above there's a free **museum** offering insights into local preoccupations such as weaving, photography and painting. It's a small collection and something of an odd one, varying in range from serious anthropological and historical exhibits, traditional craftwork and Romanesque fragments, to an array of old dolls.

The town **Pelorinho** is affectionately referred to as the *forca* or scaffold. You, like me, might think it looks rather un-scaffold like, but it was in fact the site of a large number of executions during the Inquisition. The base of the structure is original; the metalwork top was added later.

Rooms and festivities

Finding a **room** in Vouzela shouldn't be much of a problem – it's the thermal spa which attracts most of the visitors and high prices. *Pensão Ferreira* (☎032/77650) on the main street (Rua Barão da Costeira) has a number of reasonably priced rooms on its top floor. There are also a couple of local **campsites**: the nearest is on an attractive site one kilometre up towards **Senhora do Castelo** (3km), a low hill which is the location for much merry-making and picnicking on the first Sunday after August 5. An alternative is at SERRAZES, 8km north. Follow the station road and then turn right in order to reach either of these.

Another **feira** happens on May 14 when flowers are strewn in the streets in honour of **São Frágil**, and everyone drives up into the hills to witness the blossoming of the rare *loendreiros*, a kind of rhododendron peculiar to this wild flower reserve area (see the following entry on the *Reserva Botânica de Combarinho*).

Other details are easily summarised. There is a streetmarket every first Wednesday in the month; the *Snack-Bar Pub* (Rua Teles Loureiro) is a friendly place where you can eat or play cards until late; the *Casa de Camilinha*, not far from either of these stops, offers cheap food and has the bus timetables.

Buses for Viseu leave from the train station; for Caramulo from the cross-roads just beyond the viaduct.

São Pedro do Sul

Eight kilometres north of Vouzela, **SÃO PEDRO DO SUL** is, without a doubt, one of the oldest spas in Portugal. It was a great favourite with the Romans, a popular haunt of Portuguese royalty, and is today one of the grand-est and most exclusive around.

The spa's position beside the Vouga certainly lends it a charm, and it makes for a pleasant brief stop between buses (it is on the Lamego road), or an afternoon trip from Vouzela. Don't consider staying, however, unless you are prepared to pay luxury hotel prices.

The Reserva Botânica de Combarinho

South of Vouzela stretches the **Reserva Botânica de Combarinho**, a vast area of great natural beauty. In the central valley of Lafões, covered by vineyards, it is reminiscent of the terraced hills of the Minho; other parts are densely wooded and dark, more like the Beiras countryside around Luso.

There are three tiny villages at the heart of the reserve – Cambarinho, Alcofra and Caramulo – all within easy striking distance of Vouzela. **Combarinho** and **Alcofra** are of interest really for their environs, full of rhododendrons, brightly coloured azaleas and thick green shrubs growing wild on the hillside. If you feel like staying off the beaten track, both have numerous possibilities of rooms to stay in, since the villagers have wised up to the financial advantages of taking an interest in tourism. The third village, Caramulo, has similar attractions, plus a couple of wonderful museums.

Caramulo

Tucked beneath the peaks of the high Beiras serra, **CARAMULO** is a great walking base – the loftiest Serra de Caramulo peak, *Caramulinho* (1062m), is less than an hour's walk away – and a thoroughly surprising village. A diminutive, rather ghostlike place, apparently in the middle of nowhere, it seems an almost surreal setting for a couple of the country's major museums.

The principal museum is the **Fundação Abel Lacerda**, a wonderfully jumbled art collection, with everything from primitive religious sculpture to sketches by the greatest modern masters – minor works by Picasso and Dali among them. There's an exquisite series of sixteenth-century Tournai tapestries depicting the earliest Portuguese explorers in India, full of weird animals and natives based on obviously very garbled reports. A painting by British portraitist Graham Sutherland, donated to Portugal by the Queen of England and symbolising the long alliance with Britain, is accompanied by its letter of authenticity from Buckingham Palace. Elsewhere there's a large *John the Baptist*, painted by Grão Vasco (see p.124) and quantities of beautiful furniture and jewellery.

Next door and even more incongruous, is a collection of **vintage cars** and motorcycles, including a pack of chrome-plated American dream machines.

Rooms, getting to Caramulo – and the Dão Valley

Caramulo used to have a fine pension, the *São Cristovão*, though over the last year it seems to have gone out of action; if it reopens, it's by far the best place to stay. Alternatives are **rooms** in private houses – not easy to negotiate – or the (very expensive) **pousada**, just outside the village. If you're on a budget, it might be better to reckon on staying in nearby TONDELA, where there's no shortage of accommodation.

Public transport links to Caramulo are easiest **from Vouzela**. On weekdays, two buses daily run as far as VARZIELAS, 4km north; from there you can either walk, hitch, or (with a lot of luck) pick up a connection. **From the Buçaco/Coimbra side**, something of a detour is involved. You need first to take a bus to Tondela, where you should be able to pick up one of the three

daily buses that serve the village on the way to ÁGUEDA, a majestic if rather
bumpy drive straight across the centre of the Serra do Caramulo.

The route from Buçaco leads through the **valley of the Rio Dão** which it
follows, the river on the right, the Serra do Caramulo on the left, all the way
to Tondela (and on to Viseu). This is the heart of the region where **Dão
wines** – some of the country's finest – are produced. Where they're not
covered with vineyards, the slopes are thickly wooded with pine and eucalyptus trees, though all too often there are bare tracts where forest fires have
raged. Crossing this part of the country in late summer or autumn, it's rare
not to see the smudge of smoke from a fire somewhere on the horizon.

Figueira da Foz and the Costa de Prata

FIGUEIRA DA FOZ has an enormous beach. Not so much in length as in
width: it's a good five-minute walk across the sand to the sea and unless you
wear shoes or stay on the wooden walkways provided, the soles of your feet
will have been burned long before you get there.

The town itself is one of the liveliest on the west coast, a major resort and
deep-sea fishing port. At the mouth of the Mondego, roughly equidistant from
Lisbon and Porto and only an hour by train from Coimbra, it attracts people
from all over the country. And with good reason – even when it's packed to the
gills there's a bubbling good humour about the place which is really enjoyable.

Rooms and food

It can take time to find a room in Figueira in high season, but with persistence you should be able to get something – there's no lack of places to try. If
you need help, the **Turismo**, on the seafront promenade Avenida 25 de Abril,
is even more helpful than most, and also a good source of information on the
region's many festive events (such as the *Romaria* at Buarcos on Sept 8).

A couple of the cheaper **pensions** are just in front of the railway station on
Rua Fernandez Tomás and Rua da República, but these are some way from
the beach. It's better, if you've arrived by train, to keep walking next to the
river until you see the ocean, then cut down into the town centre. Along here
both **Rua Bernardo Lopes** and **Rua da Liberdade** are lined with possibilities, though the nearer they are to the casino the more they tend to turn up
their noses at the suggestion of a room without a reservation. If you arrive
early in the day, try the beautiful *Hotel Universal*, near the casino, which is
run by a Portuguese Indian retornado from Mozambique, or the *Pensão
Miramar* on Rua dos Buarcos, virtually on the seafront. Otherwise, hunt
around the side streets for smaller places; the *Pensão Paris* on Rua Dr. Lopes
Guimarães is one of the best I found. There are also two **campsites**, one with
a swimming pool which is about two kilometres inland, and the other at Gala,
some four kilometres down the coast; both are well run.

The centre of town is packed with **places to eat** – you can get superb
Goan food at *O Escondidinho* which, as the name suggests, is hidden away,
on Rua Dr. F. A. Dinis. *Restaurante Tahiti* (Rua do Fonte 86; 5mins from the
casino) and *Snack-Bar Marujo* (Rua Dr. Calado 51A; just up the street from

the Turismo) both have good food and friendly staff. *Dory Negro* (Largo Cavas Direitas 16, on the way to Buarcos) is pricey but great for fish.

Around the Town and entertainment
The town doesn't offer much in the way of sightseeing – the most impressive sight is the beach – but there are a couple of places to look out for. The brand new **museum** on Rua Calouste Gulbenkian has an impressive archaeological section, as well as a large number of photographs of nineteenth-century bathing belles. The inside walls of the **Casa do Paço** are covered with thousands of Delft tiles, part of a ship's cargo which somehow got stranded in Figueira. Just along the river from the latter on Rua 5 de Outubro is the **market**, good for food and just about anything else you might need.

For the wealthy, **nightlife** centres on the **casino**, open only to those who are properly dressed and prepared to buy gambling chips. Otherwise, *the* place to go is *Flashen* disco in **QUAIOS**; try and get a lift up the *Serra de Boa Viagem* on a Friday or Saturday night. The disco is hidden in the pine trees outside the village (no admission fee, but you're obliged to buy drinks). As for events, there's almost always something going on – Figueira likes to promote itself. One of the best of the year's parties is **St. John's Eve** (June 23/24) with bonfires on the beach and a 'Holy Bathe' in the sea at dawn.

Bullfights are often held during the season and in the first couple of weeks of September the casino hosts an **International Film Festival** – a little ramshackle in its organisation, but always with a good selection of new films shown (at around 200esc a shot) in their original language.

North of Figueira – Praia de Mira

The coast **north of Figueira** is remarkable for its total desertion. Beyond **BUARCOS** – a fishing village which has become more or less part of the resort of Figueira – there's very little, hardly even a road.

Off the main north–south road you can get to the coast at just three points before Aveiro: Quaios, Tocha and Praia de Mira. With a car you can find virtually empty beaches around either Quaios or **TOCHA**, though the low-lying coastal plain offers no protection against the Atlantic winds. There are occasional buses to both places but not necessarily more than one a day. Nor is there much accommodation once you get there; sleep either on the beach, or at the excellent campsite at Quaios, which has its own swimming pool.

Praia de Mira
Set on a small lagoon – the southernmost point of a system of waterways and canals centred around Aveiro – **PRAIA DE MIRA** has seen a certain amount of fitful development. It is also, however, much more accessible, with four buses a day from Figueira da Foz and five daily from Coimbra, as well as being a fairly easy hitch from the main road (8km). You couldn't describe Mira as a beautiful place, but the beach that stretches around it is seemingly endless and backed by dunes where you can camp without anyone bothering you.

There are two official **campsites** a short way from town – the municipal one is closer and considerably cheaper, though less well equipped. Alternatively pick from a couple of 3-star **pensions**, *Arco-Iris* and *Pensão do Mar*, both overlooking the sea, or any number of places offering cheap, basic *dormidas* along the main street. For the latter, just ask in any bar.

TRADITIONAL FISHING METHODS

Praia de Mira is one of the very few places in Portugal where traditional fishing methods have survived entirely, presumably out of poverty rather than any desire to please the tourists. Even if it's too cold to swim, you can spend a day or two on the beach, watching the techniques in motion.

There is no real harbour, so the fishing boats are hauled across the beach, rolled on small tree trunks. They have very high prows and slightly lower sterns, so that they can be launched through the crashing breakers. Once clear of the surf they head out a kilometre or two offshore, drop their nets and come back in – the nets are then slowly trawled in by teams of oxen marching up and down the beach. This can take more than an hour and once the haul has come in the fish are taken out, sorted and auctioned there and then on the beach. It's a process that involves the whole village, either in the boats, driving an ox-team, coiling ropes or sorting the catch.

On a good day you can pick up a huge fish for virtually nothing and cook it yourself over a fire on the beach. Not surprisingly the local restaurants also have really good seafood, especially the thick, bouillabaisse-like soups and stews.

Aveiro

Like Figueira da Foz, **AVEIRO** is a sizeable resort, but it's also a place of some antiquity and of interest in its own right. A thriving port throughout the Middle Ages, the town was badly hit when the mouth of the Vouga silted up in 1575, closing its harbour and creating vast fever-ridden marshes. Recovery only began in 1808 when a canal was cut through to the sea, reopening the port and draining much of the water; only the shallow lagoons you see today were left.

These form the backbone of a modern economy based on vast salt-pans, fishing and the collection of seaweed (*moliço*) for fertiliser. The occasional pungent odour wafting across town, seemingly from the lagoon, is actually from the large paper factory nearby – this is one of Portugal's chief industries.

Practicalities

The town is on the main Lisbon to Porto rail line, as well as at the start of the Vouga line to Viseu, so the **railway** is by far the easiest way to arrive; the bus companies use the train station as their terminal anyway. From the station, walk straight down the broad main street in front of you and you'll eventually hit the river and the centre of the town.

Finding a room isn't easy. The **Turismo** in the central Praça da República can help, but most of the cheap places are just across the bridge on Rua José Estevão, and in the alleys around the nearby Praça 14 de Julho – try *Pensão*

Palmeira, just off Rua Palmeira. The Turismo also has good maps of the area and information on anything that's going on.

The main event is the **Festa da Ria** in the last two weeks of August when there are boat races, folk-dance festivals and competitions to find the best decorated of the *barcos moliçeiros*, the characteristic flat-bottomed lagoon boats that collect the seaweed. During July and August there are organised **boat trips around the Rias**, and at any time of year a group of people can hire a boat to tour the river; information, again, from the Turismo.

Around the Town – and food

The **Regional Museum** (Tues.–Sun. 10am–12.30pm and 2–5pm) in the Convento de Jesus is well worth a visit. Its finest exhibits all relate to Santa Joana, a daughter of Afonso V who lived in the convent from 1475 until her death in 1489. She was barred from becoming a nun because of her royal station and her father's opposition, and was later beatified for her determination to escape from the material world (or perhaps simply from an unwelcome arranged marriage). Her tomb and chapel are strikingly beautiful, as is the convent itself, and there's a fine collection of art and sculpture – notably a series of seventeenth-century naive paintings depicting the saint's life.

The main action in town otherwise is hanging around in the cafés watching life on the Ria: try some of the celebrated local sweets, especially *ovos moles*, candied egg yolks which come in little wooden barrels. More substantial **food** is surprisingly hard to come by for a town with pretensions to being a resort. Restaurants are few, far between and often full. Good standbys are *El Mercantel*, just off the Rossio, the *Zico Snack Bar* on Rua José Estevão and the **vegetarian** restaurant below the Tourist Office. Specialities include all sorts of fish and shellfish from the lagoons (eels above all), washed down with the powerful *Bairrada* wine.

The coast from Barra

There's no beach in Aveiro itself but the coast all around is a more or less continuous line of sand. Both Barra, right at the mouth of the Vouga, and Costa Nova are regularly served by buses from the centre of Aveiro.

Barra, São Jacinto and Torreira

BARRA has a campsite and several pensions, but it's an unsettlingly ugly (and expensive) concrete development, and you're probably better off making the effort to cross the lagoon for the beach settlements along the northern peninsula. There are **campsites** at São Jacinto, Torreira, Furadouro and – considerably further north – Cortegaça. It's worth using them because the endless flat country of sand dunes and pine forests, offering seemingly limitless possibilities for unofficial camping, in fact shelters several military bases.

There's also a bus link from Aveiro, via FORTE, to **SÃO JACINTO**, a thriving little port with good swimming and dockside cafés. Beautiful it's not, but São Jacinto is atmospheric and a good place to camp, and has a bird reserve, offering two-hour guided tours each morning and afternoon. **TORREIRA** – a lively little resort with several small pensions – has a direct ferry link with

Aveiro as well, but it's far from cheap. North of here the coast starts to get more developed; there are no buses running along the peninsula but it should be easy enough to hitch, or even hike, between the towns.

Ovar

FURADOURO marks pretty much the northern extent of the system of waterways (with rooms above the *Café Amadeo*): from here it's not a long walk inland to **OVAR,** which is back on the main rail line. The helpful Turismo in the main square of this attractive market town can direct you to its **Ethnographic Museum**, which has a surprisingly comprehensive international collection of pottery; there's also traditional clothing and the usual folklore displays. Nearby is the **Sacred Art Museum**, open only on weekends. And while you're here try some of the local *pão-de-ló* (sponge cake) – every bit as good as it looks.

Feira

An alternative to taking the train from Ovar is the local bus from Aveiro to **FEIRA**. Here there's a quite spectacular **castle**, its Moorish keep forming a surprisingly coherent whole with later, more whimsical additions. There are even a few Roman inscriptions incorporated into the walls, and you can make out the familiar straight line of a Roman road through the wooded hills above. The **Great Hall** within the keep is a magnificent Moorish structure, and you can climb above to the curious domes which give the castle such a fanciful air. Beyond the keep a fantastic tunnel links the two parts of the castle in such a way that no direct or easy access can ever have been offered to intruders.

The tumbledown *Hospedaria* at Dr Santos Carneiro 5 in VILA DA FEIRA offers exceptionally cheap rooms, though not much happens here apart from the annual *Festa das Fogaceiras* on January 20. There are convenient **bus** connections north to Porto or Espinho, and **trains** (the station is a kilometre above the old town) to Viseu.

While you're in the area, watch (or listen) out for the local geological phenomenon of '**jumping stones**'. A 'parent' rock literally gives birth to a small disc of 'baby' rock, flinging it into the world with an impressive **pop**.

travel details

Trains

Beira Baixa Line 4 daily from Guarda to Covilhã (1 hr. 10 min.), Castelo Branco (3 hr. 20 min.), Belver (4¾ hr.), Abrantes (5½ hr.), Entroncamento (6½ hr.), Santarém (6 hr. 45 min.) and Lisbon (8 hr.).

Norte Line 5 daily from Lisbon to Coimbra B (2½ hr.), Aveiro (3 hr.) and Porto (4 hr.). Also 5 daily fast trains to Porto stopping at Coimbra B (2 hr.) and Aveiro (2½ hr.), and *Tranvias* from Aveiro to Porto every 45 min. from 6am to midnight. 2 daily trains from Lisbon to Braga (5¼ hr.)

Oeste Line 6 daily from Figueira da Foz to Leira (1¼ hr.), Óbidos (2¾ hr.) and Lisbon (4¾ hr.). Figueira to Coimbra A, 15 daily (1 hr.).

Vouga Line Aveiro to Viseu, 2 daily (4 hr.).

Buses

All the major towns have an express service at least once a day to **Lisbon**, usually three or four times. **International** buses from Lisbon to Paris also pass through Coimbra, Viseu and Guarda, and you can pick them up there, though seats must be reserved in advance.

CHAPTER FOUR

MOUNTAIN BEIRAS

omposed of two provinces, the Beira Alta and the Beira Baixa (a higher and a lower), the **Mountain Beiras** region offers some of the least explored country in the Iberian peninsula. Arguably, it is also the most quintessentially Portuguese part of the country. Little touched by outside influence, it is historically the heart of **ancient Lusitânia**

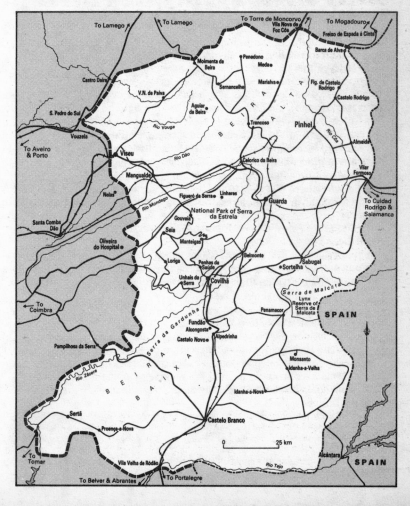

where Viriatus the Iberian rebel (a symbol of the spirit of independence in neo-classical literature) made his last stand against the Romans. You'll see many signs of this patriotism in the fine old town of **Viseu**, in **Beira Alta**, where every other place of refreshment is the *Café Viriate* or the *Restaurante Lusitânia*. Here too, in the heights of the **Parque Natural de Serra da Estrela**, lies the source of the **Rio Mondego**, that most Portuguese of rivers: the only one (bar the insignificant Rio Zêzere) to run right to the sea without having its origins in Spain.

All around here is excellent walking country, especially if you strike off from one of the two main routes which cross the range. As far as towns go, **Guarda** is a must. Though diminutive in size for somewhere of such renown, it has one of the highest locations of any provincial capital in the country and it bristles with life, especially on *feira* days. To the north and east stretch a whole series of high-sited castle-towns and some of the country's most remote villages.

Over to the south lies the more sombre plain of the **Beira Baixa** with its capital at **Castelo Branco**, and, its most obvious highlight, the ancient hilltop town of **Monsanto**.

Viseu

From its high plateau, **VISEU** surveys the country around with the air of a feudal overlord; and indeed, this dignified little city is capital of all it can see and a place of great antiquity to boot. There was a Roman town here and you can still see, on the outskirts, the remains of an encampment locally claimed to be the site where Viriatus fought his final battle. In fact it was almost certainly a Roman fortification; aside from a statue of Viriatus there's not much there.

The Old City
The heart of the medieval city has changed little, though it's approached now through the broad avenues of a prosperous provincial centre. Parts of the walls survive and it's within their circuit, breached by two doughty gateways, that almost everything of interest lies.

One of the most enjoyable pastimes in Viseu is to wander the old streets around the cathedral square. On the main approach, from the Rossio up through the Porta de Soar or along the shop-lined Rua Dr Luís Ferreira (still shown on some maps as Rua do Comércio), a certain amount of restoration and 'beautification' has been undertaken, but the jumble of alleys behind the cathedral remain virtually untouched. You suddenly come across sixteenth-century stone mansions proudly displaying their coat of arms in the middle of a street of crumbling shacks.

At the very centre, on the city's highest point, is the huge **Praça da Sé**, the paved square in front of the cathedral. It's lined with noble stone buildings, but the white Baroque facade of the **Igreja da Misericórdia** is much the most immediately striking. Silhouetted against a deep blue sky it looks like a film set without substance – you expect to walk round the back and find

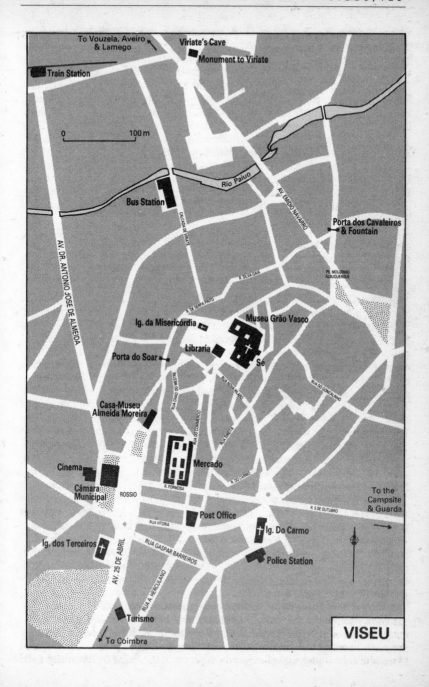

To Vouzela, Aveiro
& Lamego

Viriate's Cave

Monument to Viriate

Train Station

0   100 m

Rio Paiuo

AV. EMIDIO NAVARRO

Bus Station

Porta dos Cavaleiros
& Fountain

AV. DR. ANTONIO JOSE DE ALMEIDA

CALÇADA DE VIRIATE

PÇ. MOUZINHO
ALBUQUERQUE

R. SILVA GAIA

R. DE SERPA PINTO

Ig. da Misericórdia

Museu Grão Vasco

Libraria

Porta do Soar

Sé

RUA NOVA MISO

RUA DO GONÇALINHO

RUA CHÃO DO MESTRE

Casa-Museu
Almeida Moreira

RUA DO CHIÃO

RUA DO CHÃO

RUA DIRE

Mercado

R. FORMOSA

R. DO CARMO

Cinema

Câmara
Municipal

ROSSIO

To the
Campsite
& Guarda

R. 5 DE OUTUBRO

Post Office

RUA VITORIA

Ig. Do Carmo

Ig. dos Terceiros

AV. 25 DE ABRIL

RUA GASPAR BARREIROS

Police Station

RUA A. HERCULANO

Turismo

To Coimbra

VISEU

wooden props holding it up. There's something to that feeling: inside it's a very ordinary, rather dull church. Best to preserve the illusion of perfectly symmetrical beauty by not venturing beyond the door.

There's nothing two-dimensional about the **Cathedral**, a weighty twin-towered Romanesque base on which a succession of later generations made their mark. The granite frontage, remodelled in the seventeenth century, is stern and makes the church look smaller than it actually is – inside it opens out into a great hall with intricate vaulting, twisted and knotted to represent ropes.

The cathedral's Renaissance **cloister**, of which you get no intimation from outside, is one of the most graceful in the country. The rooms of its upper level, looking out over the tangled roofs of the oldest part of the town, house the treasures of the Cathedral's art collection (50esc admission) including naive sculptures, two thirteenth-century Limoges enamel coffers and a twelfth-century Bible.

Museu Grão Vasco

The greatest treasure of Viseu, though, is the **Museu Grão Vasco** (Tues.–Sun. 10am–5pm, free at weekends), right next door to the Cathedral in the *Paço dos Três Escalões* – once the Bishop's palace. Vasco Fernandes (known always as *Grão Vasco*, The Great Vasco) was the key figure in a school of painting which flourished at Viseu in the first half of the sixteenth century. The style of these 'Portuguese primitives' is influenced heavily by Flemish masters and in particular Van Eyck, but certain aspects – the realism of portraiture and richness of colour – are distinctively their own. Vasco and his chief rival Gaspar Vaz have a fair claim to being two of the greatest artists Portugal has produced.

The museum is spread over three floors with the works of the Viseu School on the uppermost. The centrepiece of the collection is the masterly *St Peter on his Throne*, one of Grão Vasco's last works and painted, it is said, to rival Gaspar Vaz's treatment of the same theme for the Convent of São João de Tarouca (see "Lamego"). It shows considerably more Renaissance influence than some of the earlier paintings but its Flemish roots are still evident, particularly in the intricately – and sometimes bizarrely – detailed background. Other works attributed to Vasco include a Calvary and a Pentecost, but there's considerable argument over what is actually his. Several pictures are clearly the fruit of collaboration – most obviously the fourteen panels of the former cathedral altarpiece. These, now exhibited in a room of their own, depict the life of Christ and some sections are clearly better executed than others – notice *The Adoration of the Magi* in which Balthazar, traditionally an African king, is depicted as an Indian from newly discovered Brazil.

Some practical details

The **train station** is at the bottom of the long Av. António José de Almeida, straight down from the Pr. da República; you pass the **bus terminus** on the way. Buses leave hourly for MANGUALDE on the Beira Alta Line. There are regular buses on to Lamego via Castro Daire (see Trás-os-Montes) and both bus and train connections to Guarda, high up in the Serra de Estrela and the

capital of the Beira Alta. The **Turismo**, up from the Rossio, is a good source
of information both for Viseu and for the Beira Alta region as a whole.

All the cheaper restaurants and **places to stay** are in the old quarter, but
accommodation in Viseu seems uniformly poor. The *Pensão Europa* (Rua
Direita 51), *Casa de Hospedes Central* (R. do Comercio 65) and *Pensão Bocage*
(Travessa de São Domingos 5) are right in the centre, and at least tolerable,
though you might be better off asking around for rooms to be had in private
houses. A number of cafés on the Rua Direita (try no. 205) have rooms and
there are **dormidas** at 107 Rua Chão do Mestre, so ask around. Three
pricier places with the odd cheaper room are the *Viriato* (Praça Mouzinho
de Albuquerque 24), the *Lusitânio* (Avenida Emídio Navarro) and the
Viseense (Avenida Alberto Sampaio), all of which, as you will note, profess to
be particularly patriotic. Rather more expensive pensions are clustered
around the Pr. da República.

There's a **campsite** in the Parque do Fontelo, about ten minutes' walk
from the centre, and a municipal **swimming pool** in the same direction, on
Av. José Relvas.

Some of the best **food** in the province is to be had (at not too inflated
prices) at *Contico* (47 Rua S. Hilário), popular enough for tables to be hard to
get. Better value if you're on a tight budget is *Restaurante Solar de Gonçalo*
(Rua do Gonçalo) with its huge helpings. Wherever you eat, or drink, bear in
mind that locally produced **Dão wines**, especially the reds, are some of the
best you'll find anywhere in the country.

Viseu's **Feira de São Mateus** – throughout September – is largely an
agricultural show, but enlivened by occasional bullfights and folk-dance
festivals.

Into the Serra da Estrela: Celorico

All along the train route from Santa Comba Dão to Guarda, the barren and
unwelcoming territory of the **Serra da Estrela** spreads itself as far as the
eye can see: a landscape of great jagged boulders and rough, dry grass –
often singed in patches by summer fires. The wilderness of the area, as so
often in the mountains, belies its inhabitants. The people of the serra, if a
little abrupt, have none of the suspicion of outsiders which you often encounter in Portuguese cities and coastal regions.

Celorico da Beira, the first main stop on the line, lies at a nexus of routes,
with bus connections to **Linhares**, perhaps the most attractive of the villages.
Guarda, beyond, has a more extensive network of trains and buses to the
outlying villages, as well as connections east into Spain.

Celorico da Beira

Most approaches to Guarda, whether by rail or road, will be via **CELORICO
DA BEIRA**. An unprepossessing town – its one claim to fame is as the birthplace of the aviator Sacadura Cabra – it is not the most attractive serra base,

split as it is by heavy traffic along the east–west road from Spain and the north–south route to Lisbon. It does, however, have a fine castle and, if you're passing through at the right time, it's the best place to pick up a pungent *queijo da serra*, the famed round cheese of the Serra da Estrela district.

The Castle and Town

Around the town, and best viewed from the **Castle**, stretches the extraordinary wasteland of the mountains, split only by a small river and a couple of Portuguese highways. You can obtain a key from the *Câmara Municipal* to open the more southern of the castle's two gates. If you trust the rickety construction strung up outside the large keep you can climb to impressive views from the roof – on a clear day the Sé and single tower of the castle at Guarda are both visible. The circuit of the walls might be lofty enough for those of less dare-devil inclinations.

The encampment within the walls has a long **military history** since, together with Trancoso and Guarda, it formed for several centuries part of the triangle of defensive fortifications against Spain. In its day, a garrison of three hundred, well-equipped with arms and an ample supply of food, were able to hold out with relative ease against border skirmishes: on all but one occasion in 1198, when the stout men of nearby Linhares (see below) were called in to help. Today, the town council is forced to keep the place locked as kids try to relive their town's gory history on the way home from school; a young but rather antagonistic mob made the castle their meeting-place but their plans to move in for good were thwarted.

Feiras (alternate Fridays for the cheese; Tuesdays for the ordinary covered market) are the times to be in town to catch its feel of cheery provinciality. You'll see some of the more rugged mountain types coming in to sell their *quiejo da serra*; market-going is their only form of income, enabling them to reinvest in their impoverished hilltop farms. The farmers of the Serra da Estrela must have the harshest agricultural lifestyle in Europe.

Practicalities

Celorico's **train station** is 4km along the road towards the north; on weekdays two daily **buses** pass along this road (towards Celorico or Lamego) but you'll probably need to hitch or share a taxi up to town.

The **bus-stops** in Celorico are along the main road, one in front of the *Residencial Parque*, the other in front of the *Café Central* where you can also find out about some of the timetables. Daily, three buses travel in the Guarda and Gouveia directions, others are mostly school buses (ask in the *Café Central* if in doubt).

The cheapest **pensions** in town are on the road out towards Viseu – try the *Nova Estrela* or the *Boa Hora* – but you can sometimes find an averagely priced room at the *Residencial Parque* (☎071/72880) in the centre. There is a possible rough **campsite** by the river, near the station, and a short-cut up to town across the fields, though it would be a hot walk in the middle of the day. The nearest official site is at LAJEOSA DO MONDEGO, off the road to Guarda (7km; no bus connection).

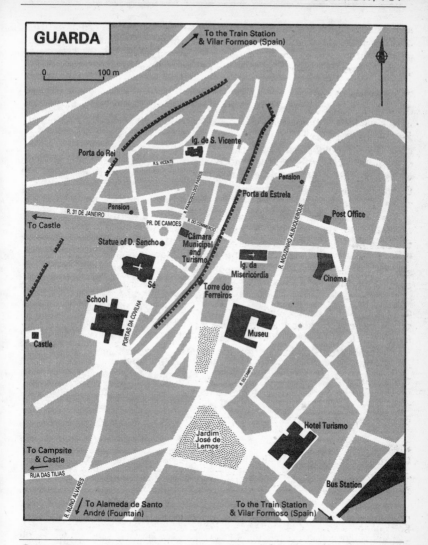

GUARDA

0   100 m

To the Train Station & Vilar Formoso (Spain)

Porta do Rei

Ig. de S. Vicente

R.S. VICENTE

Pension

Porta da Estrela

R. 31 DE JANEIRO

Pension

To Castle

PR. DE CAMOES

R. DO COMMERCIO

R. FRANCISCO DOS PASSOS

Post Office

Câmara Municipal and Turismo

Statue of D. Sancho

R. MOUZINHO ALBUQUERQUE

Ig. da Misericórdia

Cinema

Sé

School

Torre dos Ferreiros

PORTAS DA COVILHA

Museu

Castle

R. 32 CAMO

Jardim José de Lemos

Hotel Turismo

To Campsite & Castle

RUA DAS TILIAS

Bus Station

R. NUNO ALVARES

To Alameda de Santo André (Fountain)

To the Train Station & Vilar Formoso (Spain)

Guarda

GUARDA, at over 1000m, is claimed by its inhabitants to be the highest city in Europe – an assertion to be taken with a pinch of salt. It is high enough, though, to be chilly and windswept all year round and to offer endless views, especially to the east into Spain. The city was founded in 1197 by Dom Sancho I, to guard (as the name implies) his borders against both Moors and Spaniards. It was a heftily fortified place and, despite the fact that castle and walls have all but disappeared, it still has something of the grim air of a city permanently on war footing. It was known, according to an ancient *Murray's Guide to Portugal*, as the city of the four Fs – *Fria, Farta, Forte e Feia* – cold, rich, strong and ugly.

The Town

The last, at least, of these proverbial anecdotes is unfair. With its arcaded streets and little praças, the centre of Guarda can be distinctly picturesque. At the heart of it all is the dour grey **Cathedral**. It's one of those buildings that took so long to complete (1390–1540) that several architectural styles came and went during its construction, all of them incorporated somewhere into the work. The castellated main facade, with its two heavy octagonal towers, looks like the gateway of some particularly forbidding castle, but around the sides the design is lightened by flying buttresses, fantastic pinnacles, and grimacing gargoyles – the ones facing Spain are particularly mean-looking. Inside it's surprisingly long and lofty, with twisted pillars and vaulting influenced by the Manueline style of the later stages of its development. The huge carved stone *retablo* is the work of João de Rouão, a leading figure in the sixteenth-century resurgence of Portuguese sculpture at Coimbra.

It's amazing, for a place of its size and importance, that, cathedral aside, there's so little to see in Guarda. The displays of local archaeology, art and sculpture in the **Museu Regional** are, frankly, dull; of the **Castle**, on a bleak little hill nearby, only the plain square keep survives, while the **walls** are recalled by just three surviving gates – the most impressive of them the **Torre dos Ferreiros** (Blacksmiths' Tower). The cobbled streets of the old town, though, are fascinating in themselves – the tangled area between the other two portals (the **Porta da Estrela** and **Porta do Rei**) can have changed little in the past 400 years.

Practicalities

Guarda's main **railway** station is miles out of town but there's a bus at the stop opposite to meet all the major trains. The main **bus station** (such as it is) is fairly central. Services are operated by a variety of companies such as *Viúva Monteiro* who run to places like Sabugal and the Spanish border. For information on *RN* services, contact their office behind the museum at Rua do Campo 17.

Places to stay are fairly easy to come by if not especially cheap. Try the attractive *Pensão Moreira* (Rua Mouzinho de Albuquerque 47, ☎071/24131), or the somewhat down-at-heel *Residencial Gonçalves* (Rua Augusto Gil 17, off the central square). Guarda's open-all-year **campsite** is in a park a short way from the castle; remember, though, that the nights can get extremely cold. The town's heated **swimming pool** is in the same park.

An alternative base could be the pension or cafés with rooms **around the railway station**, from where you can catch a bus up into town during the day – it's quite a speedy journey to the centre.

By the bus station is an excellent food **market** – busiest on Saturdays. *Queijo da Serra*, the local mountain cheese made traditionally from ewe's milk (see "Celorico", above), is delicious and much cheaper here than in the tourist shops and roadside stalls which also hawk it. If you don't want to get your own food, try one of the **restaurants** between the Porta da Estrela and the church of São Vicente for basic but good fare.

There is a **Turismo** behind the Cathedral on Praça Luís de Camões, which should be a good source of information for the many festivals in the area. The biggest events are the great **Feiras** (June 24 and October 4), extended versions of the food market mentioned above, which are full of life and character. The **Festas de Cidade** (usually end of July) are a more cultural affair with exhibitions and folk-dancing, though a little too highly organised for their own good.

Serra Villages

The peaks of the **Serra da Estrela**, the highest mountains in Portugal and the last of the four central Iberian serras (the others are Guadarrama, Gredos and Gata), spread out to the south of Guarda. Road and railway hug the eastern slope through **Covilhã** and **Belmonte** into the Beira Baixa, while the main road from Spain cuts north towards Viseu, and then branches off south to Coimbra, past the industrial towns of **Gouveia** and **Seia**.

Don't whatever you do miss **Linhares**, a cranky little village with a castle and a stretch of Roman road which makes idyllic walking. If you're into more serious hiking the best base is probably **Penhas de Saúde,** where there's a large year-round hostel and from where you can strike off into the valleys which stretch north to Manteigas or south to **Unhais da Serra**. Public transport into the area is erratic at the best of times, though a little easier in the winter when Penhas de Saúde has Portugal's only skiing facilities.

Linhares

LINHARES is perched on a sunny slope overlooking the valley of the Rio Mondego. It's one of the most accessible of the villages in this mountain region and its great attractions, apart from the castle, are the **troglodyte-like dwellings** which nestle under large boulders in the centre of the village, and the nearby **Roman road**.

To reach the village take a through **bus** either from Celorico de Beira to Gouveia, or vice versa, and stop at CARRAPICHANA. Walking is a pleasant way to approach or you could look out for school buses (from Celorico at 5pm; Gouveia at 6.15am) which go directly to the centre of the village (2km).

If you want to **stay**, ask in the village's only café, the *Linharense*, in the central square not far from the church. They will know who has a spare room or where best to pitch your tent (most probably above the village near a rustic football pitch).

The Castle and Village
Barely distinguishable at first, the lofty Afonsino keep of the **Castle** (keys from the hairdresser who lives above the church) soon rises into reality, with

the serra as a back drop, in command of all that lies before it. It dates from 1169 when Linhares, then more of a town, was claimed for Portugal. Afonso Henriques realised its potential as a defensive post, and soon the men of Linhares were trained up and equipped to carry out such feats of bravery as the rescue of Celorico da Beira from the Spaniards in 1198. In the walls are traces of the *cisternas* which would have given the village a constant supply of water at times of siege. You can still see the course of the spring which now runs along the gully beneath the great slabs of rock on which the castle was constructed.

If you arrive in Linhares in the early morning the place appears deserted, its only sounds of life the animals grunting and kicking their stable doors to be let out. Later in the day you'll see the donkeys being brought in from the fields and, depending on the time of year, seeds laid out to dry in the sun, wine casks being washed for the next year's vintage and, whatever the season, village gossips on their doorsteps, keen as ever to meet a stranger.

A little known secret of the village's **church** is that it contains three paintings almost certainly executed by **Grão Vasco** and belonging to a larger series which is now lost. Propped up behind vulgar wooden statues and, in one case, stuck in one of the side aisles, the panels, depicting the 'Adoration of the Magi', 'Descent from the Cross' and the 'Annunciation', shine out in the obscurity. They reveal all the qualities of the great painter – his skill as a portraitist and his deft handling of tone and colour, particularly in the depiction of clothing and folds of material.

The Roman Road

Near the schoolhouse in Linhares a path branches off the road toward Figueiró da Serra. Following along it, you'll soon realise that you are walking along an old **Roman road** – part of the one which ran to Braga – with heavy slabs of rock for paving stones looking like something out of an Asterix cartoon. The walk is a beauty, the hedgerows lined with flowers in the spring and blackberries in the autumn.

Gouveia and Seia

These two towns crop up regularly on bus routes, particularly on the Coimbra–Guarda lines, though they are nothing to go out of your way for. Now large industrial towns, both have lost that feeling of Serra da Estrela provinciality – unless you coincide with Gouveia's Thursday **market** – which was once their charm.

Gouveia

On the positive side, if you are passing through anyway, **GOUVEIA** has an interesting modern art museum, a helpful Turismo to hand out maps and an elegantly-sited park headquarters in the seventeenth-century *Casa da Torre* (Rua Direita), which also provides maps and leaflets about the area.

Walking up from the **bus-stop** by the bridge, veer right and you'll soon come across the **Turismo**, established along with the municipal **library** in the basement of a *casa brasonada*. Portugal's sense of heraldry comes out in manor houses of every shape and size, where sets of arms are tacked up over doorways, on cornices, beneath the corners of the roof and any other empty space. Gouveia boasts a number of these houses, of which maybe the finest example is the **Câmara Municipal**; this hosts open-air concerts in its courtyard during the summer months, but you are generally free to walk in.

Above the Turismo (entrance in Rua Direita) you'll find the **Museu de Abel Manta**, a modern art museum with a broad selection of contemporary Portuguese pictures all donated by Gouveian-born artist **Abel Manta** (1888–1982). There's a small room dedicated to the man himself, a figure of some stature who frequented groups which included Amadeo de Sousa Cardoso (see Amarante) and Almeida Negreiros (see "Museu da Cidade" in *Lisbon*) – some of whose works are also here – and represented Portugal in the Biennale in Venice. The selection of Manta's actual works is poor, with only one picture of any great merit, but the collection as a whole is enjoyable.

At the entrance to the town there's a **statue** of a shepherd with his dog, not perhaps the most finely executed sculpture, but proudly illuminated at night and significant for what it represents. The people in the hills round here live a harsh and impoverished existence and have, as the Portuguese put it, 'an unlimited capacity for suffering'. There is never a break in the agricultural year, for when the summer is over and the harvest is stored away it is time to begin the cheesemaking, an activity which brings in their only serious income. One friend to the shepherd in his harsh lifestyle is his dog – the *Cão da Serra da Estrela* is a fearsome looking species said to be cross-bred from wolves.

Staying in Gouveia, ask for **rooms** from Maria Rodrigues in the *Café Cruzeiro* (Avenida 25 de Abril), on the way up to the Câmara Municipal, or try above the (excellent) restaurant, *A Regional* at Avenida da República 45. Opposite the latter is *Pensão Estrela* (at no. 36), a dusty old hotel with modern prices, but a restaurant with something of a reputation. The road to the **municipal campsite** at CURRAL DO NEGRO is after the Câmara Municipal (turn immediately right and right again then fork left 2km).

Seia

Cut out **SEIA** from your itinerary and you would miss very little, but it can be, like Gouveia, a useful jumping-off point with bus connections to the Serra de Lousã (see Beira Litoral) and for the Estrela National Park. Roads from Seia branch off to MANTEIGAS at the centre of the range, and to PENHAS DE SAÚDE (where there's a large youth hostel) on the way to COVILHÃ (see below), making the town an inevitable stop on a circuit of the province.

Staying in Seia, you'll find rooms above the restaurant *Miranda*, next to the town hall. **Campers** should consider moving on to wilder scenery as the nearest official sites are at Penhas de Saúde (towards Covilhã) and Valhelhas (towards Belmonte), both a steep 40 kilometres into the range. If you are headed deeper into the Estrela, the park office (Casa da Janela Bonita, Praça da República 28) can advise on transport into the area; a number of small private companies operate services other than those offered by *RN*.

Covilhã and Belmonte

COVILHÃ, immediately below the highest peaks of the Serra, is a more obvious place to base yourself. The train station is 5km from the town, but buses shuttle new arrivals from there into the centre. **Turismo**, in the main Praça do Município, can advise you where to stay (there's no shortage of places; try the *Pensão Avenida*) and will arrange routes and guides for serious hikers. For food, the *Hôtel-Restaurante Sol Neve* is excellent value.

The chief beauty spots of the range are above here, and the highest peak in Portugal – **Torre** (1993m) – can be climbed quite easily from halfway along the Seia road. A little further on is the narrow rock cone known as the **Cântaro Magro** (Slender Pitcher), which conceals the source of the Rio Zêzere, and further still the waters of the **Lagoa Comprida**, a huge artificial lake. Also up near Torre is **Nossa Senhora da Boa Estrela**, a vast statue of the Virgin carved into a niche in the rock, to which there's a massive procession from Covilhã on the second Sunday in August.

Two buses a day run in both directions between Covilhã and Seia but they follow the lower, longer road via UNHAIS DA SERRA. Walkers should consider taking the route up the glacial valley from here to Penhas de Saúde, an energetic hike, but well worth the effort.

Belmonte

BELMONTE was the birthplace of Pedro Álvares Cabral, the discoverer of Brazil, and is a village of considerable charm, commanded by a heavily restored thirteenth-century castle. It has a few pensions and is in direct line for the barren and medieval region of the Beira Baixa (see later in this chapter), particularly the two main towns of Fundão and Castelo Branco – to which *RN* runs a regular service. For public transport to SABUGAL and the Transylvanian-like fortress-village of SORTELHA, you'd do better to return to Guarda. Despite Belmonte's proximity to both of these, the region between them is deserted and wild with roughly surfaced roads and few cars.

North of Guarda: The *Planalto*

North and east of Guarda, and beyond the mountains of Estrela, stretches a rough and barren-looking territory known as the *planalto* (tableland) of the Beira Alta. Here there were once prosperous Jewish settlements such as **Trancoso** and **Sernancelhe**, whose trade decreased from the Age of Discoveries onwards as business moved to the coast. Villages are still quite large but spread far apart, and much of the land between remains untamed by agriculture, strewn as it is with boulders and great slabs of granite. The valleys and settlements though are green and fertile – the speciality in this area is roast or dried **chestnuts**. Once a replacement for potatoes, and now a dessert, they come from vast, shady trees growing beside the roads on almost any approach to a village.

The *planalto* towns are closely associated with Portuguese independence from Spain, and in particular with Afonso Henriques' march south down the length of the country. **Penedono**, **Trancoso** and **Pinhel** are just three of the towns which he fortified.

Their **castles** are today the highlight of the region. Penedono's *castelo roqueiro* is especially magnificent, with seventeenth-century reconstructions on top of the original article. Spectacular, too, is the star-shaped fortress at **Almeida**, the site of the penultimate battle in the Peninsular Wars against Napoleon.

If you're travelling in the **winter**, take to heart the proverb that *O frio almoça em Penedono, merenda em Trancoso e ceia em Guarda* – 'The cold lunches in Penedono, takes tea in Trancoso and dines in Guarda' – and come suitably prepared. The frost (*sincelo*) can have an extraordinary effect on the countryside, creating a Narnia-like landscape as massive trees are linked by boughs of crystal and metre-long icicles hang from every house.

Trancoso

TRANCOSO takes its place in Portuguese history through the legend of the **Bandarra**, a shoemaker who lived in the town in the fifteenth century. The shoemaker gained fame for his prophecies, which began with local horoscopes and poems, but after a while moved to more national matters – foretelling, among other things, the end of the Portuguese kingdom. In an age of religious dilemma and disillusionment with monarchical rule, they struck a chord in the region, but also attracted the attentions of the authorities. Their circulation was banned and the Bandara himself condemned to death, a sentence commuted, due to popular outcry, to a punishment of walking barefoot around town carrying a massive candle until it burnt to the wick. There the matter would perhaps have rested, but twenty years after the shoemaker's death, King Sebastião did indeed die on the battlefield, at Alcaçer-Quibir in Morocco, leaving no heir to the throne. Portugal was plunged into civil war and the Bandarra pronounced the **Nostradamus** of his time.

The Town

Trancoso today is a provincial sort of place, standing within a circuit of townwalls, and with an appearance that can have changed little since the days of the prophetic cobbler. Wandering the dark alleys of the old quarter, it's easy to envisage his hold on the villagers' imaginations.

The presence of a large **Jewish Community** during the Middle Ages is apparent from the **architectural details** on the facades of the ancient homes. They have two doorways: one broad for trade, the other narrow for the family; the stonework is carefully crafted and bevelled. Above some doors, clumsy crosses were later inscribed by the Inquisition to indicate that the family had converted to Christianity. Near the modern-day restaurant *São Marcos*, the former **Rabbi's house** (locally referred to as the house of the *Gato Negro*) is decorated with three emblems; the Lion of Judae, the gates of Jerusalem and the figure of *Preguiça,* or Sloth.

Within the circle of **town walls**, where four out of five of the original gateways still stand, a **Castle** with its squat, almost triangular, tower completes the distinctive silhouette visible from many miles away. It's a

Moorish design and a reminder of the Saracen domination of the town in the tenth century.

Judging by a few significant victories – Almansor in 985, Fernando Magno in 1033 and Afonso Henriques in 1139 – Trancoso's early history was troubled. Shortly after the last conquest, the town was sacked by the Moors again. Dom Afonso was recalled from the Minho, and Egas Moniz saved the day by arriving quickly with fresh supplies of men; the monastery at São João de Tarouca (see "Lamego") was built in celebration of the event. Trancoso's later military history includes the usual invasions and billeting during fourteenth-century Castillian trouble-making and nineteenth-century Peninsular Warring – look out for a charming corner house with an open stone stairway on the central square, with the tellingly British name, *Quartel de Generale Beresforde*.

Another of Trancoso's contributions to Portugal's illustrious history is the fact that Dom Dinis married Isabel of Aragon (see "Coimbra" for their history) in the small **chapel of São Bartolomeu**, on the side of the dusty Avenida which is the main entrance to town. The football pitch behind must have been the site of the wedding celebrations afterwards.

Outside the walls, in front of the law courts, **Celtic tombs** attest to very early origins indeed. Here and there a coffin-cover lies askew; the rest of the mound is a carved mass of human-shaped pits of varying sizes – one obviously for a child.

Practicalities

Staying in Trancoso you have only a few options; either to **camp** on the patch not constituting the football pitch over by the fountain, or to select one of two **pensions**. *Residencial Rico* (Rua Dr. Fernandes Vaz, ☎071/91411) is central, old-fashioned and down-at-heel, whilst *Residencial Dom Dinis* (outside the walls next to the *Correio*) is modern, clean and quite reasonably priced. Or you could ask for **rooms** in the *Café Bandarra*, near the main gateway, from Senhor Simões Rodrigues, who lives above it.

Buses leave regularly for the north: at 3.15pm via Pinhel and Almeida to Figueira de Castelo Rodrigo (from where the 1.40pm bus departs Mon–Thurs/2.45pm Fri for Moncorvo and Mogadouro); at 10am and 1pm to Pinhel only; and at 1.45pm to Penedono. Lamego-bound buses for Sernancelhe pass by several times a day – you may have to go out to the main road to catch them. For Guarda and major towns en route to Lisbon there's a 5.15pm weekday service. The ever-helpful **Turismo**, opposite the Bartolemeu chapel, can fill you in on other details – or odd facts about Trancoso.

Feiras are on Fridays, with an extra large one, Feira de São Bartolomeu, on August 20–22, following the **Festa de N.S. da Fresta** on August 15.

Sernancelhe

Midway between Guarda and Lamego, **SERNANCELHE** is not exactly the hub of Beira Alta. But it has a fine and ancient parish church, is said to have the region's best chestnuts, and makes a pleasant stop-over. You can **camp** not far from town down by the river, or stay in one of a couple of friendly **pensions**, the *Flora* or the *Trásmontana*.

The **chestnut trees**, broad-boughed and spreading across the road, are the most striking feature of the landscape as you approach the village. Carnivals, love songs, recipes and folk tales are all wound around the fruit, and if you coincide with the **Festa of N.S. de Au Pé da Cruz** on May 1 you'll witness a curious mixture of religious devotion, general springtime merrymaking and, above all, folkloric superstition. There's a dance of the chestnuts, a blessing on the trees, and the exchange of handfuls of blossom by local lovers, aside from the religious procession. Should you want to know more, the local cultural expert Padre Cândido Azevedo, in his majestic, castle-like home overlooking the town is more than pleased to greet a stranger.

On the way up to the padre's house, you pass the **Igreja Matriz**, an attractive Romanesque church with a curious facade. Fixed into twin niches either side of the main doorway, six weathered apostles lay claim to being the only ones of their kind in the whole of Portugal. Of course, Romanesque carvings of this calibre do exist elsewhere (on many a portal in the Minho for example) but you usually find them entwined around architectural features such as capitals or columns – not free-standing as these are. Inside the church are several sixteenth-century panels, including a magnificent *John the Baptist*.

Wandering about this old quarter of town you'll see the same features of an **ancient Jewish settlement** as in Trancoso – canted lintels, pairs of granite doorways of unequal size, the occasional cross for the converted. More noticeable are a number of large **town houses**, one marked with the Maltese cross, another supposed to be the birthplace of the Marquês de Pombal. A further house was the birthplace of Padre João Rodrigues, an eminent and influential missionary who founded a series of mission houses in Japan in the sixteenth century. Japanese tourists often make the pilgrimage here to see the building. The quarter today, however, is not a popular place to live and a new Câmara Municipal has sapped some of the life out of the more antique administrative establishments up here. Only on alternate Thursdays does the place comes to life, when farmers bring in their wares to a lively **feira**.

Buses on to Lamego (see Trás-os Montes) leave from the main *Rota Nacional 226* which is 4 kilometres away – there are four a day in the week, fewer at the weekend. There are weekday connections only to Penedono (1pm and 7pm) and Trancoso (9am).

Penedono

PENEDONO is another one-horse town, but again a likeable place, and with a fantastic **castle** – visible from miles around.

The Portuguese call the fortress a **castelo roqueiro**, since it soars out of a solid granite base as if the rock and the walls were one and the same. From the top, as you might imagine, there are grand views, with the village's old quarter laid out below. The castle is home to a flock of pigeons, so make plenty of noise unlocking the door (key from the shop at the bottom) or you'll have them flapping into your face the moment you enter. Nearby, a look-out post has been transformed into a clocktower which chimes the hours persistently through the night.

The castle, in times of war, and the **Solar dos Freixos** (now the Town Hall), in times of peace, were supposed to have been home to the legendary king **Magriço**, Álvaro Gonçalves Coutinho ('the Lean One'), sung of in Camões' *Os Lusiadas*. It's a claim to fame fought over fiercely with the inhabitants of Trancoso, who likewise are prepared to swear he is their man. Penedono, though, has the better claim: its name, from *pena* and *dono*, literally 'King of the Rock', merits the attribution. According to Camões the *Magriço* led eleven other men to England to champion the cause of twelve noble English ladies, who found themselves without knights, and fought a joust on their behalf. Such tales of chivalry made them the subjects of numerous allegorical murals and panels of *azulejos* around the country.

Practicalities

The village has just one **pension**, the *Solneve* (☎054/54239), with friendly patrons, though you could also find rooms above the *Café Gomes* or the *Café Avenida* on the main road; the latter has excellent food.

Buses leave at 2pm and 7.30pm on weekdays for Vila Nova de Foz Cóa, and at 8.30am for Trançoso (connection to Coimbra). **Feiras** happen on alternate Wednesdays and there's a **Romaria** on September 15–16.

Pinhel

PINHEL is big enough to run both a wine cooperative (producing an excellent red) and a cake factory (churning out less delectable sweetmeats, or *cavacas*). But, digestibles apart, it's also small enough to have left the old centre of town virtually untouched. You can walk right round the crumbling castle walls, across the top of five intact archways, through vegetable plots and back gardens, and remain almost unaware of the twentieth century. From one corner of the **walls** you look down on the shell of a ruined **Romanesque church** whose facade alone merits closer inspection. On another stretch you will discover what is left of the original fortress, a soaring tower with an intricately carved **Manueline window** high up one side.

Down in town further treats are in store, with numerous **manor houses** clustered about the magnificent gardens. One of the largest is now the **Câmara Municipal**, its hallway bedecked with a series of excellent photographs of local buildings of interest. An adjacent building, possibly the Câmara mansion's old stables, houses the town **museum** (free entrance). Two major contributions form the backbone to the collection. On the ground floor a pile of **Celtic tombstones**, some of real interest, others of less ancient origin await cataloguing. Upstairs are the remnants of the local convent, with an altarpiece alleged to be of the school of João de Ruão.

Practicalities

Staying at Pinhel, you can **find rooms** at the *Residencial Pinhalense* (☎071/42373), set back off the main street not far from the museum, or **camp** – no one seems to mind tents being pitched around the castle walls. Either way, **eat** at the *Residencial* where the food is fabulous.

Buses leave from the centre of the municipal gardens – ask in the museum or shop nearby for schedules. One useful connection is the *Barrelhas* coach which you can flag down at about 4.15pm (every day) to go to Almeida or on to Figueira de Castelo Rodrigo.

The town **festa** is on the Sunday closest to June 13 (São António).

Almeida

ALMEIDA is perhaps the most attractive of all the fortified Portuguese borderland towns. A beautifully preserved Vaubanesque stronghold, it was designed by the Dutch Jesuit, Cosmander, in the form of a twelve-pointed star. A 4km walk round the walls takes in all the peaks and troughs. There's a museum and barracks but, putting the military history aside, the town has a relaxed feel about it that induces you to stay much longer than you intended.

Inevitably, perhaps, tourism is catching on to the place. A new government *pousada* was built here a couple of years ago and already the number of cafés in town has risen from three to twenty-three. Locals are intrigued by the phenomenon of rich tourists and foreign ministers turning up in their long-forgotten town, to fork out more than a villager's weekly earnings to ride in a souped-up pony cart, or to pay through the nose (relatively speaking) for a coffee on the balcony overlooking the humble dwellings below.

The Casa das Matas and Fortifications

The arrival of the pousada, sadly, resulted in the hacking out of a fourth gateway in Almeida's **fortifications**. The original three are the town's most splendid features – long shell-proof tunnels with emblazoned entrances and sizeable guard rooms – and for years they have stood as an effective barrier against modernisation within the walls. However the new pousada gateway, smashed through eighteenth-century walls, is coach-size, lorry-size, delivery-van-size – in fact the size and price of door-to-door service to a pousada in a 'quaint village setting'.

The barracks is second in size only to Elvas, with the capacity to hold 5000 men together with supplies. In the **Casa das Matas** (9am–noon and 2–5pm; tips gratefully received) you'll see why the fort withstood such lengthy sieges. With its own water supply, rubbish shoot, breathing holes, hidden escape routes, munitions chamber (there's a range of cannonballs and gunshot still on view) and dormitory space, the possibilities were limitless.

One hazard which no one foresaw, however, was the potential for an explosion within the fortress itself. In 1810, after the Luso-Brittanic forces had held out for seventeen days against Massena, a leaky barrel of gunpowder, carried from the cathedral-castle in the centre of town to the **Praça Alta** (an artillery platform on the northern walls), left a fatal trail of powder. Once ignited this began a fire that killed hundreds, and the survivors gave themselves up to the French. Wellington, on his victorious return from Buçaco, subsequently took the fortress with no bloodshed. The French army scuttled away during the night, probably making use of one of three **portas falsas** – narrow slits in the ramparts allowing for a discreet exit. You can find out more about the campaign from the **museum** (same management as the Casa das Matas) in the old guard's room within the main town gates.

One other curiosity, not far from the pousada, is the inscription on the side of a small house declaring it to be the dumping ground for illegitimate children. At the **Rodo dos Eispostos** (literally the 'Circle of the Deserted') anyone could come and claim an unwanted child for themselves – a convenient arrangement for both mother and foster parent.

Around the Town and the River Cô

Almeida's great charm lies in watching the sun go down and the lights come on in a hundred tiny villages across the plateau of the Ribacôa. This was one of the last stretches of land to be recognised as officially Portuguese, in the Treaty of Alcanicies with the Spanish in 1297. It's easy to see why boundaries were not clearly staked out in this broad, flat territory; definition of the border, even in this day and age, is less than strikingly obvious.

Down by the Rio Cô itself (2km downhill on the Pinhel road, a gentle stroll, but you can hitch back into town quite easily) is an idyllic spot, a little above the old Romanesque bridge (and its present-day equivalent), for **camping** and **swimming**. It's a popular place with emigrants in the summer, but you'll have the place to yourself out of peak season. Swim below the barrier; the water above is for town consumption.

Practicalities

For those without the means to stay in the pousada, **staying in the old town** is a question of getting talking with the villagers. A good first stop is the Casa da Amelinha, which serves as the *RN* booking office and unofficial gathering place. Ask for Amélia, who has a number of rooms and, if full, will probably be able to direct you elsewhere; try her famous *ginginha* (cherry liqueur) while you're there. Otherwise, the official **residencials** are outside the fort by the crossroads. *A Muralha* and *Morgado* are two new ones, or ask in the *Café Tertúlia* for Dona Maria Augusta who lets out rooms. **Eat** here or at the *Restaurante Portas de Almeida* nearer town. A personal favourite from the **cafés** within the fort is the *Terreiro Velho*, near the market stalls; it stays open till 2am most nights and, despite fairly modern tastes in music, seems popular with old as well as young.

If you can possibly do so, try to coincide with one of the twice-monthly **feiras** (on the 8th and the last Saturday) or go at Pentecost (50 days after Easter) for the grand **picnic** at the Convento da Barca, a former Franciscan monastery, with a distinctively Tuscan feel about its domed chapel and setting. It's the only time you can visit, but at other times of the year you can try the excellent red wine, apples, peaches, nuts and various other produce for which the convent is famous, at shops in town.

Buses on to the north come from Vilar Formoso twice on weekdays and go as far as Figueira de Castelo Rodrigo. One sure service to catch is the *Barrelhas* bus which passes through on the main road 200 metres from the gates to Almeida at about 5pm every afternoon. Going south there are local services as far as Vilar Formoso (14km), which has trains to Guarda or Spain, and three daily buses to Sabugal and Castelo Branco.

South of Guarda

Heading south from Guarda there's a choice of routes: west to Belmonte (see earlier entry) and Fundão, or east to Sabugal and Sortelha.

Fundão and the villages of **Alpedrinha** and **Castelo Novo** to its south lie sunk into a ridge, the **Serra de Gardunha**, facing Spain. All have magnificent views and are healthy, rural places, with delicious local fruit and, at Castelo, healing waters.

Sabugal, over towards the Spanish borderland, makes an interesting alternative mainly for its access to **Sortelha**, whose amazing circuit of walls (*sortelha* means 'ring') rise amid one of the bleakest locations in all Portugal.

Sabugal and Sortelha

SABUGAL itself, like most towns in Beira Alta, has a **castle**. It's a good one, too, with massively high walls, a vast hollow centre and a pentagonal tower with three arched chambers piled one on top of the other. Trust the rickety staircase and you could be on top of the world; trust the wobbly stonework (personally, I didn't) and you could walk right round the walls.

The village has a couple of **pensions**, the *Sol-Rio* and *O Século* (both a bit overpriced in summer), or you can **camp** along the meandering river which winds right round the town. In June there's a **festa** on the 24th and a grand **feira** on the 29th; at other times of year it's all pretty quiet.

To **get to Sortelha**, 15km west, public transport is limited to school buses (5.30pm Mon., Tues., Thurs., Fri.; 1pm Wed.); these, obviously, don't run during the holidays. If you decide to try and hitch, start walking and be prepared to possibly continue for the distance.

More regular **buses** run by *Viúva Monteiro* leave from the main square for Guarda, and others run by *RN* go north to Vilar Formoso and south to Castelo Branco via Penamacor.

Sortelha

SORTELHA is isolated and very eerie, especially when mist drifts down from the serra. It is an ancient town, with Hispano-Arabic origins, and was also the first *castelo roqueiro* (see "Penedono") to be built this side of the Côa. Mystery and legend have grown up with the castle and its fortifications, with stories spun round the figure of an old lady, *a velha*, whose profile you can see on rocks from outside the top gates.

The walls are the main sight. Within them, in the old town, take a look at the **Igreja Matriz** (keys from the neighbour), whose ceiling is pure Moorish. Arabic script can be seen, too, on several house lintels near the top of town. It's also worth taking some time to browse around the **antique shop** on the road up to the castle, and the **carpet workshop** on the route back down towards Sabugal. Both offer insights into the way life used to be, but above all they show a healthy attitude to present-day tourism. Even if their continuing existence depends entirely on the foreign visitor, you never get the feeling that the show is laid on just for you. The chance to work with the fine materials and coloured wools seems to be enjoyed by all in the workshop, and the antique dealer seems just as happy to chat about the curious customs and folk tales belonging to this distant region as strike a bargain.

The village's major event is a **bullfight**, which takes place once every two or three years, depending on when the local council has the money to stage it. This is a very peculiar version of the *Capeia Arraiana*, retaining the ancient custom of the *forca* – a rudimentary defence against the bull using branches – which has been handed down from father to son. The order of events for the day has never changed, beginning with a *forca* involving all the young boys of the village – at least 25 of whom are needed to carry the device to prevent it from being tipped up by the bull. Later on solo performers with their red capes strut the stage alone with the beast. Onlookers are also involved, not only vocally, but physically – many a young bull has hopped up on to the terrace of rocks, only to find himself sniffing at discarded hats and bags while nervous laughter rises up from behind the safety of the nearest wall.

In non-bull-fight years there's still a **festa** on August 15, and a **romaria**, shortly after Easter on the day of São António, when everyone treks 4km up to the nearest hill.

Rooms and practicalities

If you are lucky, book in advance (ask at any major tourist office), or arrive out of season, you can find **Turihab accommodation** in Sortelha. This is a similar scheme to the manor houses promoted elsewhere in the country, though more relaxed and far less expensive, involving the letting of traditional stone houses in the village. On arrival, ask for Maria da Conceição Marquês, one of three women in charge; she will send you on to one of the other local ladies if her own charming stone house is occupied. Each house lies within the old town and has wonderfully thick walls, wooden furniture, hot baths, cobwebs – a wonderful mix of modern comforts and medieval surroundings. If you're out of luck, or can't afford the rates, try asking for **rooms** at the *Restaurante Celta*. The alternative is to **camp**. There are any number of promising areas to pitch camp above and beyond the old town, where the terrain is rocky and sheep take shelter beneath massive boulders.

Buses back to Sabugal leave at 7.30am on a school day, and sometimes at 9am on Tuesdays and Thursdays – check times the day before in the café.

Lynxes: the Serra da Malcata

If you have your own transport another possible excursion from Sabugal would be into the **Serra da Malcata** – believe it or not, a **lynx reserve**. The team at the reserve's headquarters in PENAMACOR (Rua dos Bombeiros Volunteiros) are full of advice about how to approach this area and where best to go at different times of the year. The lynx is notoriously difficult to see, especially without the aid of the park keepers, but the countryside is probably enough compensation if you don't get a sighting. If you're fortunate you might also see the back of a wild boar disappearing into the forests of black oak.

Staying in **PENAMACOR**, there are several small **pensions** to choose from and numerous cafés where you can get a snack. There's also a **castle**; it's nothing out of the ordinary if you've come from Sabugal and Sortelha, but the climb up is rewarded by views over the Serra da Malcata towards Spain and by tremendous sunrises and sunsets.

Otherwise Penamacor is a dull place, split in two by the constant noisy traffic, and you would do better to move on for the night to the extraordinary villages of MONSANTO and IDANHA-A-VELHA which lie off the route to Castelo Branco (see following sections). For **bus times** consult the **Turismo** (next to the main through-road) and with any luck you'll be there on the right day. The buses are rather erratic, and hitching the 20km on such small roads is only advisable in the summer. Before you set off, ask around in bars or at the petrol pump for lorry-drivers and trippers who might be going that way.

Serra da Gardunha: Fundão, Alpedrinha and Castelo Novo

The **Serra da Gardunha** is the last real mountain range of the Beiras. South of here, into Beira Baixa, the landscape flattens out, in a gradual progression towards the broad plains of the Alentejo.

Fundão
FUNDÃO is the largest town in the area and a pleasant place to stock up on supplies. As far as sights are concerned, though, even the local tourist pamphlet admits that Fundão has 'no monuments of note'. The town's rural tranquility, however, more than makes up for its other touristic shortcomings, as does its glorious abundance of fresh fruit and vegetables. The villages around the serra are celebrated for their produce and this is the local market centre.

Moving on to Alpedrinha is a pleasure in itself: a three-hour walk along an old, cobbled Roman road via the hamlet of ALCONGOSTA. Given this option, it seems a shame to use the bus, though the train (Beira Baixa Line) will deposit you on the plain below town – with an approach along another section of Roman road.

Alpedrinha
ALPEDRINHA is set into the side of the serra, overlooking fields of olives and fruit trees. In spring the hillside flowers, fruit-tree blossom and fresh springwater oozing from every crack in the road make it as idyllic a spot as you could hope to find – notwithstanding the rumbling juggernauts crashing through the village on the main road to the south. It is easy to escape the noise though, if you wander up to the older quarters and on into the serra.

A good first stop is at the museum in the former **Pacos de Concelho**. This displays an interesting collection of tradesmen's tools – from cobbler to baker to tinsmith – and traditional clothing, including a striking, black wedding dress – customary in this part of the world. A short way beyond the museum, the **Capela de Leão**, in the courtyard of the Casa de Misericordia, provides Alpedrinha with its current talking-point. Something of a mystery surrounds a series of valuable **sixteenth-century panels** which disappeared from the chapel. The panels were last spotted at a primitivist exhibition in Lisbon, which coincided with renovation work due to be carried out on the chapel.

At the top of the same street, above the plain Igreja Matriz, you'll come across Alpedrinha's highlight: an elaborate fountain known as the **Chafariz de Dom João V**. When the king passed through in 1714 he found the water so good that he commissioned the chafariz as a sign of royal approval. The little village flourished and grand houses such as the now-deserted **Palácio de Picadeiro**, which towers above the fountain, were constructed during the eighteenth century. In front of this spectre of a palace the old Roman road (from the times when Alpedrinha was called Petratinia) begins to wind its cobbled way up the side of the serra towards Fundão.

Other architectural delights abound, all detailed in the 'Friends of Alpedrinha' booklet, (available from the library below the museum). The **furniture workshop**, situated below the main road on the way out of town towards Castelo Branco, is an interesting visit. Ask inside and someone will show you round António Santos Pinto's **sala de arte**, with some of the most consummate singlehanded marquetry a craftsman ever produced. Pinto moulded Louis XV chair-legs to Napoleonic dressers and threw the odd, carved, black page-boy into his structures for good measure. There's even a set of tableaux depicting the first six *cantos* of Camões' Lusiads in the most incredible detail.

Of the **pensions** in Alpedrinha, *Clara* (☎075/57391), run by a sprightly old lady of the same name, is the cheapest and most welcoming – there's an old wing in the centre and a modern block on the road in from Belmonte. The *Estalagem São Jorge* (☎075/57154) has pricier rooms, but a **restaurant** to savour – their pizzas and huge salads make a refreshing change from the usual solid country fare. **Campers** can pitch tents near the **swimming pool**, also off the main road in from the north.

The annual **Festa do Anjo da Guarda** takes place on August 3 each year, while on the first Sunday in every month a massive **feira** fills Alpedrinha's streets.

Leaving, get information on **buses** from the newspaper kiosk on the side of the main through-road. The Alpedrinha train station, on the plain below, is unstaffed but you can buy tickets on the trains (Beira Baixa Line).

Castelo Novo

In northern Portugal **CASTELO NOVO** is best known as the source of *Alardo*, a bottled mineral water reputed to possess healing properties. A single café-restaurant marks the **spa**, as does the sparkling, clear water gushing from every crack in the earth's surface.

The village, like Alpedrinha, has ancient origins, but you'll find it more scenically than architecturally invigorating. In the centre are a few crumbling remains of a **castle**, an attractive **Paços do Concelho** (above the main square), and a Manueline **pelourinho**. Off to the sides of the square, narrow alleyways and heavy stonework constitute the village's principal charm.

Coming from or returning to Alpedrinha you can pick up one of the four daily *RN* **buses** which run along the main road as far as the crossroads, 4km from the village. There is no accommodation, but there's scope for **camping** and above all plenty of water!

Castelo Branco and Beira Baixa

After the surpassing beauty of most of Beira Alta, the flat plain of the lower province comes as something of a disappointment. For the most part it's monotonous parched country, dotted here and there with cork and carob trees or the occasional orchard. From **Castelo Branco** however, the capital of **Beira Baixa** and the only place of any size, you can make rewarding and fairly easy excursions to two very ancient, strange and atmospheric villages – **Monsanto** and **Idanha-a-Velha**.

Castelo Branco

Not much of **CASTELO BRANCO** has survived the successive wars of this frontier area, but the modern parts are set out around wide boulevards, large squares and small parks. There is a general air of bustling prosperity, in complete contrast to the somnolent villages round about.

What's left of the **old town** is centred around the narrow cobbled alleyways and stepped sidestreets leading up to the ruins of the **castle**. Around its twelfth-century walls a garden – the **Miradouro de São Gens** – has been laid out, affording vistas of the town and countryside in every direction.

They're particularly proud of their gardens in Castelo Branco, and one of them, the formal eighteenth-century garden of the **Palacio Episcopal**, well deserves the esteem. It's not very large, but is packed with elaborately shaped hedges, baroque statues, little pools, fountains and flowerbeds. The balustrades of the grand staircase are peopled with statues – the Apostles on the right, kings of Portugal on the left. Two of the latter are much smaller than the rest: the hated Spanish rulers, Felipe I and II.

The **Bishop's Palace** itself houses the **regional museum** (open 9.30am–noon and 2–5.30pm). There's the usual local museum miscellany of archaeology, art, traditional crafts and so on, but here it's filled out with a large collection of finely embroidered bedspreads. Castelo Branco's *colchas* are renowned throughout Portugal – traditionally all the young women of the village would make one as part of their trousseau. The finest in the museum date from the seventeeth and eighteenth centuries, with designs clearly based on cloths brought back from the east. There are also some modern examples; the same building houses a school of embroidery which is striving to revive the craft.

Worth seeing, too, are the elegant sixteenth-century **Câmara Municipal** in the Praça Luís de Camões and the many seventeenth- and eighteenth-century mansions in the streets around it.

The **Turismo** is right in the centre of town in a little park off the Alameda da Liberdade. There are two **pensions** on the Alameda, and several more along the street which leads from here to the cathedral and the bishop's palace. Some of the cheapest are on the Praça do Rei Dom José, and down to the right on Rua J.A. Mourão.

The **bus station** is on the corner of Rua R. Rebelo and Rua do Saibreiro, the latter leading straight up to the Alameda. It's a little further to the railway station, but equally simple – straight down the broad Av. de Nuno Álvares.

Monsanto and Idanha-a-Velha

MONSANTO, to which there are two buses a day from Castelo Branco, is a place barely changed since the Iron Age; indeed, it claims to be the most ancient settlement in Portugal.

The old village – there's a newer settlement at the bottom of the hill – cowers under a huge fortified granite outcrop and its houses, made of the same stone, are tiny but powerfully built. From only a few hundred yards away they disappear entirely into the grey, boulder-strewn background, and in less peaceful days there was safety in such camouflage; now one or two more adventurous villagers have adopted a splash of whitewash to make their homes stand out. It is all incredibly basic, though at the same time very beautiful – flowers are everywhere and the streets, barely wide enough even for a mule, are simply carved out of the rock.

The **Castle** too is impressive, though tumbledown. As you climb up through the village you're quite likely to meet someone who'll insist on guiding you up, showing you the views and expounding some of the legends. A big celebration takes place in the castle every May 3 when the village girls throw baskets of flowers off the ramparts. The rite commemorates an ancient siege when, in desperation and close to starvation, the defenders threw their last calf over the walls: their attackers, so disheartened at this evidence of plenty within, gave up and went home.

There is a small **bar** on the road below Monsanto which claims to have rooms, though when I was there they refused to let me stay on the grounds that it would be too hot indoors. They'll give you a meal anyway, and if you're stranded no one will mind if you camp.

Idanha-a-Velha

IDANHA-A-VELHA only sees one bus a day from Castelo Branco, and that turns round and leaves within half an hour of arriving. Hitching, however, is very easy on these minor roads – there's not much traffic but almost anyone who passes will give you a lift.

Now a tiny backwater, Idanha was once a major Roman city (known as Igaetania) and, under Visigothic rule (when it was known as Egitânia) the seat of a bishopric – which endured even during Moorish occupation. Wamba, the legendary King of the Goths, is said to have been born here. During the reign of Dom Manuel, however, a plague of rats forced the occupants to move to Monsanto or nearby Idanha-a-Nova.

The old village has remained much the same since that time. The massive Roman walls now dwarf the few houses left within their circuit, and there are odd Roman relics lying about everywhere – the **Roman bridge** is still in use. In the very ancient **basilica**, which is at least partly Visigothic, there's a collection of all the more mobile statues and lumps of inscribed stone found about the place; another small chapel contains an exhibition of coins, pottery and bones, all found more or less by accident.

travel details

Trains

Beira Baixa Line 4 daily from GUARDA to Covilhã (1hr. 10min.), Fundão (1hr. 40 min.), Alpedrinha (2hr. 20 min.), Castelo Branco (3hr. 20 min.), Belver (4¾hr.), Abrantes (5½hr.), Entroncamento (6½hr.), Santarém (6¾hr.) and Lisbon (8hr.).

Beira Alta Line 5 daily from GUARDA to Celorico da Beira (1hr.), Nelas (1¾hr.; change for buses to Viseu), Sta Comba Dão (2hr. change for Viseu — one night train only), Luso-Buçaco (2hr. 40min.) Pampilhosa (3hr.; change for Figueira da Foz, Aveiro and Porto), Coimbra B (3½hr.), Entroncamento (5hr.) and Lisbon (6½hr.). Most of these trains also run from Guarda to the border at Vilar Formoso-Fuentes de Onoro (1hr) from where there are two onward connections to Salamanca (2½hr.) and an Express to Paris (20hr. — currently the 10pm from Guarda).

Buses

From Coimbra Castelo Branco (3 daily; 5hr.); Guarda (2; 4hr.); Viseu (3; 3hr.); Covilhã (1; 4hr.)

From Covilhã Castelo Branco (4; 2½hr.); Guarda (4; 1½hr.).

From Guarda Lamego (4; 4hr.); Viseu (4; 2hr.).

From Viseu Lamego (5; 2hr.); Porto (2; 5hr.).

All the major towns have at least one express service a day to **Lisbon**, usually three or four. **International** coaches from Lisbon to Paris also pass through Coimbra, Viseu and Guarda and you can pick them up there, though seats must be booked in advance.

CHAPTER FIVE

PORTO AND THE DOURO

The **River Douro** (*Rio d'Ouro* – river of gold) dominates each aspect of this region. Its valley, a spectacular rocky gorge as it approaches the sea, nourishes in its upper reaches the **port** vineyards. Sadly the wine no longer shoots down the river's rapids in the traditional 'Barcos Rabelos', but even without the boats a trip up the valley is one of the best scenic routes in the country. Although services have been dramatically reduced, you can still cover this much of the way by train, while to the north a couple of equally fine (and even more reduced service) **rail lines** cut along the Rio Tamega to Amarante and along the Corgo to Vila Real.

In addition, there's **Porto** itself, an enticing, atmospheric city, with its port-producing suburb of **Vila Nova de Gaia**, and, to the north, a couple of excellent beaches at **Vila do Conde** and **Póvoa de Varzim**.

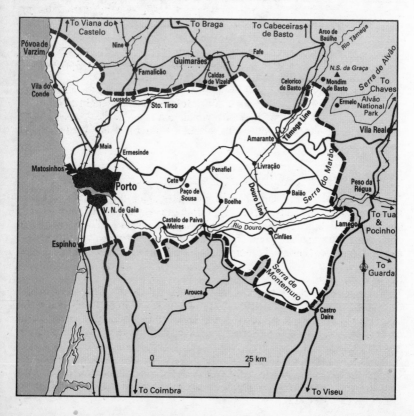

Porto (Oporto)

Portugal's second largest city, **PORTO** is magnificently situated on the great gorge of the Douro, its old quarters scrambling up the rocky north bank in tangled tiers. Although the capital of the north, it's a very different city from Lisbon – unpretentious, inward-looking, unashamedly commercial. As the local saying goes: 'Coimbra sings; Braga prays; Lisbon shows off; and Porto works'.

The Douro, always the city's lifeblood, is spanned here by three truly spectacular **bridges**: the Maria Pia railway bridge, designed by Eiffel; the vast, modern span of concrete which carries the road across the mouth of the Douro; and best of all, the two-tiered Ponte de Dom Luís connecting the city with **Vila Nova de Gaia**, home of the port wine trade. There are few more pleasant ways to while away an hour or two than to walk across here to sample some of the great liquor so influential in shaping everyone's conceptions of Porto.

In the city 'proper', there are few important monuments or grand public buildings. Its fascination lies very much in the life of the place: a bizarre mix of First and Third World, with its prosperous business core, surrounded by smart suburbs and elegant villas, side by side with a heart of cramped streets and ancient alleys, untouched by the planners, that seem almost Dickensian in their poverty. A first sight can be quite a shock. However, it remains hard not to like the place in spite of its obvious problems, and to respond to the crowds, the wealth of tiny bars and antiquated shops.

The city is at its earthiest and finest, if you can possibly plan a visit to coincide, during the riotous celebration of **St. John's Eve** (the night of June 23–24). At this time seemingly the entire population takes to the streets, hitting each other over the head with leeks, plastic hammers, or anything else that happens to be handy.

Orientation and points of arrival

Although modern Porto sprawls for some miles along the north bank of the Douro, most sights of any interest are within the very compact centre – if you don't mind the hills, these are all within walking distance. The main exceptions are the campsites, youth hostel and the new modern art museum – details of buses to these and other places are included in the relevant sections.

Orientation

The 'centre' of Porto is perhaps best considered as the **Estação de São Bento**, the city's grand principal railway station, sited immediately below the cathedral. If you arrive or leave here, look for the building's magnificent *azulejos* by João Colaço depicting the history of transport and Portugal's greatest battle.

Just a few yards away from São Bento lies the **Avenida dos Aliados**, Porto's main commercial centre, fronted by various banks and, at its north end, by the central post office and the main **Turismo** (a smaller tourist office is on Praça Dom João I).

The streets off the avenue lead to the city's commercial centres: to the left the busy **Rua da Fábrica** with its stationers and bookshops, to the right the elegant **Praça Dom João I** and the area up to **Rua Santa Catarina**, with the leading clothes and shoe shops.

Trains

São Bento is one of two major stations – most trains will drop you at the **Estação de Campanhã**, which is some way out. You should change here for a local train into São Bento – it takes about five minutes and there should never be more than a twenty-minute wait.

Certain trains from Minho (Guimarães) and the north coast (Póvoa do Varzim) also use the smaller **Estação da Trindade** from where it's a short walk down Rua da Trindade, past the town hall and into the centre.

If you're leaving Porto on an international connection – Paris especially – in the summer, be sure to book a ticket several days in advance.

Buses

Buses are somewhat more complicated since there's no terminal and each company seems to operate from a different street in a different part of town. Most are fairly central though. As a general rule, buses **heading south** leave from around Rua Alexandre Herculano, and those **heading north** (Viana do Castelo, Barcelos, Braga) from the Praça Filipa de Lencastre.

Rodoviária Nacional (Praça Filipa de Lencastre) is the most useful to know and goes everywhere, north and south, while *Cabanelas* (Rua Ateneu Comercial do Porto, off the Rua Passos Manuel) runs a rapid service to Trás-os-Montes (Vila Real, Chaves, Bragança).

International buses – to France, Germany and Switzerland but not direct to England – are operated by *InterNorte* from their head office on Praça da Galiza and, more conveniently, from Rua das Carmelitas, where there are also express buses to Lisbon.

The Airport

The airport is some 20km out, but there's a regular shuttle service, #56, to and from **Cordoaria** (see below); the journey usually takes around forty minutes but allow a good hour at peak times of day. On the way into Porto, the bus also passes the Museu Soares dos Reis, the youth hostel, and the *Centro Comercial Brasília* at Boavista.

City Bus Stops

A brief word on Porto buses and **bus stops** will help you get around more easily. There are three main areas:

● **Cordoaria:** Campo dos Martires da Pátria, Praça Gomes Teixeira (with a tram stop) and the narrow street which links them; buses for the airport leave from in front of the market.

● **Praça:** the central Praça da Liberdade, at the bottom of the Avenida dos Aliados.

● **Bolhão:** Rua Sá da Bandeira, where there are stops in front of the theatre and halfway up at Bolhão itself.

You can buy **blocks of tickets** (*módulos*) and a four- or seven-day *Passe Turístico* (Tourist Pass) at kiosks near these bus stops and in the *papelaría* on Avenida dos Aliados, next to the swish *Café Imperial*.

Like Lisbon, there are also antiquated **trams** of the type one sees in transport museums – the best of these are #18 (from *Cordoaria*) and #1 (from *Alfândega*) to the sea.

Accommodation

The **cheapest rooms** in the city are on the Rua do Loureiro, around the corner from São Bento, but be warned that it's also Porto's red-light district – if that counts for much.

For slightly more salubrious places, your best bet is to ignore hagglers at the stations and head for the areas west or east of the Avenida dos Aliados.

West of Aliados

Avenida dos Aliados: *Pensão Monumental*, in the top floors of a huge turn-of-the-century building, has huge, excellent value rooms. Good value, too, is the unnamed pension next door – above the *Bel Arte*.

Rua Conde de Vizela: *Novo Mundo* (no. 92, ☎02/25403) and *União* (no. 62, ☎02/23078) are both clean and popular (reservations wise in high summer).

Praça Gomes Teixeira: higher up and a noisy location. The pensions, *França* and *d'Ouro* (Praça Parada de Leitão 41, ☎02/381201) have a variety of prices; or try the nearby *Duas Nações* (Praça Guilherme Gomes Fernandes 59, ☎02/26807) and *Grande Oceano* (Rua da Fábrica 45, ☎02/382447) – both dingy and cheap.

Rua de Cedofeita: *São Marino* (Praça Carlos Alberto 59, ☎02/325499; new), *Nobreza* (Rua do Breiner 6, ☎02/312409; grotty) and *Estoril* (Rua de Cedofeita 193, ☎02/22751; lots of foreigners).

Rua do Almada: Options include the 2-star *Pensão Europa* (no. 398, ☎02/26971), the 3-star Pão do Azucar (excellent value for its class) and numerous workers' cafés for cheap, basic meals.

East of Aliados

Rua Fernando Tomás:*Pensão Norte* (579, ☎02/23503; on the junction with Rua Santa Catarina). A rambling old place with tiny wooden rooms – recommended.

Rua Arnaldo Gama: *Pensaão Astória* (56, ☎02/28175). Lovely, old-fashioned place behind the city wall in an un-touristy, terraced part of town; be sure to book in advance.

Campsites

Prelada (☎02/62616; bus #9 from Bolhão until 9pm, bus #50 from Cordoaria until midnight). The closest site and open year round.

Angeiras (town bus #76, change to larger bus in front of the Turismo in Matosinhos or take a direct bus run by *A Maia*, Campo dos Martires da Pátria, 11.30am–6pm). On the coast to the north, above Matosinhos.

Madalena (bus #50 from Rua Mouzinho da Silveira below São Bento). On the coast to the south – three official campsites but a less attractive beach.

Medas (buses run by *Gondomarense*, Rua São Victor – 10 min. from Praça da Batalha along Rua Entre Paredes, Avda. Rodrigues de Freitas then second right; 11.30am–6.30pm). The best option of all, on the less-crowded, terraced campsite by the Douro.

Youth Hostel

Pousada de Juventude (Rua Rodrigues Lobo 98, ☎02/65535; buses #3, #20, or #52 from Praça da Liberdade, ask for Praça da Galiza). Large and clean but, like most city hostels, lacks atmosphere.

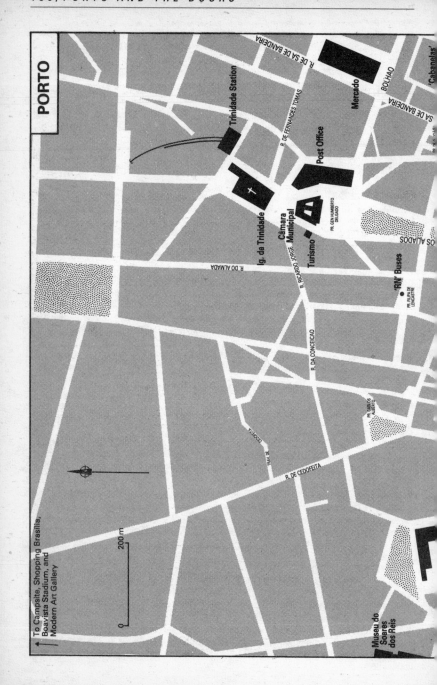

PORTO

R. DE SÁ DE BANDEIRA

Trinidade Station

R. DE FERNANDES TOMAS

Mercado

BOLHAO

Cabanelas'

SÁ DE BANDEIRA

Post Office

Ig. da Trinidade

Câmara
Municipal

PR. GEN HUMBERTO
DELGADO

OS ALIADOS

R. RICARDO JORGE

R. DO ALMADA

Turismo

RN Buses

PR. FILIPA DE
LENCASTRE

R. DA CONCEICAO

PR. CARLOS
ALBERTO

TRAV. DE
CEDOFEITA

R. DE CEDOFEITA

200 m

0

To Campsite, Shopping Brasília,
Boavista Stadium, and
Modern Art Gallery

Museu do
Soares
dos Reis

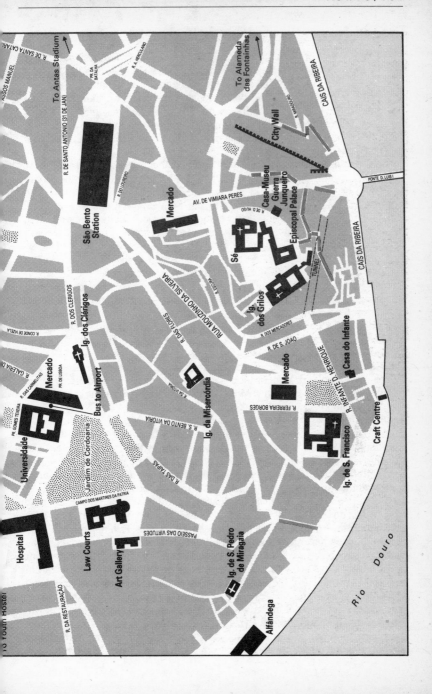

To Antas Stadium

R. DE SANTA CATARI...

...SSOS MANUEL

R. DE SANTO ANTONIO (31 DE JAN)

PR. DA BATALHA

R. A. HERCULANO

To Alameda das Fontainhas

CAIS DA RIBEIRA

R. DO LOUREIRO

São Bento Station

Mercado

AV. DE VIMIARA PERES

Casa-Museu Guerra Junqueiro

City Wall

R. DE D. HUGO

Sé

Episcopal Palace

PONTE D. LUIS I

CAIS DA RIBEIRA

R. DOS CLÉRIGOS

Ig. dos Clérigos

R. CONDE DE VIZELA

R. DAS FLORES

RUA MOUZINHO DA SILVEIRA

L. ESCOLA...

Ig. dos Grilos

TUNNEL

R. GALERIA D...

Mercado

PR. DE LISBOA

R. DAS CARMELITAS

Bus to Airport

Ig. da Misericórdia

R. DA VITORIA

R. DOS MERCADORES

R. DE S. JOAO

Casa do Infante

PR. GOMES TEIXEIRA

Universidade

Jardim de Cordoaria

R. S. BENTO DA VITORIA

Mercado

R. FERREIRA BORGES

R. INFANTE D. HENRIQUE

Craft Centre

CAMPO DOS MARTIRES DA PATRIA

R. DAS TAIPAS

Hospital

Law Courts

Art Gallery

PASSEIO DAS VIRTUDES

Ig. de S. Pedro de Miragaia

Ig. de S. Francisco

R. DA RESTAURAÇÃO

Alfândega

Rio Douro

To Youth Hostel

The Old Town

The stifled streets of the old town rarely permit any sort of overall view of the city, so it's a good idea to climb the Baroque **Torre dos Clérigos** (10.30am–noon and 3–5pm; closed Wed.) to get your bearings. This landmark, which above all else characterises the Porto skyline, was designed, like the curious oval church beneath it, by the Italian architect Nicolau Nasoni. It was once the tallest structure in Portugal, and the dizzying vistas from the top take in the entire city, Vila Nova de Gaia, and sometimes even the distant mouth of the Douro and the coast.

There are fine views too from the tower of the **Paços do Concelho** or Town Hall (weekdays 9.30am–noon and 2.30–5pm), and from the broad flagged courtyard in front of the **Sé** (9am–12.30pm and 3–6pm). The Cathedral itself is externally similar to the Sé Velha at Coimbra – a bluff, austere building standing four-square and fortress-like on its rocky outcrop. Despite attempts to beautify it in the eighteenth century it retains the hard, simple lines of its Romanesque origins – more impressive from a distance than close up. Inside it's depressing, even the vaunted silver altarpiece failing to make any impression in the prevailing gloom. For a small fee, however, you can escape into the neighbouring cloisters, and climb a Nasoni-designed Renaissance staircase leading up to a dazzling chapterhouse, with more views from the casement windows over the old quarter.

Beside the Sé stretches the fine facade of the **Archbishop's Palace** (no admission) while around to the back, along Rua de Dom Hugo, is the **Casa Museu de Guerra Junqueiro** (Tues.–Sat. 11am–12.30pm and 2.30–6pm). This, the former home of the poet Guerra Junqueiro, houses his impressive collections of artwork and furniture, though the mansion and its gardens outshine their contents. (Other *casa-museus* are detailed in the next section).

Down to the Riverside

Rua de Dom Hugo curls back around to the Sé and into the midst of the crumbling, animated old alleys which lead down to the riverside. From the prancing statue of Vimara Peres, **Calçada de Vandoma** plunges downwards, lined with the stalls of an authentic **flea market**, a few of them selling fruit or homemade foods, most simply junk – torn clothes, broken transistor radios, used batteries . . . It's the most fascinating and atmospheric part of the city, even if the medieval ghetto of back streets is deeply poverty-stricken, and, anywhere else, would have been demolished long ago. Tall, narrow and rickety, the houses have grown upwards into every available space, adapting as best they can to the steep terrain. Not much goes on down at the waterfront since the big ships stopped calling here, but along the **Cais da Ribeira** old men still sit around as if they expect to be thrown a line or set to work unloading some urgent cargo.

From the Praça da Ribeira Rua da Alfândega leads back towards the centre, past the house where **Prince Henry the Navigator** is said to have been born. An impressive mansion, it is used now for temporary exhibitions and opens to the public on weekdays from 10am to noon and 2 to 5pm.

São Francisco and the Bolsa

Henry's statue stands in the nearby Praça do Infante Dom Henrique, facing the Bolsa and the back of **São Francisco** (Tues.–Sat. 10am–12.30pm and 2.30–5pm), perhaps the most extraordinary church in Porto. From its entrance on Rua de São Francisco it looks like an ordinary enough Gothic construction, but the interior has been transformed by an unbelievably ornate attack of eighteenth-century refurbishment. Altar, pillars, even the ceiling, drip with gilded rococo carving which reaches its ultimate expression in an interpretation of the Tree of Jesse on the north wall.

Don't miss São Francisco's small **museum**, either. It's housed in a separate building next door and consists largely of artifacts salvaged from the monastery which once stood nearby. Beneath the flags of the cellar is an **osseria** – thousands upon thousands of human bones, cleaned up and stored until Judgment Day. The aged guide keeps up a wry running commentary on everything you see.

The **Bolsa**, or Stock Exchange, is a pompous nineteenth-century public building with a vast neoclassical facade, and its keepers are inordinately proud of the place. As you join the guided tour (weekdays 9am–noon and 2–5pm, Sat. am only) they dwell, with evident glee, on the enormous cost of every item, the exact weight of every piece of precious metal, and the intimate details of anyone with any claim to fame ever to have passed the doors; President Kennedy, apparently, was one. The tour's nadir is the 'Arab' Hall, an oval chamber that misguidedly attempts to copy the Moorish style of the Alhambra; here the guide's superlatives achieve apotheosis. Should you not want to bother with the tour you can see the main courtyard, easily the most elegant part, without having to buy a ticket.

Other Churches and the Centro Comercial

Other churches in the old town also have small museums. At the Igreja de **São Pedro de Miragaia** there's a fifteenth-century triptych; the church is kept locked but someone with a key is usually near at hand. More compelling is the **Igreja da Misericorida**, where you can see a remarkable **Fons Vitae**, depicting King Manule I with his wife Leonor and eight children, richly clothed, kneeling before the crucified Christ. It's an exceptional example of fifteenth-century Portuguese Realism – a style which was heavily influenced by Flemish painters like Van Eyck and Van der Weyden. To gain admission, knock at the government offices next door and ask for permission to enter the *Sala das Sessões*.

One other church of interest – remarkable for its simplicity and age – is the **Igreja de Cedofeita** (from *cito facta*: 'built quickly'), on the top left of our map. This is reputed to be the oldest Christian building in the entire Iberian peninsula and was built orignally by the Suevi king Theodomir in 556. It was later rebuilt in the twelfth century and makes a refreshing change from the heavy Baroque styles that dominate so much of Porto's religious architecture.

Nearby the Cedofeita is the modern shopping centre of the **Centro Comercial de Brasília**, overlooking the rotund **Praça Mouzinho de**

Albuquerque. The square itself is overlooked by a huge column, with a lion astride a much flatttened eagle, erected to celebrate the victory of the Portuguese and British victory over the French in the Peninsular War.

From here you can catch a **#18 eléctrico** tram all the way to Matosinhos (see "Beaches") and then back into town to the Cordoariá. It's three sides of a rectangle, but a good ride all the same.

Museums and Galleries

Ethnography and History

From the Bolsa it's not far to the **Museu de Etnografia e História** (Tues.–Sat. 10am–noon and 2–5pm) in the quiet Largo de São João Novo. It occupies another beautiful noble house with a fascinating mixed collection of jewellery, folk costumes, ancient toys and almost anything of interest that has defied easy definition. In one room there's a collection of nineteenth-century childbirth chairs, in another a reconstruction of a rural kitchen, and in yet another a display of boats used on the Douro. It's the most attractive of Porto's museums but unfortunately was considerably damaged by a fire in 1985: much may still be closed off.

Soares dos Reis

The **Museu Nacional Soares dos Reis** (Rua de Dom Manuel II), open again after restoration and rearrangement, was, interestingly enough, the first national museum in the country (1933) and comes highly recommended. Its excellent art collection includes glass, ceramics and a formidable collection of eighteenth- and nineteenth-century paintings by such artists as Henrique Pousão (Sicilian portraits), as well as the late nineteenth-century sculptures of Soares dos Reis (*O Desterro* – The Exile – is probably the best known in Portugal) and Teixeira Lopes, his pupil.

The building, a former Royal Palace – *Palácio das Carrancas* – was Marshal Soult's headquarters in the Peninsular War and it was from here that he fled so hurriedly that The Duke of Wellington, leading his troops across the Douro, was able to sit down and eat the celebratory banquet that had been laid out for the French. Hours are from 10am to 5pm daily except Monday, with free admission on Sunday or with an ISIC card.

Casa-Museu de Fernando de Castro

While at the Soares dos Reis, it's worth enquiring about the currrent opening hours of the Casa-Museu de Fernando de Castro, which the museum maintains in a nearby city suburb. This extraordinary house is crammed with treasures and in particular with pieces of gilded woodwork salvaged by De Castro (1888–1950) from the city's convents following the 1910 Dissolution of the Monasteries. The culmination of De Castro's own gothic vision is a minute ballroom, which lies beyond a richly bedecked stairwell. It's wonderful and dreadful and shouldn't be missed.

The museum, at Rua Costa Cabral 176 (an extension of Rua Santa Catarina), can be reached on any of the buses leaving from opposite the café O Brasileiro on Rua Sá de Bandeira. Admission is at present Tuesdays only.

The Palácio de Cristal and Solar do Vinho do Porto

Follow the road past the Museu Soares dos Reis away from the centre, or take any bus from *Cordoaria* except #6 and #18, and you'll come to the **Jardim do Palácio de Cristal**, a beautifully peaceful park dominated by a huge domed pavilion built to replace the original 'Crystal Palace', and which now serves as an exhibition hall. In summer the park is home to a vast funfair.

On the far side, across Rua Entre Quintas, stand the **Quinta da Macierinha**, which houses both the **Romantic Museum** (a collection of mid–nineteenth-century furniture and artwork; Tues.–Sat 10am–5pm), and the **Solar do Vinho do Porto**.

Here, in air-conditioned splendour, you can **sample one of hundreds of varieties of port**. The list is the same as at the Port Wine Institute in Lisbon but the service is considerably friendlier and the wine, after all, is at home. It's open daily, except Sunday, from 11am until midnight. It's a good prelude to a visit to the port lodges across the river in Vila Nova de Gaia (see section following).

Museu de Arte Moderna

About half an hour's bus journey from the centre is a more recent addition to the art scene of Porto – the highly contemporary **Museu de Arte Moderna** (Rua de Serralves 977; Tues.–Sun. 2–8pm; bus #78 from *Cordoaria* or from near the Palácio de Cristal).

Established and administered by the Gulbenkian Foundation (see the *Lisbon* chapter), and housed in a 1930s palace known as the *Casa de Serralves*, this displays the work of a number of Portuguese architects and designers. No public collection in the country gives you a more accurate picture of Portugal's modern art scene, and the setting manages to be at once majestic and yet very personal.

Exhibitions run for a month at a time, and the **gardens** (meriting a visit in themselves) remain open from 2pm to 5pm daily 7.30pm in summer), even during the two-week closures of the gallery for rehanging.

Commercial Modern Art Galleries

Other galleries of modern art are scattered about the centre of town. One street which is dedicated to them – an equivalent, say, of London's Cork Street – is the **Rua Galeria de Paris**. The main dealers here are **Galeria Nasoni** at no. 68-80. Summer tends to be a time of redecorating and restocking, so you may find everything closed in August and September. Otherwise, you're free to wander in and take a look at four floors of the best (and priciest) painting on sale in the country today.

Across the Cordoaria from Nasoni's, you are also welcome to stroll around *ARVORE* on Passeio das Virtudes. This is a cooperative of painters, sculptors and designers, who run their own art school in close competition with the official Escola das Belas Artes (in a nearby mansion). They pride themselves on the vitality of the teaching and the freedom they allow their pupils to explore new ideas, the results of which you can see in a punchy summer degree show in June and July.

Vila Nova de Gaia

This suburb is taken over almost entirely by the port trade – the names of the old **port houses**, spelled out in huge white letters across their roofs, dominate even the most distant view. Most of them were established in the eighteenth century, following the treaty of 1703 between England and Portugal, and although on the whole they have long since been bought by multinational brewing companies, they still try hard to push a 'family' image.

A Tour of the Lodges

Almost all the companies offer free **tasting** and a tour of the manufacturing process, though none are entirely honest about it – they deny emphatically that anything is added to the wines despite the overpowering chemical stench in some of the less respectable establishments.

It's interesting to contrast one of the large manufacturers, *Sandeman* or *Real Vinícola* – which operate virtually a production-line process – with the smaller, more traditional lodges such as *Croft*, *Taylor*, or *Kopke*. *Calém* has a particularly pleasant riverside bar; *Taylor* (not easy to find) gives a very informative talk on the processes and is happy to take just a couple of visitors at a

VILA NOVA
DE GAIA

time. There are distinct contrasts, too, between the more familiar 'British' names with the exclusively Portuguese establishments, like **Ramos Pinto** or **Borgès**. Their attention tends to be concentrated on French and Nordic, rather than British, tourists.

At **Companhia Velhá** you find the Swedish Embassy actually tucked into the lodge's grounds. The company led the first Portuguese attempt to challenge the British monopoly in the nineteenth century. Also in the grounds, apart from the numerous warehouses storing casks for the rich and famous (the King and Queen of Sweden, General Franco — or his descendants – to name just a couple), there is a six-kilometre-long tunnel which might once have formed part of a rail link, had it not been built at the wrong angle. It now serves as a perfect cold storage for Velha's famed sparkling wines and vintage ports.

Not all of the lodges are open to visits year-round, but in summer, at least, they are generally all open on weekdays until 8pm and one or two on Saturday; in winter most shut around 5pm. There's little pressure to buy anything – if you do, try the dry white ports which they serve cold here.

Casa-Museu de Teixeira Lopes

A more sober visit in Gaia could be made to the house-museum devoted to Teixeira Lopes (9am–12.30pm and 2–5.30pm, free admission; bus #36 across the bridge as far as 'Hospital'). Lopes was Soares does Reis's principal pupil and was at the centre of an important artistic and intellectual set that lived in Gaia at the turn of the century. You can see examples of much of their work in the second half of the exhibition. Teixeira Lopes's own preoccupation in his work was the depiction of children. His masterpiece, however, is *A Inglesa* – a large-nosed Englishwoman with an enigmatic expression.

The museum has a wonderful courtyard, full of sculpture. It's a good place for a picnic lunch and a couple of hours rooting around.

The Bridge and River Trips

You can walk to Gaia across the **Ponte Dom Luís**. The most direct route to the wine lodges is across the lower level from the Cais da Ribeira, but if you've a head for heights it's an amazing sensation to walk over the upper deck some 200 feet above the river. There's a beautiful view of the tiered ranks of Porto's old town from here and an even better one from the terrace of **Nossa Senhora do Pilar** high above the bridge. From this former convent Wellington planned his surprise crossing of the Douro in 1809, and it's a barracks again today. The round church is open to the public, but sadly the unusual circular cloister rests in a sort of no man's land between church and army territory. It's being restored, so perhaps there's a chance of its being opened soon.

While you're over here you could also embark on a small boat for the *Cruzeiro das Três Pontes* **river trip** (every hour from 10am to 6pm, May–Oct.; weekdays and Sat. am only). This will take you on a brief ride from the dock outside the *Ferreira Port Company*, through most of the city and under all three bridges. Longer (3-hr.) journeys along the Douro leave twice daily from the Cais da Ribeira, across the river.

Eating and Drinking

Porto is a city where you can eat well and where the average bar lunch is a bottle of chilled white port with fresh sardines on bread. You may be shocked to discover that the town's speciality is *Tripas á Modo do Porto* (tripe) and that the people are affectionately referred to by the rest of the country as *tripeiros* – little tripe. Don't let this put you off – there's always plenty of choice on the menu, and there are plenty of places where you can eat cheaply.

Workers' Cafés

At the basic level, there are workers' cafés galore, all with wine on tap, and often with a set menu for the day. Try the area above **Rua da Fábrica** and around **Praça Carlos Alberto** (*Casa Expresso* at no.73), or **Rua da Picaria** (*Refeição Económica* at no. 23), or walk right up the **Rua do Almada**, a street where three-course meals are advertised for little more than a pound (all closed Sun.).

Off the **Campo das Mártires da Pátria** (with *Casa Costa* at no. 166; open until 10pm), there's the Dickensian **Rua São Bento da Vitória** with *Casa das Colunas* (no. 66; particularly seedy) and others. And on the far side of town, just up **behind the Central Post Office**, there's *Vigo no Porto* at Rua Fernandes Tomás 959. All of these are busy in the middle of the day and invariably close early in the evening (around 7.30pm).

Restaurants around Cais da Ribeira

An area that bustles later at night is down at the **Cais da Ribeira** where numerous cafés and restaurants have been installed under the arches of the first tier of Porto's ranks of dwellings. There's a day-time **market** here along the waterfront and a post-modern cube of a fountain – a strange sight in so old a quarter. *Casa Pesa do Arroz* (no. 41–42) is one of the more authentic of the restaurants here.

Other good restaurant possibilities in the centre of town include: Rua do Bonjardim near the post office for roast meat; *O Assador Típico* (Rua Dom Manuel II 15; near Museu de Soares dos Reis; closed Mon.), a bustling cavern of a restaurant; *A Tasquinha* (Rua do Carmo 23; open until 9.30pm closed Sun.), an olde-worlde sort of place; and, best of the lot, *Montecarlo* (Rua Santa Catarina 17-2°; open every day until 10pm or later) with views over the Praça da Batalha, the appearance of a 1930s tea room, a buzzing television, good food and, particularly at Sunday lunchtime, noisy locals.

Cafés and Bars

Porto's cafés include some elegant rivals to the turn-of-the-century places in Lisbon. For their atmosphere and appearance, try: the *Imperial* (Avda. dos Aliados), with art-deco stained-glass; the *Majestic* (Rua Santa Catarina 112), all mirrors and bent wood, but now housing the equivalent of a family-style steakhouse; and *O Brasileiro* (Rua Sá de Bandeira), named after Lisbon's arty café and now a cafeteria.

Less majestic interiors but more life can be found down on the **waterfronts** on either side of the river and particularly in the area around the Cais da Ribeira, where you'll also find numerous clubs and **live music** – try Rua São João or Rua Reboleira.

The *Casa Casais* on Avenida Rodrigues de Freitas (no. 359; beyond Batalha) has marble-topped tables and wine in barrels – but an exclusively male clientele; they also serve food on the other side of the partition.

Food Shops

Whether you're buying anything or not, some of the city's food shops are worth looking inside. A personal favourite is the **bakery** at 20b Travessa de Cedofieta. This is one of the oldest in the country, using traditional methods such as burning *casqueija* – a fuel which reaches high temperatures whilst producing very little ash. Specialities are *pao de lo*, a round sponge cake, and the *marmelada*, or quince jelly, sold in beautiful old jam jars.

Casa Africana, at 112 Rua dos Clérigos, is another delight, a combined **bacalhau and port wine shop** which advertises itself by hanging its wares outside. The bacalhau (codfish split open to dry and be salted) is bundled up in stacks all around the counter, alongside just about every type of port available.

Directory

Airport Information ☎948/2141; for buses see "Points of Arrival".

American Express at *Star Travel*, Av. dos Aliados 202.

Bookshops There is an English bookshop in Rua da Picaria; try also *Livraria Internacional*, Rua 31 de Janeiro 43 or the lovely old shop at 144 Rua Clérigos.

Banks Main branches, including *Lloyds*, are concentrated around Pr. da Liberdade.

Bike Hire From *Taverna do Bebolos* at Cais da Ribeira 21-25.

Car Hire From *Jumbo Travel* (see below), *Inter Rent* (Airport or Rua do Bolhão 182, ☎381964), *Avis* (☎315497) and others.

Car Repairs Addresses from the *Automóvel Clube de Portugal*, Rua Gonçalo Cristovão 2 (☎29273). They also run a breakdown service.

Chemists Late night services are detailed in the *Jornal de Notícias*, next to the TV section.

Cinemas As in Lisbon, there are numerous cinemas showing films in their original language (*VO* in newspaper listings) and there are always a number showing the most recent American/British offerings.

Consulates UK, Av. da Boavista 3072 (☎684789); USA, Rua Júlio Dinis 826–3° (☎690008); **Holland**, Rua da Reboleira (☎36200); **Sweden**, Largo do Terreiro 4 (☎27243).

Emergencies ☎115 (free). Red Cross ☎60720.

Festivals The biggest event is St John's Eve (23–24 June).

Football *F.C. Oporto* are recent winners of the European Cup and remain Portugal's leading team in rivalry with *Benfica*. To see them play at their 90,000 capacity Antas Stadium catch bus #6/78 from 'Praça'.

Funfair There's a permanent funfair site from July–September at Luna Park, at the Palácio de Cristal.

Hospital Santo António, Rua José de Carvalho (☎27254).

Launderette *Pingouin* at the Centro Comerical Brasília is the only self-service place in the city.

Maps Ex-army ordnance survey maps are available, to Portuguese nationals only, from *Porta Editora*, Rua da Fábrica.

Markets General market daily in the Praça de Lisboa by the Torre dos Clérigos and in the market building on Rua Sá da Bandeira, behind the main Post Office. Flea Market (best on Saturday mornings) at Calçada de Vandoma, below the cathedral, and at the Alameda das Fontainhas, overlooking the river.

Newspapers English papers are available from *Livraria Bertrand* in the Centro Comercial Brasília, Praça Mousinho Albuquerque (bus #3 from 'Praca'). Porto's local paper, the *Jornal de Notícias*, includes information on clubs, football matches, late-night chemists, etc.

Police ☎26821.

Post Office Main post office (open until 10pm weekdays, 8pm weekends) is opposite the town hall in Praça Gen. Humberto Delgado; *posta restante* mail is held here, and you can also make international phone calls.

Tourist Offices At Praça Dom João I no. 1 (☎317514), Praça Gen. Humberto Delgado, opposite the town hall, and in Vila Nova de Gaia near the top of the bridge.

Travel Agencies Most are gathered around the Praça da Liberdade and Av. dos Aliados. *Jumbo* student/youth travel service at Rua de Ceuta 47 (☎381561); *TAP* (Air Portugal) at Praça Mousinho de Albuquerque 105 (☎699841); *British Airways* at Rua Júlio Dinis 778, 2nd floor (☎694575).

Women's Cooperative At *Lojinha dos Mercadores*, Rua dos Mercadores 164, near the Cais da Ribeira.

Beaches around Porto

If you read the Tourist Board handouts in Porto they'll tell you there are splendid beaches just around the coast at **FOZ DO DOURO** and **MATOSINHOS**. Don't believe it. Not only is the coast around the mouth of the river heavily polluted but Matosinhos, especially, is spectacularly ugly – built around the big port of Leixôes which nowadays serves Porto and most of the north's industry. True, it's a very pleasant ride on the tram (#1 from the Rua Nova de Alfandega; 18 or 19 from the Pr. da Liberdade), along the river and up the coast to the port, but it's best to leave it at that or, if you're desperate for a swim, to use the pool at the mouth of the river Leça.

There are much better beaches within easy reach at **Vila do Conde** and **Povoa do Varzim**, either of which makes a good day-trip, or an alternative to staying in Porto, with which they are well connected. Trains leave Porto from the Estacão da Trindade; buses from the Praça Filipa de Lencastre – arriving in Vila do Conde by the parish church, in Povoa at the Praça do Almada.

Vila do Conde and Povoa do Varzim

VILA DO CONDE is not exactly a secret as a resort, but it has lost little of its character through being discovered by tourists. It remains an active fishing port and, as well as a long sandy beach, boasts several fine churches and an atmospheric medieval quarter (complete with traditional boat-building industry) jutting out into the sea beside the River Ave. All in all, a distinctly charming and very enjoyable place.

The town is dominated physically by the enormous bulk of the **Convento de Santa Clara**, on a rise just behind. The convent is now a boys' reformatory but is open to visits. One of the boys will be designated to show you around its early Gothic church, which contains some excellent relief carvings, especially on the tombs of the founders. There's an elegant cloister too, with a fountain fed by the long aqueduct – now partly ruined – which stretches from here to the foot of the mountains.

The sixteenth-century **parish church** (*Igreja Matriz*) is also a beauty, with a soaring, airy interior and – thanks to the Basque workmen who helped with its construction – an unusual but very effective mix of Spanish and Portuguese styles.

Much of your time at Vila do Conde, however, is likely to be spent on the beach, or in the bars and restaurants. For the latter, take advice from the extremely helpful Turismo, who are also a good source of advice on where to stay. The most attractive **accommodation**, if you can afford high season prices of around 4500esc (3500esc out of season) is the *Estalagem*, excellent value for a hotel furnished like a *pousada*.

Povoa do Varzim

You could easily walk from Vila do Conde to **POVOA DO VARZIM**, but the two couldn't be more different. Although Povoa does retain a small harbour and the ruins of a fortress, it has been heavily developed as a resort. A casino and a line of concrete hotels open on to the beach, and it's crowded throughout the year with Portuguese holidaymakers.

Far from being oppressive, though, the crowds add to the atmosphere. It's an extremely lively place, and one with a fair chance of finding **accommodation** – cheaper and more plentiful than in Vila do Conde. Try Rua Paulo Barreto, where there are four or five pensions and rooming houses, or Rua Caetano de Oliveira. The **Turismo** on Avenida Mousinho de Albuquerque has complete listings.

South of Porto: Espinho

Beaches to the south of Porto are less worthwhile. At **MIRAMAR** and **AGUDA** they're small, scrubby and none too clean, while the major resort of Espinho is windswept and overcrowded.

Less of a town than an extension of the sprawling suburbs south of Porto, **ESPINHO** boasts a casino, a few high-rise hotels (with more on the way), hordes of tourist shops, an amazingly dull grid of numbered streets, and a railway right through the centre of town. But most of all Espinho is characterised by the piped Eurodisco blaring out along the main road behind the beach.

If you're heading this way anyway, keep going to ESMORIZ, or better still to CORTEGAÇA or FURADOURO (see*Coimbra and Beira Litoral*).

Along the Douro

Around the valley of the **Douro** are some of the most spectacular landscapes in the whole of Portugal, and the valley itself, a narrow, winding gorge for the majority of its long route to the Spanish border, is the most beautiful of all.

If you're driving you can follow minor roads along the river practically all the way from Porto to the border-crossing at Miranda do Douro. The **railway route**, which joins the course of the river about 60km inland and sticks to it right across the country, here cutting into the rocky face of the gorge, there crisscrossing the water on a series of rocking bridges, is even more dramatic – one of those journeys that need no justification other than the trip itself. And indeed there are no great monuments to be found along the banks, just a series of tiny, rural villages and a couple of (currently threatened) branch lines heading north into the Minho and Trás-os-Montes.

The Douro Line to Regua

The villages along the **Douro line** are so small, and so little visited other than by their inhabitants, that the train stations are scarcely signposted – Livraçao, for example, the junction with the Tâmega Line, has its name painted on an old water tower. You need to be sharp-eyed (or prepared to ask people) to get the right stop. At present there are quite regular connections along the line as far as Regua, though you will most likely find yourself on a single carriage train – which, rather amazingly, has one First Class row of seats. Beyond Regua, the schedules are in a state of flux, with most services towards the Spanish border replaced by bus.

Paço de Sousa and Penafiel

If you're on one of the slow trains, it will stop at CETE, half a dozen stations out of Porto. This is just a mile away from the vilage of **PAÇO DE SOUSA**, a former headquarters of the Benedictines in Portugal, and, set beside a stream, a popular picnic spot for Porto locals.

The village's sight, inevitably, is its **church**, a dank and dark medieval building in the process of restoration. In one corner is the **tomb of Egaz Moniz**, the tutor and adviser to the first king of Portugal, Afonso Henriques. Portuguese history treats Egaz as the great symbol of loyalty. In 1127, shortly after Afonso had broken away from his grandfather, the King of León, Egaz was sent to negotiate a settlement that would enable Afonso to concentrate his efforts away from the Spanish and onto the Moors in the south. Within three years, the king of León considered the treaty broken on the Portuguese side and threatened all-out war. Egaz made his way to León, presented himself to the king and, as can be seen on the panels around the tomb, offered to receive the punishment due his master. Mercy was granted and the king sent the loyal minister home unscathed.

There are a couple of cafés in Paço and plenty of possible camping spots. If you're looking for a bed, it's not much further down the line to Penafiel.

Penafiel

At Penafiel you enter Vinho Verde country, where the Benedictine monks were once famed for their laboriously worked terracing along the valley slopes. In the surrounding hamlets are a dozen of the finest **Romanesque churches** in the country, hidden away in folds of the countryside and hard to reach without your own transport. One, however, at BOELHE – reputedly the smallest of such churches in Portugal – can be reached by bus from Penafiel (departure at 11am; return mid-afternoon). It's a simple building, without much architectural detail, but sits well in its stunning location on the brow of a hill.

PENAFIEL itself, split by main road traffic, is not that enticing a place, and getting to it involves a connecting bus from the station – some way down the hill. But, in addition to access to the churches, it has a saving grace in its fabulous local wine, served from massive barrels in the down-at-heel but good value **adega** in the central Largo do Padré Américo. The *adega* offers basic fare, washed down with pints of wine at a time; a stream of old men in black hats move regularly through its doors. Right next door is the best and cheapest **hotel**, *Casa João da Liza* (☎25158).

For the more sober or healthy, Penafiel also has a fine covered **market**, by the **Turismo** (in a modern complex at Av. Sacadura Cabral 50: stacks of leaflets on the Romanesque churches), and an open-air one on the way up to the white church on the hillside (you'll pass the bus station on the way). The local **festa** is on August 15.

Livraçao and Regua

At **LIVRAÇÃO**, about an hour from Porto, the antiquated narrow-gauge **Tâmega Line** (see below) cuts off for Amarante and the mountains, hugging the ravine of a tributary, the Rio Tâmega.

Shortly after, the main line finally **reaches the Douro** and heads upstream until, at MESÃO FRIO, the river temporarily leaves its confined channel and broadens into the little plain commanded by **RÉGUA** (see *Trás-os-Montes* chapter). This is the terminal for trains up the lovely Corgo line to Vila Real and Chaves (again, see *Trás-os-Montes*); the station itself is charming, with a tiny snack bar serving draught local wine.

Just beyond Régua is the massive dam of a hydroelectric power station and from here on you begin increasingly to see the terraced slopes where the **Port vines** are grown. They're at their best in August, with the grapes ripening, and September when the harvest has begun. The country continues in this vein, craggy and beautiful, with the softer hills of the interior fading dark green into the distance, past PINHÃO (the main centre for quality ports; two pensions), TUA (where a third narrow gauge rail line heads north – to Bragança), and on to **POCINHO**, where passenger trains come to a halt and buses take over for routes east towards Miranda do Douro.

It is a shame that it's no longer possible to follow the Douro line into Spain. If you are headed across the border by rail, you'll need to head well to the south, following the Beira Alta line through Guarda to Vilar Formoso – and thus to Fuentes de Onoro and Salamanca.

THE TÂMEGA LINE

The narrow-track **Tâmega Line** from Livração to Arco de Baúlhe follows the course of the Rio Tâmega north as it climbs into the Serra do Marão, through to the villages of Celorico and Cabeceiras de Basto. Like the other narrow gauge lines in the north, however, it has had its services severely curtailed. At present, there are eight trains daily from **Livraçao to Amarante**, the first leaving Porto at 7.41am; last back to Porto at 6.28pm. There is one train a day still running between Amarante and Arco, though it is not timetabled – it is either the first of the day, or the last (not much use, leaving Amarante at 11.40pm). Otherwise, buses run instead, four times a day.

The real pleasure, like the Douro line, is in the ride itself and the scenery. If you are lucky, changing at Livração, you may find yourself boarding the old-style single-carriage local train, with wooden seats which on a market day accommodate as many animals as they do humans – though most of the services now use newer rolling stock. From the start it's impressive: pine woods and vines clinging to incredible slopes, and as the train continues northwards into the foothills of the Serra the gradients become increasingly unlikely, the track poised high above dizzying valley sides. Goats scramble across the steep terrace walls, to nibble at the haystacks constructed to hang from the branches of living trees.

If it turns out that you can't get one of the trains north of Amarante, you might want to walk along a section of the line – Celorico to Mondim, for example, is a pleasant hour's hike, through woods and over viaducts along the sides of the valley.

Amarante

AMARANTE, half an hour up the Tâmega line, is set immaculately along the river, the wooden balconies of its old houses hanging out over the water. It's a fine place to stop, with any number of bars and cafés along the riverside (mostly on the opposite side from the station) where you can sample some of the exquisite local cakes. Sadly, though, the river beaches can no longer be recommended – at least for swimming – as they have become heavily polluted. If you're tempted, best limit yourself to a ride in one of the *pedalos* or rowing boats rented out in summer.

The Town

The **Convento de São Gonçalo**, beside the elegant bridge across the Tâmega, is Amarante's most prominent monument. It forms the heart of an ancient fertility cult – probably with pagan origins – which still persists here at the grand *Festa de São Gonçalo*, celebrated on the first Saturday in June, when the local unmarried youth exchange phallus-shaped cakes as tokens of their love. In the church itself the saint's tomb is said to guarantee a quick marriage to anyone who touches it – his face, hands and feet have been almost worn away by hopeful suitors. Another chapel, devoted to Gonçalo's healing miracles, is festooned with wax models of every conceivable part of the body as well as entire artificial limbs, bottles full of gallstones, and other votive offerings.

Around the side, in the cloister of the former monastery, there's a surprisingly good **Museum of Modern Art**. It's dominated by the Cubist works of local boy Amadeo de Sousa Cardoso – one of the few Portuguese painters of this century to achieve international renown.

Accommodation and Festivals

Rooms can be hard to come by in July or August but are easy enough to find at other times of year – there's quite a choice of pensions. The *Hotel Silva*, just past the **Turismo** (Rua Cândido Reis) on the way from the station, is pleasant and comfortable, but not specially cheap. Alternatives on the other side of the river include *Residencial Rio*, the best value with a riverside location, the *Conselheiro* or the *Príncipe* in the nearby Largo Conselheiro António Cândido. The cheapest **rooms** are above *Casa Avião* (Rua 31 Janeiro) where there is also *vinho verde* on tap from massive barrels. Additionally there are a couple of **campsites**, one on the riverbank, another, newer and more spacious, a little further upstream on the right bank. Most pensions have restaurants. The best of the regular restaurants is behind the *Casa Avião*.

Should you happen to be in Amarante on a summer Saturday evening (July–Sept.) you could also join in one of the **festivals** in the gardens of the Casa da Calçada, with as much food and wine as you can handle. They're touristy (though mainly for Portuguese) and relatively pricey (around 1000esc) but undeniably fun. There's also a Wednesday **market** on the right bank of the river.

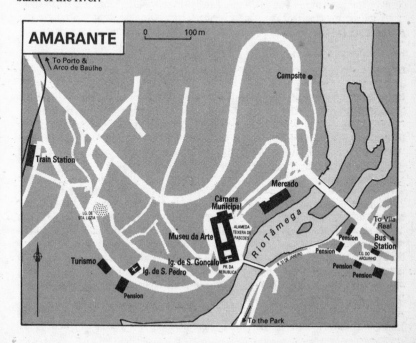

On from Amarante: Celorico and Mondim

Beyond Amarante you really feel the climb into the **Serro do Marão**. If you're on the train, you'll need to count the stops here as many are quite unmarked or at best obscurely so.

CELORICO DE BASTO is five stops up the line, an attractive little village with two pensions and a hotel. Neatly trimmed lawns and formal flower beds testify to a civic pride that one can't help feeling is conspicuously outdone by the area's natural beauty. There's great walking among a labyrinth of paths that head off through the woods from behind the church, but good as it is, the distant prospect of Monte Farinha is more alluring even from here, and if you're into hiking, that is where you should be headed.

Mondim de Basto

MONDIM DE BASTO, two stops further, but a good 2km from the station, is the best base for Monte Farinha, although there's little for you to do there if you're not keen to hike off into the hills. It's more dramatic even than Celorico and has its own tourist office, as well as several rather primitive **pensions** (try the *Mondinense* – huge rooms, but no running water – or *Parque Dormidas* near the station), an excellent **campsite** about 1km from the centre along the Vila Real road, and unofficial camping by the river (follow the path to the left, just before the bridge walking from the station).

The **Parque Natural de Alvão** headquarters (Rua do Retiro) are here too with a small exhibition and information on the park, which lies beyond the Monte Farinha (see below), stretches to Vila Real, and has some striking national features such as the waterfalls (or *fisgas*) at Ermelo; there are plenty of other less visited spots as well.

Monte Farinha and the Cabril Valley

Monte Farinha, to the east of Mondim, is by far the most striking of the surrounding peaks. It is also surprisingly easy to climb – not much over two hours from the centre of Mondim. If you follow the Cerva road out of town you can take a path up to the right shortly after Pedra Vedra; you may lose this among the pines, but on the whole the way is clear enough. Once you begin to approach the final leg, there's a stone path that leads straight to the summit. Alternatively, and somewhat easier, you can follow the longer, twisting route of the road until you see this better path (shortly after the final turn). The panoramic views well repay your efforts, and at the summit is the attractive parish church, **Senhorá da Graça**, centre of a major **festa** on the first Sunday in September.

Another good hike from Mondim is into the **valley of the Cabril**. Only about twenty minutes beyond the campsite, this small river is crossed by a **Roman bridge** – impressive in itself and set near a small waterfall where there's a good swimming hole. From here follow the river upstream to a working watermill or follow the stone track (about 200m upriver) along what must once have been a Roman road. Take this, cross a road, and you're at the start of a maze of small paths cutting between the fields and vineyards of the Cabril valley, and leading higher into the pine-forested slopes.

On from Mondim: Arco de Baulhe

There are regular bus connections from Mondim to Vila Real (a spectacular ride, skirting the Alvão National Park; for the town, see the *Trás-os-Montes* chapter), Guimarães (another beautiful route; see *The Minho*), and Porto.

At the end of the Tâmega line itself comes **ARCO DE BAÚLHE**, a strangely bleak and unwelcoming village. The station-master is especially so but you'll have to ask him to let you see the **transport museum**. There are just two trains in the collection, but both are of great interest: the first steam train to travel down the line, and the royal carriage of Portugal's second-to-last king, Dom Carlos.

If you're not heading back down to Amarante, catch one of the regular **buses**, hitch or walk the 7km on to CABECEIRAS DE BASTO (see *The Minho*), a lively provincial town, from where there are regular buses to Braga in the Minho and, via Venda Nova, to Montalegre and on to Trás-os-Montes.

travel details

Trains

Norte Line 5 trains daily from Porto to Espinho (¾ hr.), Ovar (40 min.–1 hr.), Aveiro (1–1¾ hr.), Coimbra-B (2 hr.–2¾ hr.; change for Coimbra, 4 min.), Entrocamento (3 hr.–4¾ hr.) and Lisbon (4–6 hr. 20 min.). **Change** at Aveiro for Viseu (2 daily with additional buses; 4 hr.); at Pampilhosa for the Beira Alta; at Alfarelos (2 hr.) for Figueira da Foz (15; 20 min.); and at Entrocamento for the Alto Alentejo, Baixa Alentejo, Beira Baixa and Madrid (2; 15 hr.). **N.B.** There are also '*Rápido*' (express trains) from Porto to Lisbon – twice as fast (3–3½ hr.) but twice as expensive – and *Tranvias* to Aveiro, every 45 min. from 6am to midnight.

Douro Line 13 daily from Porto to Livração (1½ hr.; change for Tâmega Line) and Régua (2½ hr.; change for Corgo Line); 7 continue to Tua (3½ hr.; change for Tua Line) and 4 to Pocinho (4½ hr.).

Tâmega Line 8 daily from Livração to Amarante (½ hr.); only one a day at present continues to Mondim de Basto (1½ hr.) and Arco de Baúlhe (3 hr.). In place of trains, there are four daily bus connections north from Amarante.

Corgo Line 5 daily from Régua to Vila Real (1 hr.) and 3 to Chaves (3½ hr.).

Tua Line 4 daily from Tua to Mirandela (1 hr. 40 min.), one or two daily continue to Bragança (3 hr. 40 min.).

Minho Line 12 daily from Porto to Lousado (20 min.; change for Guimarães), Nine (1 hr.; change for Braga), Barcelos (1½ hr.) and Viana do Castelo (2 hr.). 8 continue to Caminha (3 hr.) and Valença do Minho (3 hr. 40 min.), 3 to Vigo (Spain) and 3 to Monção (4½ hr.).

Póvoa Line Hourly from Porto to Vila do Conde (50 min.) and Póvoa de Varzim (55 min.). From Póvoa 7 trains daily go to Famalicão (¾ hr.) for connections along the Minho Line.

Guimarães Line Hourly from Porto (Trindade station) to Santo Tirso (1 hr.) and Guimarães (1¾ hr.).

Porto–Paris Once daily in 26 hr. (via Pampilhosa).

Buses

From Porto to Vila do Conde/Póvoa de Varzim (½–hourly; 40/45 min.); Viana do Castelo (3 daily; 1 hr. 10 min.); Braga (10; 1 hr. 20 min.); Guimarães (5; 1 hr.); Amarante (hourly; 1½ hr.); Vila Real (6; 3 hr. 40 min.); Viseu (2; 4½ hr.); Coimbra (4; 2½ hr.).

There are also frequent express buses to Lisbon (4–5hr), to various destinations in Galicia (Spain), and, most days, to Paris (30 hr.). See beginning of chapter for bus terminals.

THE MINHO

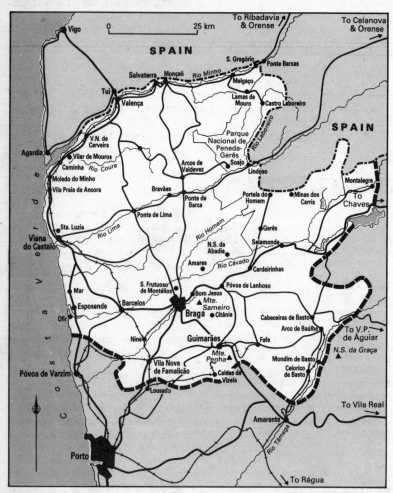

The Portuguese consider the **Minho** to be the most beautiful part of their country, and with its river valleys, wooded hills, trailing vines and wild coastline, the attractions are obvious. It's a small, thoroughly rural province, conservative (and at times reactionary) in politics, and deeply suspicious of change. Wooden-wheeled ox-carts still creak down its lanes, and there are huge country **markets** (above all the one at **Barcelos** every Thursday) and dozens of local **festas** and ancient **romarias**. In summer you'll probably just happen on these village carnivals or saint's days but most of the larger events are detailed in the text: they're worth coinciding with.

Minho towns tend to be more like large villages – ludicrously picturesque and full of quiet charm and interest. Monuments and museums are concentrated in **Braga** and **Guimarães**, while between them lie the extensive Celtic ruins of the **Citânia de Briteiros**, the most impressive archaeological site in Portugal.

To the north, where the River Minho itself forms the border with Spanish Galicia, the highlights are scenic, with the waterfalls, river gorges, reservoirs and forests of oak and cork contained in the protected **Gerês National Park**. This is good camping and hiking territory, with a spa at **Caldas do Gerês** to recuperate afterwards.

The Minho coast, the **Costa Verde**, offers wonderful beaches, though the sea here is cold – and weather too can be uncertain, temperatures rarely rising above 70°F even in midsummer. However, **Viana do Castelo** is an enjoyably low-key resort, and, if it's isolation you're after, there are strands to north and south that scarcely see visitors.

Approaches to the Minho

There are any number of possible **approaches to Minho**. Coming **from Porto** the best initial destinations are probably **Barcelos**, **Braga**, or **Guimarães**, though if time is no object – and you're into train rides or hiking – you might consider the **Tamega line**, veering up from the Douro (and covered in the *Porto and the Douro* chapter).

From Spain, the most straightforward border crossing is at **Tuy–Valença**. A little used and inexpensive alternative is the **car ferry** between **Vila Nova de Cerveira**, east of Caminha, and **Goyan** (in Spanish Galicia); this runs hourly through the day.

EMIGRATION IN THE MINHO

Travelling around the Minho, you'll see much new building – even in the smallest and most rural villages. This is accounted for mainly by Minho emigrants, who return to their homes after working abroad in France or Germany, sometimes the United States. Minho, more than any other area of Portugal, suffered severe depopulation from the late 1950s, as thousands migrated in search of more lucrative work.

The new-found prosperity of the emigrants has transformed their homeland in two ways: money sent back from abroad to support the family members left behind (a mainstay of the Portuguese economy), and the return of some of the emigrants themselves to enjoy a well-heeled retirement in *minha terra* (my land). August is the time when most people race back from abroad to see their families – making it a particularly hairy period on the region's roads. If you drop in on a *festa* don't be surprised to see groups of well-dressed emigrant kids speaking American, German or French.

Barcelos

It's worth a little planning to arrive in **BARCELOS** for the great Thursday market, the **Feira de Barcelos**. Southern Minho's big weekly event – and a perfect introduction to the region – it takes place from around dawn until mid-afternoon on the **Campo da República**, a vast open square that's about the first place you come upon walking into town (and it's a long straight walk) from the railway station.

The Feira
The Minho's markets are always interesting and that at Barcelos, which is probably the largest in Europe, is both a spectacle and a crash course in the region's economics. There are stalls for virtually everything – yokes for oxen, sausage skins, whole avenues of ducks and rabbits (treated as live meat and enough to turn you vegetarian) – but they're outnumbered by row upon row of village women squatting behind baskets of their own produce. Minho is made up of hundreds of tiny, walled smallholdings, rarely more than allotments, so most people here are just selling a few vegetables, some fruit, eggs, and maybe even cheese from the family cow. It all looks unbelievably wholesome and, presumably, will steadily disappear now that Portugal has joined the Common Market.

The *feira*'s other big feature is its local **pottery** and handicrafts, for Barcelos is the centre of Portugal's most active *artesanato* region. The crockery or *louça de Barcelos*, which is brown with distinctive yellow dots, has been well known in the region for some time, but the town was put on the map in the 1950s by the imaginative earthenware figurines of Rosa Ramalho, whose work can be seen in the town's small ceramics museum. In comparison most of today's pieces look rather derivative but the other crafts are impressive – especially the basketwork, traditionally carved yokes (*cangas*), and wooden toys. There's a permanent display in the old town **keep**, a conspicuous tower near the corner of the square, which houses a shop and **Turismo**.

The Town
As far as other sights go, Barcelos, like most other Minho towns, has an interesting **pelourinho**, some imposing late medieval mansions and a scattering of impressive, if modest, churches. The most striking of these, **Nosso Senhor da Cruz**, stands just across the Campo, fronted by a Baroque garden of obelisks and box-hedges. Built in 1708, its distinctive exterior, created by a simple contrast of dark granite and white plaster work, was to be influential in the design of churches throughout the region. It sets an odd tone to the old part of town, though, which is essentially Gothic and medieval – a small, hillside web of streets spun above the River Cávado.

Whichever way you walk from here you'll soon end up at the **river**, as beautiful as any in the Minho, overhung by willows, fronted by gardens, and spanned by a fifteenth-century bridge. Just above it loom the ruins of the **Palace of the Counts of Barcelos**, wrecked by the Great Earthquake of 1755 (the same quake that struck Lisbon) and now providing a shell for the

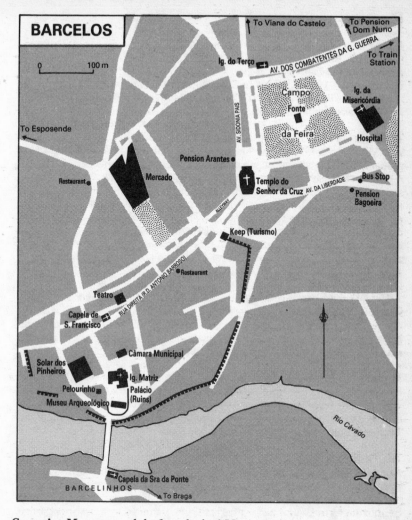

BARCELOS

0   100 m

To Viana do Castelo

To Pension
Dom Nuno

Ig. do Terço

AV. DOS COMBATENTES DA G. GUERRA

To Train
Station

Campo

Fonte

da Feira

Ig. da
Misericórdia

Hospital

To Esposende

AV. SIDONIA PAIS

Pension Arantes

Restaurant

Mercado

Templo do
Senhor da Cruz

AV. DA LIBERDADE

Bus Stop

Pension
Bagoeira

ALLEYWAY

Keep (Turismo)

Restaurant

Teatro

RUA DIREITA (R.D. ANTONIO BARROSO)

Capela de
S. Francisco

Solar dos
Pinheiros

Câmara Municipal

Pelourinho

Ig. Matriz

Museu Arqueológico

Palácio
(Ruins)

Rio Cávado

Capela da Sra da Ponte

BARCELINHOS

To Braga

Ceramics Museum and **Archaeological Museum** (entrance below; 10am–noon and 2–6pm).

The latter, a miscellaneous assembly of stone crosses, includes a fourteenth-century crucifix locally famed for its connection with the *Senhor do Galo* (Gentleman of the Cock). It depicts the legend of the **Galo de Barcelos** (Barcelos Cock), a miraculous roast fowl which rose from the dinner table of a judge to crow the innocence of a pilgrim he had wrongly condemned to the gallows. The pilgrim, having wisely proclaimed 'I'll be hung if that cock don't crow', got his reprieve. It's a story that occurs in different forms in northern Spain – at Santo Domingo de Calzada a cock is even kept in the church – but the Barcelos rooster has taken a special hold on popular folk art, becoming a national symbol of Portugal (or at least of Portuguese tourism).

Rooms and Practicalities

The town has two **pensions**, each alongside the Campo da República: the *Bagoeira* (Avda. Sidónio Pais 57) is the most attractive, a real old market inn, with spotless (though somewhat overpriced – 2500esc double) rooms. If you're on a tighter budget, stay at the *Arantes* (Avda. de Liberdade 32, by the *Templo*), which is the cheapest place in town. There is a third pension, the *Dom Nuno*, off to the right as you approach the Campo da República from the station, but it has pretensions to being a luxury hotel and prices to match.

On market days, be sure to have lunch at the *Bagoeira*, which sees a constant stream of stallholders bringing in pots, pans and containers for take-aways. Other places to **eat** include a very cheap café-restaurant around the corner from the Campo in the alleyway opposite the Templo; *Dom António* (Rua Dom António Barroso), which has built up something of a reputation; and *Restaurant Furna* (Largo da Madalena, closed Mon.), a busy upstairs room opposite the municipal market, where the cooks will spit-roast almost anything you like.

Buses (mostly *RN*) leave from the bottom corner of the Campo da República, not far from the *Bagoeira*; among other services, there's an hourly run to Braga.

THE COSTA VERDE

Spurred by the flow of foreign currency into the Algarve, the Portuguese Tourist Board is energetically trying to promote Minho's almost continuous line of sandy beaches – the **Costa Verde**. So far it hasn't worked, for despite the enticing promises of 'unpolluted beaches with a high iodine content . . . health for the whole year' and even 'gay summerhouses', Costa Verde is green for a reason. It can be drizzly and overcast right through midsummer and the Atlantic here is never too warm. Still, if that doesn't bother you and the weather's looking good there's amazing potential; you can pick almost any road, any village and find a great beach virtually to yourself.

Viana do Castelo

VIANA DO CASTELO is the one town in the Minho you could describe as a resort – but it's all the more attractive for it. A lively, elegant place, it has one of the best beaches in the north, a stylish old centre, an active fishing harbour, and above-average restaurants. It's also beautifully positioned, spread along the north bank of the Lima estuary and shaped by the thick wooded hill of Monte de Santa Luzia, which is strewn with Celtic remains. If you can be in the area towards the end of August, Viana's *Romaria* (see overpage) is the biggest and most exciting festival of the Minho.

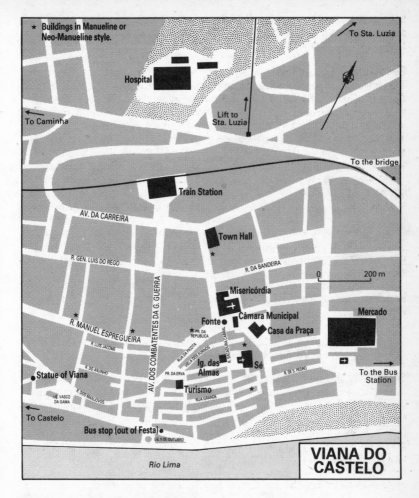

★ Buildings in Manueline or Neo-Manueline style.

To Sta. Luzia

Hospital

To Caminha

Lift to Sta. Luzia

To the bridge

Train Station

AV. DA CARREIRA

Town Hall

R. GEN. LUIS DO REGO

R. DA BANDEIRA

0   200 m

Misericórdia

Mercado

Fonte ● Câmara Municipal

R. MANUEL ESPREGUEIRA

PR. DA REPUBLICA

Casa da Praça

R. LUIS JACOME

AV. DOS COMBATENTES DA G. GUERRA

RUA DA PICOTA

VIELA DOS FORNOS

R. SÃO JOÃO CABRAL

Statue of Viana ●

R. DO ANJINHO

Ig. das Almas

Sé

R. DE S. PEDRO

R. VASCO DA GAMA

R. DOS MANJOVOS

PR. DA ERVA

To the Bus Station

To Castelo

Turismo

RUA GRANDE

Bus stop (out of Festa) ●

R. 5 DE OUTUBRO

Rio Lima

VIANA DO CASTELO

The Town and Montes Santa Luzia

Viana has long been prosperous and seafaring. It produced some of the greatest colonists of the 'discoveries' under Dom Manuel, and in the eighteenth century was the first centre for the shipment of port wine to England. Many of the buildings reflect these times and, unusually for the north, you'll notice Manueline mouldings around the doors and windows of Viana's mansions. The **Turismo** (Praça da Erva) is next to a fine example and makes a good first stop, with free maps and lists of anything you might want or need.

At the heart of the old town is the distinctive and beautiful **Praça da República**. You'll see copies of its Renaissance fountain in towns throughout the Minho, but few buildings as elegant and curious as the old **Misericórdia** (almshouse) that lines one side. Built in 1598, this is one of the most original and successful buildings of the Portuguese Renaissance, its upper storeys supported by deliberately archaic, primitive-looking caryatids. The town **museum** (9.30am–noon and 2–5pm; closed Mon.) adds further to these impressions of Viana's sixteenth- to nineteenth-century opulence with a notable collection of ceramics and furniture. It stands near the end of Rua Manuel Espregueira, ten minutes' walk from the square on the far side of the Avenida dos Combatentes da G. Guerra.

Wherever you stand in Viana, **Monte de Santa Luzia** makes its presence felt, an ugly modern basilica glowering from the summit like an evil eye. But don't let this heap – the ostensible highlight of the town – put you off. It's a great walk up through the pines and eucalyptus trees (take the shortcut over the railway tracks) or you can be hauled to the top by an old funicular, which runs (hourly 10am–noon, half hourly 12.30–6pm) from just above the railway station. There are tremendous views down the coast and along the River Lima.

Amid the woods here, just below a luxury hotel, lie ruins of a Celto-Iberian **citânia** (see "Citânia de Briteiros", below). These include the foundations of dozens of small, circular stone huts, a thick village wall, and partly paved streets. They were probably occupied from around 500 B.C. and only abandoned with the Roman pacification of the north under Emperor Augustus (ca. 26 B.C.). The ruins have recently been fenced off but there should be access.

Viana's **market**, held on Friday, is smaller than the one at Barcelos, but not much, and many of the same stallholders set up shop near the old fort by the sea, in an area known as the Campo do Castelo. There is a permanent market at the other end of town for general provisions.

Praia do Cabedelo

Praia do Cabedelo, the town beach, lies across the river, connected by a seasonal and very rickety ferry, the *Saudade*, which leaves from the harbour at the end of the main street. The only road access from town to beach is over the old metal bridge, with its eighteen-inch pavements nudged by juggernauts. Given sun the beach is more or less perfect – a low curving bay with good (but not wild) breakers, and a real horizon-stretching expanse of sand.

THE *ROMARIA*

Viana's main *romaria*, dedicated to **Nossa Senhora da Agonía**, takes place for three days around the **weekend nearest to August 20**. A combination of carnival and fair, fulfilling an important business function for the local communities, it's a great event to be in town for.

The best day is **Saturday**, when there's a massive parade of floats with every village in the region providing an example of a local craft or pursuit: a marvellous display of incongruities, with threshers pounding away in traditional dress while being pulled by a new Lamborghini tractor. If you want a seat in the stands, get a ticket well in advance. Each of the days, though, there are processions with *gigantones* (carnival giants), folk dancing and pipe bands, and, needless to say, concerted drinking.

The beach in fact extends, virtually unbroken, to the Spanish border at Caminha, to the north, and to Povoa do Varzim to the south. For the energetic, either of these routes makes a memorable and enjoyable hike. For details of the routes, see overpage.

Rooms, Restaurants and Transport

Pensions in Viana are easy enough to find, but some are very pricey. Three cheaper options are *Pensão Guerreiro* (Rua Grande 14, ☎058/22099), which is down-at-heel but friendly and has very good meals; *Nova Floresta* (Rua do Anjinho 34–36, ☎058/22386), where, though the service is unfriendly, there is wine on draught in china bowls; and *Terra Linda* (Rua Luís Jácome 11–15) where they try harder to please. If you can afford it, the *Vianamar* is one of the more luxurious pensions in town, with warm rooms in winter.

All these streets have other options and there are **rooms**, particularly during the *Romaria*, advertised in the windows of private houses (or consult the Turismo). Try Rua Grande 72 (☎058/25118) or, for the occasional inexpensive room, *Residencial Laranjeira* and *Residencial Magalhães* (Rua Manuel Espregueira 24, ☎058/22241, and 62, ☎058/23293). An alternative not worth bothering about is **camping** – at least at Viana's two official campsites by the Cabedelo beach. The *Inatel* is for carnet-holders only, and used by Porto families for summer-long tents; the other, *Orbitur*, is overpriced for what you get. Head towards MAR (see overpage) if you want to sleep out.

The Rua Grande and the Rua Manuel Espregueira (full of workers' places) have a wide choice of **restaurants**. One incredibly low-cost establishment is *Casa de Pasto Trasmontano* (Rua Gago Coutinho 12), behind the old town hall in the Praça da República. For better food, at restaurant prices, try: the *Dolce Vita* (Rua do Poço 44), good value food (pizza and pasta for vegetarians) and an excellent house red wine – if it looks full, there is plenty of space downstairs; *Laranjeira* (Rua Manuel Espregueira 24), basic but fine; or *Os Tres Arcos* (Largo João Tomás da Corta 25, by the Jardim Marginal), the best of the lot, with excellent food and vinho verde, and a bar with cheap snacks.

Viana is a good **base** for exploring much of the Minho: there's easy and regular access by **bus** to Ponte de Lima (16 daily; note the Monday fair every other week) and to Arcos de Valdevez (12.30pm, 1.30pm, 4.05pm, and 6pm), and by **train** south to Barcelos or up the coast towards Caminha (see below). Aside from *festa*-time, there is a bus stop in the centre on the Largo 5 de Outubro; the main station, the *Central de Camionagem*, is right at the top of the Rua da Bandeira. The agency, AVIC (Rua dos Cambatientes; ☎24081) run boat trips up the Lima river.

The Costa Verde: South and North of Viana

The **Costa Verde** between Póvoa de Varzim (see *Porto and the Douro* chapter) and Caminha is almost continuous beach, with the road for the most part a kilometre or so inland. There are at least four buses a day in each direction, most using Viana as an axis; in addition there are trains along the coast from Viana to Caminha.

South of Viana

Fifteen kilometres south of Viana, the little fishing village of **MAR** (or, more fully, SÃO BARTOLOMEU DO MAR) fronts one of the best stretches of the Costa Verde. There is little to the place: just a church, shop and café (with a few rooms to let), and good unofficial camping amid the sheltered pines behind. As well as fishing, the local economy revolves around gathering seaweed. Whole families harvest it on the beach using huge shrimping nets, which are then hauled across the sands by beautiful wooden carts pulled by oxen. The seaweed is finally stacked on the edge of the village before being spread as fertiliser on the coastal fields.

Development along these reaches is limited by law, as the coastline between the Rio Neiva estuary (halfway between Viana and Mar) south to Apúlia comes under the *Área de Paisagem Protegida do Litoral de Esposende*. Walk south from Mar, past another busy little fishing community, and you probably won't see another tourist all the way to Esposende. **ESPOSENDE** itself is a rather drab sprawl of buildings, sited inland on the estuary of the Rio Cávado. Its nearest beaches are 4km by road across the estuary at **OFIR**, where a couple of large luxury hotels have been built on a beautiful spit of pine-backed sand. This, if you are driving, could be a good place to stop and swim, but not really to stay.

North to Caminha

North of Viana the **Minho railway line** follows the coast all the way to Caminha. It's cheap, stops at all the villages en route, and offers easy access to a sequence of, for the most part deserted, beaches. An alternative to the train, if you're feeling active, is to **walk**; one of our readers covered the stretch in a couple of days, camping overnight among the sheltered dunes at Afife.

AFIFE, whichever way you get there, is certainly a good goal: a tiny village with a fort and a small **pensão-restaurante** (3-star) and cheap, useful café-cum-shop at the railway station. The dunes – and a particularly wonderful expanse of beach – are fifteen to twenty minutes' walk from the village, the least frequented parts being to the south. On the north side, there is an official **campsite** in the pine woods at GELFA.

Five kilometres up the coast, and the next stop on the railway, is **VILA PRAIA DE ÂNCORA**. This is larger – almost a real resort – and popular with local Portuguese at weekends. The beach, which is right alongside the railway line, is again superb, sheltered by hills and drifting back into a beautiful river estuary, where you can swim enjoyably even when the Atlantic breezes are blowing towels around the sands. Finding a **room** for a few days should not be hard: there's a 2-star *pensão-restaurante*, a 2-star hotel, and a summer **Turismo** that arranges *quartos* in private houses. There's also unofficial camping by the fort on the beach. **Restaurants** are plentiful, if somewhat standard, with good fresh fish; the *Café Central*, opposite the train station, has cheap meals too.

North of here, **MOLEDO** offers the railway traveller's last chance of sea swimming (there are river beaches all along the Minho). Very much in the

Vila Praia mould, it again has a fort – this time half ruined, guarding the river from a long, sandy spit – and is predominantly a Portuguese family resort. If you're heading on to Caminha, Valença, or Spain, you could easily stop off here, wander down to the beach, and then catch the next train.

Caminha to Valença

Rather like a small version of Viana do Castelo, **CAMINHA** is a quiet river port with a few reminders of better days, principally in the main square, with its battlemented town hall and Renaissance clock tower. In previous years it had a ferry link across the river to La Guardia in Spain, though this is currently suspended (there are plans to revive it); a service still operates to the east meanwhile at Vila Nova de Cerveira.

Caminha's most distinguished building is the **Igreja Matriz**, a couple of minutes' walk away towards the river. (Take the street through the arch – past the Turismo.) This church was built towards the end of the fifteenth century when Caminha was reputed to rival Porto in trade, and stands within part of the old city walls. Try and find someone with a key, for it has a magnificent inlaid *artesanado* ceiling – a rare burst of Moorish inspiration in the north. Note also the figures carved on the two Renaissance doorways, one on the north side giving the finger to Spain across the river!

The town is a pleasant stopover, either for a night, or for a meal between trains. The *Restaurante Caminhense* (in the main square) has superb regional specialities, and there's good food, too, at the more reasonably priced *A Lareira* and *Adega do Chico* on Rua Visconde de Sousa Rego (head up the right-hand side of the main square, away from the clocktower).

There is one upmarket **pension**, *Galo d'Ouro* (Rua da Corredoura 15, ☎058/921160), and the possibility of **rooms** in a couple of houses near the station (turn right and head for the water, then turn left). Of the two local **campsites**, the one inland at VILAR DO MOUROS (weekday buses 11.30am and 6.30pm from the café/stop 200m left out of the station) is nicely positioned, by a small river. The alternative, usually a little crowded, is the *Orbitur* site, next to the river 2km south of Caminha (weekday buses from the town hall in the main square at 11.30am, 1pm, and 6pm stop close by).

The *Orbitur* site faces the island of the **Fortaleza da Ínsua**, to which fishermen run trips on Sundays. If you want to arrange something during the week (for the next morning), ask in the *Café Valadores* (fourth right down Rua Visconde de Sousa Rego) for directions to António Garrafão's house. He will only go if there is a reasonably large group gathered.

Vila Nova de Cerveira

More or less hourly **trains** run along the banks of the River Minho to **VILA NOVA DE CERVEIRA**, a small walled town, with a car and passenger ferry – little more than a floating platform – which drifts hourly across the river to GOYAN in Galicia. The ferry (40esc passengers, 250esc cars) has turned the village into something of a shopping centre for Spaniards. Staying in Portugal, the Minho rail line continues to the east to Valença and Monção.

Valença and around

More village than town, **VALENÇA** is quite absurdly quaint, clumped amid perfectly preserved and multi-layered seventeenth-century ramparts on a hillock above the river. In the daytime its 'charm' is exploited by border souvenir shops, catering to the day-trippers who cross the border from Spain to pick up Portuguese linen and low-duty electrical goods. (Small-scale smuggling of such items is probably Valença's major industry). By late afternoon however the crowds are gone and at night it's almost a ghost town. There are great walks down by the river and along the ramparts (watch out for hidden stairwells), and, an equally fine sight just inside the walls, a fire station with a couple of gleaming red engines straight out of a 1950s children's book.

The town is not a bad place to stay, either, if you can find a **room**. Try asking at the *Bar Cantinho* (Rua Conselheiro Lopes da Silva) or in any of the countless **restaurants**. Alternatively you could **camp** below the ramparts at the western end, as everybody else does, or find your own hidden corner between the fortifications themselves. The town's only **pension**, the *Rio Minho* (Largo da Estação, ☎051/22331; on the other side of the road from the station, almost 2km away), is a bit the worse for wear and often full, but offers a good restaurant.

There is a huge Thursday **market**, beside the **Turismo** (open until 7pm in summer), between the station and town.

Crossing to Spain: Tuy

Just a mile distant from Valença, Spanish **TUY** is an ancient, pyramid-shaped town with a grand battlemented parish church. It, too, is partly walled and it looks far sturdier than Valença, though the first English *Guide to Portugal* (Murray's in 1855) reported that 'the guns of Valença could without difficulty lay Tuy in ruins'. If you're not planning to go on by train, walk across the frontier bridge to explore Tuy's old quarter by the river.

By **rail** you can go direct from Valença, with a passport stop at the border, to Vigo, in easy reach of Santiago de Compostela, the great and beautiful pilgrimage town of Galicia. Don't forget to get your passport stamped.

Paredes da Coura

PAREDES DA COURA, 28km inland from Valença, claims to be the oldest village in Portugal – and also declares itself a centre of trout fishing. The first claim is conceivable, the second a bit stretched, as it's all done from a feedpen these days. If you are headed for Ponte da Barca or Ponte de Lima, it's a pleasant enough detour, nonetheless. You can climb up to the top of the town for views over an almost Swiss landscape, with chalet-style houses and white church spires, or follow the track down beyond the football pitch to the river for the town's best swimming spot (at lunchtime no one is around).

The best **place to stay**, with a range of prices, is *Pensão Miquelina* (Rua Conselheiro Miguel Dantas, ☎058/92103), which is not far from the **Turismo**, an old prison. A daily bus runs to the town from Valença, leaving, at around 5pm, from the old Mercado, on the way to the train station.

Along the Minho: Monção and Melgaço

The best section of the Minho, in Portugal at least, is the route from Valença east to Melgaço, a minor border crossing, with buses on the Spanish side to Orense. The Minho rail line runs as far as Monçao, with buses taking over along the last stretch to Melgaço. At the latter town, you are also well poised for an exploration of the northern reaches of the Parque Nacional da Peneda Gerês – covered later in this chapter.

Monçao

Visually the **fortress** at **MONÇÃO** doesn't quite match up that of Valença – there being only one doorway (*Porta de Salvaterra*), a section of walling above the bus depot, and a high defensive walkway that runs along the northern, river-facing side of town. But the town's history, in which two local women played a prominent part, provides a colourful backdrop to the fortifications.

The principal figure is **Deu-la-deu Martins**, who is commemorated by a statue in the Largo da Loreta (opposite the **Turismo**, close to the central Praça da República). Her tale, similar to a number of other siege accounts across Portugal and Spain, recalls a crucial moment in the mid-seventeenth-century Wars of Restoration, when the Spanish troops had besieged the townspeople to the point of starvation. Deu-la-deu, the judge's wife, baked some cakes, using much skill and next to no flour, and had them presented to the Spanish camp with an offer to 'make more if they needed them'. The psychological effect of this bluff was so great that the enemy promptly gave up and went away. Local *pãozinhos* (little bread cakes) are still baked in her honour; her birthplace is off the Praça, above the butcher's shop on the arched side road.

A second siege later in the same war was relieved in 1659 when the **Countess of Castelo Melhor**, perhaps inspired by earlier example, resorted to psychological warfare once again. The story goes that having negotiated a ceasefire on condition that full military honours be given to her men, the Countess relinquished her 236 surviving fighters to the Spanish army; knowing nothing of the town's 2000 fatalities, the enemy assumed they had been kept at bay by this paltry platoon, and duly retreated in shame.

In the town, behind the mask of new paint and building work, there are a couple of interesting older places to visit. The seventeenth-century **Misericórdia** on the central square contains some magnificent *azulejos*, as does the Romanesque **Matriz** (at the centre of a maze of ancient streets), which houses various tombs, including that of Deu-la-deu herself.

The Spa, Cortes and Lapela

The presence of a **thermal spa** to the east of the town (follow the walls) has turned Monção into something of a resort for Spanish day-trippers and Portuguese weekenders. Aside from the dubious pleasures of the alkaline water, there's a park and a free **campsite** by the river; if you swim in the latter, take care with the currents.

Further afield to the west of the town, a pleasant walk trails off into the woods from the stop at *Senhora da Cabeça* to the hamlet of **CORTES**, which was Monção's medieval site. About 3km further west (or a couple of stops back on the railway from Valença) is **LAPELA**, whose river beach is safer for swimmers. The village is dominated by a lofty **tower**, all that remains of a fortress destroyed in 1706 to provide materials for the restoration of the battered walls of Monção.

Accommodation and Food

Pensions in Monção raise their rates with each passing day, but you can still find a reasonably priced bed at the *Central* (Largo da Loreta, ☎051/52314); above the *Pastelaria Raiano* next door; at *Residencial Esteves* (Praça da República, near the station, ☎051/52386); or above the *Galleria Melis* (Praça Deu-la-deu). Better still for price and atmosphere is the *Casa Constantino* (Rua da Independência 24) with a couple of rooms overlooking the river. Or finally, in the rock-bottom range, there's *Ponte da Lima* (near *Esteves*), which promotes itself as 'an ancient house with modern service' – don't believe it!

The best place to **eat** is with the locals on the first floor of the other *Central*, diagonally opposite in the same square, or at the Spanish-run *El Pollo Rico* (opposite the station), 'the restaurant which Monção is proud to have'. Fancier, though not expensive, is *Restaurante Mané* (Rua General Pimenta de Castro), with the best fish dishes but no atmosphere, and the pleasanter *Quinta da Oliveira* (Estrada dos Arcos), 400m down the road to Braga.

Minho trout and salmon are always tremendous (even if the eggs do come from Sweden), and between January and March the rich, eel-like **lamprey** are in season – avoid them in other months, as they can be toxic if they're not absolutely fresh. The local *vinho verde,* the finest in the country, is available on draught in a couple of bars off the main square. Most delicious of all is the *Palácio de Brejoeira Alvarinho*, which, as another splendid Monção one-liner puts it, 'someone in France once classified as being the best in the world'.

The local **festas** of *Corpo de Deus* (Corpus Christi; June 18) and particularly of *N. S. das Dores* (Sept. 19–22) are interesting times to visit – though you are unlikely to find a room. The former perpetuates medieval superstition in an elaborate enactment of the Fight against Evil, a battle that looks something like the tale of St. George and the Dragon.

Leaving Monçao, trains to Valença leave at 6.25am, 11.20am, and 6.45pm only, and **buses** for Melgaço go from outside the train station at 9.15am (Mon.–Sat.), 11.50am, 2.20pm, 5.35pm (Mon.–Fri.), and 6.30pm. From the **bus station** (turn right out of the train station) you can reach Braga (twice a day) and most other main towns. Monção has a Thursday market.

On to Melgaço

An historic incident in Anglo-Portuguese relations took place on the fragile-looking bridge over the Rio Mouro just before **CEIVÃES**, 8km along the road to Melgaço. Cascades of rubbish tumble down the banks below the spot where John of Gaunt, the Duke of Lancaster, arranged the marriage of his daughter Philippa to King Dom João I in 1386, an arrangement that resulted in the signing of the **Treaty of Windsor** (see "Batalha", in *Estremadura and Ribatejo*) between the two countries. It gave rise to an alliance lasting over five hundred years and to the naming of numerous public places as 'Praça Felipa de Lencastre'.

Thermal spa enthusiasts might want to ask the driver of the Monção–Melgaço bus to stop at **PESO** (5km short of the journey's end). This is a tiny spa town, spread along the main road and looking down on a magnificent curve of the river. There's a lovely (and free) **campsite** set in lush riverside gardens, a **Turismo**, and some **pensions**, of which *Rocha* (☎051/42356) and *Águas de Melgaço* (☎051/42262) are marginally the cheaper.

Melgaço and around

MELGAÇO is a small town sitting high above the Rio Minho, and if its rural origins are somewhat obscured by the modern developments that sprawl along the main road, the accent and the mentality remain unchanged. With the exception of a few *festa* days in mid-August when a display of tractors, an array of the town's long-reputed smoked hams (*presunto*), a craft exhibition and a performance from the school banjo band are organised, little happens. Try to arrive for the **Friday market** when chickens, ducks, sticky buns, furniture, pottery, cabbages and corsets cover the stretch around the old walls.

At other times the best reasons for coming to Melgaço are that it is so obviously off the tourist track – and that it gives easy access to the northern part of the **Parque Nacional da Peneda-Gerês** and to Spanish Galicia (see below for access details). Its one historic feature are the ruins of a fortress, much fought over during the Wars of Restoration, but now little more than a **tower** and a few walls handy for hanging out washing.

In the alleys below, a couple of **café-restaurants** offer good food at reasonable prices and there are two **pensions** towards the main road, *Flor-Minho* (quieter and more pleasant, in the central square) and *Pemba* (near the bus stop; ☎42555).

Buses leave for Monção every day (7.45am, 2.30pm, 4.40pm, and Mon.–Fri. 8.40am and 11.45am), and connect for Braga, Coimbra, Porto and Lisbon.

Romanesque Churches and the Spanish Border

Short **excursions** from Melgaço might include the two **Romanesque churches** of PADERNE (3km, off the road to Monção) or NOSSA SENHORA DA ORADA (1km east).

The **border post** at PONTE BARXAS (open Apr.–Oct. 7am–midnight, Nov.–Mar. 8am–9pm) is 1km away from **SÃO GREGÓRIO** (8km; inexpensive taxis from Melgaço). Across the frontier in Spain, buses leave for RIBADAVIA and ORENSE at 7am and 1pm (weekdays only).

Both Ribadavia (along the Minho and with wonderful red wine) and CELANOVA (on a different route to Orense and dwarfed by a vast medieval monastery) are within striking distance, and are two of the most lovely and characteristic towns of Spanish Galicia. The Minho itself – or Miño as it becomes known – is more placid in the further reaches, as it is dammed shortly after the point when both of its banks are within Spain.

Into the Parque Nacional da Peneda-Gerês

The route from Melgaço into the **Peneda** area of the **Parque Nacional da Peneda-Gerês** is one of the best approaches to this region of staggering scenery and awesome rock formations. For details of the region, see the section on Gerês at the end of this chapter.

Weekday **buses** leave Melgaço for Castro Laboreiro between 5 and 7am (with additional noon service on Friday) and return at 6.45pm – check times with the parcel depot just around the corner from the *Pemba*.

South to the Rio Lima

The route **south from Monção** takes you first across the **Rio Vez**, then to the broader and more beautiful **Rio Lima**, the legendary "River of Forgetfulness". The most rewarding towns to base yourself, or visit, are **Arcos de Valdevez, Ponte da Barca** and **Ponte de Lima**. From any one of these you could have fine walks into the hilly and wooded countryside around, perhaps exploring one or two of the many **Romanesque churches** – such as that at Bravães (see opposite).

If you are headed for the **Parque Nacional da Peneda-Gerês**, Arcos offers bus connections to **Soajo**, at the edge of the park, and Ponte da Barca to **Lindoso**, further to the east. These are covered in the Gerês Park section.

Arcos de Valdevez

ARCOS DE VALDEVEZ ('Arches of the Valley of the Vez') comes alive in mid-August with a three-day **festival**, featuring *gigantes*, red-caped drummers, horse races and fireworks. Traditionally these celebrations should take place on the last weekend of the holiday month, but they've been shifted to take account of local emigrants who return to work abroad at the end of August; one of the festival days is actually named the *Dia do Emigrante*.

At other times, it is a sleepy little town, with a weekly spot of animation for the Wednesday market. As the name implies, it spreads along the banks of the Rio Vez, a tributary of the Lima – here just 4km south. You can **camp** unofficially on the banks of the Vez, downstream from the town, or there are several good and reasonably-priced **pensions**. In the upper part of town, known as Valeta (second left up to Largo da Lapa and down the left-hand side of the church), there are several excellent cheap **restaurants** on the Rua de São João. At the end of the street and on the right, the small and unpretentious *Pensão Flor do Minho* (Largo da Valeta 11–15, ☎058/65216). The second pension is by the riverside pension across the bridge. It is an attractive place to spend a night, though don't expect much more than a taste of the local *pão de ló* (sponge cake) and a walk by the river.

The **Turismo** opposite the bridge (July–Sept. 9am–1pm and 2–7pm, except Sun. 9am–noon) has free maps and advice on the nearby Parque Nacional da Peneda-Gerês. For information on the **bus** service to Lindoso and Paredes da Coura ask at the *RN* depot above the Largo da Lapa, where there are also regular buses to Monção, Ponte de Lima and Viana do Castelo (7.40am,

8.50am, 12.05pm, 1.05pm, and 6pm). Buses to Braga (15 each weekday, fewer on weekends), Sistelo (Mon.–Sat. at noon), and Soajo (Mon.–Sat. 12.20pm, plus 5.30pm Mon.–Fri.) leave from a stop by the Turismo.

On to the Lima: Ponte da Barca

The **Rio Lima**, whose valley is perhaps the most beautiful in Portugal, was thought by the Romans to be Lethe, the mythical River of Oblivion. Beyond it, they imagined, lay the Elysian Fields; to cross would mean certain destruction, for its waters possessed the power of the lotus, making the traveller forget country and home. The Consul Decimus Junius Brutus, having led his legions across most of Spain, had to seize the standard and plunge into the water shouting the names of his legionaries from the far bank before they could be persuaded to follow.

There are roads along both banks of the Lima from Viana do Castelo but the valley has more impact if you come upon it from inland. Coming down from Monção and Arcos or up from Braga the most obvious town to approach is Ponte da Barca.

Ponte da Barca

Ignoring the modern suburbs of **PONTE DA BARCA**, and heading for the river, the small old town quarters form a quintessential pastoral vision. The Lima is spanned here by an imposing old bridge; alongside is a seventeenth-century *mercado* and, on the corner, a seasonal **Turismo**. On Wednesdays there's a superb market, which again spreads out by the river banks.

You can camp (fairly discreetly) along the river bank and enjoy perfect, pink-hazed, evening light. There are also two good **pension-restaurants** overlooking the bridge; the place run by Maria Gomes (Rua Conselheiro Rocha Peixoto 13, ☎058/42288) is especially recommended, and worth phoning ahead to book. The town's *romaria* takes place around the weekend closest to August 19.

From the **bus stop** by the bridge, near the arches of the town hall, you can reach Lindoso (Mon.–Fri. 7.35am, 5.20pm, and 6.30pm, plus 12.10pm every day) and Braga (5 daily).

Bravães

Walking in the Lima region, amid pine and eucalyptus forests, is a treat, and in almost any village you'll come upon a **Romanesque church**, simple and rustic in design but often with beautiful naive carvings on its doorways and columns. Most were built in the twelfth and thirteenth centuries under the supervision of the Cluniac monks, who brought their architecture to Spain and Portugal along the pilgrimage routes to Santiago de Compostela in Galicia; the main Portuguese route ran through Braga and so Minho has the highest concentration.

They are really best encountered by chance, hidden among the trees of some once-remote roadside village: and this, even if you plan the visit, is what it feels like to arrive at the twelfth-century church of **São Salvador** at **BRAVÃES**. It stands just to the right of the road in this small hamlet (6km out of Ponte da Barca along N203 to Ponte de Lima) – a lovely walk through low hills traced everywhere with vines, often suspended in trellises above some other crop. The church's two sculpted **doorways** are perhaps the best in the country, filled with carvings of doves, griffins, monkeys and two of the local wide-horned oxen. The interior is kept locked but ask at the cottage behind and the doors will be flung open for you, lighting up medieval murals of St. Sebastian and the Virgin.

There's a bar in Bravães where you can debate the chances of a bus going on to Ponte de Lima, though you'll probably find it's easier to hitch – most drivers stop even if they do tend to be going just a couple of kilometres.

Ponte de Lima

Like Ponte da Barca, **PONTE DE LIMA** lies at the end of a low stone bridge – Roman in origin, it is said to mark the path of their first hesitant crossing. The river here offers pleasant swimming and has wide sandbanks where the town's bi-monthly Monday **market**, the oldest in Portugal, has been held since a charter of 1125. So too have the curiously named '**New Fairs**' (second/third weekend of September), a tremendous festival and market, seemingly attended by half the Minho, with a traditional bull-taunting game by the bridge, fireworks, an amusement park, wandering accordionists and *gigantes*, and a large brass band competition.

At other times the evening focus is a long riverside **alameda** shaded by magnificent plane trees; it leads to the rambling old convent of Santo António, which has a small museum of treasures in its church. In the town itself there are sixteenth-century **mansions** with stone coats of arms, and interesting remains of the old **keep**, used into the 1960s as a prison (the occupants were allowed to hang cups down from the windows for money and cigarettes).

But the real attraction lies once again less in buildings than in the place itself. And, not least, in the bars, which serve wine straight from the barrel into handleless porcelain cups. There are lots of inexpensive café-restaurants along the riverfront, though only one **pension**, the *São João* (Rua do Rosário ☎058/941288) near the Roman bridge; this is inexpensive, excellent and with good food downstairs.

There is also a **Turismo**, combined with the headquarters of the Manor Houses Association, which deals in cosy (and expensive) accommodation with Portuguese aristocrats. Alternatively, you could camp across the bridge on the riverbank, where during the New Fairs a rainbow site emerges, with families washing clothes, auctioning cattle and letting off fireworks through the night.

Braga

BRAGA, the Turismo pamphlet claims, is the Portuguese Rome. This clearly is going over the top – though it is a useful illustration of the city's ecclesiastical pretensions. One of the most ancient towns in Portugal, founded by the Romans in 279 B.C., Braga was an important Visigothic

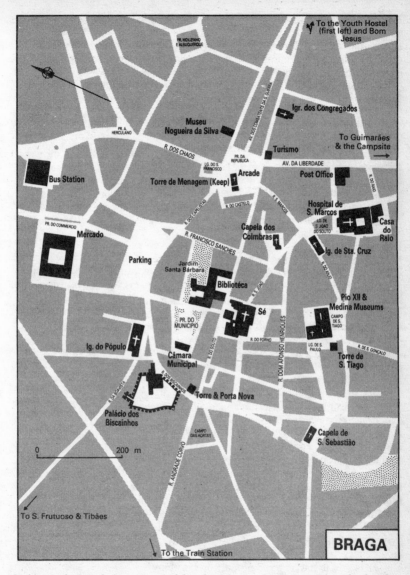

To the Youth Hostel (first left) and Bom Jesus

PR. MOUZINHO E ALBUQUERQUE

Museu Nogueira da Silva

Igr. dos Congregados

R. DOS COMBATENTES DA G. GUERRA

PR. Á. HERCULANO

R. DOS CHAOS

Turismo

To Guimarães & the Campsite

LG. DO S. FRANCISCO

PR. DA REPUBLICA

Arcade

AV. DA LIBERDADE

Bus Station

Torre de Menagem (Keep)

Post Office

R. DO CASTELO

R. MARCOS

Hospital de S. Marcos

R. DO JANO

PR. DO COMMERCIO

Mercado

R. DOS CAPELISTAS

Capela dos Coimbras

LG. DE S. JOÃO DO SOUTO

Casa do Raio

R. FRANCISCO SANCHES

Parking

Jardim Santa Bárbara

Ig. de Sta. Cruz

Bibliotéca

R. D. JANO

Sé

Pio XII & Medina Museums

PR. DO MUNICIPIO

CAMPO DE S. TIAGO

R. DO FORNO

Ig. do Pópulo

R. DOM AFONSO HENRIQUES

LG. DE S. PAULO

R. DE S. GONCALO

Torre de S. Tiago

Câmara Municipal

R. DO SOUTO

R. S. JOÃO

Torre & Porta Nova

R. ANDRADE CORVIO

Palácio dos Biscainhos

CAMPO DAS HORTAS

Capela de S. Sebastião

0   200 m

To S. Frutuoso & Tibães

To the Train Station

BRAGA

bishopric before being occupied by the Moors. Reconquered early, by the end of the eleventh century its archbishops were pressing for recognition as 'Primate of the Spains', a title they disputed bitterly with Toledo over the next six centuries.

It is still Portugal's religious capital – the scene of spectacular **Easter celebrations** with torchlit processions and weirdly hooded penitents – and the bastion of its reactionary politics. It was here, in 1926, that the military coup leading to Salazar's dictatorship was launched, while in the more recent past, a year after the 1974 Revolution, the Archbishop of Braga personally incited a mob to attack local Communist offices. Today, however, a socialist majority council struggles against the immediate and slightly oppressive feel of a cathedral city, of churches and buildings endowed by archbishops who often wielded only slightly less power and wealth than the nation's kings.

The City

Whatever your interests, looking around Braga you won't be able to miss the old **Archbishop's Palace**, a great fortress-like building, right at the centre of the old town. In medieval times it actually covered a tenth of the city, and today it easily accommodates the municipal library and various faculties of the university. The library is open weekdays and inside you can inspect the ornate ceilings of the medieval reading-room and the *Sala de Dr. Manuel Monteiro*.

The Sé

Immediately opposite the palace is the **Sé** (cathedral). Like the palace, it encompasses Gothic, Renaissance and Baroque styles – though in origin it is Romanesque, founded in 1070 with the restoration of the bishopric. Its original south doorway is a survival from this earliest building, carved with rustic scenes from the legend of Reynard the Fox.

The most striking element of the building, however, is the intricate ornamentation of the roofline, commissioned by Braga's great Renaissance patron Archbishop Diogo de Sousa and executed by João de Castilho, later to become the architect of Lisbon's Jerónimos Monastery, greatest of all Manueline buildings.

Inside, the cathedral complex is disorienting: you enter through a courtyard fronting three Gothic chapels, a cloister and, most prominently, a ticket desk. Everything that can be locked at Braga has been, so you shuffle around behind a guide with a fistful of keys (9–11.30am and 2–5.30pm; nominal charge). The tour aside, each of these three outer chapels is worth the visit, particularly the fourteenth-century **Capela dos Reis** (King's Chapel), built to house the tombs of the cathedral's founders – Henry of Burgundy, first Count of Portucale, and his wife Teresa – the parents of Afonso Henriques, founder of the kingdom. Exposed beside them is the mummified body of Archbishop Lourenço, found 'uncorrupt' when his tomb was opened in the seventeenth century; he had fought in the great victory over the Castilians at Aljubarrota (1385), riding around bestowing indulgences on the ranks, and there sustained a scar on his cheek – which he himself is said to have carved proudly on his effigy.

Beyond the chapels is the treasury, now the cathedral **museum** (9am–12.30pm and 1.30–6pm). One of the richest collections in Portugal, it has pieces from the tenth to the eighteenth centuries, though the display does its best to make it all look dull. Eventually you emerge alongside magnificent Baroque twin organs in the **Coro Alto** to gaze down into the cathedral proper – unexpectedly small and, when you descend, remarkably uninteresting.

Elsewhere in the Old Town: Cafés and Mansions

Unless you have an academic interest, you're unlikely to find Braga's other churches very inspiring: most, like the cathedral, were stripped and modernised in the late-seventeenth and eighteenth centuries. The most interesting, architecturally, is the small Renaissance **Capela dos Coimbras**, another of De Sousa's commissions, sited on the Largo Carlos Amarante.

Time is better spent at Bom Jesus do Monte, just outside the city (see overpage), or among the **coffee houses** on and around the Avenida da Liberdade. The *Café Astória* and *O Nosso* (both on the Avenida) and *O Brasileiro* (Rua Dom Marcos) are majestic old places, mahogany-panelled and with cut-glass windows, going very beautifully to seed. And there's the *Café Avenida*, in the gardens of the Avenida Central, all Art Deco curved glass, chrome and black leather.

The **mansions** from earlier ages are interesting, too, at least in passing, with their extravagant Baroque and Rococo facades. The Câmara Municipal and Palácio do Raio, both by André Soares, are good examples, as is the Hospital de São Marcos with its apostle-roofline. Best of all perhaps, and visitable, is the mid-seventeenth-century **Casa dos Biscainhos** – its flagstoned ground floor characteristically designed to allow carriages through to the stables. Nowadays it houses a small museum (Tues.–Sun. 10am–noon and 1–5.30pm).

In the Campo de São Tiago, a former seminary has been turned into the town **museum** (10am–noon and 2–5pm; closed Mon.). It in fact consists of two distinct collections: the *Pio XII*, housing dusty religious regalia, and the *Medina*, named after the Portuguese painter and donated on the understanding that it would be housed separately from any other exhibits. Save your energy for the collection of fonts and capitals gathered in a courtyard like standing stones, or for the small excavation of a first-century Roman water tank – and try persuading the guide to hold back on a few of the endless locked doors. If you feel in a mood for museums, the contents of the **Casa Nogueira da Silva** (Avda. Central; closed Sun.), with its variety of paintings, Chinese porcelain and carpets, might be more rewarding.

One last, if extremely modest, curiosity in the old town is the so-called **Fonte do Idolo**, a rough-hewn fountain with a Roman inscription, possibly of Celtic origin.

Practicalities

The **Turismo** (at the corner of Avda. Central) has copies of the local *Correio do Minho*, good for advice on most events in the region. It also offers an impressive large-scale map of the city – a useful supplement to ours.

Accommodation

The least expensive places to stay are the **rooms** above the *Restaurante Marisqueira* (Rua do Castelo 15, ☎053/22152), or, better, at no.128 on the Avenida. There are also pleasant and inexpensive rooms at the church-run *Casa Santa Zita* (Rua São João 20, ☎053/23494), and a well-equipped **youth hostel** (Rua Santa Margarida 6, off Avda. Central; closes midnight).

Regular **pensions**, if they have space, are more enticing. Cheapest is the *Hotel Francfort* (Avda. Central, ☎053/22648), decaying but charming and friendly. Moving a little upmarket, pick from the *Pensão Económica* (Largo São João do Souto 131, ☎053/23160), *Residencial Inácio Filho* (Rua Justino Cruz, left off Rua do Souto heading from the Turismo; ☎053/23849) or *Pensão Comercial* (Rua dos Chãos 33, ☎053/22628).

The local **campsite**, *Parque da Ponte*, is a fairly long walk out of town along the Guimarães road – but very cheap and right next to the municipal **swimming pool**.

Restaurants and Bars

Restaurants are pretty sparse and the central ones tend to be expensive. Four very positive recommendations, however, are:

A Ceia, Rua do Raio (closed Sun.). Always crowded with locals, so arrive early.

Above the Co-op Supermarket, Avda. Central. Lunchtime only, but rock-bottom prices.

Conde Dom Henrique, Rua do Forno. At the heart to the old town and therefore more expensive, but worth it.

Rio Este, Rua das Barbarosas (first left having crossed the river down Avda. da Liberdade). The house speciality – possibly the nastiest dish in Portugal, and by a long way the most disgusting taste I've ever experienced – is *Papas de Sarrabulho* (giblets in pig's blood), but they serve seafood dishes as well.

Festivals

In addition to the Semana Santa (Easter Week) celebrations, the whole city is illuminated for the **Festas de São João** (June 23–24; ancient folk dances, an amusement park, general partying). The main **pilgrimage to Bom Jesus**, probably best avoided, takes place over Whitsun (six weeks after Easter). At SÃO BENTO DA PORTA ABERTA, near the Parque Nacional, there's a weekend of picnicking around August 7, with regular buses running from the station.

There is a regular **Tuesday market**.

Buses

You can go by **bus** from Braga to almost anywhere in Minho, including Ponte da Barca, Ponte da Lima (via Frutuoso), Arcos de Valdevez, Guimarães, Barcelos, Póvoa de Varzim and Gerês (all 7–9 buses daily). Some useful **times** are Viana do Castelo (7am, 10.05am, 4.05pm, 7.10pm, plus 12.35pm Sun.), Monção (9am, 12:55pm, 4pm), Melgaço and border post (6.15pm weekdays), Lindoso (5 between 9.45am and 5.20pm), Cabeceiras do Basto via Póvoa de Lanhoso (7.15am, 10.35am, 3.40pm, 6pm), and Chaves via Montalegre (7.25am, 9.25am, 1.15pm, 4.15pm). All of these depart from the main bus station (see plan); some make an additional stop on the Guimarães road, at the bottom of the Avenida da Liberdade.

Exceptions are local buses to Bom Jesus (from near the Hospital de São Marcos, by the fountain), and to São Frutuoso/Tibães (from the corner of Rua do Carvalho/Rua de São Vicente: take the bus marked *Ruães*).

If you are heading for **Gerês**, the park headquarters in Braga are at Rua de São Geraldo 19 (closes 5.30pm and weekends).

Bom Jesus and other Sights outside the City

BOM JESUS, one of Portugal's best-known images, is as much concept as building, a monumental place of homage created by Braga's archbishop in the first decades of the eighteenth century. It is a vast ornamental stairway of granite and white plaster cut into the side of a densely wooded mount high above the city. There is no particular reason for its presence, no miracle or vision, yet it remains the object of devoted pilgrimage, penitents often climbing on their knees.

Buses run the five kilometres from Braga about every half-hour (the #5 direct from the station is another possibility), more frequently at weekends when half the city piles up there to picnic. You're dropped near the base of the stairway, but most of the local families, armed with immense baskets of food, ride straight to the top in an ingenious hydraulic funicular.

If you resist temptation and make the climb up the **stairway**, Bom Jesus's simple **allegory** unfolds. Each landing has a fountain: the first symbolises the wounds of Christ, the next five the Senses, and the final three represent the Virtues. At each corner, too, are chapels with mouldering wooden, larger-than-life tableaux of the Life of Christ; these are arranged chronologically, leading to the Crucifixion at the altar of the church. As a design it's a triumph – one of the greatest of all Baroque architecture – and was later copied with even greater success at Lamego.

Bom Jesus is also a very pleasant place to spend an afternoon or, best of all, early evening. There are wooded gardens, grottoes and miniature boating pools behind the church, and (at the far end) several cheap, lively **restau-**

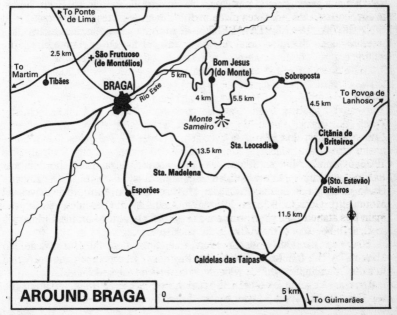

rants – filled on Saturdays with parties from a literally constant stream of weddings. If you want to stay up on the mount there's a 1-star **hotel** overlooking the steps (the *Sul Americano*; ☎053/22515) and a couple of simple, less well-sited **pensions** by the restaurants.

São Frutuoso and Tibães

Slightly closer in – 3½km northwest of Braga – is another worthwhile church excursion: **São Frutuoso**, built by the Visigoths in the seventh century, adapted by the Moors, and then restored to Christian worship after the Reconquest. It is a gem of a church, set in open countryside with a flanking eighteenth-century chapel, and it should be open Tuesday to Sunday until 5pm, though keys are kept in a nearby house if need be. The approach is from SÃO JERÓNIMO REAL down a track to the right (marked).

Half a kilometre beyond the Frutuoso turning, to the left of the main road, a paved track also leads to the **Monastery** of **TIBÃES** (9am–noon and 2–5pm; closed Mon.), formerly the grandest Benedictine establishment in the land. A vast and ruined hulk, its abandoned medieval buildings, cloisters and rambling gardens were once occupied by gypsy families, but it is now private, the entrance to the courtyards guarded by a couple of alsatians. It is an evocative place though, if you feel like the walk, and you can look around the monastery **church**, which has been maintained. On some days there is a guided tour, on others you have to knock for the priest.

On the Road to Gerês – Nossa Senhora da Abadia

Turning off the Braga–Gerês road at BOURO SANTA MARIA (which has a shell of a monastery and a large Baroque church), you arrive at the shrine of **Nossa Senhora da Abadia**, said to be the oldest sanctuary in Portugal.

The site, like Bom Jesus, is a centre of pilgrimage, and loudspeakers can be heard along the approach calling the faithful to prayer. The focus is a twelfth-century wooden statue of the Virgin and Child, which the devoted kiss. The church itself is largely an eighteenth-century rebuilding. Outside are two elegant wings of monks' cells and usually some market stalls.

Buses run to Bouro on Sundays only at 10am, returning at 1pm.

Citânia de Briteiros

Citânias – Celtic hill settlements – lie scattered throughout the Minho. Remains of 27 have been identified along the coast, some 16 in the region between Braga and Guimarães alone. Most seem to date from the arrival of northern European Celts in the Iron Age (ca. 600–500 B.C.), though some are far earlier – having merged with an existing local culture established since Neolithic times (ca. 2000 B.C.). They were conquered late by the Romans (ca. 26–19 B.C.) and often appear to have been little affected by the invasion.

The **CITÂNIA DE BRITEIROS**, midway between Braga and Guimarães, is the most spectacular – and is reputed to have been a last stronghold against the Romans. It's an impressive and exciting site, including the foundations of over 150 huts, a couple of which have been rebuilt to give a sense of their

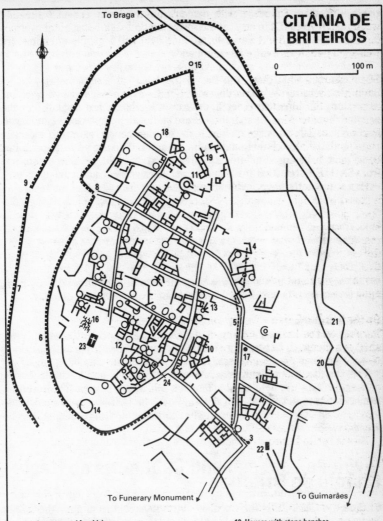

CITÂNIA DE BRITEIROS

To Braga

0   100 m

15

18
19
11
8
2
4
7
6
13
5
16
23
12
10
21
17
20
1
24
14
3
22

To Funerary Monument

To Guimarães

1. Area reserved for chickens
2. Main street with ducts for water supply
3. Early fountain
4. Water source (now defunct)
5. Ingenious method of transporting water
6. Inside wall
7. Second (of four) walls
8. Gateway
9. Gateway
10. House with various rooms
11. House with helix
12. Houses reconstructed by Martins Sarmento

13. Houses with stone benches
14. Circular house belonging to community
15. Single, isolated house outside inner walls
16. Small paved area
17. Cistern
18. Tunnel possibly leading to River Ave
19. Law courts(?), prisons(?)
20. Entrance
21. Parking
22. Guard's room
23. Chapel of S. Romão
24. Cross and Christian cemetery

scale and design. There's a clear network of paved streets and paths, two circuits of town walls, cisterns, stone guttering, and a public fountain (*fonte*). Most of the huts are circular with porches for their fires, though some are rectangular – among them a larger meeting house (*casa tribunal*) or prison.

The site is open 9am to dusk; don't miss the **funerary chamber** (no. 17 on the plan: a fair walk down the hill to the left of the settlement) with its geometrically patterned stone doorway. Similar examples, along with carved lintels from the huts and other finds from the *citânia*, are displayed at the Sarmento museum in Guimarães. These indicate that the settlement was abandoned as late as A.D. 300 and – unlike Conimbriga, another Celtic site near Coimbra – show little Roman influence other than the presence of coins. Strabo gave a vivid description of these northern tribes in his *Geographia* (ca. 20 B.C.). They organised mass sacrifices, he recorded, and consulted prisoner's entrails without removing them, but otherwise:

> *live simply, drink water and sleep on the bare earth . . . two thirds of the year they live on acorns, which they roast and grind to make bread. They also have beer. They lack wine but when they have it they drink it up, gathering for a family feast. At banquets they sit on a bench against the wall according to age and rank . . . When they assemble to drink they perform round dances to the flute or the horn, leaping in the air and crouching as they fall.*

Entrails aside – and they may have been Strabo's literary imagination – none of this seems far removed from the Minho and Trás-os-Montes of today.

Getting to Briteiros
There are just two **buses** direct to Briteiros from Braga (at 8.15am and 6pm). Otherwise you have to **hitch or walk**: either from Bom Jesus (set out along the road beyond the gardens and pensions; 9km), or from CALDAS DAS TAIPAS (on the Braga–Guimarães bus route; 6km).

Alternatively, you might be able to catch one of the buses which run from Guimarães through Caldas das Taipas to Póvoa de Lanhoso. Leaving the site, hitching a ride with other visitors, either to Braga or Guimarães, should be fairly easy.

Póvoa de Lanhoso and Cabeciras de Basto

If you are heading from Braga to the Gerês park (see last section in this chapter), you will pass through **Póvoa de Lanhoso**. This small provincial town also provides a transport link to the east into **Trás-os-Montes**, or south to the **Douro**, via the village of **Cabeceiras de Basto**.

Póvoa de Lanhoso

PÓVOA DE LANHOSO is a small, modern town sandwiched between two ancient sites. At the northern end of town (the approach from Braga), a steep mound rises up to one of the smallest **castles** in Portugal (open afternoons) and a scattering of chapels and picnic tables. In the fourteenth century, the lord of the shire was reported to have locked up his adulterous wife, her lover and their servants in the castle and ordered it to be burned; it was substantially rebuilt in the eighteenth century. The **restaurant** nearby keeps a set of keys and offers reasonable food and good views, if you can squeeze in between the parties of christening and wedding guests.

In the opposite direction, 3km out of town, the small church of **Fonte Arcada** is a short walk from the main road (past the white statue). The simple interior, characteristic of the Romanesque style, is in marked contrast to the complications of the doorway whose centrepiece is a relief of a large sheep.

Lanhoso has a central **pension**, though you would be wiser to move on. **Buses** connect the town with Braga (9.15am, 1.10pm, 3.35pm and 5.05pm), Caldas do Gerês (pick up one of four Chaves buses, 3km out on the main road to Cerdeirinha), Guimarães (ask at the newspaper kiosk) and Cabeceiras de Basto (7.50am, 11.10am, 4.15pm and 6.35pm).

Cabeceiras de Basto

CABECEIRAS DE BASTO is in the heart of the **Terras do Basto**, a fertile region that produces a strong *vinho verde*. The area's name comes from the Celtic statues, symbolic of power ('basto' meant 'I claim'), which have been dug up in several local spots. All of the unearthed figures have been headless, but the Cabeceiras *Basto* – proudly displayed in the gardens across from the bus depot – has sported a French head since a prank during the Napoleonic Wars. Equally esteemed in Cabeceiras is a local doctor whose reputation has soared to saintly heights, owing not only to his skill but also to his honesty and generosity. Senhor Doutor Francisco is said to accept as payment for his attentions whatever the patient can afford, be it a sack of grain or a chicken – astounding in a country where financial corruption is commonplace; the paragon's likeness stands outside the local hospital.

The Baroque **Mosteiro de Refojos**, the town's main sight, dominates the central square. It is one of the few religious institutions not to have succumbed to the temptation to bludgeon faith into the populace through a quartet of loudspeakers attached to the church. If you pay your respects to the sacristan, not only can you visit the treasury (a collection of statues and religious garments) but also gain privileged access to the clock tower, from which you can view the church's highlight, the *zimbório* (dome).

Rooms, Food and Festas

You can **stay** above one of the modern **café-restaurants** in the new part of Cabeceiras – try *A Cafil* or *São Miguel*. A short way up the road at the back of the Refojos Monastery, good food is to be had at *O Avenida*. Another area to explore is beyond a patch of ground set aside for the Monday **feira** – a left turn after the school takes you into the Campo do Guinchoso, where there's a **nightclub** (Thurs.–Sat. 10pm–2am and Sun. 4–7pm), a friendly **pastelaria**, and **swimming** in the river down beyond the new housing development.

As the centre of a very traditional and rural area (spot the *medas de palha* or haystacks woven around a central pole), Cabeciras's big event on the social calendar is the **agricultural show** in late September, known as the *Festas de São Miguel*. It's also an area whose landowners were hard hit by the

Revolution, and whose peeling houses are now reminders of the glory and elitism of Portugal's Age of Absolutism.

Buses

Three useful **bus routes** are to Celorico de Basto (8am, noon and 6.20pm), to Chaves (7.05pm, or 9.05pm on Sun.) and to Porto (9.25am Mon.–Sat.). ARCO DE BAULHE, the nearest **train station**, has eight daily connections enabling you to reach Mondim, Celorico or Amarante on the Tâmega Line (see *Porto and the Douro*).

South to Fafe

The routes south from Cabeceiras are enjoyable, leading through magnificent countryside, dotted with huge boulders, to Fafe. On the way you might want to stop between buses at ERVIDEIRO or GANDARELA (look out for the topiary). Four kilometres along the Gandarela road (6 daily buses) there is a **basket weaver**, running the only such cottage industry in the area.

FAFE itself is little more than an overgrown **bus station** with connections to almost anywhere you like (most regularly to Guimarães). It has a couple of pensions and a large revolutionary statue of a worker violently clubbing his bowler-hatted boss.

Guimarães

Birthplace of Afonso Henriques and first capital of Portucale, **GUIMARÃES** remains one of the most interesting towns in the country. It is also one of the most enjoyable – a lively, provincial place that comes as a relief after the somewhat stolid monumentality of Braga.

The Old Town and Museums

At the old centre of Guimarães are small enclosed squares and a handful of narrow medieval streets – among them the beautiful **Rua de Santa Maria** with its iron grilles and granite arches.

The natural place to head first is the **Castelo** (9am–12.30pm and 2–5pm; closed Mon.), whose great square keep and seven castellated towers are an enduring symbol of the emergent Portuguese nation. Built by Henry of Burgundy, it became the first court and stronghold of his son, Afonso Henriques. From here began the Reconquest and the creation of a kingdom which, within a century of Afonso's death, was to stretch to its present borders.

Afonso is said to have been born in the keep of the castle, and was probably baptised in the font of the diminutive Romanesque chapel of **São Miguel** (erratic opening times), on the grassy slope below. The third building here, the **Paço dos Duques**, was once the ruined medieval palace of the Dukes of Bragança, but under the Salazar dictatorship was 'restored' as an official residence. It looks ludicrous – like a mock-Gothic Victorian folly – and now houses rather dull collections of portraits, furniture and porcelain.

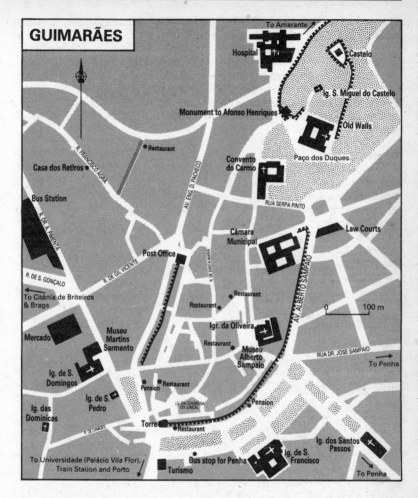

GUIMARÃES

(map labels)
To Amarante
Hospital
Castelo
Ig. S. Miguel do Castelo
Monument to Afonso Henriques
Old Walls
Convento do Carmo
Paço dos Duques
R. FRANCISCO AGRA
Restaurant
Casa dos Retiros
AV. ENG. D. PACHECO
RUA SERPA PINTO
Bus Station
Câmara Municipal
Law Courts
R. DA PIMENTA
Post Office
R. DE GIL VICENTE
R. DE S. GONÇALO
R. DE SANTA MARIA
Restaurant
To Citânia de Briteiros & Braga
Restaurant
Igr. da Oliveira
AV. ALBERTO SAMPAIO
0   100 m
Mercado
Museu Martins Sarmento
Restaurant
Museu Alberto Sampaio
RUA DR. JOSE SAMPAIO
To Penha
Ig. de S. Domingos
Pension
Restaurant
IG. DA CONDESSA DO JUNCAL
Ig. de S. Pedro
Pension
Ig. das Dominicas
R. DE CAMÕES
Torre
Restaurant
Ig. dos Santos Passos
To Universidade (Palácio Vila Flor), Train Station and Porto
Bus stop for Penha
Ig. de S. Francisco
Turismo
To Penha

Considerably more attractive than the latter exhibits are the children's toys – hammered out from old tin and no doubt lethal, but beautiful objects nonetheless — on sale in a number of shops opposite the castle.

The Sarmento and Sampaio Museums

The other two museums in Guimarães are, in contrast to the Paço, among the best outside Lisbon. Both insist on accompanied if not guided tours so you can't be in too much of a rush.

Finds from the *citânias* of Briteiros and Sabroso are displayed in the **Museu Martins Sarmento** (10am–noon and 2–5pm; closed Mon.). They include a remarkable series of bronze votive offerings (note the 'coach', pulled at each end by men and oxen), ornately patterned stone lintels and door jambs from the huts and – most spectacularly – the two *Pedras Formosas* and the *Colossus of Pedralva*.

The *Pedras* (literally, 'beautiful stones'), once taken to be sacrificial altars, are in fact the portals to funerary monuments, like that in situ at Briteiros. The colossus is more enigmatic and considerably more ancient, a vast granite hulk of a figure with arm raised aloft and an outsized phallus. It shares the bold, powerfully-hewn appearance of the stone boars found in Trás-os-Montes (in Bragança, for instance) and like them may date from pre-Celtic fertility cults of around 1500 to 1000 B.C.

The Sarmento museum is housed in the former convent of São Domingo, its larger exhibits arranged in the fourteenth-century Gothic cloister. Another convent, the seventeenth-century Santa Clara, is now the town hall and a third, the oldest and most beautiful, has become the **Museu Alberto Sampaio** (10am–12.30pm and 2–5.30pm; closed Mon.). This is mostly just the treasury of the collegiate church and monastery but it is outstandingly exhibited and, for once, has pieces of real beauty as well as weight-value. The highlight is a brilliantly composed and humanised silver-gilt *Triptych of the Nativity*, said to have been found in the King of Castile's tent after the Portuguese victory at Aljubarrota (1385). Nearby is displayed the tunic worn in the battle by João I.

At the heart of this museum-convent is a simple Romanesque cloister with varied, naively-carved capitals. The church to which it's attached, the **Colegiada**, was (like the Mosteiro de Batalha) built in honour of a vow made by João I before the decisive victory over Castile. It is interestingly dedicated to 'Our Lady of the Olive Tree' and before it stands a curious Gothic canopy-shrine. This marks the legendary spot where Wamba, unwillingly elected king of the Visigoths, drove a pole into the ground swearing that he would not reign until it blossomed. Naturally it sprouted immediately. João, feeling this a useful precedent of divine favour, set out to meet the Castilian forces from this very point.

Among the other churches in Guimarães, the finest is **São Francisco** (closed noon–3pm) with its huge eighteenth-century *azulejos* of St. Francis preaching to the fishes, and elegant Renaissance cloister and fountain. Once again, this was a convent until the 1834 dissolution. On a smaller scale and less well-kept, the **Capela de Nossa Senhora de Conceição** (past the bus station and apartment houses, left then right) is another jewel of Baroque gilt and flamboyant tile-painting. The difference is that it is crumbling away and few people go there. The couple who look after it are delighted to open up, and will continue with their chores next door while you enjoy the shade of the chapel's front porch, a kind of three-sided loggia.

Practicalities

There are more tourists coming to Guimarães now than there used to be, but apart from some coats of paint and a marginal increase in admission fees, little has changed, and the choice of **accommodation** isn't much better than before. Restaurants, however, are good, as are transport links.

Accommodation

Probably the most attractive place to stay is the *Casa dos Retiros* (Rua Francisco Agra 163, ☎053/412253). Attached to the church of São Francisco, this is run by padrés, but there's no proselytising. It does, however, have an 11.30pm curfew and is sometimes booked up by groups.

Otherwise, the *Oriental*, on the Praça do Toural, has a few cheap rooms above the restaurant, or you could try *São Mamede* (Rua de São Gonçalo 1) or *O Imperial* (Alameda da Resistencia) – though only the restaurant can really be recommended at the latter. The *Toural* (Praça de Toural), listed as a 1-star hotel in town is at present closed, and due to reopen in considerably upmarket form.

The town's **campsite** is 6km away up at PENHA, a pilgrimage mount and chapel; it is well located, cheap, and has a small swimming pool; buses leave every half-hour between 6am and 10pm (8pm Sun.).

Restaurants and Bars

Guimarães has no shortage of good cheap places to eat and drink. In the centre, try *Solar da Rainha* (Rua de Rainha D. Maria II) with a daily set menu, *Carramão* or *El Rei* (both Largo de São Tiago), *Alameda* or *Juncal* (both Largo da Condessa do Juncal) and *Casa dos Capuinhos* (Trav. de Arrochela behind Praça de Toural). Further out try *Dona Teresa* (Rua de São Torcato, to the left of the castle) or *Pinguim* (up the steps off Rua Francisco Agra), with local dishes but little atmosphere. Just into the Rua da Rainha, opposite the tower, there's a bar serving wine straight from the barrel in massive mugs.

As a provincial capital, the city also boasts a few **clubs**. The *Crocodile Club* (Rua de São Gonçalo; July–Sept. Fri.–Sun. 10.30pm–3am; 600esc men and 300esc women) is the big young hangout. Possibly more enjoyable, for foreign tastes, is the *Casa de Arco* (opposite the town hall; 3–7pm and 9.30pm–2am), with an art gallery, live music and lower admission charge.

Festivals

Guimarães' biggest **festa** is for São Gualter (Aug. 5–8, celebrated since 1452), when all public buildings are closed. Next in importance is the long-established *romaria* to São Torcato (6km northeast, first weekend of July), which, in the curious lingo of the Turismo leaflet, 'includes procession with archaic choirs of virgins'. If you miss the Festas Gualterianas you can catch most of the same stall-keepers, and something of the atmosphere, the weekend after in CALDAS DE VIZELA, a thermal spa with a park and boating-lake. Caldas has just lost its campaign for independence from the municipality – at one stage separatist fever rose so high that bus routes were severed between the two towns.

Buses and Trains

The **bus station** is located near the football stadium (Guimarães has a First Division football team). It looks deserted on weekends, but you can still buy tickets on the bus itself – just check the times before everything closes up. There is regular service to Amarante, Cabeceiras, Mondim de Basto and Póvoa de Lanhoso (via Briteiros).

The **railway station** is south of the **Tursimo** and past the University (set in the grounds of the former Palácio de Vila Flor), with regular trains to Porto and the north (changing at Lousado).

Santa Marinha da Costa

The former monastery of **Santa Marinha da Costa**, now converted into a luxurious *pousada*, can easily be reached by taking the SÃO ROQUE bus from the Guimarães tourist office (every half hour until 11.15pm). Get off at COSTA, and then follow the signs. The church is open to the public. Strictly, the *Pousada* is closed except to guests, but you can peek into its magnificent **cloister** (note the *Moçarabe* doorway in one of the walls); shelling out for a drink will give you greater licence to look around.

Dona Mafalda, the wife of Afonso Henriques, ordered the monastery to be built in 1154 to honour a vow to Santa Marinha, patron saint of pregnant women. Originally Augustinian, the monastery passed into the hands of the Order of Saint Jerome in the sixteenth century.

At the far end of the first floor rooms (rebuilt after a fire) a tiled, wooden **veranda** is named after *Frei Jerónimo* and elsewhere, especially in the **church** (July–Sept. 9am–1pm and 2–7pm; small fee), Jerome's twin emblems of the skull and the lion are recurring motifs in the decoration. The church's mixture of styles blends well, as each generation who came to build on it respected what they began with – there are tenth-century doorways on the south wall, sixteenth-century panels in the sacristy (look out for Jerome beating his breast with a stone against the temptation of women), and an eighteenth-century organ and stone roof in the choir.

Parque Nacional da Peneda-Gerês

PENEDA-GERÊS, the largest nature reserve in Portugal, is hardly a secret. Caldas do Gerês, the main centre of the park, attracts more tourists than anywhere else in the Minho, with the possible exception of Viana, and at weekends, when Portuguese campers arrive in force, parts of it can seem a bit like Windermere on a Bank Holiday.

The park as a whole, though, is large enough to absorb the great numbers of visitors, and the northern sections, particularly the area known as **Peneda** (best approached from Melgaço) remain largely undiscovered.

A **survey map for the Gerês** is available in Lisbon, through the army office (see "Directory" in *Lisbon and Around*), or from *Porta Editora* (Rua da Fábrica) in Porto, though you will need to get a Portuguese national to obtain one for you. It is not very reliable, dating as it does from 1959, since when dams have been built and whole areas submerged, but it's all that's available. The Portuguese themselves are reluctant walkers and the plans dished out by the Gerês Turismo are of little use; the park's head office in Braga (Rua de São Geraldo 19) can, however, be helpful. Maps aside, if you plan a long hike, go in July (less chance of fog) and take boots, a compass, food (for the remoter areas) and a water bottle (plenty of streams).

Hotels and pensions in Gerês are concentrated exclusively on Caldas do Gerês and the best campsite is there too. Other **campsites** are at Lamas de Mouro, Lindoso and Mezio; at Albergaria there is now *no* campsite and camping in the area is not permitted. On longer walks don't be too obvious about camping and no one will mind; in the villages (Ermida, for example) ask around for a *dormida*.

Picking flowers and, more important, **lighting fires** are forbidden in Gerês. The Portuguese have an alarming habit of lighting them whenever and wherever they picnic, no doubt a factor in disastrous fires such as those that destroyed over 80,000 hectares of forest in 1985 alone – a spate that caused particular damage to the landscape of the Minho.

From the North: Melgaço to Castro Laboreiro

The route from Melgaço into the **Peneda** area of the **Parque Nacional da Peneda-Gerês** (see "Melgaço" for transport details) runs, after 19km, through **LAMAS DE MOURO**, which has a beautifully situated but minimally equipped **campsite**.

On from Lamas you pass the sanctuary of **Nossa Senhora da Peneda** (9km), flooded with devotees at the beginning of September (especially the 7th and 8th), but pretty much deserted the rest of the year. You can take a two-hour **walk** from the sanctuary up to the peak of **Penameda** (1258m), where there are freshwater lagoons and extraordinary views across the whole of the Parque Nacional.

Alternatively, you might consider setting out on the first stage of a **two-day hike** (approximately 25km, allow an extra day in case of fog) to either **Soajo** or **Lindoso**, from both of which you can cross the Serra Amarela to Gerês. The Soajo route, marginally the easier, follows the Rio Peneda until it meets the Rio Veiga (7km), crosses over to the tiny village of TIBO, and takes the dusty road to Soajo (18km). The second trek continues down the Rio Peneda to the *Mistura das Águas* (Mixing of the Waters, 11km); from there use the Rio Laboreiro as a guideline down to the Rio Lima (15km), where you can cross over the barrage to Lindoso. You will need survey maps.

Castro Laboreiro

The main road through Lamas takes you up to the ancient village of **CASTRO LABOREIRO** (9km farther), a place that's best known for the species of mountain dog to which it gives its name. The village is practically deserted in summer, being made up of *inverneiras* (winter houses), the pastoral community having gone off to find greener fields and build *brandas* ('soft' houses) for the warmer months. If you can speak Portuguese and want to learn more about the area, contact the village priest, who knows everything. There are **rooms** at *Pensão Abrigo* (☎051/45126).

To get to the ruins of the town's Afonsino **castle** you have a twenty-minute steep walk: past a large rock known as the *Tartarúga* (Tortoise) and through heather and between boulders, with sheer drops to each side and steps hacked out of the rock face.

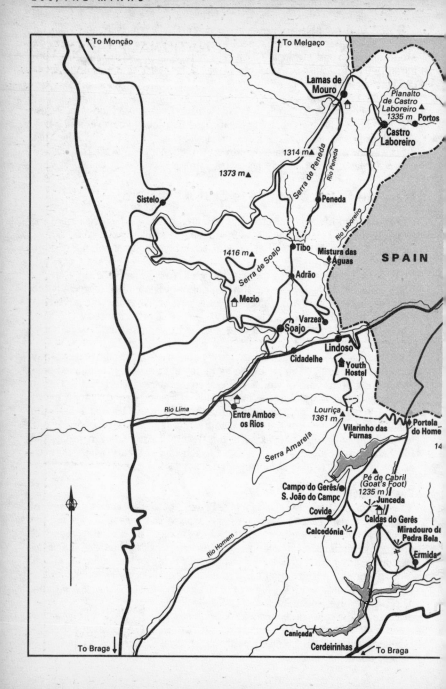

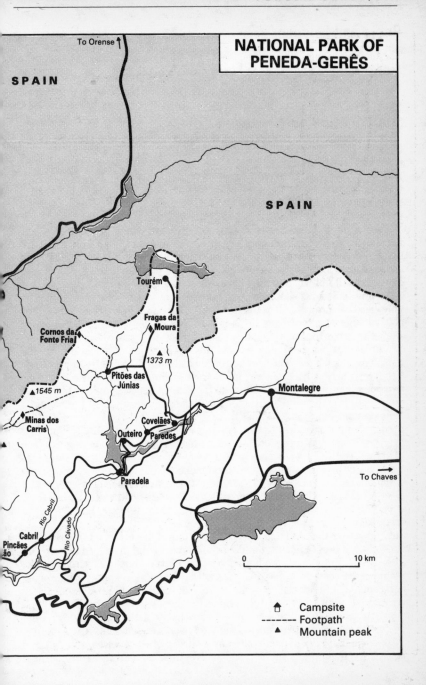

NATIONAL PARK OF
PENEDA-GERÊS

To Orense

SPAIN

SPAIN

Tourém

Fragas da
Moura

Cornos da
Fonte Fria

▲ 1373 m

Pitões das
Júnias

▲1545 m

Montalegre

Minas dos
Carris

▲

Covelães
Outeiro
Paredes

Paradela

To Chaves

Rio Cabril

Rio Cávado

Cabril
Pincães
ão

0   10 km

⌂ Campsite
------- Footpath
▲ Mountain peak

Soajo and Lindoso

The neighbouring villages of **Soajo** and **Lindoso**, halfway between the Peneda and the Caldas areas of the park, are reached most easily from (respectively) Arcos de Valdevez and Ponte da Barca.

Soajo

SOAJO is a small village tucked into the folds of a hilly landscape. Its highlight is a collection of eighteenth- and nineteeth-century **espigueiros** (grain houses), over twenty of which are clumped together on a stony platform, their roof-crosses (intended to bless the annual crop) giving them the eerie look of a graveyard. In addition to providing a ready-made, breezy threshing ground, the site offers a degree of protection from rats as well, but the tall stone mushrooms that raise the houses from the ground do not appear to keep vermin entirely at bay.

Their grouping together is a vestige of the days when the isolated village depended heavily on communal effort for its survival. Even now there are several flocks of sheep and goats that belong to the whole community and are tended by the village shepherds. If you set off on a hike at the crack of dawn you will walk up into the hills to the sound of small brass bells.

Staying in Soajo is simple as long as there aren't many others in town. The only café-restaurant (next to the bus stop) has **rooms** upstairs and should be able to suggest alternatives if it's full. (There is also a campsite 8km west along the Arcos road at MEZIO).

The lack of places to stay reflects the villagers' indifference towards the outside world. Changes are not accepted easily and the village takes its traditions very seriously. Folkloric groups are maintained by those who stay behind, while the emigrants all try to inculcate a sense of 'minha terra' (my homeland) into their modern-minded (and in this case American) offspring.

Festas are fun anywhere, but there is a special feel about one in a small, hard-working village, where the period of 'madness' seems more essential for everyone's sanity and the fun and games more spontaneous. Owing to a lack of horses, the Soajo *corrida* is a race on foot – balancing blue plastic amphoras full of water on their heads, the contestants compete for the honour of being ceremoniously drenched by all the others. Large, homemade fireworks, set off all over the place without warning, enhance the vitality of the occasion.

Lindoso

Set high above the Rio Lima, **LINDOSO** is one of the most attractive villages in Gerês. It's best reached from Ponte da Barca, though buses do run directly from Braga; to the east, the border post with Spain is open in summer only. All along the route from Ponte da Barca there are perfect spots for swimming and camping (the official campsite at ENTRE-AMBOS-OS-RIOS is open very erratically), until you reach the turning to Soajo, where the banks rise high above the gorge that stretches to the hydroelectric dam below Lindoso. Here you can cross on foot and walk up the Rio Laboreiro (see "Lamas de Mouro").

Lindoso, like Soajo, is dominated by a cluster of espigueiros, and its life is again very traditional. The rearing of **livestock** is central. Every morning starts with the lowing of cows or the clattering of the communally-herded sheep and goats, and the smell of animals lies thick on the air. The traditional method of baking bread in these parts involved removing the hot coals and sealing the oven door with a mixture of ash and dung, and it's a technique still in use today in the old part of Lindoso. You can see a restored oven in the **castle** (keys from the restaurant), which is heavily restored itself, and boasts a working drawbridge and a selection of Parque Nacional leaflets for sale.

The village has one **restaurant**, the *Castelo* (☎058/47405), which also has overpriced **rooms**; guests are likely to be disturbed by the noisy camaraderie of the dam-workers who often drink downstairs until 2am. A better bet is the seasonal **youth hostel** (May–Sept.), a three-kilometre walk out of the village; follow the trail of pale red arrows. This is well equipped (a barrel of wine and an open fire!), but take your own food.

A Hike across the Serra Amarela

The Lindoso Youth Hostel is the starting-point for a **two-day walk across the Serra Amarela** via PORTELA DO HOMEM or VILARINHO DAS FURNAS to GERÊS, an adventure for which you should take provisions for three days, in case of fog.

The journey is in two stages: the dirt track (13km) to the bottom of the **Louriça summit** (1361m), and two less obvious routes across the hills to Portela (14km), or Gerês (15km). You'll need walking boots, a water bottle (last water for the second day is below the road up to Louriça or up at the top for those going on to Vilarinho das Furnas), a stick (to drive off cattle or wild horses), and something warm (for the night cold).

On the second sighting of the Louriça television aerials you could take a short cut, roughly in line with the pylons, up to the next bend, or else put your trust in the road and follow its winding course all the way to the deserted cottage below the summit. This is where the two routes split.

If you're going on to Vilarinho, the **forest guard** and his family, who live on top of the hill, will point out the reservoir from the plateau in front of the station, and advise you on the best route down. Ignoring their suggestions could get you stuck behind the sheer cliff faces above the deserted, half-sunken village of Vilarinho. Once at the reservoir, you can cross the dam and join the route detailed in the Gerês section (see following account) to Campo do Gerês.

The **alternative route to Portela do Homem** follows the road (so overgrown as to be barely distinguishable) that lies below the more obvious track from the cottage to the old lookout post. After a large zigzag down into the valley, a wooded patch, and a long stretch pushing through chest-high tree heather along the other side, you break out into a rocky landscape. From here, follow the dry stone wall a short way (200m), turn left (north) along the ridge or just behind it, and walk down into the first valley. Before descending, you'll catch sight of the glacial rounded valley of the Rio Homem (up to Minas dos Carris); a useful landmark away in the distance, Portela do Homem is tucked into a fold of land at its foot.

Cutting across country, you should hit the old road (you can see part of this from back up on the ridge), which ends at the border post (open June–

Oct. 7am–9/12pm). Those in difficulty should use the Spanish border, a stone wall with marker posts (E and P) as a guideline, but cut down to the road as soon as you see it. A couple of hours later you should come upon the border café. At **PORTELA DO HOMEM** there is a collection of Roman mile-stones. Gerês is 13km farther, but you can hitch; don't miss the **river pool** nearby at the bottom of the Minas dos Carris valley.

Caldas and Hikes in the Central Gerês

The Parque Nacional is centred around the old spa town of **Caldas do Gerês**, reached most easily by bus from Braga (1½–1¾ hr.; 6 daily). From here, there are a couple of interesting and accessible **hikes** – though, frus-tratingly, this central section is not well equipped with footpaths, and walking off the tracks can be difficult and painful, with small shrubs slashing the legs. Keep in mind, too, that if you get lost there are only a few old stone huts here and there for shelter.

If you've no **map** of any kind, you can pick up a vaguely functional free plan from the tourist office in Caldas.

Caldas do Gerês

Weekends aside, when Portuguese picnickers arrive en masse, **CALDAS DO GERÊS** is a relaxed and very elegant base. 'The Spa of Gerês', it became fashionable in the early years of the last century – an epoch convincingly evoked by a row of Victorian grand hotels along the sedate old main street. The **spa** still functions, ensuring a summer spectacle of infirmities, though most visitors nowadays are younger and healthier, up from the northern cities to picnic in the woods – or, in the case of eccentric foreigners, to hike.

There is no shortage of **pensions**. The *Pensão da Ponte* (behind the main street) is a good deal, or try *Pensão Baltasar* (past the park office). If you have the option, though, I'd recommend **camping**. The site at VIDOEIRO, well maintained by the park authority, is just on the edge of town, set along-side a gushing river, with terraced areas for tents and good facilities. Open campfires are permitted here and most evening life takes place around them. Cafés and restaurants in Caldas are few, poor and expensive.

West of Caldas: Around the Mountain

This is a fairly tiring day's hike (6–7 hr.) but a good one, taking you along the way of the **old Roman road** that began at Braga and stretched ultimately to Rome and Byzantium. The route also runs alongside the **Rio Homen**, now a reservoir with obvious swimming potential. In the height of summer you can see the submerged village of Vilarinho das Furnas (turn right after crossing the dam) and even swim through its doors and windows. From there you could reach the Louriça summit (5 hr.) by following the path above the ceme-tery along the brook and heading for the TV aerials (see "Serra Amarela").

Setting out from Caldas, follow the road north towards Portela do Homem. You'll have to keep on it, despite apparent shortcuts, past the defunct campsite at ALBERGARIA and beyond, veering left, by which time the signs are for Campo de Gerês and the **reservoir** looks increasingly enticing. There is a road off to it, but the main road continues north – first along gladed paths and then suddenly into the open. Fires here have seared the foliage and given the granite crags an almost apocalyptic grandeur. Staying with the road (past an old stone building housing a weaving project run by the park), you veer left into **CAMPO DE GERÊS**, a small group of houses with a pension, a café and, nearby, a bus stop (4 or 5 daily buses to Braga).

Soon after Campo you come to the crucifix of **São João de Campo**. Turn off the road here, to the left, on to a dirt track. This will take you around the southern tip of the mountain and, apart from the occasional obsessive car driver, you'll be pretty much alone – eerily so at times, amid the Neolithic and often obscenely-shaped boulders. This stretch can be hard going in the midday heat, as there is no shelter, so save it for the late afternoon. At the end of the circuit the way back to Caldas is signposted (right at the first junction, then right again at the water fountain).

To the Miradouro and Ermida

An hour's walk southeast of Caldas, the **Miradouro do Gerês** is *the* destination for Portuguese weekend picnickers. And small wonder, with its site overlooking the vast reservoir of Caniçada and a good part of the Gerês range. The only catch, if you're intent on following suit, is the extent of local enthusiasm. This is not a road to walk unless you're immune to inhalation of exhaust fumes and dust; better to hitch up and then start hiking. The quickest approach to the Miradouro road is to follow the road behind the petrol station at Caldas, where it becomes an uphill path.

The most obvious, and probably the most attractive, route to follow **beyond the Miradouro** is the road to ERMIDA and CABRIL. For, though this is indeed marked as a road on the maps, and has sections of tarmac, it is to all intents and purposes a country path. Walking in early September, between the Miradouro turning and Cabril (nearly 30km – 5½–6 hr.), I was passed by only one car and one tractor – well outnumbered by oxen. Just before arriving at Ermida you'll pass a sign to CASCATO DO ARADO, left off the main track; follow this and a brief walk leads to the magnificent **Arado waterfalls.**

Ermida and East

ERMIDA, despite its proximity to Caldas (1½ hr.) and the Miradouro (½ hr.), has an immediate air of seclusion about it. If you're looking for a quiet base, this could be a good choice: there's a scattering of **dormidas** and a couple of cafés, but little outward sign of tourism. A granite village, like all in the Gerês, it is still very much a farming community.

Continuing **east from Ermida**, along a blackberry-lined lane above the reservoir, you'll pass a small group of waterfalls and cross a distinctly unsafe-looking bridge before coming to **FAFIÃO,** a tiny farming hamlet. Past here the countryside becomes more fertile, terraced with vines and maize, the road winding down to another hamlet, **PINCÃES**, and through it (turn right at the end of the houses) to the slightly larger **CABRIL.** A lovely, isolated place with odd attempts at modernity (100m of tarmac), its centre is still sauntered through by oxen, goat and flocks of sheep.

From Cabril, if you're backpacking or driving, you could go on to OUTEIRO, PITÕES DAS JUNIAS (with a prominent monastery) or MONT-ALEGRE via another vast dam, the **Barragem de Paradela**. Montalegre can also be reached by bus from Caldas do Gerês via VENDA NOVA.

On to Montalegre

Travelling from Gerês on into Trás-os-Montes, Montalegre provides a suitably remote and dramatic link. The appeal lies as much in the road up as the place itself. Bumpy, narrow and at all points incomplete, it's one of those journeys that seem to trigger madness in bus drivers, simultaneously delighting and terrifying unaccustomed passengers. You can get on to the bus route either from BRAGA/GERÊS or from ARCO DE BAULHE at the end of the Tâmega line (see p.167).

Either route takes you through **VENDA NOVA**, a tiny group of houses (with a single, very friendly **pension**) on the edge of a reservoir, and on past the hydroelectric plant of **PISÕES** – the largest dam in the country, and an unexpectedly modern development in this otherwise very remote region.

Montalegre

MONTALEGRE, which appears suddenly, commanding the plains all around, seems to be hovering between centuries. There is a fair amount of new development (and a cold, cosmopolitan café), stimulated by the Pisões dam. Yet at the same time the town, with its medieval centre and castle, remains at least in part in the old frontier tradition, bringing its cattle in at night with a wary eye towards Spain. There must have been a good deal of border banditry over the years.

There is just one **pension** at Montalegre, the slightly fancy (3-star) *Residencia Fidalgo*. There is very little tourism here, less still in the hills around – all good walking territory, scattered with dolmens and the odd Templar and Romanesque church.

Heading east there are daily buses on to CHAVES, as good an approach as any to Trás-os-Montes.

travel details

Trains

Minho Line 12 trains from PORTO to Lousado (30 min.: change for Guimarães, 1 hr. later), Nine (1 hr.: change for Braga, 25 min. later), Viana do Castelo (2 hr.); 8 continue to Caminha (2–3 hr.), Valença (2 hr. 30 min.–4 hr.) and 3 go to Monção (30 min. later). Irregular intervals between 5.10am–6.55pm, with big gaps both mid-morning and mid-afternoon.

Tâmega Line 5 daily from LIVRAÇÃO to Amarante (1½ hr.) and Arco de Baulhe (2 hr.).

Vigo (Spain) Line 3 daily from VALENÇA to Vigo (3 hr.). Connections to Santiago de Compostela and La Coruna.

Buses

Porto to Fao/Esposende/Viana (3 daily; 50 min./1 hr./1 hr. 10 min.), Vila Real (6; 3 hr. 40 min.), Braga (10; 1 hr. 20 min).

Braga to Guimarães (half-hourly until 8.30pm; 45 min.), Ponte de Lima (7; 1 hr.), Caldas do Gerês (6; 1½ hr.), Barcelos (7; , hr.), Monção (4; 2½hr.).

To Spain Saturday buses leave Porto (3.30pm) and Valença (5.30pm) for Vigo/Santiago (2 hr./4 hr. 15 min. from Valença). Tues., Thur., and Fri. buses pass through Monção (11am), Melgaço (11.30am) for Ponte Barjas in Spain and for France.

CHAPTER SEVEN

TRAS-OS-MONTES

Trás-os-Montes – literally 'Beyond the Mountains' – is Portugal's Lost Domain. For centuries this remote and rural province has been a place to hide and practise one's beliefs in peace: its peculiar traditions and dialects have been formed by a diversity of populations, from the prehistoric tribes who carved the *porcas* (stone pigs) to Jews who sought refuge here from the Inquisition. The extremity of the climate – 'Nine months of Winter and three months of Hell' – and the aridity of much of its land have kept it well apart from the mainstream. Even today, with new highways being built, and some industry coming to the major towns, the province has half the Minho's population in an area almost twice its size.

A sharp **natural divide** cuts across the province. In the **south** is the fertile territory officially labelled the Upper Douro, but known unofficially as the **Terra Quente** (Hot Land). Encompassing the terraced stretches of the Douro, Corgo and Tua rivers, and extending down to Lamego, this area produces peaches, oranges, melons and wine. The bitter winters of the **north** have earned it the name of **Terra Fria** (Cold Land). North of Macedo de Cavaleiros and Mogadouro, the most visible features of this wild and rugged terrain are the countless pony carts, pigeon houses (*pombais*) and almond trees, whose fleeting blossoming in late February and early March draws thousands of weekenders to the border town of Miranda do Douro.

Travelling in Trás-os-Montes can be a slow business, with erratic trains and very localised buses. However, almost any route into the province has its own rewards. The highlights of any trip must include one of the **narrow gauge railway lines** cutting into the *serras* from the Douro: the **Corgo** (from Régua to Chaves) and the **Tua** (from Tua to Bragança). If you're pushed for time, the latter is easiest; the Corgo services have been cut back to the point of near extinction in recent years. At the ends, the fortified old frontier towns of **Chaves** and **Bragança**, the capital, provide suitable targets. Making a loop around the province, you might also take in the tiny frontier villages of **Miranda do Douro** and **Freixo de Espada á Cinta**, their appeal as much in their remoteness and situation as any low-key sights. For hikers there are the even less visited trails of the **Montesinho** and **Alvão national parks**.

As most approaches to Trás-os-Montes will be **from the Douro**, to the south, this chapter begins with a section of the Douro rail line, its major junction at Regua, and the elegant Baroque town of **Lamego** (technically in Beira Alta) nine kilometres to the south. The region south again from Lamego, towards Guarda and Viseu, is also covered here – a rival for Trás-os-Montes in its wild, rural splendour.

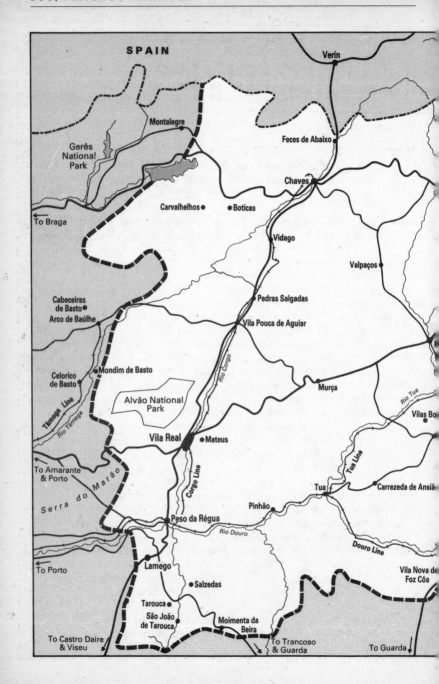

SPAIN

Verín

Montalegre

Feces de Abaixo

Gerês
National
Park

Chaves

Carvalhelhos ● ● Boticas

To Braga

Vidago

Valpaços ●

Cabeceiras
de Basto ●
Arco de Baúlhe

Pedras Salgadas ●

Vila Pouca de Aguiar ●

Celorico
de Basto ● ● Mondim de Basto

Rio Corgo

Murça ●

Rio Tua

Tâmega Line

Rio Tâmega

Alvão National
Park

Vilas Bo

Vila Real ● Mateus

Tua Line

To Amarante
& Porto

Corgo Line

Serra do Marão

Tua ● ● Carrezeda de Ansiã

Pinhão ●

Peso da Régua

Rio Douro

Douro Line

To Porto

Lamego ●

Vila Nova de
Foz Côa

● Salzedas

Tarouca ●

São João
de Tarouca

Moimenta da
Beira

To Castro Daire
& Viseu

To Trancoso
& Guarda

To Guarda

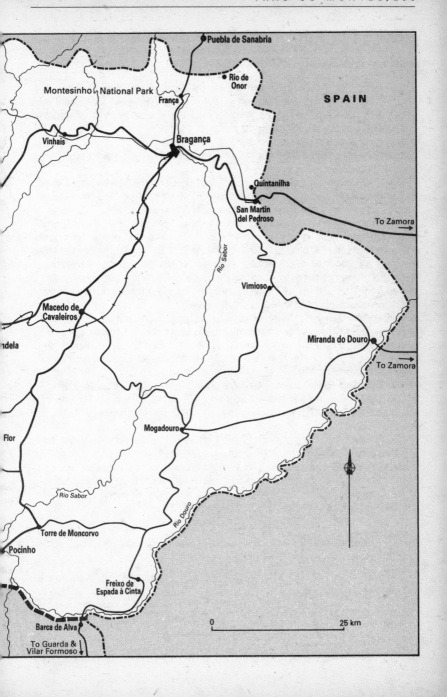

Puebla de Sanabria

Montesinho National Park

Rio de Onor

França

SPAIN

Vinhais

Bragança

Rio Sabor

Quintanilha

San Martin del Pedroso

To Zamora

Vimioso

Macedo de Cavaleiros

Miranda do Douro

ndela

To Zamora

Mogadouro

Flor

Rio Sabor

Rio Douro

Torre de Moncorvo

Pocinho

Freixo de Espada à Cinta

0   25 km

Barca de Alva

To Guarda & Vilar Formoso

Douro Connections: Peso da Régua and Torre de Moncorvo

To go almost anywhere by train in Trás-os-Montes you have to follow the Douro line through to the junction at **PESO DA RÉGUA**. This small and very provincial town has been known for over two centuries as the 'Capital of the Upper Douro', after its role in the port industry. In fact, the centre for quality port wines is now at Pinhão, half an hour further up the line; Régua is simply the junction and the depot through which all the wine must pass on its way to Porto.

The **Turismo** on the river bank can, nonetheless, inform you about **visits to local cellars**. The *Casa do Douro* and *Ramos Pinto* (east of the station), are open to visitors and run more personalised tours than their Porto equivalents. Quotas for wine production have been in force around here since the mid-eighteenth century, and some terrace walls from that period have withstood the assault of the diggers and dynamite that are used nowadays to clear the way for the vineyard tractors. Grape-treaders and *barcos rabelos* have generally been replaced by machines and cistern trucks, but there's still a demand for large groups of hand-pickers (*rogas*) when there's a bumper crop, and some treading still goes on in small villages.

Apart from these alcoholic diversions, there's not much to do in Régua except wander through the upper village and along the river bank. It's as well to be sure of your next train or bus out. There are four public transport alternatives. You can take the **train** along the Corgo Line to Chaves; continue to Tua (for the line to Mirandela and Bragança), or keep on to the end of the line at Pocinho (bus connections take over for the journey on to Torre de Moncorvo, Freixo de Espada à Cinta and Miranda do Douro). Or you can catch the **bus** in front of the station to Lamego, to the south (every hour until 9pm).

If you need to stay at Régua, the high-rise *Pensão Império* (Rua José Vasques Osório 8) offers good **accommodation**, breakfast and views. The *Pensão Borges* is cheaper but too near the noisy railway line for comfort. There are plenty of **restaurants** along the main street. Camping is possible, free of charge, below the swimming pool down by the river; ask in the Turismo for Senhor Pereira, who owns the land.

Torre de Moncorvo

TORRE DE MONCORVO is the nearest town to POCINHO, the end of the Douro passenger line. It is also the last place in Portugal where you can still see **steam engines** at work – they shuttle freight to DUAS IGREJAS on Tuesday and Thursday. Moncorvo's other claim to fame is its almond trees, which draw crowds of Portuguese in February and March to witness the blossoming. At other times, aside from the **cathedral**, there is little to see.

As far as **pensions** go, the *Campos Monteiro* (Rua Visconde Vila Maior 55, ☎079/22355) is excellent value, with a good **restaurant** downstairs. The

Roboredo (Rua Constantino) has the cheapest rooms in town and occupies the top two floors of a traditional *adega* called *O Caneco* (The Mug). Sadly, the place doesn't reflect Moncorvo's high reputation for wine – which is due to the 'Barca Velha' from the nearby and internationally renowned Quinta do Vale de Meão – but the stuff comes in jugs and the prices are fair enough.

The 12.10pm and 6.52pm arrivals at Pocinho are met by buses to Moncorvo that continue on to Mogadouro and Miranda do Douro – useful for those on an anti-clockwise trek around the province. **Heading for Porto,** there are also connections to meet the 9.12am and 6.55pm trains from Pocinho. In Moncorvo, buses operate from the central square, just across from the *Santos* office; other departures run south to Vila Nova de Foz Côa, and thence into Beira Alta.

Lamego

Nine kilometres south of Régua lies the wealthy town of **LAMEGO**, technically outside the Trás-os-Montes region, but most conveniently regarded as the edge of the *Terra Quente*. The town is spread over the gentle slopes of the rich agricultural land fed by the Douro, a terrain which produces such gastronomic delights as hams, melons and *Raposeira* – the closest thing to champagne you will find in Portugal. (The *Caves Raposeira*, 1km out of town on the Castro Daire road, are open for free tours and tasting.) The graceful white *quintas* and villas on the hillsides around are echoed in the luxuriant architecture of the centre, where Baroque mansions seem to stand on every corner and lavish decorations are found within the smallest chapel.

The Town

The most celebrated of Lamego's monuments is the shrine of **Nossa Senhora dos Remédios**, whose healing miracles make it a target for pilgrims from all over the country. Standing on a hill overlooking the city from the west, it's approached by a magnificently elaborate eighteenth-century stairway, modelled on the one at Bom Jesus near Braga. Punctuated by a series of devotional chapels, *azulejos*, and allegorical fountains and statues, some 700 steps lead up to the facade of the church.

The great **pilgrimage** is on September 8; the most devout ascend the staircase, slowly and painfully, on their knees. It is an occasion for several weeks' celebration in Lamego, starting in the last week of August and continuing into mid-September, the busiest days being those immediately prior to the big one. Apart from the pilgrimage and its associated processions – some with cavalcades of young children in white – there's a traditional 'Battle of Flowers', torchlit parades, rock concerts with some of the country's top bands, dances, car races and a fair on the Recinto da Feira, below the sanctuary.

At the other end of town there's an excellent **Museu Regional**, housed in an eighteenth-century palace off the Largo de Camões (10am–12.30pm and 2–5pm; Tues.–Sun.). Its exhibits include five of the remaining panels of a

polyptych commissioned from Grão Vasco by the Bishop of Lamego in 1506. Judging by the lack of correlation between the various panels – for instance between the *Creation of the Animals* and the prodigiously executed *Annunciation* – some of the work must be attributed to the great man's school. Other things to look out for include a series of sixteenth-century Flemish tapestries (especially a *Life of Oedipus* sequence), three curious statues of a conspicuously pregnant Virgin Mary (peculiar to this region), a fine assembly of *azulejos*, piles of ecclesiastical treasure from the Episcopal Palace, and a group of chapels rescued from the decaying *Convento das Chagas*. It's all beautifully laid out and more than justifies the small fee.

The **Cathedral** is just across from here on the Largo da Sé. It is largely a Renaissance building, but the twelfth-century tower survives from an earlier church on the site while the main facade is Gothic. The mixture works well and its **cloister** is a beauty. On the opposite side of the Avenida near the **Turismo**, the Rua da Olaria, a narrow street crowded with little shops, leads into the somewhat more upmarket Rua do Almacave, which ends at the Praça do Comércio. From here you can pass through the walls of the ancient citadel and climb up to the castle, a route that takes you by many of the other churches in Lamego. The **Igreja do Almacave**, a very ancient foundation said once to have been a mosque, is particularly beautiful.

The **Castle**, surrounded by a cluster of ancient stone houses, has become the local boy scout hut (open to visitors from 10am–noon and 2–5pm). The fellows do have a fairly legitimate claim on the place, having – so they say – cleared eighteen truckloads of rubbish away in the 1970s and saved the building from ruin. For a small entrance fee you can watch their displays of knotting and campcraft on your way up to admire the view. Sadly, what you'll probably see are a lot of burnt hillsides; once known as the *Vila Verde*, Lamego suffers up to three forest fires a day in the height of summer.

Below the castle and still within the upper town, there's a thirteenth-century **cisterna**, one of the strangest buildings in the country. If your powers of persuasion are up to it (French may help), the Chief Fireman's wife, down below at Rua do Almacave 30, will lead you up four storeys to the top of her house and out into the back garden – and there stands what appears from the outside to be a semi-sunken toolshed. Inside, it looks more like a perfectly preserved Romanesque chapel, its walls still bearing the original stonemasons' marks; it is in fact the town's ancient water source. Even today, in emergencies, it proves useful as an extra supply.

Accommodation and Food

Though the old Baroque town is a very pleasant place to stay, **finding a room** can be difficult. There's a well-turned-out government *pousada*, but something of a dearth of more modest places. A couple of rather pricey *residências* can be found on the Avenida (Visconde Guedes Teixeira) – the *Império* and the *Solar* (☎0541/62060), the latter with fine views over the cathedral. *Pensão Silva* (Rua Trás-da-Sé 26, ☎62929) is cheaper and almost as good, or try the rooms farther up the Avenida (ask in the *Restaurante Espírito-Santo* on the street above the post office). The least expensive

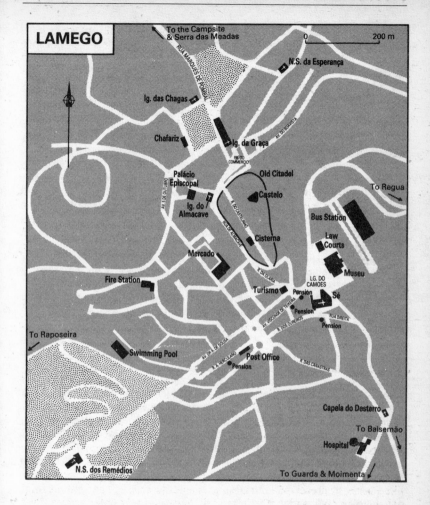

LAMEGO

To the Campsite & Serra das Meadas

0   200 m

N.S. da Esperança

RUA MARQUES DE POMBAL

Ig. das Chagas

Chafariz

Ig. da Graça

AV. DO ROANSA

Palácio Episcopal

Old Citadel

Castelo

To Regua

Ig. do Almacave

Bus Station

Cisterna

Law Courts

Mercado

Museu

Fire Station

LG. DO CAMOES

Turismo   Pension   Sé

To Raposeira

Pension

RUA DIREITA

Pension

Swimming Pool

Post Office

Pension

R. DAS CANASTRAS

Capela do Desterro

To Balsemão

Hospital

N.S. dos Remédios

To Guarda & Moimenta

dormidas of all are to be found nearby at Rua Santa Cruz 15 (☎62556), or above the smoked-ham shop and café at Rua da Olaria 61.

The local campsite is four kilometres out along the Rua Marquês de Pombal (past the garden); a lofty position on the Serra das Meadas, where there is a weekend of pilgrimages, picnics and general revelry on the second Sunday in June. There are no buses, but hitching in summer is no problem.

Restaurants, like pensions, are on the expensive side. The *Império* is probably the best, if funds will stretch. If not, try the *Novo* (opposite the cathedral), or put together a picnic from the ham shop and nearby grocers. A couple of saloon-door **drinking** places are on the way to the castle (at the top of Rua do Almacave, and Rua do Castelino 25), but both close at 9pm.

Transport

For **transport** to Régua (almost hourly between 7am and 7.30pm), Viseu (*RN* 8.10am every day, all year), Guarda (6.10am and 1.35pm Mon.–Fri.), and almost anywhere you want, head for the efficient **bus station** behind the museum. It also has an early morning café if you are there for a connection to the Régua train station.

Balsemão

BALSEMÃO, site of a seventh-century **chapel** founded by the Suevi, is a three-kilometre hike from the back of the Lamego cathedral. The route requires three left turns in all: the first is at the Capela do Desterro down into the old quarters of town and across a bridge; the second is a fork on to the hillside road; and the third comes a little while later, taking you down into the valley and above a rushing river. After three large curves a village school, a collection of outhouses, and the chapel appear.

The undistinguished facade and dark interior of the **Capela de Balsemão** give it the air of a family vault, an impression strengthened by the imposing **sarcophagus** of Dom Afonso of Porto. The florid fourteenth-century capitals that encircle the tomb make the few remaining Suevi curls on the archway into the choir seem rather subdued by comparison. The profoundly pregnant statue of **Nossa Senhora do Ó** (that's Ó as in *O! Nossa Senhora, Mãe de Deus* . . .) is being restored, but is due to be returned shortly.

South from Lamego

Continuing on south of Lamego in the direction of Viseu, the country is high and wild and virtually uninhabited. This territory was among the earliest to fall to Afonso Henriques, the first king of Portugal, in his march south against the Moors. It is said that he laid the first stone of the monastery of **São João de Tarouca** after his victories at Trancoso and Sernancelhe in Beira Alta; the monastery of **Salzedas**, the fortified bridge at **Ucanha**, and the church at **Tarouca** were also founded at this time.

Hourly buses connect Lamego with Tarouca, and three to five a day run on to São João, Salzedas and Ucanha.

São João de Tarouca

The small village of **SÃO JOÃO DE TAROUCA**, off the southeast route from Lamego to Guarda, was the site of the first Cistercian monastery to be founded in Portugal (1124). Only the simple **Romanesque church** is really intact, and even here the greatest treasure – Gaspar Vaz's renowned altarpiece of Saint Peter – is no longer on display. Villagers complain that the authorities in Lisbon removed the painting for cleaning in 1978 and have ever since refused to return it. Being less portable, the medieval tomb of Dom Dinis's bastard son, the Count of Barcelos, with elaborate hunting scenes carved into the sides, still lies in a side aisle.

Buses leave Lamego every Thursday at 8am and 1.30pm to pick up shoppers from São João. On other days, you have to take one of the daily Guarda-

or Moimenta-bound buses as far as MONDIM DA BEIRA and then walk for half an hour high above the brook that waters the remote valley. In summer there are usually students working on the site, one of whom will probably be happy to show you around.

Ucanha

In **UCANHA** – north of Tarouca, on the opposite side of N226 – life revolves around the water. Down below the main road, two ingenious ducts have been made to tap the river upstream in order to provide adequate washing facilities in the centre of the village. The wash houses are practically in ruins, but the system of one tank for suds and another for rinses, common to the Mediterranean, has been preserved. Running below the pools, the river looks so tempting that on a sunny day, regardless of what rubbish might be floating by, the village children are constantly nipping in and out.

The real beauty of the scene stems from the majestic **tollgate** (free admission) and single-arched **bridge**. They date from shortly after 1163, when the diocese of Salzedas was awarded to Teresa Afonso, erstwhile nursemaid to Afonso Henriques' five sons and heirs, and widow of Egas Moniz, the first king's tutor and closest advisor. Besides marking and protecting the border of her domain, these structures were also, of course, an ostentatious mark of manorial power. Today, clothes are hung out to dry under the arches.

Salzedas

SALZEDAS lies four kilometres further along the Ucanha road, past another 'champagne' cooperative, a rival to *Raposeira*. The **monastery** here was once the greatest of its kind, grander even than São João. The complex was rebuilt with money donated by Teresa Afonso in 1168, when the order was Augustinian; it became Cistercian during a later period of administration from Alcobaça.

Unfortunately, eighteenth-century renovation has largely altered its original appearance into a clumsy mixture of baroque and pseudo-classical styles. The monastery's main facade presides over the small square of the diminutive village. As at São João de Tarouca, students work here in the summer, and though they may seem surprised to see casual visitors, they will follow you around and open the relevant doors.

The smell of decay is strong inside – water draining off the raised road feeds a rich growth of mould. The two dark and dusty **paintings** of *Saint Peregrine* and *Saint Sebastian* by Grão Vasco, which hang either side of the choir, are easily overlooked. More conspicuous are the two fifteenth-century tombstones of members of the Coutinho family near the entrance; the Coutinhos were a dominant noble family in the Beira Alta region during the early years of the Portuguese nation.

Out through a side door, a succession of courtyards bear the scars of a period of extensive pillage and decay, which began in 1834 at the dissolution of the monasteries. A caring gardener has planted a mixture of vegetables and roses in the dry earth, where once there were formal gardens.

THE CORGO LINE

At Régua the **Corgo branch line** begins a memorable journey. The track follows the course of the River Corgo from its confluence with the Douro through **Vila Real** up to **Vila Pouca de Aguiar** (famous for its bread), finally running alongside the Rio Tâmega on the approach to **Chaves**. The journey is slow (3½ hr.), but you wouldn't want it to be any quicker: the views are constantly magnificent over a landscape where everything from cowsheds to vine posts seem to be made from granite, and where the luscious green of the vines belies the apparent barrenness of the earth.

One or two trains daily make the whole trip to Chaves, but depending on time of year you may have no choice but the **6.24am from Regua**, calling at Vila Real at 7.23am; services are more regular along the section from Regua to Vila Real (5 daily) and Vila Pouca de Aguiar (2 daily through the year). At the same time as cutting back on services, the rail company has, unfortunately, introduced new carriages. If you're lucky, you may still ride in one of the ancient wooden coaches, open at either end, and standard on the line until the late 1980s; if not, they're to be admired at the station in Regua.

Vila Real

VILA REAL is the one break from the pastoralism of the Corgo – the largest industrial town in the northeast, it is bordered on three sides by sprawling suburbs. The setting, however, is magnificent, the twin **Serras** of **Marão** and **Alvão** (the so-called 'Gateway to Trás-os-Montes') forming a natural amphitheatre behind the town, and it's quite a lively place, too, if you need to stay. **Festas** take place on June 13 (Santo António) and 29 (São Pedro).

The old quarter, built on a promontory above the junction of the Corgo and Cabril rivers, is attractive, though there is little to see other than the main **Avenida**, which runs down the spine of the promontory – the view from the bottom, past the fourteenth-century chapel of **São Brás**, is not for vertigo sufferers. The only house of architectural interest on the Avenida is no. 94, the former palace of the Marqueses of Vila Real, which has four simple Manueline windows – it now houses the **Turismo** (9.30am–7pm; Oct.–June closed noon–1pm and Sun.).

The **Cathedral** opposite has modern stained-glass windows but the interior is fifteenth-century and simpler. Diogo Cão, who discovered the mouth of the Congo in 1482, was born above the café near the town hall.

Practicalities

For **food and drink** (and the wine here is good) the streets behind the Turismo have the best cafés. The liveliest **nightspot** is the bar at Largo do Pelourinho 11 (open until 1am; Fri. and Sat. 2am), which, for this part of the country at least, is distinctly avant garde. Another good bar, open until midnight, is the *Excelsior* at Rua Serpa Pinto 30–36 – a huge, elaborate pool hall featuring the strangest timing meters for your game you'll ever see.

The *Excelsior* (☎059/22422) also has **rooms**, and there is an excellent restaurant around the corner on Rua Texeira Sousa. The next best restau-

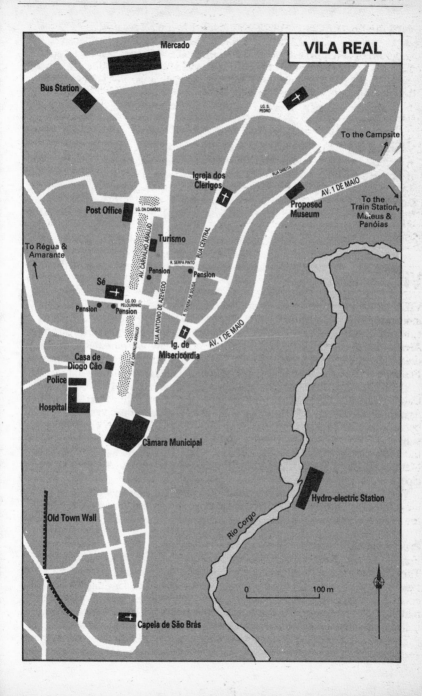

VILA REAL

Mercado

Bus Station

LG. S. PEDRO

To the Campsite

RUA DIREITA

Igreja dos Clerigos

AV. 1 DE MAIO

Post Office

LG. DA CAMÕES

Proposed Museum

To the Train Station, Mateus & Panóias

Turismo

AV. CARVALHO ARAÚJO

RUA CENTRAL

To Régua & Amarante

R. SERPA PINTO

Pension

Pension

Sé

RUA ANTÓNIO DE AZEVEDO

R. TRAVESSA DE SOUSA

Pension

LG. DO PELOURINHO

Pension

AV. 1 DE MAIO

Ig. de Misericórdia

Casa de Diogo Cão

AV. CARVALHO ARAÚJO

Police

Hospital

Câmara Municipal

Hydro-electric Station

Old Town Wall

Rio Corgo

0   100 m

Capela de São Brás

rant, the *Encontro* (no. 78 on the Avenida), also has rooms upstairs. Opposite, down the side of the cathedral, the *Mondego* is a clean, cheap pension. For other options consult the helpful tourist office or look in the Praça de Camões, up the Avenida. The **campsite** (with pool) is by the river, off the Avda. 1 de Maio – if you're coming from the station, take a right after crossing the bridge (turn left for the centre of town).

Most **buses** depart from the top of the Avenida, but local ones run from the bottom, at no. 26.

Mateus

The **Solar de Mateus** is just 4km from Vila Real along the Sabrosa road (signposted 'Palazio Mateus'), and easily reached on the regular *Cabanelas* bus service. Described by Sacheverell Sitwell as 'the most typical and the most fantastic country house in Portugal', it's certainly the most familiar, being reproduced on each bottle of *Mateus Rosé*, the most popular exported Portuguese wine.

The villa charges a handsome admission fee for a limited – in every sense – tour of its interior (9am–1pm and 2–6pm in summer), but the gardens are a delight. The palace's facade is true enough to its soft-focus image, the twin wings 'advancing lobster-like towards you', in Sitwell's phrase, across a formal lake.

Panóias and Sabrosa

You might combine a visit to Mateus with the Roman site of **PANÓIAS**, 5km farther along the same road. The sole remnant of the once powerful *Terras de Panóias*, the ancient forerunner of Vila Real, it doesn't at first appear much of a site – a few slabs of rock with odd-shaped cavities that are often full of water and rubbish. However, if you know a little French or Portuguese, the guided tour offered by the old man in the nearby house is worth accepting (tips gratefully received). He brings the three **sacrificial slabs** to life with gory descriptions of the filter systems for the blood and viscera created by the offerings to Serapis, a deity with pre-Roman origins.

As a digression, your guide may also elaborate on the harsh times under Salazar, when he was brought up in extreme poverty and lived off potatoes and grass soup. The region, in fact, happens to be where the first potatoes from South America were introduced, and appropriately enough, **Magellan's birthplace** is nearby at **SABROSA**, a village now better known for its wine.

Cabanelas operates a weekday bus to the Panóias site at 3pm from town, but you have to walk back down to the stop on the main road for a lift back.

Alvão National Park

The **Alvão National Park** can be glimpsed if you are travelling by road between Amarante and Vila Real. A granite basin formed around the Rio Olo – a tributary of the Tâmega – the park has some spectacular waterfalls at FISGAS DE ERMELO, and a few quiet, rural hamlets, with houses made from the schist of the hillsides. Good targets might include LAMAS DE OLO, with its mill and primitive aqueduct; the waterfall (and another mill) at GALEGOS DE SERRA; and the dammed lakes of Alvão itself.

The problem in exploring Alvão is transport. Without a car, you're dependent on very sketchy bus services: *Tâmegatur* goes only as far as LORDELO, and *RN* to nearby BORBELA. Serious walkers intending to cross the whole reserve should obtain maps from the Army in Lisbon, and consult the Park Headquarters in Vila Real (Rua Alves Torgo 22, °3 ; turn left after the bus station).

Chaves

CHAVES, the last stop on the Corgo line, stands only twelve kilometres from the Spanish border. Its name translates as 'Keys', reflecting a strategic history of occupations and ownership. Between 1128 and 1160 it was an Islamic enclave, and in the following seven centuries it was fought over by French, Spaniards and Portuguese in turn. One of its greatest overlords, **Nuno Álvares Pereira**, was literally awarded the 'keys' of the north by João I for his valiant service at *Aljubarrota*, and from him the town passed into the steady hands of the House of Bragança. However, as recently as 1912 Chaves bore the brunt of a Royalist attack from Spain – two years after Portugal had become a Republic.

The town is today rather less significant, a market centre for the villages of the fertile Tâmega plain – the richest agricultural lands in Trás-os-Montes. Its principal attractions are its setting and gastronomy. Chaves is famed in Portugal for a strong red **wine**, a famous smoked **ham**, and delicious meat cakes (*bôlas de carne*) and stuffed sausages. It also has a winter *feira*, held on November 1.

The Town

Chaves's military past is clearly felt today. There are two Vaubanesque **fortresses** (one before and one beyond the train station), an ancient keep (near the bridge) housing a small **military museum**, and a **Museu Regional** (Praça de Camões), which details the history of the town and its customs.

The town has an older name, indicative of another aspect of life in Chaves: *Aquae Flaviae* was an important point on the Roman road from Astorga (in Spanish León) to Braga, and two milestones remain on the Trajano bridge. It was the Roman army under Aulus Flaviensis in the first century A.D. who was also responsible for bringing the region's **thermal stations** to prominence. Despite changing fashions, the waters of Pedras Salgadas (Vila Pouca da Aguiar), Carvalhelhos (Boticas), Vidago and Chaves are still drunk today. The Chaves water is alkaline, warm (73°F), and not very tasty – if you want to try it, visit the building that houses the *nascente* (spring) below the city walls towards the river.

Unfortunately, the river itself is polluted – frustrating any chance of a swim – though the gardens around are well-kept and attractive. As far as architecture goes, there are two interesting **churches** on the central Praça de Camões. The **Matriz** is partly Romanesque; the **Misericórdia** is distinguished by vast *azulejo* panels.

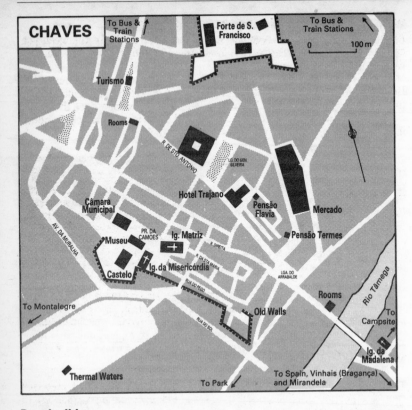

Practicalities

Despite its glittering background, the town can be disappointing, especially in the height of summer when the **campsite** may be crowded, the river too dry for swimming, and the **pensions** full or overpriced.

Cheapest bets for rooms are generally *Pensão Jorge* (Rua do Loureiro, off Rua S. António), *Pensão Jaime* (Avda. da Muralha, ☎076/21273; below the city walls) or *Pensão Imperial* (Rua Direita 158, ☎076/23142; near Praça de Camões), or the *dormidas* signposted just past the **Turismo** on the corner of Rua de Santo António (marked on the map). Other rooms are usually advertised near the bridge – look for signs in the windows. A little more upmarket, try the *Hotel Trajano* (marked on the map) or the *Pensão Flavia* opposite.

Most pensions also have **restaurants**. Recommended are those attached to the *Pensão Jorge* (cheap) or the *Hotel Trajano* (less so).

Buses leave regularly for Mirandela, Vinhais (6am, 12.30pm and 5pm; connections to Bragança) and Braga (via Montalegre). Heading **into Spain**, you could pick up an *Internorte* express coach from Porto on a Thursday or Sunday (leaves Chaves at 3.15pm, arriving Vérin 4.45pm and Orense 6.15pm), but it would be wise to make an advance reservation. Other days, hitching should be feasible.

West and East from Chaves: Montalegre and Vinhais

Almost any route from Chaves has something going for it. To the west, you can get buses to **Montalegre** (see *The Minho*), a fine approach to Braga or the Gerês National Park.

To the east, buses roll through the hills along a superb scenic route to Bragança. Midway is the dusty roadside village of **VINHAIS**, dominated by the Baroque convent of **São Francisco**. North of the village rises the **Serra de Montesinho**, now protected as a National Park (see "Bragança", following). There are a couple of **pensions** if you get stuck in Vinhais.

THE TUA LINE

The **Tua valley** by rail is a magnificent approach to Trás-os-Montes. All the way to **Mirandela** (70km; 1 hr. 40 min.), the line accompanies the rocky course of the river; thereafter it crawls across the Serra de Nogueira (65km; 2 hr. 45 min. to Bragança), at times coming too close to the construction work on the new highway for comfort. Occasionally passengers are politely requested to step down and walk along an unstable section of track, to another train which takes over for the rest of the way. It is hard to believe that anybody would have tried to construct a railway in such difficult terrain; the British, apparently, take the honours.

Fortunately, unlike other lines in the north, the railway company maintains a reasonably **full service**. There are five departures daily from Tua to Mirandela, with four of these continuing along the whole route to Bragança.

Mirandela and the Tua Valley

Midway along the Tua, **MIRANDELA** is an odd little town with a medieval centre, a scattering of Baroque mansions and a brand new museum of modern art. It makes a good place to break the journey – with the option of staying, or continuing on a later train to Bragança.

The **Museu de Arte Moderna** (Mon.–Fri. 2.30–6pm) is in fact combined with the town's library. It has two collections of paintings: one dedicated to local boy Armindo Teixeira Lopes's images of Mirandela and Lisbon; the other, rather more exciting, to a fairly representative – if slightly too slick – display of twentieth-century Portuguese painting and printmaking.

In contrast to the clean lines of this modern building, the **old town** is in a state of decay. The chapel next to the town hall, at the summit of the ancient citadel, simply fell down six years ago. Scavengers have pilfered the most useful or attractive pieces of stonework, but there is still a pile of rubble and an altarpiece open to the skies.

The grandeur of the **Câmara Municipal** – the former *Palácio dos Távoras* – and of several other flamboyant townhouses here, is due to the dominance of the **Távora** family between the fourteenth and seventeenth centuries. Pêro Lourenço de Távora rose to power in 1385 at the Battle of Aljubarrota, where he fought against the Castilians at the side of the future João I. Unfortunately, his distant grandson, Luís Álvares Távora, was to accompany Dom Sebastião in 1578 on the disastrous trip to Morocco, and the subsequent decline in the family fortunes went so far that in 1759 Pombal ordered the Távora insignia to be removed from all the palaces.

Prior to this activity in town, the Romans, as usual, were building bridges. Mirandela's **bridge** – renovated in the fifteenth century – is by far its most striking feature, stretching a good 200m across the sluggish river.

Practicalities

The best **pension** is the *Sá Moreno* (Avda. das Amoreiras, ☎078/22434), on the right coming from the station to the Turismo; further along the avenida is the much cheaper, unstarred *Residencial Flórida* (Rua da República 77; ☎078/22254). The *Sá Moreno* has a fair restaurant, too, or try the *Universo* (Travessa de S. Cosme, above the *Florida*). The **campsite** is several kilometres out of town (marked on the left off the Bragança road).

Mirandela is at a crossroads in central Trás-os-Montes, with **buses** twice a day to and from Chaves and Vila Real (via Murça). *Cabanelas* operate from beyond the fire station on the Rua da República, while *RN* is back between the **Turismo** (by the bridge) and the train station (second on the left).

If possible, visit Mirandela during its **festa** – one of the longest in Portugal (July 25–Aug. 15), or for one of the weekday **markets**, held as close as possible to the 3rd, 14th, or 25th of every month.

Towards Bragança: Macedo de Cavaleiros

At Mirandela the Tua broadens and the railway branches off along the Rio Azibo to **MACEDO DE CAVALEIROS**. However, unless the shooting and fishing parties at the *Estalagem* are in your line, Macedo is not a box of delights. For those unfortunate enough to be stranded here, delicious Italian **pizzas** at the *Marisqueira* (Rua Fonte do Paço 5), swilled down with the local wine, could help to diffuse your sorrows. You can also save a few pennies by staying above the *Churrasqueira* restaurant or at the cheap **pension** on the main street.

For **trains** on to Bragança (under 2 hr.), the station is out of town on the Moncorvo road.

Carrezeda de Ansiães and Vila Flôr

Travelling by road between the Douro and Bragança, the main route runs to the southwest of the Tua, through **Carrezeda de Ansiães** and **Vila Flôr**, before joining the rail line at Macedo.

Carrezeda de Ansiães

CARREZEDA DE ANSIÃES is summarised in an old Gulbenkian Guide to Portugal as 'dull and flat', but three-and-a-half kilometres south of it you'll find the far from dull ruins of an **ancient walled town**. Little remains within the perimeter of walls except rocks and boulders, but two **chapels** stand right outside, the newer of which – the twelfth-century church of *São Salvador* – deserves a close look. Its Romanesque **portal**, extravagantly carved with leaves, animals, and human figures, including Christ and the four Evangelists, forms a sharp contrast to the simplicity of the church.

Local myth has it that a tunnel connects the town to another castle beyond the Douro, 12km away; a gaping, fly-ridden hole beneath an impressive slab is the principal piece of supporting evidence. What is undoubtedly true, however, is that the town was a base for five different kings, including the King of Léon and Castile, before Portuguese independence; they're listed by the gateway on a plaque unveiled by Mário Soares in February 1987.

People lived in this ancient town until the mid–eighteenth century. Then, in 1734, a gentleman named Francisco de Araújo e Costa managed to transfer the official council seat to the new town below. He replied to protests by ordering the castle *pelourinho* to be destroyed. With this symbol gone and without a sufficient supply of water, the hill community had no hope of putting up effective resistance. The medieval town went into decline and was soon totally abandoned.

There is one **pension** in the modern town if you need to stay, but it is preferable to move on. **Buses** run between Vila Flôr and Tua station in both directions, but at irregular times. Check with *José Lages* in town, or hitch a lift with one of a number of grocery vans that supply the area.

Vila Flôr

Bafflingly described as 'airy and progressive' by the Gulbenkian guide, **VILA FLÔR** merits a visit if only for its eccentric **museum** (9.30am–12.30pm and 2–5pm; closed Mon.; admission free, but donations are gladly accepted). Three eminent Vilaflôrians donated the contents of their houses to the museum when it was founded in 1946, and the result is an incredible rag-bag: a much-glued *porca* (see "Bragança") and a few dusty pictures by Manuel Moura are the only items of value. The enveloping clutter contains typewriters, sewing machines, snake skins, a set of broken percussion instruments, religious sculptures, teacups, stuffed animals, and an ensemble of zebra-hide furniture.

Dom Dinis passed through here on his way to meet Isabel of Aragon in the thirteenth century, and in a display of *largesse* eminently befitting a young man in love, he renamed the small village 'Town of Flowers'. His favouritism was short-lived in practical terms. Soon Vila Flôr was forced to contribute a third of its church revenue to rebuilding the walls of rival Torre de Moncorvo. Nowadays the only striking features of the Vila Flôr townscape are a piece of old town wall known as the *Arco Dom Dinis*, and a so-called 'Roman' fountain.

There are three **pensions** at the new end of town. *Pensão Campos* (☎079/52311) is fine, and has a good **restaurant**, though you have to warn them in advance that you're coming. Otherwise, cafés will occasionally cook a Sunday spit-roast with *piri piri* sauce out on the pavement; the three most likely to do this are down by the museum. A little to the south, 2km along the Moncorvo road, is an excellent **campsite** – one of the first in the area, it's clean and has a swimming pool.

The local **festa** runs from August 22 to 28, with amateur live bands and open-air stalls on the last weekend. Couples still insist on traditional slow dancing whatever the rhythm of a song. There's also an extensive **street market** on the weekday closest to the 15th and 28th of every month.

Lying in the heart of the *Terra Quente*, but a little way from port territory, the Vila Flôr **wine cooperative** produces one of the most palatable red wines in the north. The town also boasts a good **bus company**, *Soc. de Transportes* (Avda. Marechal Carmona), with pale green buses and the resources to print their timetables.

Vilas Boas

Nearby at VILAS BOAS, 8km northwest, a raised sanctuary attracts pilgrims on August 15 (Nossa Senhora da Assunção). If you climb the ridge behind Vila Flôr, there is just as impressive a view (without the pilgrims) over vast stretches of undulating land covered in plantations of olive trees.

Bragança

On a dark hillock above **BRAGANÇA**, the remote capital of Trás-os-Montes, stands a circle of perfectly preserved medieval walls, rising to a massive keep and castle, and enclosing a white medieval village. This, the Citadel, is an extraordinary place – seemingly untouched by the centuries, with crops still grown within the walls – and, along with the fine local museum, the principal reason for a visit to the town.

'Modern Bragança', below, is a pleasant and functional base, but very small, quiet and provincial – and at odds with the ancient royal connotations of its name.

The Citadel and Town

Bragança is famed for the last line of **Portuguese monarchs** (and Charles II of England's Queen Catherine), who replaced the Spaniards in 1640 and ruled until the death of the monarchy in 1910. To the Portuguese, the name of Bragança also represents the defence of the liberty of the people, for the Braganças were the first to muster a popular revolt against Junot in 1808, and have always defended their power to make their own decisions.

The twelfth-century council chamber, the **Domus Municipalis**, stands in the heart of the Citadel. Very few Romanesque civic buildings have survived, and no other has this pentagonal form. Its traditional function as a gentlemen's club and watering hole has prompted the local nickname 'The House of Water'. Rising up at its side is the church of **Santa Maria**, with its eighteenth-century barrel-vaulted, painted ceiling – a feature of several churches in Bragança. Keys for both are kept locally if you find the doors shut.

Towering above these two is the **Castle**, which the royal family rejected as a residence in favour of their vast estate in the Alentejo. Ironically it reached the nadir of its decay under the militia in the last century, but was one of the first tasks of restoration for the Society of National Monuments in 1928. At its side a curious *pelourinho* rises from the back of a prehistoric granite pig. The town's museum has three more of these crudely-sculpted *porcas*, the most famous of which is to be seen at Murça. They are thought to have been

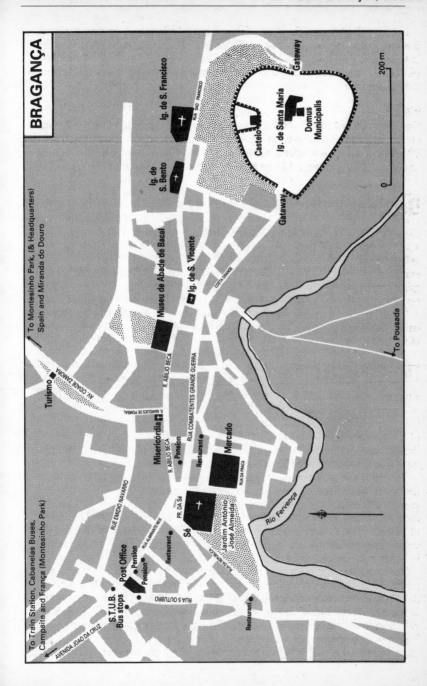

BRAGANÇA

To Montesinho Park, (& Headquarters)
Spain and Miranda do Douro

To Train Station, Cabanelas Buses,
Campsite and França (Montesinho Park)

Ig. de S. Francisco

RUA SÃO FRANCISCO

Ig. de
S. Bento

Gateway

Castelo

Ig. de Santa Maria

Domus
Municipalis

Gateway

0   200 m

AVENDA JOAO DA CRUZ

Turismo

AV. CIDADE ZAMORA

Museu de Abade de Bacal

Ig. de S. Vicente

COSTA GRANDE

R. ABILIO BECA

R. MARQUES DE POMBAL

Misericórdia

RUA EMIDIO NAVARRO

R. ABILIO BECA

RUA COMBATENTES GRANDE GUERRA

Pension

Restaurant

Mercado

RUA DA PRAÇA

Sé

PR. DA SÉ

Jardim Antonio
José Almeida

Rio Fervença

RUA ALMIRANTE REIS

Post Office

Pension

Pension

S.T.U.B.
Bus stops

RUA 5 OUTUBRO

Restaurant

Restaurant

To Pousada

the fertility idols of a prehistoric cult, and it's easy to understand the beast's prominence in this province of wild boars and chestnut forests, where the staple winter diet is smoked sausage.

Look over the furthest walls and you'll see the **Parque Natural de Montesinho** stretching across to Spain, making the town seem smaller and more remote than ever. The group who took the most advantage of this isolation were the **Jews**, who escaped over the border in the sixteenth century from the terrors of the **Inquisition** in Spain. Despite the common rule by Spaniards over the two countries during this period, the Inquisition in Portugal was relatively inefficient – administered in municipalities, the organisation spread slowly northwards with ever-decreasing zeal. The Jewish community has left its mark in the names of Bragançan families and in the town's cuisine (the *alheira* sausage is no longer kosher, but is still paler than its more sanguinary brothers); the thriving synagogue was opened in 1927.

The Town: São Vicente and the Museum

Doubling back to the middle ground between citadel and cathedral, the narrow, stepped Rua Serpa Pinto leads down to the church of **São Vicente**, where Pedro I claimed to have secretly married Inês de Castro (see the "Alcobaça" in *Estremadura and Ribatejo* for their legend).

Veer right after the church and you come to the **Museu do Abade de Baçal**, installed in the former Bishop's Palace in Rua Abílio Beça (10am–12.30pm and 2–5pm; closed Mon.). Celtic-inspired medieval tombstones rub shoulders with a menagerie of *porcas* in the palace gardens. Inside, the collection of sacred art and the topographical watercolours of Alberto Souza are the highlights, along with the displays of local costumes – especially the female dress of the (male) *Pauliteiros* ('stick dancers'), who still perform at festivals around Bragança and Miranda do Douro.

Further down the same street is the fine Renaissance **Misericórdia** (founded in 1418), but the best church in Bragança is undoubtedly **São Bento**, back up at the top of Rua Abílio Beça and close to the castle. This again is Renaissance (1590); simple, small and exceptionally beautiful, with three contrasting ceilings.

Practicalities

Bragança is a good base, especially if you are considering exploring the wild and lonely hills of the Montesinho. **Lodgings** are mostly close to the cathedral square, though the cheapest pension, the *Transmontano* (Avda. João da Cruz 168, ☎073/22899) is opposite the station. You'd be better advised to pay a little more and stay at *Residencial Poças* (Rua Combatentes da G. Guerra 200, ☎073/22428), the best in town at the price. Alternatively, the old-fashioned and friendly *Pensão Rocha* (Rua Almirante Reis 42, ☎073/22672) or the down-at-heel *Hospedaria Bragantina* (next door) are also very reasonable. The **campsite** is 6km out of town on the França road (left out of the station; no bus and sparse facilities), but there are also plenty of open spaces beyond the walls of the upper town. If you need to **change money** outside normal banking hours, the *Poças* will usually oblige.

Restaurants are good but not very cheap. At the top end of the range are the *Solar Bragança* (in Praça da Sé), an excellent *casa típica*, and *O Manel* (Rua Orobio de Castro 27, near the market), which has the best local dishes. Two personal favourites are *O Bolha* (Jardim Dr. António José de Almeida), which has cheap set menus and a homemade pink liqueur, and the basic but disarmingly friendly *Machado Cure* (Rua Almirante Reis). There's also excellent food at the *Residencial Poças* – opposite which is *Bô*, the best late **bar** in town, with live Brazilian bands and local guitarists in summer. There are numerous dives around, too – at the bottom of the Rua Combatentes da G. Guerra, for instance – and the bar of the *Solar* (see above) is also good.

For details on the Bragança **festa** – largely a cultural event with exhibitions, ballets and films – from August 14 to 22, consult the helpful **Turismo** on the Avenida Cidade de Zamora.

Transport

Buses leave from outside the train station, where *Cabanelas* has a kiosk – and an office up the opposite street. There are various buses to Vinhais, including one at midday (change for Chaves), and more regular ones to Miranda do Douro at 5.45am, 11.35am, and 5pm (Sat. 11.35am only). This is an advisable route to take for hitchers since traffic is poor on the Vimoso route to Mogadouro, and it turns out to be just as quick the longer way round.

If you head down south by **train**, remember to take provisions for a journey which is long (often over 4 hr.), but spectacular for the last hour and a half from Mirandela to Tua.

Getting to Spain

For various reasons the two Iberian nations do not communicate on the subject of cross-border transport, and as a result a smooth crossing from one to the other is almost unheard of. Give yourself two days wherever you are.

From Bragança the most obvious route is **via Quintanilha** (34km). *Cabanelas* leave at 5pm on a weekday, but any bus to Miranda Do Douro will take you to a crossroads from which you can hitch the 12km to the San Martin border post; you can stay here, if need be, above the *Evaristo* (the place's only shop, restaurant and pension). At 7am there is a bus to ZAMORA (or you could hitch) and from there *Condes de Alba y Aliste* runs a weekday service to MADRID at 7am, 10.15am, 2pm and 5.15pm.

In Bragança there's also the possibility of reserving a seat on the *Internorte* **express bus** which passes through from Tuesday to Saturday at 2.45pm (arriving Quintanilha 3.15pm and Zamora 6.15pm).

Alternatively, **buses to Portela**, at the top of the National Park, are run by *Cabanelas* on Monday, Wednesday and Friday at 2.15pm, but there are no connections to PUEBLA DE SANABRIA (20km away; on the train line and with accommodation) except from CALABRIA (4km into Spain) on a weekday. From PUEBLA there are weekday buses to MADRID at 11.15am, 2.30pm and 5pm. Hitchhikers will find the **Miranda do Douro** route to ZAMORA marginally busier than either of these.

Parque Natural de Montesinho

Occupying the extreme northeastern tip of Portugal, the **Parque Natural de Montesinho** is the only sector of the *Terra Fria* where the way of life and the appearance of villages have not been changed by the new wealth of the emigrant workers. The *Terra Fria*'s predominantly barren landscape is here disrupted by microclimates which give rise to hills of heather, wet grass plains and thick forests of oak. Another curious feature of the region is the round *pombal*, or pigeon house – a structure which, no matter how well-established its position, invariably seems to have dropped in from another world.

The **National Park Headquarters** in Bragança (Rua Alexandre Herculano 11159; 10am–noon and 2–5pm) has leaflets and advice for walkers of all grades of seriousness. As far as **transport** into the area is concerned, the buses to Vinhais or better still to Rio de Onor can help. It is also possible to hitch on the França road in summer. Walking beyond França alongside the **Rio Sabor** is idyllic, and there are deserted spots for swimming and camping which the Park Headquarters will point out.

Rio de Onor

RIO DE ONOR is a good introduction to the village life of the area. There are in fact two Rio de Onors, one in Spain, one in Portugal. A simple chain slung between two stone blocks labelled 'E' and 'P' marks a border that in practice means very little, as the villagers have come and gone for generations, intermarrying and buying goods. Out of this blending of the two tribes comes the dialect of *Rionorês*, a curious hybrid of the two tongues.

Both villages are set above a stream: the granite steps and wooden balconies of rough stone houses line the narrow alleyways, and straw creeps out across the cobbles. The extreme isolation of these villages encouraged systems of justice and mutual cooperation which are independent of the state and which still exist. The aging villagers share land, flocks, wine-presses, mills and ovens.

The ethnographical museum in Miranda do Douro can fill you in on aspects of traditional village life such as the black cape and the cloaks of straw – as much protection against heat as against cold. In anticipation of the harsh winter to come, the inhabitants move out onto their front doorsteps in autumn to pod and shred a curious selection of hard beans for storage.

Transport

Naturally the transport service is suited to the villagers and not to day trippers: **buses** leave here every weekday at 7.15am and 4pm and return at 2pm and 5.35pm (1.35pm Sat.) from Bragança. Ask near the post office for the correct *STUB* bus stop, as they are liable to vary in accordance with the school timetable. These times may entail pitching a tent, but there is also the possibility of basic shelter in the *Casa do Povo* (parish rooms) if you contact the village president on arrival.

Border Towns

The route from **Bragança to Miranda Do Douro** runs across the *Planalto Mirandês* – a breathtaking journey in late February and early March, when the sudden blossoming of the **almond trees** transforms the countryside.

Miranda do Douro

For several centuries past, **MIRANDA DO DOURO** played an important role as a **border post**. Some say that it was the beauty of Miranda that decided Afonso Henriques, the future first king of Portugal, to turn against his Spanish kinsmen, refortify the towns that are now on the border, and begin his victorious sweep across Lusitânia at the start of the twelfth century. Facing Spain across the deep gorge of the Douro, the town played a key role in all of the country's subsequent wars. After valiant service in the Independence, Spanish Succession, and Seven Year wars, it ended its fighting days in 1762 when an explosion during a Spanish attack destroyed the castle, the town and 400 inhabitants.

Today, with a population of less than 2000, Miranda is scarcely more than a village. Yet it once had the status of a city, and a sturdy sixteenth-century **Cathedral** overlooks its cobbled streets and low white houses. This peculiar honour came about in the twelfth century with the Church's decision to make Miranda the capital of the diocese, in order to counteract the feudal power of the House of Bragança in Trás-os-Montes. At the end of the eighteenth century, however, the see was transferred to the larger of the two towns, leaving Miranda with its cathedral as a cumbersome memento of past glory. To the bitter comment, 'The sacristy is in Bragança, but the cathedral is in Miranda'; the astute Bragançans reply, 'If ever you go to Miranda, see the cathedral and come home'.

As a town, Miranda seems a bit too clean and pricey to be very Portuguese. However, there is a certain neat charm in the tidied-up **ruins of the Episcopal Palace**, which is now a café, or in the medieval **Rua da Costanilha** (to the side of the museum). Beyond the **gateway of Santo do Amparo** there is a small medieval bridge over the diminutive Rio Fresno, and an eighteenth-century fountain set above the road to the **campsite** (not as clean or neat as the town). The **museum** (9am–noon and 2–4.45pm; closed Mon.), bursting with curiosities, from lumps of stone to pistols, has a couple of rooms arranged in Mirandês style – an illustration of local life that's inaccurate only in that the agricultural labourers of the region generally live, sleep and die in a single room.

Apart from the **festa** periods (Santa Bárbara – 3rd Sun. in Aug.; Romaria N.S. do Nazo – Sept. 7–8; Pauliteiros – Dec. 27–28) and the *feiras* on the first weekday of every month, not a lot happens in Miranda besides the odd football match. A folk group from Duas Igrejas, the *Pauliteiros de Miranda*, occasionally perform the 'stick dance' in a whirl of dust and to the sound of the tambourine and the bagpipes, but their world tours (if you can believe that) have put an end to their regular Sunday afternoon displays.

Practicalities

The only **pension** in the old part of town is the *Santa Cruz* (Rua Abade de Baçal 6l, ☎073/42474), which is fine; the **Turismo**, back towards the main road, can advise you on the selection on their side of town. Nothing is very cheap. *O Mirandês* or the cheaper *Balbina* are both, however, excellent **restaurants**. The latter has wine in jugs and a local *posta assada á mirandesa* (beef), which does amply for two or three.

Moving on, there are reasonable **bus connections**. *Santos & Co.* operates from the museum square to Mogadouro, Moncorvo and Pocinho at 5.45am and 3.15pm (every day) and 11am (Mon.–Fri. only). Change at Freixo station for the town itself (14km farther on), from where there are connections to Figueira de Castelo Rodrigo and to Guarda. A weekday would be best for Guarda.

The **Spanish border** lies just the other side of a vast **hydroelectric dam** – at 528m the highest in the country, and the last before the Douro becomes the Duero. You might take advantage of this crossing (3km to the border post) to approach Zamora, but you'll have to hitch (not impossible with regular parties of Spaniards coming to Miranda for duty-free goods). Outside the Spanish tourist season, it makes more sense to cross at VILAR FORMOSO, 170km south.

Mogadouro

For a more unkempt picture of town life in the *Terra Fria*, take a look at **MOGADOURO** – and, more specifically, head for the **Castle**. It's unexceptional as a monument, but the ground in front of it is a common where children play and farmers sort out their produce. During the harvest period the area is often stacked high with dried *tremoços* bushes – which are consumed as beer-time snacks and used in soups. The castle hill also commands terrific views over a long, low horizon and a crazy patchwork of fields and *pombais*.

Mogadouro would never be listed for its ancient buildings, though the **Town Hall** is in a former convent. The townspeople treat it as their own backyard, herding cows home in the evening, saddling up pony carts and playing at tossing coins for hours at a time. The only building to visit is the **Cultural House** (*CCM*) which has small exhibitions upstairs (on Avda. da Espanha – follow the signs for the hospital and walk right down).

Should you want to **stay**, there's the cheap *Pensão Russo* behind the café (Rua 5 de Outubro 10, ☎079/32134) or, better still, you could ask for a room in the stone house below the far walls of the castle. Be warned that the town is busy (and full) in August, when the emigrants are back home with their families, and has a **festa** on the penultimate weekend before they leave the country again. You could **camp** overnight in the fields beyond the castle if the 18km to the site at *Ponte de Remonde* seems too far.

Buses leave from the kiosk in the central gardens, but few pass the campsite. Ask in the *Santos* office nearby.

Freixo de Espada à Cinta

The twentieth century recedes even further as you travel south to **FREIXO DE ESPADA À CINTA**, reached by changing buses off the Miranda do Douro–Pocinho route at Freixo station, 14km away.

The town feels almost end-of-the-worldish as the bus climbs down to its valley, hidden on each side by wild, dark mountains; arrive at dusk and you'll see donkeys being led back to their stables in the lower storeys of the houses. Curiously there is a very rich **Igreja Matriz** – part Romanesque, part Manueline – with a retablo of paintings by Grão Vasco (see "Viseu" in *Mountain Beiras*). Across the way is a magnificent hexagonal **keep**, a landmark for miles around. Unexpectedly too there is a good modern *hospedaria* (**pension**) in the square where you arrive.

travel details

Trains
Douro Line 18 daily from PORTO to Livração (1 hr. 30 min.; change for Tâmega Line), 15 to Régua (2 hr. 45 min.; change for Corgo Line), 7 to Tua (3 hr. 30 min.; change for Tua Line), and 4 go on to Pocinho (4 hr. 35 min.).

Tâmega Line 7 daily from LIVRAÇÃO to Amarante (30 min.), Mondim de Basto (1 hr. 30 min.), and Arco de Baúlhe (2 hr.).

Corgo Line 5 daily from RÉGUA to Vila Real (1 hr.), 3 to Chaves (3 hr. 30 min.; at 6am, 4.55pm, and 7.45pm, returning at 4.55am, 11am, and 5pm).

Tua Line 5 daily from TUA to Mirandela (1 hr. 40 min.), Macedo de Cavaleiros (2 hr. 30 min.) and 4 to Bragança (4 hr.; at 6.20am, 11.10am, 6pm and 9.55pm, returning at 5.30am, 7.25am, 12.25pm, and 5.15pm).

Buses
Sabor Line Buses follow goods-train route daily from POCINHO to Freixo de Espada à Cinta station (1 hr.), Mogadouro (2 hr.), and Miranda do Douro (3 hr.) at 12.20pm and 6.55pm, returning 6am and 3.45pm.

Chaves–Vinhais/Bragança (3 daily; 2 hr./3 hr.).

Chaves–Montalegre/Braga (4 daily until 4.55pm; 1 hr./3 hr.).

Bragança–Miranda do Douro (3 daily; 1 hr. 30 min.).

Lamego–Régua (12 daily; 30 min.).

Lamego–Viseu, for Coimbra (6 weekdays, 3 on weekends; 1 hr. 15 min./3 hr. 45 min.).

CHAPTER EIGHT

ALENTEJO

T he huge, sparsely populated plains of the **Alentejo** are overwhelmingly agricultural, dominated by vast cork plantations well suited to the low rainfall, sweltering heat and poor soil. It's an impoverished province, divided into vast estates (*latifúndios*) which provide nearly half of the world's cork but only a sparse living for the landless mass of the agricultural workforce.

Visitors to the Alentejo generally head for its central and northern section, drawn to **Évora**, the province's dominant and most historic city. Declared by *UNESCO* to be a locality of special cultural interest, Évora and its monuments are well maintained and worth seeing, though be warned that tourism here is big, on a scale with Toledo, say, in Spain. Elsewhere in the 'Upper Province' of **Alto Alentejo**, few towns see more than a handful of visitors in a day. And yet there is much to see and enjoy: the spectacular fortifications of **Elvas**; the eagle's nest hilltop sites of **Monsaraz**, **Évora-Monte** and **Marvão**; and the marble towns of **Estremoz**, **Borba** and **Vila Viçosa**, to the northeast of Évora, where even the humblest homes are made of fine stone from the local quarries. The province is also scattered with **prehistoric remains**, sheltering over a dozen megalithic sites with dolmens, standing stones and stone circles.

The plains of **Bajo Alentejo**, south of Évora, have rather less appeal, and the towns, with the notable exception of **Beja**, can seem rather dull. But the Alentejo coastline – almost as extensive as the Algarve's – more than compensates for the lack of urban pleasures and the tedium of the inland landscape. Whipped by the Atlantic winds, its **beaches** are less domesticated than those in the south, and are especially good around **Melides** and **Santo André** (near **Santiago do Cacém**), and farther south at **Ilha do Pessegueiro**, **Vila Nova de Milfontes** and **Zambujeira do Mar**.

ALENTEJO *LATIFUNDIA*

Following the 1974 revolution, much land in Alentejo – which was then (as now) the Communist stronghold – was collectivised. The workers, however, possessed neither the financial nor the technical know-how to cope with a succession of poor harvests, and increasingly the original *latifundia* owners have been clawing back their estates at depressed prices. Jobs are today scarcer than ever, with mechanisation doing away with much casual farm labour, though the government, helped by EC grants, is finally beginning to invest in modernisation programmes and new methods.

Visible reminders of the heady days of 1974 survive in scores of fading revolutionary slogans – daubed on buildings in even the smallest communities.

ÉVORA AND ALTO ALENTEJO

Unless you are headed south to the beaches, Évora provides the easiest access to Alentejo, with frequent and fast buses, or rather slower trains, from Lisbon. There is little to detain you en route though, if you are driving, the castle at MONTEMOR O NOVO (the town is not up to much) is enjoyable to clamber about. Moving into the province of Alto Alentejo, Évora and, to the north, Portalegre are very much the transport hubs.

Évora

ÉVORA is one of the most impressive and enjoyable cities in Portugal, its provincial atmosphere forming a perfect setting for a range of memorable and often intriguing monuments. Until recently it was almost as if the circuit of walls had fended off the outside world and allowed Évora to crawl into the twentieth century at its own graceful pace, dragging its feet through 2000 years of rich history. Nowadays it's becoming ever more popular with the tourists and prices have crept up – but there's a long way to go yet before the town is spoiled.

Évora's Development

The so-called Temple of Diana, at the centre of Évora, is a solitary but grand reminder of four centuries of **Roman occupation**, while the **Moors**, who were here for just as long, have left their stamp in the tangle of narrow alleys which rise steeply among the whitewashed houses.

But most of the monuments date from the fourteenth to the sixteenth century, when the city prospered under the patronage of the ruling **House of Avis**. To their wealth are owed the city's royal and noble palaces and its Jesuit **University**, founded in 1559 by Cardinal Henrique – the future 'Cardinal King'. With royal encouragement the city became one of the leading centres of Portuguese art, adorned by masters of Manueline and Renaissance architecture; the Regional Museum still contains an important collection of fifteenth- and sixteenth-century artworks.

Decline, however, set in with the Spanish usurpation of the throne in 1580 – after which time future Portuguese monarchs preferred to live nearer Lisbon – and a century later the University was closed down. For the next four hundred years, Évora drifted back into a rural existence as a provincial market centre.

Even today, the 40,000 population numbers no more than half its medieval level. However, there is a definite aspect of wealth about the place, much of it from the new-found tourism. The city continues to hold one of the biggest agricultural markets in the country – every Tuesday morning – when you'll find the main square packed with dark-suited, black-hatted farmers doing deals. And the university, re-established in 1979, with its presence of 3000 students, adds to the place an air of youthful vitality.

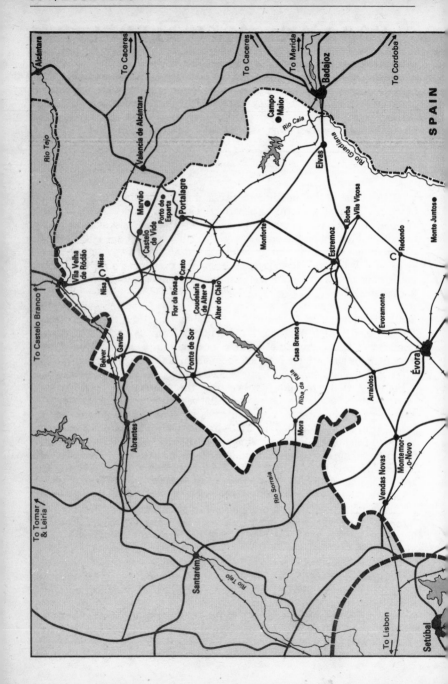

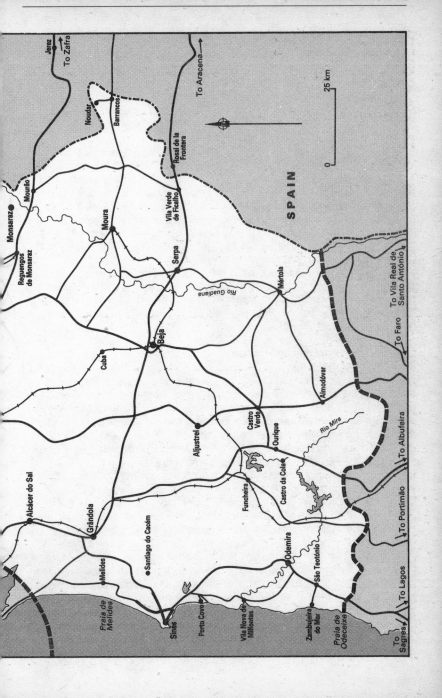

The City and Monuments

Évora is a remarkably compact city, and the **Roman Temple** in its central square stands out as a kind of progenitor of the later monuments around it. Dating from the second century A.D., it's the best preserved temple in Portugal despite (or perhaps because of) its use as a slaughterhouse until 1870. The stark remains consist of a small platform supporting more than a dozen granite columns with Corinthian capitals and marble entablature. Its popular attribution to Diana is, apparently, fanciful.

Directly opposite the Temple, the former **Convento dos Lóios** has been converted into a government-owned *pousada*. The sixteenth-century cloisters now serve as a dining area and the hotel staff can be sniffy about allowing non-residents in to look around. Dress up as formally as you can (a tie is a help for men) and walk in. The dual horseshoe arches, slender twisted columns, and the intricate carvings on the doorway to the chapter house are fine examples of the so-called Luso-Moorish style and have been attributed to Francisco de Arruda, architect of the Tower of Belém in Lisbon and of the aqueducts both here in Évora and at Elvas.

To the left of the *pousada* lies the actual church of the convent, dedicated to **São João Evangelista**. This is the private property of the ducal Cadaval family who still occupy a wing or two of their adjacent (mainly seventeenth-century) ancestral palace. Ring the bell and you should be admitted (for a fee) to see the *azulejos* within.

The Sé, Town Museum and Ermida

The **Sé** (cathedral; closed 12.30–2pm) is a good illustration of the development from Romanesque to Gothic architecture. It was begun in 1186, about twenty years after the reconquest of Évora from the Moors, and the Romanesque solidity of its two huge square towers and battlemented roofline contrasts sharply with the pointed Gothic arches of the porch and central window. The interior is more straightforwardly Gothic, although the choir and high altar were remodelled in the eighteenth century by the German Friedrich Ludwig, architect of the Convent at Mafra.

For a nominal fee you can clamber on to a terrace above the west entrance and take an unusually close look at the towers and the *zimbório* (the lantern above the crossing of the transepts). Don't miss the cathedral museum, either: it's stuffed with treasures and relics, the prize exhibit being a carved statue of the Madonna whose midriff opens out to display layered scenes from the bible.

Immediately adjacent is the former archbishop's palace, now the excellent **Museu de Évora** (10am–12.30pm and 2–5pm; closed Mon.), housing important collections of fifteenth- and sixteenth-century Flemish and Portuguese paintings assembled from the city's churches and convents. These give a good illustration of the significance of Flemish artists in the development of the 'Portuguese School', and reflect the strong medieval trade links between the two countries. Frei Carlos, probably the most important Flemish artist known to have worked in Évora, is well represented – but the real centre-

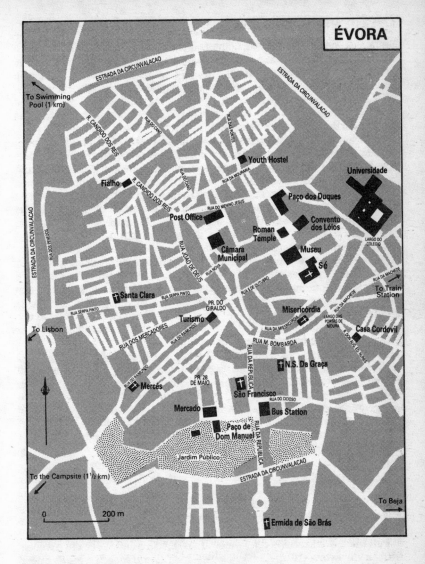

ÉVORA

To Swimming Pool (1 km)

ESTRADA DA CIRCUNVALAÇÃO

ESTRADA DA CIRCUNVALAÇÃO

R. CANDIDO DOS REIS

RUA DO CANO

RUA DA PORTEL

Youth Hostel

Universidade

Fialho

R. CANDIDO DOS REIS

RUA DO CANO

RUA DA MOURARIA

Paço dos Duques

RUA DO MENINO JESUS

Post Office

Convento dos Lóios

LARGO DO COLÉGIO

Roman Temple

Câmara Municipal

RUA JOÃO DE DEUS

RUA NOVA

Museu

Sé

RUA DA MACHEDE

ESTRADA DA CIRCUNVALAÇÃO

RUA DOS PENEDOS

Santa Clara

RUA SERPA PINTO

RUA 5 DE OUTUBRO

To Train Station

RUA SERPA PINTO

PR. DO GIRALDO

Misericórdia

To Lisbon

Turismo

RUA DOS MERCADORES

RUA DO RAIMUNDO

RUA DA MISERICÓRDIA

LARGO DAS PORTAS DE MOURA

Casa Cordovil

R. DOS DOL. 15 ALVES

RUA M. BOMBARDA

Mercés

RUA DO RAIMUNDO

PR. 28 DE MAIO

RUA DA REPÚBLICA

N.S. Da Graça

São Francisco

RUA DO CICIOSO

Mercado

Bus Station

Paço de Dom Manuel

RUA DA REPÚBLICA

Jardim Público

ESTRADA DA CIRCUNVALAÇÃO

To the Campsite (1½ km)

To Beja

0   200 m

Ermida de São Brás

piece of the museum is a series of thirteen panels by an anonymous fifteenth-century Flemish artist, portraying scenes from the Life of the Virgin. This was once the main cathedral altarpiece.

Great architects likewise gravitated to Évora, and the **Ermida de São Brás,** just outside the city walls on the road to the train station, has been identified as an early work by Diogo de Boitac, pioneer of the flamboyant

Manueline style. Its tubular dunce-capped buttresses and crenellated roofline bear scant resemblance to his masterpieces at Lisbon and Setúbal, but they certainly foreshadow the style's uninhibited originality.

No less bizarre is the mid-sixteenth-century facade of the **Igreja da Graça** (behind the bus station). At the corners of its Renaissance pediment grotesque Atlas-giants support two globes, emblem of Dom Manuel and his burgeoning overseas empire.

The Capela dos Ossos and Artesania

Such architectural extravagance notwithstanding, the most striking monument in Évora has to be the **Capela dos Ossos** (Chapel of Bones) in the church of **São Francisco**. A timeless and gruesome memorial to the mortality of man, the walls and pillars of this chilling chamber are entirely covered in the bones of more than 5000 monks. There's a grim humour in the neat, artfully planned arrangement of skulls and tibias around the vaults, and in the rhyming inscription over the door which reads '*Nós ossos que aqui estamos, Pelos vossos esperamos*' ('We bones here are waiting for your bones').

Such macabre warnings to the faithless can be encountered elsewhere in Portugal – there are similar chapels at Faro, and more especially at Campo Maior. Another interesting feature of this fifteenth-century church is its large **porch**, which combines pointed, rounded and horseshoe arches in a manner typical of Manueline architecture. Appropriately enough, the restored **Palácio de Dom Manuel** (1495–1521) – the king who gave his name to the style – lies no more than a minute's walk away, in the Jardim Público. It too incorporates inventive horseshoe arches with strange serrated edges.

Directly opposite São Francisco, on the Praça 1 de Maio, the rich craft traditions of the Évora district are well displayed in the **Museu do Artesanato Regional** (10am–noon and 2–5pm daily). The collections include pottery, weaving, tapestry and carvings in wood, cork and bone, and modern pieces are on sale, too. For purchases, however, it's a lot more fun to make your way to the **city market** (Tues.–Sat. mornings), five minutes down the hill, which is cheaper and more boisterous. If you're interested in the coarse Alentejan terracotta ware, this is certainly the place to get it.

Practicalities

The **Praça do Giraldo** is the centre of Évora's distinctly low-key social scene. Here you can find the **Turismo** (9am–12.30pm and 2–7pm) and a couple of outdoor cafés. In the evening, you'd do better taking a look at the **university** – the town goes to bed fairly early and in the centre, at least, it's hard to find a bar open after around 10pm. The university, well worth seeing in any case, has a beautiful entrance courtyard and, just beyond, a fine, dirt-cheap student bar; in term-time there may well be a band playing here or elsewhere in the complex.

Rooms and Camping

All the cheaper places to stay are within five minutes' walk of the Praça do Giraldo, although Évora's importance as a historical, cultural and tourist centre unfortunately pushes **accommodation** prices way over the norm. Cheapest options are *Os Manuéis*, just west of the square at Rua do Raimundo 35A; *Casa Portalegre*, a guesthouse at Travessa do Barão 18 (take the third alley right down Rua do Raimundo), and cheapest of all, the **youth hostel** at Rua de Corredoura 32, near the Roman Temple. If you can afford 3000esc or so for a double, try the very pleasant *Pensão Giraldo* at Rua dos Mercadores 15, or *Pensão Policarpo* at Rua da Freira de Baixo 16, near the cathedral. An even better alternative, for not much more, is *O Eborense* on the Largo da Misericórdia, a converted sixteenth-century **ducal mansion**, with a relaxing, spacious feel and an excellent breakfast included. If you're stuck for a room, the **Turismo** will sometimes arrange accommodation in private homes.

Évora's **campsite** is a couple of kilometres out of town on the Alcáçovas road. There's no reliable bus service and you're best off taking a taxi if you can't face the trudge. The campsite itself, once you get there, is clean and well-equipped. To cool down, head for the **swimming pool** just outside town (closed Oct.–Apr.).

Restaurants

There's no shortage of **restaurants** in the centre. *A Choupana* (Rua dos Mercadores 20) is recommended, as are the places at nos. 10 and 16 in the same street, and *O Túnel* (Alcárcova de Baixo 59, just off Rua de Misericórdia). Another basic but friendly place which serves enormous portions is *Restaurante Lagoa*, at Rua Cândido dos Reis 19 – five minutes' walk north of the main square, down Rua João de Deus. There's an excellent (and signposted) health-food restaurant in a sidestreet left of Rua Serpa Pinto, as you walk away from Praça do Giraldo. Or, if you're flush, the *Restaurante Fialho*, at Travessa do Mascarenhas 14 (see map), is the best in town – and, some say, in the country. Less crippling to budgets is the *Gelateria Zoka* (Rua da Misericórdia 14), which serves up superb icecream and coffee, ideal for sitting outside on a summer's evening.

Évora's Festival

The year's big event is the **Feira de São João**, a folklore, handicraft and music festival which takes over the city during the last ten days of June – well worth getting to if you possibly can. On Tuesdays there is a huge market, when farmers come into town; follow Rua da República south, past the bus station, to a large open space. It's all very colourful: part livestock market, part flea market, with pottery and all kinds of junk.

Carpets and Castles: Arraiolos, Évora-Monte and Viana

The trip out from Évora to **ARRAIOLOS**, half an hour's bus ride northwest (four buses a day each way), is well worthwhile if you can spare the time. Since the seventeenth century, the town has been famous for its tapestries, and the craft has survived. Nowadays they tend to be simple and brightly coloured but the original designs were based on elaborate Persian imports.

Some of their most luxuriant eighteenth-century creations can be seen hanging on the walls of the Royal Palace at Queluz. Apart from the carpet shops (the carpets are expensive – but a lot cheaper here than elsewhere), Arraiolos is a typical Alentejo village with its ruined castle, whitewashed houses, seventeenth-century pillory, and anti-fascist graffiti.

Évora-Monte

A similar daytrip distance from Évora, but to the northeast, on the Estremoz road, lies ÉVORA-MONTE (three buses a day each way). The sixteenth-century **Castle** here, built on the site of earlier fortifications going back to Roman times, occupies a spectacular position on top of a steep mound, around which the sleepy medieval town huddles. The keep was constructed in Italian Renaissance style with four robust, round towers, and adorned with a simple relief of Manueline stonework in the form of thick ropes. The interior contains three vaulted chambers with intricately carved granite capitals.

In the town itself, there are half a dozen interesting religious buildings, notably the *Igreja Matriz da Santa Maria*, an amalgam of styles dating from the sixteenth century.

Viana do Alentejo

VIANA DO ALENTEJO, to the south of Évora on the minor road to Beja, has another fine castle, this time fourteenth-century and full of Manueline decorative features. The village is sleepy and typically southern Alentejan.

Ancient Monuments

The administrative district of Évora contains over a dozen **megalithic sites** dating from around 3000 B.C. The dolmens, standing stones and stone circles found here have their origins in a culture which flourished in the peninsula before spreading north as far as Brittany and Denmark.

Unfortunately, they are hard to reach by public transport and are often a considerable distance from the nearest road; for full descriptions of all the sites and directions in English, ask at Turismo in Évora for the leaflet entitled *Roteiro Turístico de Alguns Monumentos Megalíticos do Distrito do Évora*.

Os Almendres

One of the sites nearest to Évora is the **stone circle** and three-metre-high **menhir** (upright stone) at a cork plantation called *Os Almendres*, about 3km out of GUADALUPE, just off the Évora–Montemor road. Ask for directions in the village, and then it's a stiff uphill walk through wild country.

Those interested in unusual birds will have the additional pleasure of seeing the **hoopoes** of the area.

Pavia

In the hamlet of **PAVIA**, 20km north of Arraiolos, is a massive **dolmen** within which the tiny sixteenth-century chapel of São Dinis has been built. The effect is a bit grotesque and out of keeping with Pavia's traditional Alentejan architecture, but impressive nonetheless.

Monsaraz and North to Vila Viçosa

'Ninho das Águias' (Eagles' Nest) is how the Portuguese refer to **MONSARAZ**, a name that conjures up suitably exhilarating and idyllic notions. It's a tiny village, fortified to the hilt and perched high above the undulating plains about 8km from the Spanish border. Once the novelty of cork trees has worn off, the scenery of the Alentejo can be mighty tedious, but from the heights of Monsaraz it takes on a magical quality. Absolutely nothing stirs amid a sensational panorama of sunbaked fields, neatly cultivated and dotted with cork and olive trees.

There's something peculiarly satisfying, too, about such a small village. From the clock tower of the main gateway, the only proper street leads past the only bar (unmarked, on the left, next to the post office) to the village square. Here you'll find an unusual eighteenth-century pillory topped by a sphere of the universe.

All seventy or so houses nestle within the thirteenth- and seventeenth-century walls, but the **Castle** proper lies at the far end of the village, dominated as ever by its *Torre de Menagem* (keep). Monsaraz forms part of a chain of frontier fortresses, continued to the south at Mourão, Moura and Serpa, and to the north with Alandroal, Elvas and Campo Maior. When the Moors were ejected in 1167 the village was handed over to the Knights Templar, and later to their successors, the Order of Christ; today their fortress has been converted into a tiny bullring.

The Monte do Xarez Stones

Between Monsaraz and the Guadiana river at MONTE DO XAREZ is a **menhir** four metres high, surrounded by a square of **standing stones**, probably the site of neolithic fertility rites. There are two more giant menhirs within easy reach of Monsaraz, just off the Reguengos road at **Outeiro** and at **Bulhoa,** where the stone is covered with symbolic engravings. Details of these sites are included in the leaflet mentioned opposite.

Monsaraz Practicalities

Two **buses** a day run from Évora to Monsaraz via Reguengos de Monsaraz, 17km away and the nearest significant settlement. This sparse service is supplemented by a twice-daily service from Reguengos to Monsaraz and back. Bus times make a day trip from Évora to Monsaraz feasible; hitching is virtually impossible. A few **rooms** are available at the bar in Monsaraz, where you can also get something to eat.

Reguengos and North to Vila Viçosa

If you find yourself stranded in **REGUENGOS DE MONSARAZ**, there are some dirt-cheap rooms (unadvertised) just off the Praça da Liberdade and directly opposite the *Café Central*, the liveliest place to sample the splendid wine of the local co-operative.

Reguengos itself is a dull agricultural town, but the journey north from here to VILA VIÇOSA (2 buses daily) is infinitely more interesting than the main approach from Évora. The first stage runs along crumbling roads through the backyards of scattered farming communities where the problems of the Alentejo are disturbingly apparent. Radical political slogans still have real meaning here. At **MONTES JUNTOS** a wall proclaims '25 APRIL FOREVER!' (the date of the 1974 revolution) and another, 'AGRARIAN REFORM! LAND! BREAD!'

Further north the pretty villages of **TERENA** and **ALANDROAL**, each with its castle, seem positively prosperous in comparison.

The Marble Towns: Vila Viçosa, Borba and Estremoz

The area around VILA VIÇOSA, BORBA and ESTREMOZ is so rich in marble quarries that the availability of beautiful white stone is taken for granted. Where other towns use brick and concrete, these three use slabs of marble, giving butchers' stalls and simple cottages the sort of luxurious finish you generally see only on churches and the grandest houses.

Vila Viçosa

At **VILA VIÇOSA** everything from the pavements to the toilets in the bus station are made of the local marble (luxury indeed!). The town is justly famous, too, for the **Ducal Palace of the Bragança Family** (signposted *Paço Ducal*), the preferred residence of the last kings of Portugal – which gives a fascinating insight into the private side of royalty.

The Ducal Palace
The dukes of Bragança were descended from the illegitimate offspring of João I of Avis, and established their seat at Vila Viçosa in the fifteenth century. For the next two centuries they were on the edge of the ruling circle but their claims to the throne were overridden in 1580 by Philip II of Spain. Sixty years later, while Spanish attention was diverted by a revolt in Catalonia, Portuguese resentment erupted and massive public pressure forced the reluctant João, eighth Duke of Bragança, to seize the throne; his descendants ruled Portugal until the foundation of the Republic in 1910.

Despite a choice of sumptuous palaces throughout Portugal – Mafra, Sintra and Queluz are the most renowned – the Bragança kings retained a special affection for their relatively ordinary home at Vila Viçosa; the town was in effect their ancestral domain. Dom Carlos spent his last night here before his assassination on the riverfront in Lisbon in 1908, and it was a favourite haven of his successor, Manuel II, the last king of Portugal.

The **Palace** (9am–1pm and 2–6pm; closed Mon.; guided tour lasts 1 hr.; 300esc) was built in the sixteenth and seventeenth centuries and has a simple rhythmic facade. The standard regal trappings of the more formal chambers are tedious, but the private apartments and mementos of Dom Carlos and his wife Marie-Amelia have a powerful impact. Faded family photographs hang on the walls, changes of clothing are laid out, and the table is set for dinner: the whole scene seems to await the sudden return of the king. In fact Dom Duarte, present heir to the nonexistent throne, spends his days in experimental eco-farming at his estate near Viseu.

The Old Town and Castle

On a hill midway between the palace and the bus station rise the walls and gates of the **old town**, built by Dom Dinis at the end of the thirteenth century and reinforced four centuries later. Originally the population of Vila Viçosa was based within these walls and a few of the cottages are still lived in.

The **Castle** occupies a corner of the old town and was the seat of the Braganças before the construction of their palace. Its interior (9am–1pm and 2–6pm; closed Mon.; guided tour 45 min.; 100esc) has been renovated beyond recognition and houses an indifferent archaeological museum, but from the roof there's a good view of the *Tapada Real* (Royal Hunting Ground), enclosed within its 18km circuit of walls.

Practicalities

Vila Viçosa is a quiet town and despite its attractions there's very little available **accommodation**. Two houses advertise *quartos*, at Praça da República 27 and at Rua Públia Hortênsia de Castro 2 (right by the church of Santa Cruz), and that's about it. Although it's officially discouraged, you could also camp around the old town.

The bus service is sufficient to make the town an easy day trip from Évora or Estremoz. The **Turismo** is by the bus station on the elongated Praça da República; nearby, at no. 35, is the popular *Restaurante Framar*.

Borba

Just four kilometres away, down a road lined on either side with enormous marble quarries, lies **BORBA**, a dazzlingly white little place: anything not whitewashed is white marble. The town seems not to have exploited the wider commercial possibilities of its quarries, and with the exception of a fine eighteenth-century fountain there are no particular signs of wealth, no extravagant mansions or remarkable churches. All this only serves to make more extraordinary the extensive use of marble in even the most commonplace cottages, shops and streets. Borba is simply an unassuming town which happens to be built of marble: its other main attribute is the wine of the local co-operative, available throughout Portugal. *Restaurante Lisbeota* at Rua de Mateus Pais 31 has **rooms** to let.

Estremoz

ESTREMOZ is the largest and liveliest of the three marble towns. It comes into its own every Saturday when the local **market** takes over the main square (**Rossio**) of the lower town, which is a classic marketplace of huge dimensions surrounded by bars, restaurants, and churches. Amongst the produce on sale are what are renowned as the best cheeses in Portugal, mainly made from ewes' and goats' milk. For centuries Estremoz has been famous, too, for the manufacture and sale of earthenware jars, and the shapes and styles of the pottery have remained basically unchanged since Roman times. The most distinctive products are the porous water coolers known as *moringues*, globe-shaped jars with narrow bases, two short spouts and one handle.

The local potteries also make earthenware figurines, examples of which can be seen in two of the town's museums: the **Museu Municipal** on Largo de Dom Dinis (in the upper town opposite the tower) and the **Rural Museum** at Rossio 62. The latter has an illuminating ethnographic collection of locally produced artifacts in clay, wood, rush, straw, cork, textile and metal. There's a third museum at Rua de Serpa Pinto 87 that specialises in **agricultural history** and has a fascinating display of old kitchen equipment. All three museums are open from Tuesday to Sunday (10am–noon and 2–6pm). Finally, next to the bus station on the main square rises the twin-towered marble facade of the **Câmara Municipal** (Town Hall). Originally this was one of the Rossio's three convents and its grand staircase is decorated with late seventeenth-century *azulejos*.

The Upper Town

In its heyday the population of Estremoz was ten times its current size and the town one of the most strongly fortified in the country. An army garrison is still stationed here, and the inner star-shaped ramparts of the **upper town** are well preserved.

On the hill within these fortifications stands a white, prison-like building, easily visible from the Rossio, which despite its external austerity was once a palace of Dom Dinis, the king famous for his administrative, economic, and military reforms. It is now a *pousada*; but you're free to wander in and look quietly around.

Beyond loom the deep-cut battlements of the thirteenth-century **Torre de Menagem** – very distinctive and bearing a close resemblance to the great tower of Beja, its exact contemporary. From this part of town the castle of Évoramonte is clearly visible on the horizon, thirty kilometres to the southwest.

Practicalities

The **Turismo** office (Mon.–Fri. 9.30am–12.30pm and 2–5.30pm, Sat. am and Sun. pm) is on Largo da República, a small square just off the Rossio at the southwest end; if it's closed, try the Turismo kiosk at the corner of Rossio. The staff are very helpful and so enthusiastic that you'll probably want to spend a couple of days in their town.

Fortunately there's plenty of inexpensive **accommodation**. Try the *Café Alentejano* at Rossio 15 for rooms with a central location, or *Casa Miguel José* at Travessa da Levada 8, near the town's Gadanha lake.

There's no shortage of **eating** places either, but the best deal has to be a tiny, nameless place at Rua Dr. Gomes de Resende Junior 15, on the way to the upper town. The excellent *Zé Varunca* on Avda. Tomas Alcaide (between Rossio and the railway station) is a more expensive alternative.

East to Elvas and Campo Maior

ELVAS is a beautiful frontier town, its houses stacked along steep cobbled streets. A deceptively peaceful atmosphere presides over the curious sixteenth- and seventeenth-century mansions here – deceptive because Elvas is of interest above all for a long and glorious history as a powerful military stronghold. Its excellently preserved **fortifications** are among the most complex and formidable in Europe. The original thirteenth-century walls were supplemented in the seventeenth century by extensive moats and star-shaped ramparts; designed along lines perfected by the French engineer Vauban, the bastions jut out at irregular but carefully-judged intervals to maximise the effects of artillery cross-fire.

Further examples of Vauban's designs are the **Forte Nossa Senhora da Graça**, a couple of kilometres north of Elvas, and the superb seventeenth-century **Forte de Santa Luzia**, a few minutes' walk to the south of the town. You'll also see echoes at Estremoz and throughout Portugal.

Elvas was the Portuguese response to the Spanish stronghold of Badajoz, a mere 17km away, and withstood periodic attacks for over three centuries before succumbing – through bribery – in 1580. It made amends in 1644 and 1658 by resisting the aggression of Philip IV and by confirming the reintroduction of self-government in Lisbon after sixty years of Spanish rule. In 1801, during the War of the Oranges that preceded the Peninsular War, Elvas withstood another memorable siege, and ten years later Wellington advanced from Elvas to launch his bloody but successful assault on Badajoz. As at Estremoz a military garrison is still stationed here.

The Aqueduct and Town

The jagged and ungainly course of the **Amoreira Aqueduct** looks like a bizarre extension of the town's fortifications. Despite its stark and awkward appearance it is nevertheless an imaginative and original feat of engineering. Monstrous piles of masonry, distinctive cylindrical buttresses, and up to five tiers of arches support a tiny water channel along its 7km course, until it is finally discharged at the fountain in Largo da Misericórdia. It was built between 1498 and 1622 to the designs of Francisco de Arruda, the famous Manueline architect.

The former **Cathedral**, at the heart of Elvas, was also Arruda's work, although alterations in the seventeenth and eighteenth centuries left a ragged hotch-potch of styles. The original Manueline inspiration is best seen on the south portal and in the unusual conical dome above the belfry.

The cathedral, which lost its episcopal status in 1882, opens on to the elegant **Praça da República**, where you'll find the sixteenth-century town hall, the **Turismo** (Mon.–Fri. 9am–7pm, weekend 9am–1pm) and the **bus station**. The **railway station** is 4km down the Campo Maior road at Fontainhas and is reached by a bus shuttle service.

Behind the cathedral lies the Largo Santa Clara, a tiny cobbled square built on a slope around a splendid sixteenth-century *pelourinho* (pillory). Criminals were chained from the four metal hooks towards the top but, aside from the grisly technicalities, it's also a work of art, with typically Manueline twisted column and rope-like decorations.

Directly opposite stands the strange and beautiful church of **Nossa Senhora da Consolação** (9am–12.30pm and 2.30–6pm; closed Mon.). From the outside it's nothing more than a whitewashed wall with a mediocre Renaissance porch, but the small interior is in the form of a sumptuous octagonal chapel: richly painted columns support a central cupola and virtually all surfaces are decorated with magnificent seventeenth-century *azulejos*. The chapel was built between 1543 and 1557, on the site of an earlier church of the Knights Templar, and its almost circular design was inspired by the particular preferences of this military order (see the "Tomar" section of the *Estremadura and Ribatejo* chapter). Elsewhere in Elvas the churches of **São Francisco** and **São Domingos** are notable for their fine interiors.

The Largo Santa Clara tapers upward to a restored tenth-century archway flanked by fortified towers and surmounted by a **loggia** or gallery. Originally part of the old town walls, this was built by the Moors who occupied Elvas from the early eighth century until 1226. The street beneath the gateway leads to the **Castle** (9.30am–12.30pm and 2.30–7pm; closed Thur.), also constructed by the Moors, on an old Roman fortified site, but strengthened by Dom Dinis and João II in the late fifteenth century.

Accommodation and Meals

Finding suitable **accommodation** can be a problem. In the absence of inexpensive pensions, the best budget bet is a *Casa de Hóspedes* (guesthouse) such as the one right next to the Arco do Bispo – turn right down the hill past the police station. Alternatively, several houses around the Largo de Olivença advertise *quartos*, but you have to look hard – the signs are not prominent. If these are full, the **Turismo** may be able to point you towards rooms in private houses, or you may be approached on the street: in both cases it's accepted practice to haggle over the price.

Cheapest of the **pensions** is the *Lidador* (though it hardly merits three stars); the *Pensão Quinta dos Aguias* (2500esc a double) is pricier but better value.

The **campsite** is about 2km along the Lisbon road behind the Quinta das Águias hotel. It's very cheap and very basic.

The best of the cheaper **restaurants** is *Canal 7* at Rua dos Sapateiros 16 (off the main square, opposite the Turismo) where there's invariably a queue and a friendly, boisterous atmosphere. More expensive, but with good cooking, is *O Alentejo* on Rua Cadeia. The place to buy fruit and cheese is the small, early-morning food **market** at the bottom of Rua dos Chilões.

The Market and Festival

Elvas's big **weekly market** – a chaotic, lively affair attracting people for miles around – is on Monday just outside town behind the aqueduct.

The **Festa de São Mateus**, which lasts a week in late September, is the town's annual cultural, folkloric and religious bash. It's well worth seeing, although accommodation is at a premium at this time.

Campo Maior

The road to **CAMPO MAIOR**, 18km north of Elvas, passes through olive groves and sunflower fields. It's an enjoyable journey to a pleasant, if unremarkable, fortress town, that warrants a short visit for its hauntingly claustrophobic **Capela dos Ossos**, a small version of the Chapel of Bones in Évora (9am–noon and 2–5pm). This stands immediately to the right of the large parish church just off Rua 1 de Maio: ask for the key in the church itself or try the door next to the chapel. Adding to the surreal effect, the entrance is through a neat local government office.

The walls and vaults of the chapel's interior are covered in human bones, two skeletons hang from the walls, and three rows of skulls are positioned on the window ledge to inspect passers-by. The chapel is dated 1766 and its purpose is implied in a Portuguese translation of the Book of Job (ch. 19, v. 20) traced out in collarbones near the window: 'My bone cleaveth to my skin and to my flesh, and I am escaped with the skin of my teeth'. Job is complaining of his horrific physical and mental suffering, but takes solace in the knowledge that 'though after my skin worms destroy this body, yet in my flesh shall I see God' (v. 26).

The chapel may have been 'furnished' by the disaster which devastated Campo Maior in 1732, when a powder magazine in the town's castle was struck by lightning, killing 1500 people and destroying 823 houses. Today the Castle is little more than a ruin but there are fine views as you scamper around the site (100esc admission).

Practicalities

The journey from Elvas takes just 35 minutes (5 buses daily, 2 on Sun.), making it ideal for a day trip. If you're intent on staying, there's a simple **pension**, *A Tentadora*, at Rua 1 de Maio, and a pleasant restaurant, *O Faisão*, opposite the parish church.

Portalegre

Crouched at the foot of the Serra de São Mamede, **PORTALEGRE**, capital of the Alto Alentejo, is an attractive town with the usual whitewashed and walled old quarters on a low hill, and some interesting reminders of an industrialised and prosperous history.

Industrial traditions survive mainly in the cork factories – prominent, with their great twin chimneys, on the edge of town. In the past, though, Portalegre was famous for the manufacture of textiles, and its single remaining **Tapestry Factory** (in Rua Gomes Fernandes) is open to the public (9.30–11.30am and 2.30–5pm; closed weekends). It's housed in a seventeenth-century former Jesuit convent on Rua Fernandes, just off the central Largo A. J. Lourinho: turn right from the bus station and it's barely two minutes' walk. There's a guided tour of the studios and weaving hall, where 5000 shades of wool are said to be used in the reproduction of centuries-old patterns.

The Portuguese textile boom reached its peak in the seventeenth century when silk factories were established here, and the ensuing wealth is immediately evident in the **old town**. Rua 19 de Junho, in particular, boasts a spectacular concentration of late Renaissance and Baroque mansions (the **Tursimo** – with much-needed maps of the town – can also be found here, at no. 40).

At one end of the street, and dominating the entire quarter, is the **Cathedral**, a plain building except for its distinctive towers with their pyramidal pinnacles. To the right, the **Museu Municipal** (10am–12.30pm and 2–5.30pm) is housed in an eighteenth-century palace: excellent collections of ceramics and ivory reliefs, along with religious statuary from the dissolved convents of Santa Clara and São Bernardo, stand out from the regular bunch of mediocre portraits, furniture and furnishings.

Practicalities

The best bets for **accommodation** are the *Pensão Alto Alentejo* (☎045/22290), opposite the Turismo, or the cheaper and decidedly down-at-heel *Nova* (Rua 31 de Janeiro 28; ☎045/21605). Alternatively, there's an excellent **youth hostel** in a converted Franciscan monastery near the Praça da República, and the *Orbitur* **campsite**, 4km into the hills.

A good and reasonably priced restuarant is *O Cortico*, near the Rossio, which serves up the typically Alentejan dish of *migas*.

The **railway station** is a good 12km out of town, just off the main road to Estremoz – there are four bus connections a day in both directions.

Castelo de Vide and Marvão

The area **north of Portalegre** couldn't be more of a change: a bucolic landscape of tree-clad mountain ranges and enchanting hilltop villages, the finest (and most accessible) of which are **Castelo de Vide** and **Marvão**.

Two **trains** a day pass through the Castelo de Vide and Marvão stations on their way from Portalegre to Madrid. **Buses** for the region leave from Portalegre five times a day to Castelo de Vide and twice to Marvão (at 9am and 6pm; return at 7.40am and 1.10pm). The 9.20am and 6.15pm trains from Castelo de Vide to Portalegre connect with the buses to Marvão at the junction of PORTAGEM.

The **border post** at GALEGOS, 10km from Marvão, is open to traffic but very few cars use it, and there's only one bus a day from Portalegre to Valencia de Alcantara in Spain.

Castelo de Vide

The spa town of **CASTELO DE VIDE** is one of the best to head for, covering the slopes around a fourteenth-century castle with blindingly white cottages in brilliant contrast to the surrounding greenery. The bus drops you at a *pelourinho* outside the **Turismo** in the centre of town; the one-star *Pensão-*

Restaurante O Cantinho Particular is on the other side of the road at Rua Miguel Bombarda 7–9 (☎045/91751), one of half a dozen parallel streets which climb sharply and picturesquely to the aptly named Praça Alta on the edge of town.

The main road, meanwhile, peters out into a narrow path, descending past a therapeutic Renaissance fountain to the twisting alleyways of the **Judiaria** (Jewish Quarter). The cottages here preserve their Gothic doorways and windows, and the thirteenth-century **synagogue** is the oldest in Portugal (the key is to be found in a special compartment on the outside wall).

On a hill above the Judiaria squats the **Castle** (8am–6pm), within the wider fortifications of the original medieval village.

Marvão

Beautiful as Castelo de Vide is, **MARVÃO** surpasses it. The panoramas from its remote, almost ethereal position are unrivalled and the atmosphere is even more whisperingly somnolent than a population of less than 1000 would suggest. No more than a couple of houses – all as scrupulously whitewashed as the rest – lie outside the seventeenth-century walls.

Originally the village seems to have been an outlying suburb of *Medobriga*, a mysterious Roman city which has vanished almost without trace. Its inhabitants fled before the Moorish advance in around 715 but later returned to live under Muslim rule, when the place was renamed after Marvan, the Moorish Lord of Coimbra. It fell to the Christians in 1166 and the present **castle** was built by Dom Dinis in 1229.

As at Monsaraz, the **Castle** lies at the far end of the village and was another important link in the chain of outposts along the Spanish border. Its daunting walls blend impenetrably into the sharp slopes of the Serra, and it comes as no surprise to discover that the castle was captured only once, in 1833 – and then by use of a secret gate.

Rooms and Transport

There are two **hotels** in Marvão but both are pricey (*Estalagem Dom Dinis* marginally the less so): go instead for rooms in private houses, available through the tourist office.

If you decide to **hitch back to Portalegre**, in the absence of buses, it's best to walk back the 5km from the village to the main road at Portagem.

Northwest from Portalegre to the Tagus Valley

The countryside northwest of Portalegre is sparsely populated, and the direct road to Abrantes is in such a state of disrepair that it's easier to get to the area's most interesting spot, **Belver**, by the train that runs between Abrantes and Castelo Branco; if you are going by road, you should turn off at GAVIÃO (28km before Abrantes).

Belver

BELVER takes its name from its **Castle**, a late twelfth-century fortress overlooking the valley of the Tagus, from which you can now see, to the west, the glittering hydroelectric dam that marks the border with the Ribatejo.

Back in the first few centuries of Portuguese nationality, Moors, Castilians and other usurpers to the throne were repulsed from Belver's walls, and in most cases never made it across the river. If you find the castle locked, search out the jovial guard who lives at no. 1 on the Praça (15 de Outubro/ Luís de Camões); he keeps the grounds spotlessly clean and for a small fee will unlock the chapel to show you its formidable fifteenth-century **reliquary**. All the pieces of bone were stolen during the French invasions in the nineteenth century, but fortunately for the villagers there was still a casket of 'spares' hidden away by the priest, and these substitutes are nowadays paraded around town at the **Festa de Santa Reliquária**, held during the last five days in August. At the beginning of August there is also a **folk-dancing** competition.

Rooms and Transport

You're very likely to track down the castle guard sharing a few jokes over a glass of *bagaceira* (Portugal's cheapest hangover) in the only **café-restaurant-pension** in town. Here you can stay cheaply all months of the year except August.

Buses leave from the Praça or from above the train station, which is directly below the village beside the river. The only useful one is the 8am on Saturday via Vale de Feiteira to Crato; otherwise stick to the train network. If you take the **train** north along the valley to Castelo Branco, look out for the striking rock faces before Vila Velha de Ródão known as the **Portas de Ródão** (Gates of Ródão).

West of Portalegre: Convento de Flôr da Rosa and the Alter Stud Farm

The sole daily bus from Portalegre to Lisbon (8.40am) takes a thoroughly roundabout route westward through the sleepy cork centre of **Ponte de Sor**. Other intermittent services stop at the small towns of **Crato** and **Alter do Chão**, both splashed with the usual white and yellow, and worth visiting for two nearby sites: the **Convento de Flôr da Rosa**, and the *coudelaria* (stud farm) of **Alter**. Both these towns offer the possibility of staying overnight.

Crato

Its ruins overrun by farm animals, fig trees and oregano plants, the once-mighty **Castle** at **CRATO** is now far from intimidating, but it does give you a splendid view over the ancient town and across the countless rows of olive trees to the distant hills of Portalegre. Keys are kept by several of the live-stock's owners in houses close by, but you might also find them hanging beneath an abandoned blue cart in the field in front.

Crato's ecclesiastical heritage has fared rather better: three large, ornate, and well-kept churches serve the faithful, and the most elegant structure in town is the mid-sixteenth-century **Varanda do Grão Prior**, from which mass used to be celebrated for the crowds in the square below. For a good display of the handicrafts and domestic traditions of Alto Alentejo, visit the **museum** installed in a small town mansion, down a narrow street across the main road from the Public Gardens. (Hours erratic – sometimes open until 7pm). Well into this century alms were still being handed out to the local poor from the balcony upstairs (*Capela de N.S. do Bom Sucesso*) – a perfor-mance that must have aroused a little envy in the inmates of the prison oppo-site (now a library).

Crato Practicalities

The town has just one small **pension**, above the *Café Parque* (Avda. D. Nuno Álvares ☎045/97223), though the seasonal **Turismo** (in a hut near the Public Gardens) can let you know about private rooms. **Campers** might find spots by the old Roman bridge near the train station or up by the castle.

On the corner of the road to Aldeia da Mata you'll find an excellent *adega*, with delicious home cooking and a crowded bar where everyone plays *belho* (not unlike a miniature version of the French *boules*). You will need a 50esc coin.

Crato's local **train station** is three kilometres away, but if you arrive with heavy bags the station master can telephone for a taxi, which is not expen-sive. **Buses** pass that way at inconvenient times (10.20am from town, 2.30pm back).

Flôr da Rosa

Two kilometres from Crato, on the Nisa road, lies **FLÔR DA ROSA**, once a village of **potters** with over seventy families in the trade. Now the distinctive *olaria* of the region is made in only two workshops, whose shared kiln is near the convent, high above the broad streets and low houses. Clay has to be sought further and further afield these days – yellow for water-proofing, grey for ovenware – but the methods of manufacture haven't changed. Your purchases may break easily, but it's nice to know that these functional (and inexpensive) pieces are not designed for the tourist trade.

The Convent

The **Convento de Flôr da Rosa** was founded in 1356, by the father of the famous warlord **Nuno Álvares Pereira** of the Order of Malta (in whose insignia the garden is laid out). The actual building is an odd mixture of styles, chiefly twelfth-century, sixteenth-century and post-1940 restoration. Its great charm stems from the colour of the stonework, whose yellow hue is best picked out by the softer light at the end of the day.

Father Pereira's tomb (dated 1382) is prominent in the narrow, soaring **Cathedral**. The rest of the building, with the exception of the Condestável's residence (in extreme disrepair), is on two levels. On the ground floor the fine brickwork of the fan-vaulting in the sixteenth-century **Sala do Capítulo** contrasts with the heavier architecture of the **Gothic cloister**; from the monks' **dormitories** on the first floor there are sweeping views from the open casements across acres of olive trees.

You can also see the vestiges of **stables** and of a **kitchen** whose water supply has flooded a whole room. The monastery was abandoned from 1897 to 1940 due to serious leaking, and it has taken recent state aid to redeem the place at least in part.

Alter do Chão

South of Crato, and served by the buses to the station, is the small town of **ALTER DO CHÃO**. A fourteenth-century **Castle** looms over the place (you can climb up the central tower), and the centre has an attractive Renaissance **marble fountain** and some large, handsome houses. Alter's main attraction is the **coudelaria** (stud farm), 3km out of town. The seasonal **Turismo** will gladly point the way, but the route is well marked by signs.

The Coudelaria

The *coudelaria* is not as dull as it sounds. Founded in 1748 by Dom João V of the House of Bragança, it remained in the family until 1910 when the War Office took it over. Today a former cavalry officer will show you around at a stately pace any time before 5pm (tips welcome), though to see the horses in action it's best to arrive in the morning.

The stud's great prestige comes from the intelligent and sensitive **Alter-Real** horses, favoured by the Portuguese mounted police and the Lisbon Riding School at Queluz, and popular with equestrians all over Europe. (Dom José sits on an Alter-Real in the Praça do Comércio in Lisbon.) Between 10am and noon there's a chance to witness the procession of grown horses filing in from the fields to feed, accompanied by the ringing of forty bells. The animals are the stars of course, but inside the buildings there are magnificent **carriages** and nineteenth-century horse regalia that you might find interesting.

If you can possibly time a visit, April 25 is the best day to be at the coudelaria, when the annual sale takes place. The town's main festival – the **Festa** of N. S. da Alegria – takes place on the following day.

Practicalities

Several **pensions** are clustered in the road opposite the castle in Alter. Ask for rooms above the *Café Simas* or at the *Pensão Ferreira* (Avda. Dr. João Pestana, ☎045/62254). Get up before 9.30am if you're interested in seeing the coudelaria coach and horses come in to collect the mail. For **meals**, try downstairs at the *Café Simas* or sample the cakes at the excellent *Pastelaria Ateneia*. **Buses** leave for Estremoz (10.50am), Crato (2pm) and Portalegre (9pm, or 6pm Sat.).

BAIXO (LOWER) ALENTEJO

The undulating scenery of the southern section of the Alentejo province and the dry, hot **inland routes** have little to offer beyond a stop at **Beja** (the most interesting southern Alentejo town), en route to the Algarve, or the frontier villages of **Serpa** or **Mertola**, if you're heading for Spain.

The **coast**, however, is another matter. There are beaches, few developed beyond the odd pension or campsite, almost the whole way down from Setúbal to the borders of the Algarve at Odeceixe. If you can take the **Atlantic winds** – which can at times make swimming dangerous or impossible with their colossal breakers – it's a simple matter to pick a beach and rest up for a few days of quiet and inexpensive living.

Beja

BEJA, a welcome oasis amid the sweltering and featureless wheatfields of Baixo Alentejo, is by far the most interesting town south of Évora and makes for a pleasant break on your way to or from the Algarve. There are peculiar churches here, a beautiful convent and a fancy thirteenth-century castle overlooking the unhurried old quarter around the Praça da República. With the town walls long gone, modern Beja has spilled over into the surrounding plain in a nondescript and often confusingly unplanned fashion. Our map, though, should enable you to orientate yourself and find all the major monuments.

The Town

Founded by Julius Caesar, Beja was later occupied by both Visigoths and Moors, but in Portugal it's best known for the love affair of a seventeenth-century nun who lived in the **Convento de Nossa Senhora da Conceição**. Sister Mariana Alcoforado is believed to have fallen in love with Count Chamilly, a French cavalry officer, and is credited with the notorious (at least in Portugal) *Five Love Letters of a Portuguese Nun*, first published in Paris in 1669. The originals have never been discovered, and a typical scholarly debate has raged over the authenticity of the French 'translation'. Nonetheless, English and Portuguese editions soon appeared and the letters became internationally famous as a classic of romantic literature.

Quite apart from its sentimental associations, the convent is well worth visiting for its fifteenth-century architecture. There are elaborate portals and the rhythmic roofline is decorated with Manueline balustrades and sharp pinnacles. The convent was dissolved in 1834 and the memorable interior now houses the **Museu Regional** (Mon.–Sat. 9.30am–1pm and 2.30–5pm). The walls of the cloisters and chapter house are completely covered with multicoloured sixteenth- and seventeenth-century *azulejos*, and present one of the finest examples of this art form. The other highlight is a magnificent Rococo chapel, sumptuously gilded and embellished with flying cherubs. The actual museum pieces are comparatively disappointing but include Roman and Visigothic stone, fifteenth- to eighteenth-century Portuguese painting, and the grille through which the errant nun first glimpsed her lover.

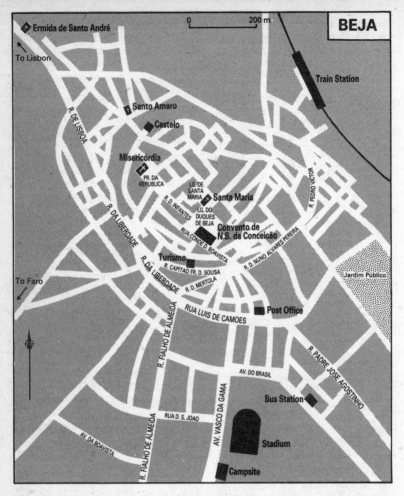

Beja's **Castle** (10am–1pm and 2–6pm) rises decoratively on the edge of the old quarter. It was built – yet again – by Dom Dinis and is remarkable for the playful battlements of the *Torre de Menagem*. Similarly, an exaggerated horseshoe window half-way up hints at the architect's artistic intent. In the shadow of the tower stands the Visigothic basilica of **Santo Amaro**, housing a small archaeological museum. This building, unexciting from the outside, is a rare survival from pre-Moorish Portugal; the interior columns are carved with seventh-century geometric motifs.

Three other churches in Beja are of interest. The most distinctive of them is the mid-sixteenth-century **Misericórdia** in the Praça da República; its huge projecting porch served originally as a meat market and the stonework is deliberately chiselled to give a coarse, 'rustic' appearance.

Finally, at the beginning of the main road to Lisbon, is the **Ermida de Santo André**, looking like an eccentric fortress with its gigantic tubular buttresses, similar and contemporary (fifteenth century) with those on the Ermida de São Brás at Évora. The same round-style towers recur on the Gothic porch of **Santa Maria**, in the heart of the old quarter of town.

Practicalities

Most of the cheap **accommodation** is to be found on the way into town from the **railway station**, five minutes from the centre. *Pensão Pax Julia*, at Rua Pedro Victor 8, and *Pensão Rocha*, at Rua D. Nuno Álvares Pereira 12, are both basic and clean. If you're prepared to pay for a prime location, head for the *Pensão Coelho*, at Praça da República 15. The municipal **campsite** – well run and reasonable – is near the **bus station** and a modern **swimming pool**.

There's no problem finding affordable **food and drink**: especially recommended are *Casa Primavera* (a real gem) opposite the post office and *Restaurante Pena*, at Praça de Diogo Fernandes de Beja 21, between the pedestrian precinct and the castle. The **Turismo** (Mon.–Sat. 9am–6pm), on Rua Capitão J. F. de Sousa 25, is very helpful and will shower you with enough information to see you through a visit of several days.

Beja has good **transport connections** to the rest of central and southern Portugal, as well as a bus link to Seville in Spain. In most cases you have a choice of bus or train: for Lisbon and the western Algarve take the **train**, while for Évora, Vila Real de Santo António (for the eastern Algarve), and Santiago do Cacém (for the west coast) take the **bus**.

East to Serpa

SERPA lies midway between Beja and the border with Spanish Extremadura, and affords visitors a pleasant overnight stay. A peaceful old walled town, it was at various times occupied by the Romans, the Moors and the Spaniards. Inevitably there's a Moorish **Castle**, offering spectacular vistas of the Alentejan plain to the north and the hills to the south.

The principal curiosities, however, are the well-preserved eleventh-century **aqueduct** (the remnants of its fifteenth-century *nora* chain-pump are at one end), and the thirteenth-century church of **Santa Maria**, right next to the castle. Santa Maria's altar is covered with intricate wood carving, faced with gold-leaf, and surrounded by seventeenth-century blue and yellow *azulejos*.

If you have time to fill, there are also two museums, a tiny **archeological museum** in the keep, and a small **ethnographic museum** near the hospital, offering an interesting account of the changing economic activity of the area. A pleasant place for a stroll, Serpa is a town of narrow whitewashed streets and twisting alleys where all the points of interest are clearly marked.

Practicalities

The **bus station**, with three departures a day to Beja and one through bus to Seville, is on Largo do Rossio, where you'll also find *Pensão Virgínia* at no. 75 (unmarked). At the southwest corner of town, a new **camping**, leisure and **swimming pool** complex is imminently scheduled to open.

Of the several cheap **eating places**, the *Restaurante O zé*, at Praça da República 10, is highly recommended for its friendly atmosphere and its *gaspacho*. The local cheese, *queijo de Serpa*, is delicious; the **Turismo** (just off the main Praça da República at Largo D. Jorge de Melo 2; Mon.–Fri. 9am– noon and 2–5pm) can put you in touch with several traditional manufacturers.

South to the Algarve: Mértola

If you're driving or hitching to the Algarve from Beja, the **direct route south to Faro**, via Castro Verde, is one of the dullest in all Portugal – passing through interminable parched tracts of wheatfields and half a dozen small agricultural towns. It doesn't brighten up until you hit the lush greenery of the **Serra do Caldeirão** around Ameixial in the Algarve. The route's only point of interest in the vicinity of Beja comes at **PISÕES**, 8km southwest of the town, just past PENEDO GORDO. Here the remains of a **Roman villa** (first- to fourth-century A.D.) include well-preserved mosaics, a heating system under the floor, a pool and baths. It's sometimes closed for further excavation, so check first with the Turismo in Beja.

Mértola

The other main route south, heading for Vila Real de Santo António, passes through the old Moorish fortress town of **MÉRTOLA**, beautifully situated on a hill above the Rio Guadiana. This is certainly worth an overnight stop, longer if you like cross-country walking among rolling hills or simply relaxing in a spot which is, and feels, extraordinarily isolated. It's a quiet place, with a small and falling population. In the earlier decades of this century the town survived largely on the copper mines a few kilometres down the Serpa road at Mina de São Domingos. These were owned by a British company of marked illiberality, who employed a private police force and treated the workers with appalling brutality. Older residents in the bars still recall these times.

As far as sights go, the highlight, inevitably, is the **Castle**, built in the thirteenth century and still, albeit in a bad state of repair, dominating the town and the valley. The view from the tower is spectacular, especially at sunset when the hills for miles around change colour by the minute. The **Igreja Matriz**, also thirteenth-century, started life as a Moorish mosque and retains its Islamic *mihrab* (prayer niche) behind the altar on the eastern wall. The church has a square plan with a vaulted roof supported by twelve pillars, each topped with a differently styled capital.

Near the south end of town on the Largo de Misericórdia, the **Museu Arqueológico** (Mon.–Sat. 9am–12.30pm and 2–5.30pm) contains a well-presented collection of recoveries from local digs, notably Roman pottery, jewellery and needles, plus a set of strange-looking religious figures retrieved from the castle.

The *Residencial Beira Rio* on Rua Dr. Afonso Costa (as it descends steeply to the river) is a simple, inexpensive **pension**, and the *Restaurante Boa Viagem*, opposite the place where buses stop at the bridge, offers a good

selection of cheap meals. There are several friendly **bars** nearby. The
Turismo (Mon.–Fri. 9am–noon and 2–5.30pm), on the Rua da República
right in the centre of town, sometimes arranges **boat trips on the
Guadiana**. Two **buses** a day connect Mértola with Beja to the north, and
Vila Real to the south.

The Pulo do Lobo Waterfall
Within reach of Serpa, if you have your own transport, is the **PULO DO
LOBO** (Wolf's Leap), a 60m waterfall in stark, wild scenery.

There are two possible approaches: the first is an 18km rough road south
from the village of SÃO BRÁS, just 4km south of Serpa; the second is a
longer and easier route that follows the signs from the hamlet of VALE DO
POÇO on the Mértola road. Around the falls the river has carved a deep
gorge through the hills, and the valley is made up of strikingly eerie rock
formations. You're almost guaranteed complete solitude here, and you could
camp out for days.

The Alentejo Coast

If you're heading south from Lisbon, by far the best route is along the coast,
where some of the towns and beaches are so inviting that you might not even
make it down to the Algarve. The area is undeveloped and perfect for camping right by the sea – though, with the proliferation of commercial campsites,
this is now officially prohibited. Admittedly, it's exposed to the winds and
waves of the Atlantic and the waters are far colder than those of the eastern
Algarve, but it's comfortable enough for summer swimming.

All the beaches are situated along minor roads, but there is an efficient **bus
service** from **Santiago do Cacém** and **Odemira**. The *Zambujeira Express*
bus from Lisbon takes you within easy range of the whole coastline and actually stops at the beaches of **Vila Nova de Milfontes**, **Almograve** and
Zambujeira do Mar. It leaves Lisbon twice a day from the bus station at
Casal Ribeira; as with all *expressos*, it's wise to buy tickets in advance.

Heading South: Alcácer do Sal and Santiago do Cacém

ALCÁCER DO SAL curves around a loop in the Rio Sado, at a junction of
the roads south from Lisbon and Setúbal. It's a slightly seedy-looking place,
but with an attractive promenade running along the waterfront to the town's
castle (10am–noon and 2–5pm). From here, there are striking views of the
lush green paddy-fields which almost surround the town, and of the storks'
nests on the church rooftops.

Four buses a day run from Lisbon (and from Setúbal) to Alcacer, and there
are reasonable connections south to Santiago do Cacém. There are a couple
of good restaurants and bakeries facing the river and, if you decide to stay
the night, the *Pensão Alcacerense* is just a few doors from the bus station. On
the first Saturday in October the town hosts a major **regional fair** which lasts
for three days – one of the best around.

Grândola

Heading south towards Santiago the road passes through the agricultural town of **GRÂNDOLA**, made legendary through the song *Grândola vila morena*, the broadcasting of which was the prearranged signal for the start of the 1974 revolution.

Santiago do Cacém

Twenty-five kilometres farther on lies **SANTIAGO DO CACÉM**, a pleasant little town overlooked by a castle. Within half an hour's walk there are the fascinating ruins of the Roman town of Mirobriga, and it's only a short bus journey to the lagoons of Santo André and Melides, two of the finest beaches in Portugal (see opposite).

If you want to base yourself at Santiago, rather than at the beaches, there's no shortage of good food and accommodation: the *Restaurante Covas*, by the bus station at Rua Cidade de Setúbal 10, is recommended both for its cheap and unpretentious **rooms** and for its meals. There are plenty of other places around town advertising *quartos*, and another great **restaurant** – *O Grelhador* at Rua de Camilo Castelo Branco 26. Finally, there's a good covered **market** in the centre of town where you can stock up for the beach.

In the town, there are a couple of minor sights to be found. The Moorish **Castle**, presently under restoration, was rebuilt by the Knights Templar and now serves as the town cemetery. There are splendid views over the town and to the sea from the battlements, whose crumbling masonry provides the habitat for a curious species of large golden beetle, found here in profusion. The **Museu Municipal** (Tues.–Fri. 9am–12.30pm and 2–5pm) is one of the most interesting of its kind – imaginatively housed in one of Salazar's more notorious old prisons, in a small park just northeast of the centre. A suitably political strain pervades its display: one of the spartan cells has been preserved while two others have been converted into a 'typical country bedroom' and 'a rich bourgeois bedroom'. Even a drawing in the section devoted to the local primary school shows a child's impression of the 'Great Revolution' of 1974.

Mirobriga

The archaeological section in Santiago's museum should whet your appetite for a visit to the ruins of **Roman Mirobriga** (Tues.–Sat. 9am–12.30pm and 2–5pm; 100esc admission for non-Portuguese): follow the Rua de Lisboa for about a kilometre up the hill, then take the marked turning to the right, and, after another ten-minute walk, turn left at a sign marking the entrance to the site, which lies isolated amid arcadian green hills.

At the highest point of the site a **Temple of Jupiter** has been partly reconstructed, overlooking a small forum with a row of shops built into its supporting wall. A paved street descends to a **villa and bath complex** whose underground central heating system is still intact.

None of the remains are individually spectacular, but there's a sense of adventure here: it's a great place to explore and let your imagination loose on the ancient streets and houses – provided you can shake off the warden, who watches visitors like a hawk.

Santo André and Melides Lagoons

There are seven buses a day from Santiago do Cacém to **LAGOA DE SANTO ANDRÉ**, and it's a short walk from there along the shore to **LAGOA DE MELIDES**. These **lagoons**, separated from the sea by a narrow strip of sand, are named after the nearest towns inland, but each has its own small, laid-back community entirely devoted to having a good time on the beach. The **campsites** at both places are of a high standard and there are masses of signs offering rooms, chalets and whole houses to let. Needless to say, there's more of a squeeze in July and August, but at other times accommodation should be no problem at all. People still camp on the beach, too, but the authorities are taking an ever-harder line on this.

At either beach, the social scene centres around the beach-cafés and ice-cream stalls. Beyond these is the sand – miles and miles of it stretching all the way to Comporta in the north and Sines in the south. The sea is very enticing with high waves and good surf, but be warned and take local advice on water conditions; the undertow can be fierce and people are drowned every year.

Sines

SINES is the one place *not* to go to on this stretch of coast. Vasco da Gama was born here, but he'd turn in his grave if he could see the massive **oil-refinery** and the sacrifice of the environment to new roads, railways, pipelines and wells.

Porto Côvo and Ilha do Pessegueiro

The ugliness around Sines is short-lived and just south of here there's a whole new set of untouched little beach settlements. The best of all of them is the furthest south, the area around Ilha do Pessegueiro, reached from the road heading down to **PORTO CÔVO** – itself a simple, unassuming little place with a small cove harbour, a few rooms to let, and a sewage plant right on the oceanfront.

Following the signs to the *Ilha* (island), it's an easy walk to **PESSEGUEIRO**. There's a wonderful bar-restaurant by the beach here – and this is definitely *the* place to try *caldeirada*, the Portuguese version of bouillabaisse. Do not be tempted by the *Delícias do Mar*: you may be expecting a platter of mixed seafood, but what you get is fish sticks and they taste as revolting here as they do from any whelk stall.

Apart from the restaurant, a small seaside **fort** nearby, and an increasing number of official **campsites**, there's very little else. Quite a few people – a good mix of Portuguese and foreign travellers – camp out at Pessegueiro, but if you want to get away from them, it's no problem at all. There are facilities in the form of toilets and showers, and basic provisions are easy to come by. All in all, it makes an excellent place to hole up for a while if the very simple (and cheap) life appeals.

Most days, too, local fishermen are around to take you to the **island** little more than a kilometre offshore, where there are interesting ruins to explore.

Odemira, Vila Nova de Milfontes and Almograve

On the southern half of the Alentejo coast, **ODEMIRA** is the main inland base. A quiet, unspoiled country town, it has bus connections to beaches at Almograve, Vila Nova de Milfontes (8 daily, taking 40–50 min.) and Zambujeira do Mar (2; 45 min.). Local buses also connect Odemira with LUZIANES railway station about 20km away, with connections for Beja and Évora. (You'll need to get to FUNCHEIRA for Lisbon and the Algarve.)

Unless you're camping you're unlikely to find anywhere to spend the night in any of these resorts from June to August, so it's not a bad idea to stay in Odemira and take day trips to the seaside. The town has several restaurants and **pensions**, including *Residencial Rita* and *Residencial Idálio* just to the left when you come out of the bus station. The older *Dionísio* is a couple of minutes away in the centre, at Rua Serpa Pinto 4. Among restaurants, try *O Escondidinho* – cheap and reasonable, at the lower end of town.

Vila Nova de Milfontes

VILA NOVA DE MILFONTES lies on the estuary of the Rio Mira, whose sandy banks gradually expand and merge into the coastline. If the waves of the Atlantic are too fierce you can always swim in the calmer waters of the estuary – though again be careful of the currents.

Vila Nova has in recent years been discovered – notably by the Germans – and it is generally the most crowded and popular resort in the Alentejo, with lines of villas radiating from the centre of the old village. It's a pretty place, though, and an ancient port, reputed to have harboured Hannibal and his Carthaginians during a storm. The village boasts a striking little castle with tremendous views out to sea. Portuguese families flock here from the big cities of the north, giving it a homely atmosphere quite distinct from the cosmopolitan trendiness of the Algarve. If you want to escape some of the crowds, take the ferry from the little jetty (*cais*) to the far side of the estuary.

All the **pensions** are fully booked in summer, but out of season you can get excellent cheap rooms, or try two more expensive alternatives: the English-run *Boavista Hotel*, 2km from the centre behind the petrol station on the main road, and the *Castle* itself, which sometimes takes lodgers: ring the bell and see what happens. There's a large **campsite** just to the north of the village and if you want to camp elsewhere, you'll have to be discreet. It's a great place for a restful holiday, though it's convenient if you have your own transport as the timing of the buses make day trips very difficult.

Almograve

The coastline south of Vila Nova de Milfontes becomes ever more rugged and spectacular. At the tiny resort of **ALMOGRAVE**, five kilometres west of the Odemira–Vila Nova road, huge waves come crashing down on the rocks and for most of the day swimming is impossible. It can get very crowded at high tide, too, when the beaches are reduced to thin strips with occasional waves drenching everybody's belongings – but, for all that, it's an exhilarating place.

You could camp virtually anywhere around the beach at Almograve, and there are a few cafés and bars, but the bus service from Odemira is just right for a day trip. If you are interested in a **month-long stay** in the village, a Danish woman, Henja Listner (Almograve, 7630 Odemira), offers bed-and-breakfast, catering mainly for writers and painters; write in advance.

Zambujeira do Mar

At the village of **ZAMBUJEIRA DO MAR**, south of Odemira and 7km west of the main road, a large cliff provides a dramatic backdrop to the beach, which, like that of Vila Nova, can get very crowded in July and August.

The scenery more than compensates for the winds and the sea – which can get positively chilly, even in summer – but can't disguise the run-down state of the village and the encircling villas. There's only one small **pension** (*Residencial Mar-e-Sol*), a few *dormidas* and a couple of bars, and the schedule of the buses from Odemira make a day trip impossible. A reasonable **campsite** is being redeveloped about 1km from the cliffs; if you want to rough it meanwhile, make sure you've got enough rocks to hold the tent down. Good seafood is alleged to be available at the harbour 3km along the road to the north of the village.

On to the Algarve

Zambujeira is the southernmost Alentejo beach, and an attractive road twists its way into the hills of the Algarve from the river crossing at ODECEIXE. For the most dramatic approach, however, take the road from Odemira through the **Serra de Monchique**, descending to the Algarve coast at Portimão.

travel details

Trains
Beira Baixa Line 6 trains daily from LISBON through Abrantes to Belver (3 hr.), and on to Castelo Branco and Guarda.

Leste Line 7 trains daily from LISBON to Abrantes – 2 go on to Ponte de Sôr (2 hr.), Marvão (3 hr.), Valencia de Alcantara (3 hr. 15 min.) and Madrid (11 hr.); 4 go on to Crato (2 hr.), Portalegre (3 hr. 40 min.) and Elvas (4½ hr.), 3 of these continuing to Badajoz, Spain (5½ hr.).

Sul Line (Alentejo) 5 daily from LISBON to Casa Branca (1½ hr.: with direct service or easy connections to Évora, ½ hr. farther on) and Beja (3½ hr.). 2 continue from Beja to Tunes (3 hr. more for connections to the Algarve line – Faro, Lagos and Vila Real etc.).

Sado Line (Lisbon–Algarve) 5 daily from LISBON to Tunes (5 hr.) via Ermidas-Sado. From here 2 connections daily to Santiago do Cacém (40 min.) and Sines (1 hr.).

From Évora 5 daily to Estremoz (1 hr. 20 min.), Borba (1 hr. 35 min.) and Vila Viçosa (1 hr. 40 min.); 3 daily to Reguengos de Monsaraz.

From Estremoz 2 daily to Portalegre (1 hr. 10 min.).

Buses
From Évora Lisbon (6 daily; 3 hr.) of which 2 go on to Porto (7 hr. 35 min.) and Braga (9 hr.); Vila Viçosa/Borba/Elvas (5; 1 hr. 25 min./1 hr. 35 min./2 hr.); Monsaraz (2; 2½ hr.); Estremoz (3; 1 hr. – via Évora-Monte); Portalegre (2; 3 hr.); Beja (2; 2 hr.); Arraiolos (4; 35 min.).

From Portalegre Elvas (3; 1½ hr.); Castelo de Vide (5; ½ hr.).

From Elvas Estremoz (4; 1 hr.); Badajoz (4; 30 min.).

From Beja Santiago do Cacém (3; 2½ hr.); Faro (4; 3½ hr.); Serpa (3; 45 min.); Seville, Spain (1; 5 hr.).

Coast Lisbon–Vila Nova de Milfontes/ Almograve/Zambujeira (2 daily expresses; 4 hr./ 4½ hr./4 hr. 50 min.). Odemira–Zambujeira (2; ½ hr.). Odemira–Lagos (2; 1¾hr.). Odemira–Almograve/Vila Nova (8; 40–50min.).

CHAPTER NINE

THE ALGARVE

With its long, sandy beaches and picturesque rocky coves, the **Algarve** has attracted more tourist development than the rest of the country put together. In parts, this has gone a long way to destroying all the charms that it was intended to exploit. The strip of coast **west from Faro to Lagos** has suffered most, with its endless villa compléxes creating a rather depressing Mediterranean surburbia. On the fringes, around **Sagres**, or **Tavira**, things are far better, with small-scale and relaxed resorts, the odd undeveloped beach or island sandbank, and some highly attractive inland towns.

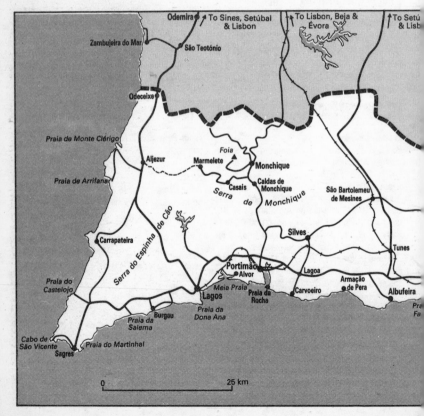

The **coastline** has two different characters. To the **west of Faro** you'll find the classic postcard images of the province – a series of tiny bays and coves, broken up by weird rocky outcrops and fantastic grottoes. They're at their most exotic around the resort towns of **Lagos** and **Albufeira**, but if you're looking for more space, and above all if you want to camp, head instead to **Salema** or to the historic cape of **Sagres**.

East of Faro, there's a complete change as you encounter the first of a series of sandy offshore islets, **the Ilhas**, which front the coastline for some twenty-five miles. Not only is this the quieter section of the coast – the developers haven't yet got to grips with the islands – but it has the bonus of much warmer water than further west. Faro, Olhão and Tavira all offer access to islands and can be attractive bases, Tavira especially.

Inland, there are scattered attractions in the Roman ruins of **Estoi**, north of Faro, or the old Moorish town of **Silves**, easily reached from Portimão. The outstanding area, however, is the **Serra de Monchique**, the highest mountain range in the south, with cork and chestnut woods, strange remote little villages, and a beautiful old spa in **Caldas de Monchique**.

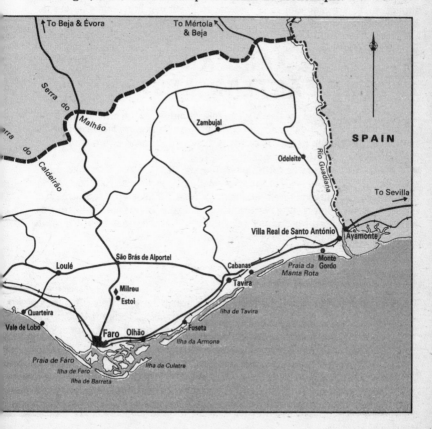

Seasons, Rooms and Transport

The Algarve is an all-year-round destination, with sunny and relatively mild winters. In many respects the region is at its best in **spring** or **winter**. Most pensions and restaurants stay open, so rooms are easy to find – if often unheated, so come prepared – and people are genuinely welcoming of visitors. May has an added attraction in the Algarve's **International Music Festival**, sponsored by the Gulbenkian, and hosting major classical artists.

If you come in the summer months, **accommodation** can be quite a problem, with hotels block-booked by package companies and pensions filling alarmingly early in the day. Fortunately, private rooms (*quartos*) or campsites can usually fill in the gaps. Rooms can be found in even the smallest of villages (places just inland are a good bet if you have transport); they're not always advertised, so ask around in bars and local tourist offices.

Transport along the main section of coast is easy and quick, with a (very cheap) rail line complemented by both regular and seasonal buses. The Algarve also has a new passenger **ferry link with Tangier** in Morocco; this currently operates from Faro (Mon., Thurs. and Sat. throughout the year), though there are plans for it to relocate to Portimão. For details phone the boat's Lisbon agent, *ACP Viages* (☎01/527858, or ☎01/560382).

FARO AND
THE EASTERN ALGARVE

The administrative core of the Algarve tourist industry, **Faro** hosts the international airport and acts as a transport hub for the region. Never a popular holiday destination in itself, the centre of the town is however more attractive than the ugly concrete suburbs might suggest.

The area of the Algarve to the **east of Faro** has suffered less from intensive tourist development than the west. Without spectacular rock formations and protected by an elongated sandbank for much of its length, this stretch of coast has several interesting old towns – principally **Tavira** and **Vila Real de Santo António** – and a number of wonderful beaches that front the *ilhas* (islands) on the seaward side of the sandbank.

Faro

FARO has been transformed from a sleepy provincial town into a centre of trade and commerce within the space of twenty years. Today it has all the facilities of a modern European town, with a bustling shopping area, chic restaurants and fashionable hotels.

Excellent beaches, too, are within easy reach, and in summer there's quite a nightlife scene, as thousands of travellers pass through on their way to and from the airport. There are certainly better places to spend a holiday on the Algarve, but for a night or two's stay at either end, it can be an enjoyable enough base.

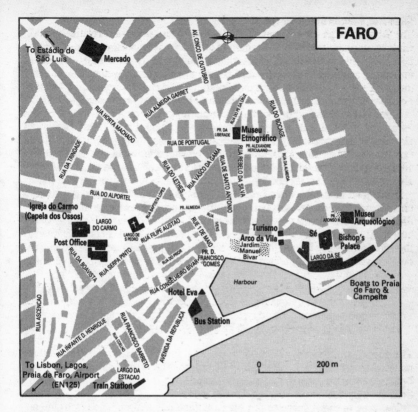

Arriving

In the summer months, flights land at Faro **airport**, 6km from the centre of town, 24 hours a day. The public transport system closes down early, however, and there's a seasonal shortage of accommodation. It's worth asking the airport Turismo desk to try and book you a room; if you arrive late at night, however, be prepared to sleep at the airport. **Taxis** to Faro cost about 700esc, and 900esc after 8pm.

Two **bus** lines run from the airport to the harbour in the centre of Faro (stop *Jardim*): the unreliable #18, with a perplexing timetable, leaves from right outside the airport buildings, and the #16 stops on the right of the main road some 200m away (Mon.–Fri. 7.30am–8pm; May–Sept. every 30 min., Oct.–Apr. hourly; weekends occasional service, same hours).

The same #16 stops on the other side of the road on its way to Praia de Faro (10 min.; see overpage for description) where there's a **campsite** (open all year; Auto Club camping card required). It is always full (and very cramped) in summer; if you want to stay, phone ahead (☎082/24876).

Arriving by bus or train is more straightforward. Both terminals are centrally located, with the old town just across the harbour.

Rooms, Restaurants and Other Practicalities

In the season, **places to stay** in Faro can be very thin on the ground, so try if at all possible to arrive early in the day. The best bet is to head for the **Turismo** (daily Apr.–Sept. 9am–8pm; otherwise 9am–7pm) on the harbour-front at Rua da Misericórdia 8. They have an efficient, pot-luck system of *quartos* allocation and are usually helpful.

If you want a bit more control, the tourist office also provides a list of pensions and hotels, but they will not phone ahead for you. The **pensions** are concentrated just north of the harbour along Conselheiro Bivar and Infante D. Henrique, and around Praça Ferreira de Almeida on Rua Vasco da Gama, Rua Filipe Alistão and Rua do Alportel. Two of the better places to stay are the *Pensão Dandy*, at Filipe Alistão 62, and the ever-expanding *Pensão Madalena*, on Rua C. Bivar.

The heart of the city is a modern, pedestrianised shopping area around **Rua de Santo António**, where you can find a multi-screen cinema and innumerable restaurants, cafés and bakeries stocked with almond delicacies, the regional speciality. There are **restaurants** to meet most budgets. The *Recife* at Vasco da Gama 32 is excellent; the *Caracoles* on Praça Ferreira de Almeida is reasonably priced and the place to try *choquinhos ma timta* (cuttlefish in ink).

Entertainments include the *Sheherazade* **disco** at the *Hotel Eva* (Wed., Fri., Sat.); occasional **fairs** on the Largo de São Francisco; and every other week, Sunday **football** out of town at the Estádio de São Luís. Faro is a major music centre and well-known **bands** sometimes appear at the football stadium – details and tickets from the tourist office.

The Town

Founded by the Moors some 8km to the south of the old Roman city of Ossonoba, Faro was conquered by Christian forces in 1249. Sacked and burned by the Earl of Essex in 1596, and devastated by the Great Earthquake of 1755, the city has few remaining historic buildings, though several churches and museums are of interest.

Chapel of Bones

By far the most curious sight in town is the Baroque **Igreja do Carmo** (Mon.–Fri. 10am–noon and 3–5pm, Sat. 10am–1pm) near the central post office on the Largo do Carmo.

A door to the right of its altar leads around to a macabre **Capela dos Ossos** (Chapel of the Bones). Like the one at Évora, its walls are decorated with human bones disinterred from the adjacent monks' cemetery.

The Old Town

Aside from the chapel, the town's most interesting buildings are all in the old, semi-walled quarter. This is centred around the majestic **Largo da Sé** and entered through the eighteenth-century **Arco da Vila** next to the Turismo.

The Largo is flanked by the old bishop's palace and, of course, the **Cathedral** (8am–noon and 3–5pm), a miscellany of Gothic, Renaissance and Baroque styles, heavily remodelled after the Great Earthquake.

More impressive is the nearby **Museu de Arqueologia** (Mon.–Fri. 9am–noon and 2–5pm) installed in a fine sixteenth-century convent. The most striking of its exhibits is a superb third-century A.D. Roman mosaic of Neptune surrounded by the four winds, unearthed a few metres back near the Faro railway station. Other items include a collection of Roman statues from the excavations at Estói (see below), a rather frightening four-foot Roman phallus, and a selection of local paintings, militaria and sixteenth-century naive multicoloured tiles upstairs in the art gallery.

The **Museu Etnográfico** (same times; entered through a municipal office building) has a mildly interesting display of local crafts and industries, including reconstructions of typical cottage interiors, and models of the net systems still used in fishing for tuna.

Beaches

Faro marks a geographical boundary on the Algarve. The whole coastline east from here to Manta Rota, near the Spanish border, is protected by thin stretches of mud flats, fringed in their turn by a chain of long and magnificent sandbanks. Often accessible only by boat, they're usually far less crowded than the small rocky resorts of the western Algarve. Ornithologists should take their binoculars, as the shores from Faro to Tavira are thick with various types of wading birds in winter and spring.

Praia de Faro

The 'town beach', **Praia de Faro**, is typical of these sandspit beaches – but atypical in that it's both overcrowded and over-developed. Hotels, bars, restaurants (*Camané* is excellent) and a campsite have all been jammed on to a sandy island far too narrow to cope, and you have to walk miles to escape the human press. The *ilhas* off Olhão are really more preferable, and a boat links Faro with Farol on Culatra (see overpage) four times daily in season.

Still, if you just want a few hours' swimming, it's quite functional. A steal at 65esc, **ferries** sail from the jetty (marked on the map) through the narrow marshy channels to the beach from June to September. (High season 8 daily; otherwise 4 daily). You can also go by bus (#16 from the harbour gardens) but it's a sweaty 9km journey and slightly more expensive.

Roman Ruins at Estói

ESTÓI, 11km north of Faro (12 buses a day; 20 min.), has two attractions – a delightful eighteenth-century country estate and the rather scant remains of the Roman settlement of Ossonoba, now known as Milreu. Also, rather unexpectedly, in Estoi's Upper Town is a live music venue, *The German Bar*, which frequently hosts minor British bands.

Milreu

The Roman excavations, 1km west of the village, are dominated by the apse of a temple. This was converted into a Christian basilica in the third century A.D., making it one of the earliest of all known churches. The other recognisable remains are of a bathing complex with fragments of mosaic. The site is open from 11am–12.30pm and 3–7pm, May 1–Sept. 30; 10am–12.30pm and 2–5pm the rest of year; closed Monday.

The Palace

The **Palácio do Visconde de Estói**, just off the village square, resembles a diminutive version of the Rococo palace of Queluz near Lisbon. Only the grounds are (sporadically) open to the public, but the palace has recently been bought by the state and there are plans to turn it into a museum.

Olhão and its Ilhas

OLHÃO, 8km east of Faro, is the largest fishing port on the Algarve and an excellent base for visiting the surrounding sandbank *ilhas*. It's an otherwise uneventful place, notwithstanding the somewhat surreal prose of the local brochure, which proclaims Olhão as home of the 'amazing poodles of the Algarve . . . strong and muscular, they are of invaluable assistance to the fishermen for whom they dive into the water to guide the fish into the nets'. Unfortunately the aquatic poodles were abandoned for more modern methods in the 1950s.

The Town

Despite the offputting run-down appearance of its outskirts, Olhão has an attractive, bustling centre that spreads out from the shore and docks. There are no 'sights' as such, but the flat roofs, external staircases and white terraces of the old town (running roughly parallel to the seafront) are reminiscent of North Africa. Indeed the town has centuries-old trading links with Morocco, as well as a small place in history for its uprising against the French garrison in 1808. Following the French departure, the fishermen of Olhão sent a small caïque across the Atlantic to Brazil to give the news to the exiled King João VI. The journey, completed without navigational aids, was rewarded after the King's restoration to the throne with the granting of a town charter.

The best view of the whitewashed cubes of the old houses is from the **belltower** of the seventeenth-century parish church of Nossa Senhora do Rosário, right in the middle of town. The **train station** and the adjacent **bus terminal** are towards the head of Avenida da República, a wide boulevard leading into the city centre, a five-minute walk away.

There are no *quartos* in town and consequently **accommodation** can be hard to find. If you walk down the boulevard, past the post office, and turn right on to Rua 18 de Junho and take the second left, you reach the average 1-star *Pensão Torres* (closed Nov.–May) at Rua Dr. Paulo Nogueira 13. Further along the boulevard take the left fork down Rua Vasco da Gama for the greatly preferable 2-star *Pensão Bicuar* at no. 5. One block to the east is the 1-star *Pensão Rosa* at Rua Carlos da Maia 56. Other alternatives are the relatively expensive *Hotel Ria Sol* by the bus station, and the **campsite** at MARIM, 3km east along the railway tracks, or 5km via the main road; the latter has a pool, and views of Armona, though frustratingly no beach.

If you're still out of luck, head for the **Turismo** on Rua do Comércio, the main shopping street and an extension of the Avenida da República. (The office is open July and Aug. Mon.–Fri. 9am–7pm, weekends 9am–noon and 2.30–5pm; rest of the year Mon.–Fri. 9am–noon and 2.30–5pm, Sat. 9am–noon, closed Sun.) They will provide a town map, advise on accommodation, and provide (not entirely reliable) sailing times for boats to the *ilhas*.

There are a number of **restaurants** and **bars** around the Rua do Comércio; try the *Taiti* at Rua Vasco da Gama 24 or the *Algarve*, the latter with good value traditional fare.

The Ilhas: Armona and Culatra

Ferries leave for the **Ilhas** of **Armona** and **Culatra** from the jetty at the far end of Olhão's municipal gardens, five minutes from the Turismo. Fares are cheap, and the kiosk near the boats sells tickets and provides up-to-date details of sailing times.

Ilha da Armona

The service to **ARMONA** leaves between nine and twelve times daily from June to September, five times daily in May and October, and twice daily in winter. The journey takes fifteen minutes.

You are dropped off at the northern end of the only settlement, a long strip of vacation chalets and huts that stretches right across the island on either side of the main path. It's a ramshackle, cosy affair, a world away from the sterility of most of the Algarve's 'holiday villages' and a delightful place to be. There are a couple of **bar-restaurants** by the beaches at either end of the village, packed with a lively mix of holidaymakers soaking up the sun and the booze.

On the **ocean side** the beach disappears into the distance and a short walk will take you to totally deserted stretches of sand and dune: the further you walk, the greater the privacy. The **beach facing the mainland** is smaller and tends to get very crowded in summer, but the water here, sheltered from the Atlantic, is always warm and perfectly calm.

There are no campsites, pensions or hotels on Armona, and the obvious solution is to bed down on the beach – but be somewhat cautious: some of the chalet owners are none too keen on this 'illegal' activity. If you prefer a roof over your head, the Turismo in Olhão will rent a **chalet** on your behalf: the more of you there are, the cheaper it becomes, but you'll be lucky to find anywhere in high season.

Ilha da Culatra

The **boats** for Culatra and Farol on the **ILHA DA CULATRA** leave seven times daily from June to September, and once daily throughout the winter (35-min. journey).

Culatra is another huge sand spit, but it's very different in character from Armona. The **northern shore** is dotted with a series of poor fishing villages that sometimes resemble Third World shanty towns, mixed with an incongruous sprinkling of holiday chalets.

The ferry's first port of call is **Culatra** – the largest settlement and a grim and distinctly unpleasant place. **Farol**, the second stop and 45 minutes from Olhão, is more agreeable – even if it doesn't have Armona's charm. A rather commonplace, untidy village of vacation homes, Farol ('the lighthouse') is edged by beautiful tracts of beach on the ocean side, though the beach facing the mainland is grubby.

Once again unofficial **camping** on the island is frowned upon, and tends to be conspicuous among the fishing villages. Basic **rooms** and **food** at not-so-basic prices are available at the all-year *Hotel Bar Tropical* – a lively, Norwegian-owned place that seems stuck somewhere in the late 1960s.

Fuzeta

Armona is also accessible from the unkempt fishing village of **FUZETA**, 10km east of Olhão. There is an official campsite here in summer, but it's very uninviting – you're better off heading straight for the islands.

There are no organised ferries over, but it's easy enough to pay for a ride across the channel. Take your own food and water.

Tavira – and more Ilhas

TAVIRA is one of the most beautiful towns on the Algarve, and a clear winner if you are looking for an urban base on the eastern stretch. It has superb island beaches in easy reach, yet despite ever-increasing visitors and encroaching development, continues to make its living as a tuna-fishing port.

The Town

The broad Rio Gilão, lined with palm trees and overlooked by ancient balconied houses, flows right through the centre of Tavira, straddled by a bridge whose origins, if not present structure, are Roman.

From the **Castle**, half hidden on a low hill in the centre of town, you can look down over the peculiarly oriental rooftops and the town's thirty-seven churches. Nearby, the whitewashed **Santa Maria do Castelo** contains the tomb of Dom Paio Peres Correia, who reconquered much of the Algarve from the Moors, including Tavira in 1224. Fittingly, the church stands on the site of the former mosque.

Transport and Rooms

The **bus** stop is in the central square, the **Praça da República**; there are good connections from here to Vila Real, Faro and other local destinations. The **railway station** is 1km from the centre of town, straight up the Rua da Liberdade.

Accommodation is tight in summer so try to arrive early in the day. The best place to stay is the *Pensão Lagoas*, east of the river at Rua Almirante Cândido dos Reis 24, with attractive rooms and rooftop views. Other reasonable alternatives are the *Pensão do Castelo* in the main square, the *Residencial*

Mirante at Rua da Liberdade 83; the *quartos* just opposite; and – for those not sensitive to noise – the pension above the *Restaurante Imperial* at Rua José Pires Padinha 22.

If these options fail to produce a bed, the **Turismo** in the Praça may be willing to help you find a private **room** (May–Sept. 9am–8pm; otherwise Mon–Sat. 9am–12.30pm and 2.30–5pm, closed Sun.).

If you want to see a bit more of the coast, **bikes** and **mopeds** can be hired; further details from the tourist office.

Bars and Restaurants

A succession of bars and restaurants line the gardens along the riverbank. Probably the best of these is the *Restaurante Imperial*, which serves some of the finest seafood in the Algarve – at fairly reasonable prices. Other recommendations are the *Ponto de Encontro* in the Praça Dr. António Padinha and the *Restaurante Bica*, Rua Almirante Candido dos Reis 22–24.

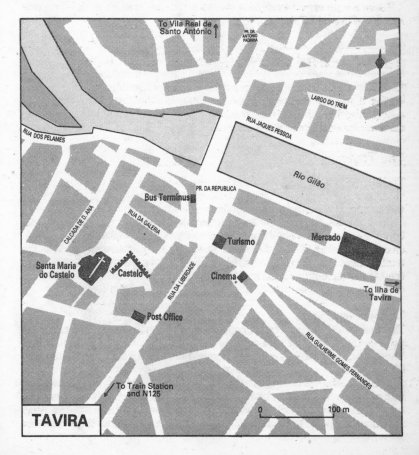

Beaches: Ilha de Tavira and Pedras d'El Rei

The **ILHA DE TAVIRA** stretches west from Tavira almost as far as Fuzeta some 14km away. For most of its length the landward side of the island is a dank morass of mud flat, but at the eastern tip the mud disappears and the *ilha* ends in a featureless expanse of sand and sea. The boats across from Tavira Beach dock at the eastern end of the island, next to a run-down chalet settlement that incorporates an unappealing **campsite**. The beach is enormous but massively popular, and you have to walk miles to escape the crowds.

Buses (marked *Quatro Águas*) leave from outside the Tavira cinema for the ten-minute trip to the ferry terminal at Tavira Beach. In summer (June–Sept.) the boats are more or less a shuttle service, in May and September there are four departures a day – and there are none for the rest of the year.

Pedras d'El Rei

If you're after isolated beach, it's better to head four kilometres west from Tavira to **PEDRAS D'EL REI**. This is a holiday village, designed expressly for the purpose, but while it's a bit sterile, it's not too big and is very pleasant for its type (and the sands spread for miles if you feel like laying down a sleeping bag for the night). Alternatively, chalets can be rented on a short-term basis at reasonable prices for small groups, though the complex is usually full in July and August. Regular summer **buses** connect Tavira with Pedras or you can walk up from the main road in about fifteen minutes.

From Pedras a **miniature railway** shuttles backwards and forwards across the mud flats to the beach of **BARRIL** on the Ilha de Tavira. It's a few minutes' walk right or left to escape the tourist facilities at the terminal, and there you are: miles of beautiful, peaceful, dune-fringed beach.

Tavira to Vila Real

Just to the east of Tavira, the sand spit that protects much of the eastern Algarve from the developers starts to thin out, merging with the shoreline beach at Manta Rota. The result is predictable: **CABANAS**, **MANTA ROTA**, **ALAGOA** and **MONTE GORDO** have all been intensively developed, robbing the coast of its charm. **PRAIA VERDE** is another place to avoid: the beach is pretty and the hills are attractively wooded, but sheltering under the branches are enough caravans to accommodate the Russian army.

Cacelha Velha

There's one surprise. For some reason, the small hamlet of **CACELA VELHA** (not to be confused with VILA NOVA DE CACELA, 2km inland) is completely untouched by tourism. Perched on a rocky bluff overlooking the sea, surrounded by olive groves, and home to an old church and the remains of a fort, it is spectacularly pretty – how much of the Algarve must have looked forty years ago. Naturally enough, the hamlet is short on 'facilities', but it's got a little restaurant and a handful of **rooms** that are snapped up in the summer. The beach is a delight and it's easy enough to arrange a lift over to the sand bar just off shore.

The only direct **bus** to Cacela Velha is from Vila Nova and it isn't at all frequent. The best bet is to walk up from the main road, 1km away.

Vila Real de Santo António

The border town and harbour of **VILA REAL DE SANTO ANTÓNIO** is a lively place to end (or begin) your travels in Portugal. The original town was demolished by a tidal wave at the beginning of the seventeenth century, and the site stood empty until it was revived in 1774 by the Marquês de Pombal. Eager to apply the latest concepts of town-planning, Pombal used the same techniques he had already pioneered in the Baixa quarter of Lisbon and rebuilt Vila Real on a grid plan. The whole project only took five months, but it was a huge waste of resources: the hewn stone that Pombal had dragged all the way from Lisbon could have been quarried a couple of miles up the road. With the exception of the main square, the end result is pretty dreary, and the rats and rubbish that line the River Guadiana add nothing to the allure.

On the other hand, with so many travellers passing through and so many Portuguese coming here for their holidays, Vila Real has something happening pretty much all the time. Rua Teófilo Braga and the riverside promenade are packed with popular bars and restaurants; there are regular bullfights and rock concerts in the Estádio do Lusitano; and there's always the odd chaotic festival with bands blaring through the streets.

Practicalities

There's a shortage of **accommodation** in Vila Real so try to arrive early in the day, when you can have your pick of the *pensions* dotted either side of the Rua Teófilo Braga. The *Residencial Felix* across from the tourist office on Avenida da República is one of the pleasanter places to stay. Alternatively, the Turismo can be persuaded to phone around for a vacant *quarto*, there's an all-year **youth hostel** on Rua Dr. Sousa Martins 40; and in an emergency you could doze off in the municipal gardens by the river.

There's no shortage of bars and **restaurants** – and the *Caves do Guadiana* at Av. da República 90 is outstanding.

Monte Gordo and Castro Marim

Vila Real's nearest **campsite** and **beach** are a few miles south at **MONTE GORDO**, an ugly tower-block resort near the mouth of the Guadiana, connected by an hourly bus service.

Far more appealing is the little village of **CASTRO MARIM**, tucked away 5km north. A key fortification protecting Portugal's southern coast, Marim was the first headquarters of the Order of Christ (1319) and the site of a huge castle built by Afonso III in the thirteenth century. The massive ruins are all that survived the earthquake of 1755, but it's a pretty place with fine views.

The area around Castro Marim has been designated as a **nature reserve**, so there's no danger of its being despoiled. There are a couple of buses a day connecting the village to Vila Real and though there's no official accommodation, ask around and you may be able to find a room.

Crossing into Spain

What will happen when the road and bridge connecting the Algarve to Spain is finally completed no one can be sure, but in the meantime **ferries** offer the only approach to Ayamonte, across the River Guadiana in Spanish Andalucía. They run every half hour, seven days a week from 7.30am to 11pm with an occasional night ferry. The trip takes about fifteen minutes and costs 60esc per person, 325esc per car; in season you may have to queue up for several hours if you want to take a car across.

From **Ayamonte** there's regular transport to HUELVA and SEVILLA – Vila Real's **Turismo** by the ferry terminal will provide up-to-date details (8am–8pm daily). The ferry terminal is next to the bus station and one of Vila Real's **two railway stations** – Vila Real-Guadiana.

THE WESTERN ALGARVE

The **Western Algarve** stretches some one hundred kilometres from **Faro** to **Sagres** and includes the most intensively developed areas in the country. Immediately west of Faro is the worst string of the developments: an almost continuous stretch of resorts all the way to Lagos. Although these are immortalised on postcards for their sandy beaches and unusual rock formations, few of them are worth a visit – **Albufeira**, **Carvoeiro** and **Portimão** are the possible exceptions. The better bases, however, are inland; places like **Loulé** or **Silves** could be enjoyable if you have your own transport to the sea.

West of **Lagos**, an attractive town in its own right, the pace of development slackens and the resorts are small and relatively manageable. The best is perhaps **Salema**, beyond which the road and land cut high above the sea, across a cliff-edged plateau, and finally down to **Sagres**, with its dramatic scenery and busy nightlife.

The tourist boom has scarcely touched the long beaches of the **western coast** – heading north from Sagres – where the sea is distinctly colder and often pretty wild. If you can brave the climate, low-key villages such as **Vila do Bispo**, **Carrapateira**, **Aljezur** and **Odeceixe** offer cheap rooms near the beaches, and camping outside established sites is generally accepted.

Faro to Albufeira

The coast west of Faro begins with very little promise. The first of the resorts, **QUINTA DO LAGO** is a vast luxury holiday village with its own leisure centre and opulent hotel. There's more of the same at **VALE DO LOBO**, next door, with golf courses, a riding school and a tennis club once run by old Wimbledon pro Roger Taylor.

Quarteira and Vilamoura

Next along the coast, **QUARTEIRA** is by contrast quite a pleasant town, though the building from adjoining VILAMOURA – one of the ugliest developments imaginable – increasingly threatens to overwhelm it, spreading to its west and north.

The older section of Vilamoura, however, centred on the seafront, has a fine (if touristy) beach, with restaurants, a permanent *mercado* and a weekly (Wednesday) market, selling a wide variety of produce, from fresh honeycomb to home-made pimento sauce. The **Turismo** is very helpful and will usually be able to direct you to vacant rooms or pensions – even in season.

A kilometre to the east lies a sequence of beaches known collectively as TRAFAT. These are far less crowded than those in Quarteira and frequented mainly by the inhabitants of the beachfront **campsite**, the entrance to which is about 2km along the Quarteira–Faro road.

Loulé

LOULÉ, 11km inland from Quarteira, has a history similar to most of the towns in southern Portugal – Roman and Moorish occupation – and castle ruins to match. In its winding backstreets, you'll find a market, bars and restaurants, and an excellent art gallery. Being slightly inland, there are plenty of rooms and pensions available, making a good base for the beaches.

Albufeira

Every inch a resort, **ALBUFEIRA** tops the list of European, especially British, package-tour destinations in the Algarve. It was once an unusually pretty resort with narrow, twisting lanes of whitewashed ancient houses crisscrossing the high grey-red cliffs above a beautiful spread of beaches. All this, however, has been engulfed by hundreds of new apartment buildings that may not be high-rise but have surely destroyed much of the character and elegance of the town, and overcrowded its beaches.

Nevertheless, Albufeira is still one of the nicer resorts. Its visitors inhabit at least two distinct social milieux: there's an aging, well-heeled clientele who dress formally for dinner at the more expensive restaurants, and then there's the younger contingent who devote themselves to downing as many beers as is humanly possible.

Practicalities

The main street, the Rua 5 de Outubro, bisects the town and leads from the **bus station** to a tunnel, five minutes away, that's been blasted out of the rock to give access to the beach. Close to the tunnel is the **Turismo** (Mon.–Fri. 9am–7pm, weekends 9am–12.30pm and 2.30–5pm). Almost opposite, in an alleyway to the right as you face the beach, is *Pensão Silva*, Travessa 5 de Outubro 18, the cheapest place to stay. If it's full (as is likely) there are few other choices and you'll have to get the Turismo to phone around for a **room**, though even these can be tight in high season. **Camping Albufeira** (2km) and the **railway station** at Ferreiras (6km) are both north of town, off N395, with regular connections from the bus station.

The whole town is jam-packed with **restaurants** to match every budget. It's difficult to single any out and you tend to get what you pay for, but for the better bargains head for the area around the old fishing harbour, east of the main beach. The *Beach Basket* on Praça Miguel Bombarda, just west of the Turismo and overlooking the beach, serves excellent but expensive meals.

The best of the **discos** are *Silvia's*, on Rua São Gonçalo de Lagos, and the more established *Silver Screen*, on Avenida 25 de Abril. Small-time British and American **bands** appear at various bars – the best are usually booked by the *Bird's Nest* in the main square, Largo Engenheiro Duarte Pacheco.

Beaches around Albufeira

The **beach** fronting Albufeira is as good as any in the area, once again flanked by strange tooth-like rock formations. But obviously it gets crowded – and a relatively short bus ride can open up a number of other possibilities.

The rocky red headlands just **to the west** of Albufeira are beautiful and were inaccessible until the development of a strip of villa resorts, principally **SÃO RAFAEL, CASTELO** and **GALÉ**. Spreading back from small cove beaches with craggy, eroded rock faces, this trio competes at the more exclusive end of the European second-home market. None of them have been finished and the whole area can resemble a building site, with great gashes of red earth exposed by the bulldozers. If the developers were to show restraint it might not be too bad, but the indications are that now that the roads to the beaches have been finished, there'll soon be a chain of villas and chalets trailing right across the hills. There are no direct buses to any of these resorts; the nearest you'll get is the Albufeira–Portimão service that drops you on the main road, a steep 2km away from the beaches.

Overall it's better to head **east**, where you have several more choices. Immediately east of Albufeira ochre-red cliffs divide the coastline into a series of bays and beaches, all within easy walking distance of the Albufeira–Faro

bus route (a dozen buses daily). Praia da Oura, which begins just two kilometres from Albufeira, is the longest and nearest, but has been terribly over-
developed. Farther along, **OLHOS DE ÁGUA**, an old fishing village, is
smaller and more manageable. Less ferociously touristy, it remains an attractive little place with a lively bar-restaurant at the west end of the beach that
often has live music at night. If the beach gets crowded, you can walk to other
more isolated coves.

Praia da Falésia

At **Praia da Falésia**, ten kilometres out of Albufeira, the character of the
coastline changes to produce one long, tremendous stretch of sand.
Unbroken red cliffs run its whole course – making it tricky to get down to,
but equally worth the effort. The simplest approach is to take the Faro bus to
the *Touring Club of Portugal* stop on the fringes of ALDEIA DAS AÇOTEIAS,
a bewildering chalet and villa complex. Here you can just hop aboard the
shuttle service to the beach and walk as far away from the crowds as you like.
There are taverna-cafés at numerous points along all of these beaches – but
reasonably priced accommodation is hard to find.

West to Portimão

Heading west from Albufeira along the main N125, you'll pass through
PORCHES, about halfway between ALCANTARILHA and LAGOA. This is
where the most famous of the Algarve's handmade **pottery** comes from.
Thick, chunky and handpainted, it has a good heavy feel, and if you're look-

SUPERNATURAL FORCE ON THE ROAD TO LOULÉ

The following account comes from an otherwise impeccably reliable correspondent.
You might like to check it out.

'Driving with a Portuguese friend along N270 from POÇO DE BOLIQUEIME to
LOULÉ, heading downhill after the *Eurocampina* factory, we noticed that the car
began to slow down erratically, as if due to some mechanical failure. As this continued we felt the sensation of driving into some "other force". Putting the car into
neutral, we slowed down and actually stopped before reaching the bottom of the
hill! No brakes!

After a few seconds of our stunned exclamations, the car began to move backwards, unaided, up the hill. We actually reached about 20mph until a truck
appeared on the horizon, at which point we slipped into gear and accelerated
through 'the force'.

I personally experienced this phenomenon on three separate occasions. Locals
have no explanation – they prefer to create a mystery to amuse themselves and
others. Nonbelievers are usually of the opinion that the whole thing is an optical
illusion, and that the rock formations and horizon play tricks with the mind. Of this,
I am somewhat dubious. I prefer the other, more inspired idea that some sort of
magnetic force is in the area, created by friction at the quarry located further along
the road. In fact many heavy-duty lorries use the road, so do pay attention while
experimenting. If you can't get hold of a car try hitching a lift with holidaymakers in
"the force".'

ing for thoroughly impractical presents to take home, this is the place to stop. Six kilometres to the south and connected to Albufeira by regular bus service (4 daily; 30 min.) is the gargantuan resort of ARMAÇÃO DE PÊRA, about which nothing complimentary can be said.

Carvoeiro

Further west the small resort of **CARVOEIRO** can be reached by bus from LAGOA and PORTIMÃO. Cut into the red sea cliffs, this is an attractive place that used to have an air of tranquil seclusion, until developers draped a line of villa-apartments across the surrounding hills. The beach is much too small to cope with this second influx, with the result that Carvoeiro's charm has begun to fade.

Rooms are out of the question in high season and go for about 2500esc in June and September. There are two small **pensions** (3500–4500esc), a number of bars and restaurants, and a helpful **tourist office** (Mon.–Sat. 9am–12.30pm and 2.30–5pm).

Follow the coast road east, and in less than 1km you'll reach the impressive rock formations of ALGAR SECO, where the cliffs form dramatic overhangs above narrow beaches.

Estômbar

A few miles inland is **ESTÔMBAR**, an unremarkable little town that's a pleasant contrast to all those coastal developments. The birthplace of the eleventh-century poet Ibn Ammãr, the town straggles down a steep hill in a confusion of narrow lanes – but at least you feel you're in Portugal.

Portimão and Beyond

PORTIMÃO is one of the largest towns on the Algarve coast. A sprawling port, a major sardine-canning centre, and a base for the construction industries spawned by the tourist boom, it's rather an ugly place, dominated by graceless tower blocks. Most of the older buildings were destroyed in the 1755 earthquake and the best part of town is the riverfront – a hive of activity with its bars, restaurants and fishing port. Day-trippers come in strength from the surrounding beaches to photograph the fishermen, buy English papers, and patronise the cafés.

Practicalities

The **Turismo** on Rua Dr. João Vitorino Mealha will help you find a **room** for about 2000esc, or provide a list of **pensions** (Mon.–Sat. 9am–7pm, or 9am–12.30pm and 2.30–5pm). Alternatively, you shouldn't have much difficulty in getting yourself set up at either the *Pensão O Pátio* (down from the tourist office at no. 5), or the spick-and-span and more expensive *Pensão Arabi* on Praça Manuel Teixeira Gomes. The best of the town's restaurants is *Don Antonio*, on the outskirts; it's not the cheapest by any means, but for the quality of cooking is fine value.

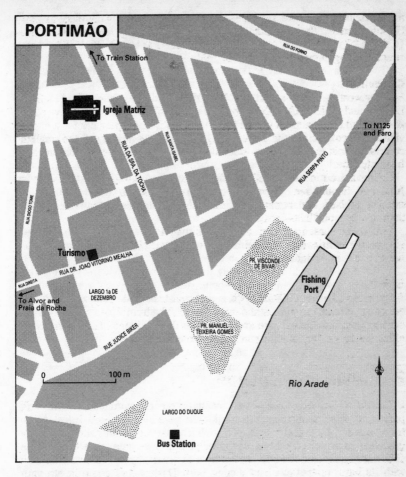

The **railway station** is inconveniently located at the northern tip of town and there's no bus connection; a taxi costs about 250esc or it's a twenty-minute walk. Other **bus services** from Largo do Dique are excellent: Lagos (hourly; 30min.); Alvor (hourly; 20min.); Faro (5 daily; 2hr.) and Monchique (8 daily; 1hr.).

Ferragudo, Praia da Rocha and Alvor

FERRAGUDO, across the estuary from Portimão and also connected by regular bus service, is very different in character: stuck on the side of a hill, it's a run-down, friendly little place that's only now beginning to be tarted up for tourists.

There are a couple of small pensions in the town and you should be able to find a **room** – ask around at the bars or at the tourist office (if it's open). There are good views of Portimão's skyline and a couple of lively bars including the *Caldeirão*.

The **beach** is about 1km to the south and popular in a small-scale way, with a windsurfing school and a few restaurant-bars. A large, dreary **campsite** slouches next to the road ten minutes further south.

Praia da Rocha

PRAIA DA ROCHA, 3km south of Portimão, was one of the first Algarve tourist developments and has since become one of the most up-market, with a spate of high-rise hotels, discos, a sports complex and a casino. The **beach** is one of the most beautiful on the entire coast, a wide expanse of sand framed by jagged sea cliffs and the walls of an old fort (now a restaurant) that once protected the mouth of the river Arade. It was even more beautiful before a great chunk of cliff was blown away to improve access.

Bus connections are excellent, with direct service to Lisbon from outside the Hotel Jupiter and a half-hourly bus to Portimão. Surprisingly, **accommodation** is rarely hard to find and cheaper than you might imagine. The **Turismo**, near the fort, will readily find you a room (Mon.–Fri. 9am–7pm, weekends 9am–12.30pm and 2.30–5pm); the only inexpensive **pension**, the *Oceano*, is nearby on the main street and charges about 3000esc for a double. Praia da Rocha has one other curiosity: the seafront **Hotel Bela Vista**, a pseudo-Moorish mansion built in 1903 as a wedding gift by the wealthy Magalhães family; the interior is an exquisite mixture of carved woods, stained glass and yellow, white and blue *azulejos*. If you've got 15,000esc burning a hole in your pocket, stay the night.

Alvor

The coast road west of Praia da Rocha has been engulfed by a series of massive tourist developments of no charm and very little interest. The ancient port of **ALVOR** may itself have been saved from this fate, but much of its appeal has been washed away under a tide of tourists from the surrounding hotels and holiday villages: the town's narrow streets and its multitude of bars and restaurants can hardly cope. Whitewashed houses and lovely views of the estuary are the last vestiges of Alvor's charm.

The **beach** is enormous and if it's a bit on the dull side, at least it's still easy to escape the crowds. The west end is also an excellent place for catching *conquilhas* (shellfish). At low tide wriggle your feet under the sand in the shallows until you feel one move, then reach down and grab it – or simply copy the Portuguese who will be out there with you. They're good fried with oil and garlic for a few minutes (until they open).

In season **rooms** at Alvor are hard to come by, but there are two **campsites**, a grim affair near the beach and the more pleasant *Campismo Dourado* about 1km north, towards Montes de Alvor. Restaurants are more promising, at least outside of peak season. The beach café *Rosemar* does good fish and basic meals.

Silves

Residence and capital of the Moorish kings of the al-Gharb, **SILVES** is still an imposing place and one of the few inland towns in this province that merits a detour. The railway station – an easy approach from either Lagos or Faro – lies 2km outside the town; there is a connecting bus, as usual, but it's better to walk, allowing the town and its dominating fortress to appear slowly as you emerge from the wooded hills.

Moorish Silves: The Castle

Under the **Moors** Silves was a place of grandeur and industry, described in contemporary accounts as being 'of shining brightness' within its three dark circuits of guarding walls.

In 1189 a mixed army of Portuguese and Crusaders led by **Sancho I** set out to put an end to this civilised splendour. It was an uneasy and unruly army: desperately in need of extra manpower, the devoutly Catholic king was forced to swallow his disgust for the rabble of 'large and odious' northerners, who had already been expelled from the holy shrine of St. James of Compostella for their irreligious behaviour. The combined force arrived at Silves towards the end of June and the 30,000 Moors retreated into their citadel. There they remained through the long, hot summer, sustained by huge water cisterns and granaries, but on September 1, the water was exhausted and they opened negotiations. Sancho was ready to compromise, but the Crusaders had been recruited by the promise of plunder, and were not prepared to accept the king's financial inducements to forego the pleasure of wrecking the town. On September 3, the gates were opened after Sancho had negotiated guarantees for the inhabitants' personal safety and goods; all were brutally ignored by the Crusaders, who duly ransacked the town, killing some 6000 Moors in the process.

The impressively complete sandstone **walls** of the Moorish **fortress** retain their detached towers and elaborate communication system, but the inside is a bit disappointing: aside from the great vaulted water cisterns that still serve the town, there's nothing left of the old citadel, and the modern gardens are as dull as the 'traditional festival' held here every Saturday night in summer. Just below the fortress is Silves' **Cathedral**, built on the site of the old mosque in the thirteenth century. Flanked by two broad Gothic towers, it has a suitably defiant and military appearance, though the Great Earthquake of 1755 and centuries of impoverished restoration have left their mark inside.

Practicalities

If you want to stay in Silves, the **Turismo** – in the heart of the town, on Rua 25 de Abril – will help you find a **room** (9am–12.30pm and 2.30–5pm daily). Alternatively, there should be space at *Residencial Sousa* at Rua Samora Barros 17 or the *Pensão Central* on Rua Comendador Vilarinho. More expensive is the *Estabelecimentos D. Sancho*, opposite the cathedral.

The *Marisqueira Rui* **restaurant**, just above the Pensão Central, has an international reputation for excellent, reasonably priced food. In the summer, tourists drive from all over the central Algarve to eat here and the queues can be amazing. If you manage to squeeze in – and you should try – order shellfish, the restaurant's speciality.

Should you decide to make Silves your base for a few days, the easiest **beach** to get to is at Carvoeiro (by bus, change at Lagos) or you could head inland to the artificial lake of the **Barragem do Arade**, 12km northeast. Here you can rent a motor boat to cruise the waters behind the huge dam and hardly see a soul.

Inland to the Serra de Monchique

Seven buses a day leave Portimão for the ninety-minute journey to **Monchique** via **Caldas de Monchique**. Eventually clear of Portimão's ugly suburbs, the main road crosses the coastal plain flanked by endless orchards of apples, pears, figs, almonds, pomegranates and citrus fruits.

At PORTO DE LAGOS the road divides, east to Silves and north into the foothills of the **Serra de Monchique**, a green and wooded mountain range of cork, chestnut and eucalyptus that gives the western Algarve a natural northern boundary. It is ideal hiking country, or a superb route to take if you can hire a moped for a couple of days at one of the Algarve resorts.

Caldas de Monchique

CALDAS DE MONCHIQUE, set in a ravine and surrounded by thick woods, has been a celebrated spa since Roman times. In 1495 Dom João II came here to take the waters (but nevertheless died soon afterwards in the nearby village of Alvor), and in the nineteenth century it became a favourite resort of the Spanish bourgeoisie. A Casino from these times still stands in the main square, serving now as a handicraft centre, surrounded by lovely, fading nineteenth-century buildings.

The setting is as beautiful as any in the country, and the village's peace and quiet is only temporarily disturbed by the coachloads of day-trippers who stop for a look and a cup of coffee. It's perhaps a shame about the modern Thermal Hospital on the edge of the nearby cliff – an eyesore, despite its well-kept gardens – and the equally ugly *Oficina de Engarrafamento* where the famous water is bottled for sale around the country. But at least it maintains the tradition, and Caldas remains an active spa rather than being simply quaint.

There are two good, cheap **pensions** in Caldas: *Pensão Central*, in the main square, and *Pensão Internacional* by the main road. Both are basic, but both also have that wonderful air of melancholic decay which seems to hang over these old spas, especially out of season – and the *Internacional* has a good old-fashioned restaurant. Climbing up from the spa you can follow the stream to sit under giant eucalyptus trees and picnic, and no doubt one could also camp around here without anyone being too bothered. Try taking along some of the local arbutus-berry-derived *aguardente* (fire water), which nicely complements the spring water.

Monchique and nearby Villages

MONCHIQUE, six kilometres to the north and 300m higher up the range, is a small market town with a huge monthly agricultural fair, famous too for its smoked hams and its furniture. There's not a great deal to see, but it's an interesting, busy town and makes a good excursion.

The **parish church**, up a steep cobbled street from the main square, has a Manueline porch and inside a little chapel with a facade of *azulejos*. The most evocative sight, though, is the ruined seventeenth-century monastery of **Nossa Senhora de Desterro**. Only a roofless shell of the old Franciscan foundation survives, apparently quite uncared for, but it's in a great position overlooking the town and shows a beautiful blend of classical Renaissance facade with Moorish-influenced vaulting.

There are a couple of rather unappealing **pensions** in Monchique – the *Bela Vista* in the main square and the *Zé de Ferro*, about 150m down the Portimão road – and several restaurants: *Restaurante Chorette* is one of the best of the worthwhile places on Rua Samora Gil. If you have the chance, try the speciality of the Serra – eel. *Ensopado de Enguias*, eels and bread baked in tomato sauce, is a lot better than it sounds.

Fóia

If you're visiting Monchique, you should also try and make it up to FÓIA, eight kilometres away and, at nearly 1000m, the highest of the Serra's peaks. There are no buses but you might be lucky in hitching a lift from a day-tripper. At the top there's a concrete obelisk, a radio tower, a few stalls selling knick-knacks and knitwear (it can be cool up here), and a **pension-café**, *O Planalto*, whose few rooms are generally full. (Camping would be possible only if you have a very wind-resistant tent).

The summit also has a **panoramic view of the Algarve**, taking in the Portimão bay, Lagos, the foothills stretching to the Barragem da Bravura, and Cabo São Vicente. The poet Robert Southey claimed to have caught a glimpse of the hills of Sintra, beyond Lisbon, but that must have been one of those legendary 'clear days' – or maybe the air is never so clear now as it was in 1801. In any event it feels fresh up here.

Marmelete

MARMELETE (2 buses a day from Monchique) is another fine excursion. It feels very remote: no pensions, nobody trying to sell you anything, old houses, old people. In short, nothing happens here, but the country around, and en route, is devastatingly tranquil; you can camp in the forest and hike among the woods or hills, and the village itself has two bars.

If you want to keep going west from here, there's a perilous dirt road (currently being improved) which leads through the hills and forests to Aljezur (see below).

Santa Clara

Back on the main road north, N266 continues through the hills, past the huge **Barragem de Santa Clara** and across the flatlands of the Alentejo to a fork with turnings for ODEMIRA and the west coast, or BEJA and the eastern Alentejo. **SANTA CLARA-À-VELHA** (just over thirty kilometres from Monchique) makes a pleasant break in the journey, a compact little town with rooms and a few café-restaurants where you can get a meal of fresh fish from the Barragem.

Lagos

Once a quiet little town, **LAGOS** has been transformed into a major resort, one of the liveliest and most expensive on the Algarve coast. It has little of the packaged provincialism of Albufeira and attracts the whole gamut of tourists – Scandinavian executives rub shoulders with American college students, back-packers, and family holidaymakers. What brings everyone here is an extraordinary network of cove beaches, sheltered by cliffs, pierced by tunnels and grottoes, and studded by weird and extravagantly weathered outcrops of purple-tinted rock.

The Town

The town is one of the most ancient in the Algarve – probably founded by Phoenicians, who were attracted to its superb natural harbour. Under the Moors it became an important trading post until its reconquest by Christian armies in 1241. Later it became a favoured residence of Henry the Navigator, who used Lagos as a base for the new African trade – which explains the formation in 1441 of the town's **slave market**, held under the arches of the old **Customs House** that still stands in the Praça da República near the waterfront.

In this same square is the church of **Santa Maria**, through whose whimsical Manueline windows the youthful Dom Sebastião is said to have roused his troops before the ill-fated Moroccan expedition of 1578. Fired up by militant Catholicism, the dream-crazed king was to perish on the desert battlefield of Alcácer-Quibir with almost the entire Portuguese nobility. It was a disaster that enabled the Spanish to absorb Portugal for sixty years, but it did Dom Sebastião's reputation a world of good among the aggressively devout. He's commemorated in Lagos by a fantastically dreadful statue in the centre of town, looking like a pink flower-pot man.

On the waterfront and to the rear of the town are the remains of Lagos's once impregnable fortifications, but most of the town was devastated by the Great Earthquake. One rare and beautiful church which did survive for restoration was the **Igreja de Santo António** and this, even if you bother with no other local 'sights', demands a look. Decorated around 1715, its gilt and carved interior is wildly obsessive, every last inch filled with a private fantasy of cherubic youths struggling with animals and fish. Next door is the **Museu Municipal** (Tues.–Sun. 9.30am–12.30pm and 2.30–5.30pm), with bizarre displays ranging from Roman mosaics and folk costumes to misshapen animal foetuses.

Accommodation

Most of the hotels and pensions are fully booked through the summer and unless you turn up very early in the day, your only chance of a bed will be in a **private house**. You'll probably get offers at the bus or railway terminal; otherwise it's a fifteen-minute walk from either to the **Turismo** in the central Largo Marquês de Pombal (June–Aug. 9am–8pm daily; otherwise Mon.–Fri. 9.30am–7pm, weekends 9.30am–12.30pm and 2–5pm). If you have a good idea of what you want and how much you're prepared to pay, they may phone around and find you a place. In summer a good room costs about 2500esc.

Alternatively, you could try two of the more convenient **pensions** just by the Turismo – the *Pensão Caravela* and the *Residencial Mar Azul*, at Rua 25 de Abril 14 and 13 respectively; they're pleasant and reasonably priced places, but rooms facing the street can be noisy.

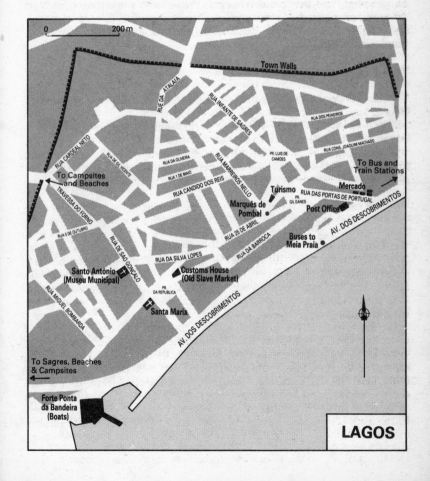

Lagos also has two **campsites**. The *Imulagos: Parque de Campismo* is dauntingly big, but uncramped, with good facilities (half-price entry to the nearby swimming pool); the alternative, *Campismo da Trindade* is not so clean and all very concrete. In season a regular bus service marked 'D. Ana/ Porto de Mós' connects the bus station with both, and *Imulagos* even provides its own free transport from the railway station. If you're walking, follow the main Sagres road around the old town and it's about ten minutes from the Forte Ponta da Bandeira to *Trindade*; fifteen for *Imulagos*.

Food, Drink and Entertainment

If you want to buy your own food there's a fish and vegetable **market** where Rua das Portas de Portugal joins Av. dos Descobrimentos (Mon.–Sat. until 1pm), and a more general affair on Saturday morning by the bus station.

Otherwise, the whole centre of town is packed with **restaurants**. Some of the better ones are the cheap, good-quality fish and shellfish places by the market, such as the *Casa do Zé*, the Dutch-owned *Ao Natural* at Rua Silva Lopes 29 (specialising in vegetarian dishes), and the *Dom Sebastião* at Rua 25 de Abril 20, one of a number of prestige restaurants. *O Muralha* at the top of Rua Infante de Sagres stays open until 4am and offers a range of live music including *fado*. Of the many **bars** around town, try the vaguely new-wave *Vitaminas* (Irish owned, with great cocktails; Rua 25 de Abril 103), or *Stones* next to it.

Bullfights, held most Saturday afternoons in the summer, are run strictly for the tourists and their 'famous horsemen' are in reality quite unknown; don't encourage them, is our advice. Less of a compromise, and probably more fun, **boat trips** are easy to arrange with the fishing boats that gather around the Ponta da Bandeira, or you can book a 'cruise' at the Turismo.

Connections

At Lagos the **Algarve Railway Line** begins its route east, with thirteen trains a day to TUNES (for connections to Évora, Lisbon, etc.) and nine continuing onwards to Faro, Tavira and Vila Real de Santo António.

Buses connect Lagos with most principal Algarve destinations, including Portimão (12 daily; 40 min.), Monchique (8; 1 hr.), Sagres (9; 1 hr.), and Luz/ Burgau/Salema (5; 15/20/50 min.).

The Beaches

The promontory **south** of Lagos is fringed by extravagantly eroded cliff faces that shelter a series of small **cove beaches**. All are within easy walking distance of the old town, but the headland is now cut up by campsites, hotels, roads and a multitude of tracks, and the beaches all tend to be overcrowded.

The most northerly is the tiny **Praia do Pinhão**, next to the **Praia Dona Ana**, one of the most photogenic of all the Algarve's beaches. Further south are the **Praia Camilo** and, right at the point, the **Ponta da Piedade**, where a palm-bedecked lighthouse makes a great vantage point for the sunset.

A couple of kilometres west of the *Imulagos* campsite is the more expensive **Praia do Porto de Mós**, where there's usually a bit more room.

Meia Praia

To the **east** of Lagos and flanked by the railway line is the huge **Meia Praia**, a vast tract of sand that extends to the delta of the rivers Odeáxere and Arão. A regular bus service leaves from the Avenida dos Descobrimentos and travels the length of the beach; alternatively there's a seasonal ferry service from the side of the Forte Ponta da Bandeira. If you're prepared to walk you can always find some privacy here but the beach is a drab and often squalid affair.

The Reservoir

If you'd rather get away from the crowds altogether, you could head instead for the **Barragem da Bravura** (or *Barragem de Odeáxere*), 15km inland from Lagos and reached by three daily buses.

A huge reservoir built in Salazar's time to water the country behind Lagos, the lake is surrounded by forests and deserted except for a few picnickers and the occasional windsurfer. There's just one seasonal café here, so it's best to bring your own food; the terrain is relatively easy for camping but, again, come equipped.

Lagos to Sagres: Salema

Five kilometres west of Lagos you arrive at the beach resort of LUZ, an unappealing mass of chalets and villas that spreads in all directions, swamping the old fishing village. There's a large luxury campsite some way from the seafront and the full range of tourist facilities, but it's a charmless place. Best keep heading west, past BURGAU (another intensively developed, very British holiday spot), and on to Salema, halfway between Lagos and Sagres. Buses cover this route several times daily from Lagos.

Salema

Unusually for this stretch of the Algarve, **SALEMA** is still a fishing community as well as a resort, and the old village trails up the hill and along the coast quite separate from the hotels. The **beach** – a wide, rock-sheltered bay – is magnificent: a little crowded around the restaurants but at its far end more or less the preserve of the campers who gather here each summer.

There are a handful of **rooms** to let in the village (ask at the bars and the post-office shop, or just stroll along the street) and there's a beautiful, quite pricey **campsite** in a ravine about 1km up towards the main road.

On towards Sagres

The beaches between Salema and Sagres are still unmarked on most tourist maps, though they are accessible by road from the village of RAPOSEIRA on N125. The turning with the sign for 'Ingrina' is the one you need; about 1km down the road, take the left fork that passes through Hortas do Tabual and after another 3km or so you'll reach two isolated, craggy beaches – **Praia do Zavial** and **Praia da Ingrina**. They have the bare minimum of tourist facilities (though a campsite is planned), and there are no public transport connections from the main road.

From Raposeira the route to Sagres passes VILA DO BISPO and the turn-off for the west coast, before heading across the flattened landscape for the town itself.

Sagres

Wild and windswept, **SAGRES** was considered by the Portuguese as the far limit of the ancient and medieval worlds. It was on these headlands in the fifteenth century that Prince Henry the Navigator made his residence and it was here too that he set up a school of navigation, gathering together the greatest astronomers, cartographers, and adventurers of his age.

Magellan, Pedro Álvares Cabral and Vasco da Gama all studied at Sagres, and from the beach at Belixe, midway between the capes of Sagres and São Vicente, the first long caravels were launched, revolutionising shipping with their wide hulls, small adaptable sails and ability to drive close to the wind. Each year new expeditions were dispatched to penetrate a little further than their predecessors, and to resolve the great navigational enigma presented by the west coast of Africa, thereby laying the foundations of the country's overseas empire. After Henry's death here in 1460, the centre of maritime studies was moved to Lisbon, and Sagres slipped back into the obscurity from which he'd brought it.

The Fortaleza

The **village** of Sagres, rebuilt in the nineteenth century over the earthquake ruins of Henry's town, has nothing of architectural or historical interest and is little more than a long single street connecting the fishing harbour with the square. The main road, built to transport tourists straight to the headlands, runs parallel, trailing a series of drab villas off to the east.

At the end of this main road, dominating the whole scene near the village, is the **Fortaleza** (Fortress) where an immense circuit of walls (of which the north side survives intact) surrounded a vast shelf-like promontory high above the Atlantic. With its explicit demands of secrecy and security together with its wild remoteness, it must have seemed a kind of Aldermaston of its day. You enter through a formidable tunnel, before which is spread a huge pebble *rosa dos ventos* (wind compass) unearthed beneath a church in 1921 and said to have been used by the Infante Henriques himself.

Historians disagree – and are equally unimpressed by the claims of the adjacent tourist office and youth hostel to have been the prince's house. Still, it is a wonderful, wild setting and the simple, much-restored chapel of Nossa Senhora da Graça is at least contemporary with Henry's explorations.

Staying at Sagres

Sagres can be a great place to stay: beautiful sunsets, wild scenery and a lively (if a bit over-studenty) social scene. Stuck at the far end of Portugal, it attracts an oddball mix of travellers and tourists who hang around the **bars** dotted all over the main street and square.

Rooms and Camping

The best views of the Fortaleza are from the balconies of the **rooms** of the *pousada*, a good example of 'New State' (i.e., Salazar) architecture, a style that mixes the traditional and the stolid in about equal proportions. It's a wonderful location, offers special rates out of season, and may be worth considering if you're looking to relieve yourself of about £30 per night.

Far more reasonable, the *Aparthotel Orquídea* overlooks the fishing port and has fine views up the coast; flashy as the place looks, it's surprisingly cheap, especially out of season. Alternatively, the *Residencial Dom Henrique* is right in the square and perfectly adequate.

Further down the scale are the *quartos* offered in dozens of the villas that trail east from Sagres; finding a spare room in summer can be a long walk and it's far better to head for the **Turismo** at the fort (summer 9.30am–7.30pm daily; winter 9.30am–6.30pm daily). They'll phone around until you're fixed up. The **youth hostel** (July–Aug. only) is a rather strictly run affair next door. The nearest **campsite** is 2km east of the village along the main road – convenient for Praia do Martinhal.

Bars and Food

The place to be is the *A Rosa dos Ventos*, a lively, loud and drunken bar on the square. Here Swedish teenagers, German bikers, and Portuguese fishermen with berets stuck to their ears conduct fractured conversations, under the hazy gaze of novice boozers who've fallen at the first hurdle.

If you want a classier **eating-place** than the *Rosa's* cheap snacks, the *Atlântico Restaurant* on the main street is excellent, and *A Tasca* right down by the fishing boats serves marvellous seafood, especially fresh tuna and '*caldeirada de peixe*' (fish stew), at very reasonable prices.

Transport

Buses go right down the main street of Sagres from the square to the terminal above the harbour. There are connections to Faro (2 daily; 3 hr.) and Lagos (10; 1 hr.) via Vila do Bispo, for Carrapateira and Aljezur (2; 20 and 35 min.; unreliable on Sun.).

Beaches and the Cape

There are five **beaches** within easy walking distance of the village. Three are on the more sheltered coastline east of the Fortaleza: **Praia da Mareta** is just below the square, the grubby **Praia da Baleeira** is by the harbour, from where it's a five-minute walk to the longest and best beach, the **Praia do Martinhal**, an ideal spot for windsurfing. The beautiful **Praia de Belixe** (see below) is the better of the two beaches on the west coast. Whichever you choose, the water is very cold and swimming must be approached with caution – take local advice about the currents.

Cabo de São Vicente

The still more exposed **CABO DE SÃO VICENTE**, across the bay, was sacred to the Romans, who believed the sun sank hissing into the water beyond here every night. It became a Christian shrine when the relics of the martyred St. Vincent arrived in the eighth century; watched over (some say piloted) by ravens, the remains were transferred by boat to Lisbon in 1173.

It was almost certainly here that Henry established his School of Navigation, founded a small town, and built his Vila do Infante. Today only a **lighthouse**, flanked by the ruins of a sixteenth-century Capuchin convent, are to be seen. The other buildings, already vandalised by the piratical Sir Francis Drake in 1597, came crashing to the ground in the Great Earthquake of 1755, the monks staying on alone until the Liberal suppression of the monasteries in 1834. It is, though, a dramatic and exhilarating walk from Sagres, the road skirting the edge of tremendous cliffs for much of the 6km.

At **BELIXE**, two kilometres down the road, there's an excellent beach and a couple of bar-restaurants, and at FORTE DO BELIXE, fifteen minutes' walk away, there are the remnants of a prim little fortress, a restaurant, and a small, four-room **hotel** perched high on the edge of the cliffs: it's a fantastic location but rooms are very expensive.

The West Coast: Sagres to Odeceixe

Unlike the southern stretches of the 'Algarve proper', the **west coast**, from Sagres to Odeceixe, is little known and little developed. There are reasons: the winds are strong, the water is cold, swimming is often dangerous, and the villages scattered over the flat countryside behind the coast have a history of neglect and isolation. In a low-key way, things have begun to change – there's the odd tourist settlement and all the coastal villages offer rooms – but the west coast remains a windswept delight, popular with young travellers for its quiet beaches and its rural, relaxed pace.

Vila do Bispo
Heading east from Sagres, the Lagos bus (9am–noon daily; unreliable on Sun.) takes about fifteen minutes to reach **VILA DO BISPO**, at the junction of the west and south coast roads. It's a pretty little town with a lovely old church (erratic opening times). Every surface of the building has been painted, tiled or gilded, the highlight of its particular blue and gold beauty being the simple geometrics of its eighteenth-century *azulejos*.

Nothing much happens in Vila do Bispo, but there are some **rooms** above the restaurant in the square and a couple of **pensions** – *Pensão Mira-Sagres* on Rua do Hospital and *Pensão Casal da Vila* on Rua General Carmona. The nearest beach, the cliff-edged **Praia do Castelejo**, is an exhilarating/back-breaking (take your pick) hike of 5km through the bleak moors and dramatic hills behind the coast. There aré no buses and you'll probably be glad of a drink at the little bar-restaurant when you finally arrive.

Carrapateira
Fifteen kilometres to the north of Vila do Bispo is the village of **CARRAPATEIRA** (2 buses daily from Vila do Bispo), a dilapidated little place that tumbles down a hillside by the side of the road. It's possible to get

a **room** here – ask around the main square or try at the *Bar Barroca* – or you can walk north for 500m until you reach the point where two dirt tracks meet N268. To the east, 1km away, is the *Residencial Casa Fajara* – a complete surprise: right here in the middle of nowhere, and overlooking an empty river valley is a spruce, modern villa with neatly arranged gardens. It's a great location, but it's no bargain – rooms go for about 6000esc in high season.

To the west of the turning, another kilometre away, is the spectacular **Praia da Bordeira**, where massive heaps of sand twist a tiny river around before it finally cuts across the beach to empty into the crashing surf – it's a beautiful place, and the sandbanks provide some shelter from the wind. Camping *is* allowed here and in summer the dunes hide all kinds of tents and sleeping bags. There's a seasonal steakhouse by the beach but, if you're after even greater solitude, you can walk around the headland to the south (4km) until you reach another tract of sand – **Praia do Amado**.

Aljezur and Vale da Telha

The village of **ALJEZUR** (2 buses daily from Lagos and Vila do Bispo) is divided into two distinct halves: to the west of the river is the drab old Moorish town, straggling along the side of a hill underneath the ruins of a tenth-century castle, and to the east lies a more modern settlement.

The old site was an unhealthy, mosquito-infested place and Francisco Gomes de Avelar, Bishop of Algarve (1739–1816), made every effort to point this out and build a new town on healthier ground. Not immediately successful, his plans have borne fruit in the present eastward expansion of the village, though no one could describe the new area as picturesque.

The **Turismo**, just by the river, will help to find you a **room** and will recommend the *Residencial Francisca Sirominho*, the only pension in the new town. (They refuse to recommend the dingy rooms over '*Ruth's Restaurant*' just near them.) The nearest **beaches** – MONTE CLÉRIGO (8km) and ARRIFANA (10km) – are accessible by road from a turning a kilometre south of Aljezur.

The only bus service leaves Aljezur for Arrifana once in the morning and once in the afternoon. En route you pass an entrance to the **VALE DA TELHA** tourist complex, a couple of kilometres from the beach and the best place to stay. It's a good twenty-five-minute walk from the bus stop to the office at the centre of the complex, where you can make a reservation for **camping** or sleep at the pension.

With planning permission for 2500 chalets and villas, the Vale da Telha would be a nightmare if it were a commercial success; instead most of the plots are empty (and probably always will be), and the site looks rather plaintive. The restaurant near the office is excellent, and whatever criticisms you could make of the place as a whole, it must be better than staying at the village of ARRIFANA – a grubby affair perched on steep cliffs overlooking its magnificent beach.

Odeceixe

ODECEIXE, hunched on a hill and cramped by the river, is the last village before the Alentejo. Situated near the head of a delightful curving estuary, it is a friendly, quiet little place that attracts more than its share of independent travellers. There are a couple of simple bars and restaurants and a number of houses offer **rooms** to let, though it's better (if your Portuguese is up to it) to ask around and rent one of the small villas by the beach.

The **Praia de Odeceixe** is a high-cliffed cove where the river meets the sea just three easy kilometres to the west; with a minimum of tourist development, good surf, a few cosy houses and a sheltered beach, it's all very idyllic.

travel details

Trains

Algarve Line 13 trains a day from LAGOS to Meia Praia (5 min.), Alvor (30 min.), Portimão (40 min.), Silves (1 hr.) and Tunes (1 hr. 20 min.). 9 continue from TUNES to Albufeira Est (10 min.), Faro (50 min.), Olhão (1 hr. 10 min.), Tavira (1 hr. 50 min.) and Vila Real de Santo António (2 hr. 35 min.). There are also an additional 4 trains from Faro to Vila Real.

Trains from Tunes Station

1) Via Sado 4 daily to Lisbon (4 hr.–4 hr. 20 min.).

2) Via Sul 2 daily to Beja (3 hr. 20 min.) with connections for Casa Branca (4 hr. 40 min.; change for Évora, 30 min.) and Lisbon (6½ hr.).

Trains **from Lisbon** continue beyond Tunes to either Lagos or Faro/Vila Real.

There are **night trains** from Lisbon to Tunes and Tunes to Lisbon, connecting with trains to/from Lagos and Faro/Vila Real.

Buses

From Lagos Sagres (9 daily; 1 hr. 5 min.); Luz/Burgau/Salema (5; 15/20/50 min.); Aljezur/Odemira (2; 1 hr./1 hr. 45 min.); Portimão (12; 40 min.).

From Portimão Silves (6; 20 min.); Ferragudo (12; 10 min.); Monchique (8; 1½ hr.); Albufeira (4; 1 hr. 10 min.).

From Albufeira All stops to Faro (11; 1 hr. 20 min. to Faro).

From Faro to Tavira/Vila Real (10; 50 min./1 hr. 20 min.); Olhão (30; 20 min.); Beja (4; 3 hr.); Estoi (12, fewer on weekends; 20 min.).

Vila Real ferry to **Ayamonte** (every 30 min.; 15 min.).

Numerous companies operate **Express Buses** between Lisbon and the Algarve: ask at travel agents. Most are quicker than the *R.N.* buses between Faro and Lisbon (3 daily; 7 hr.) and Lagos and Lisbon (1 daily; 7½ hr.).

HISTORICAL FRAMEWORK

The early history of Portugal – as part of the Iberian Peninsula – has obvious parallels with that of Spain. Division at this stage is somewhat arbitrary, an independent development becoming valid only with Afonso Henriques' creation of a Portuguese kingdom in the twelfth century.

EARLY CIVILISATION

Remnants of pottery and cave burials point to tribal societies occupying the Tagus valley and parts of the Alentejo and Estremadura as early as 8000 to 7000 B.C. – but as yet there have been no finds in Portugal comparable to the Paleolithic caves of Altamira and northern Spain. More, however, is known of **Neolithic** Portugal and its *Castro* culture based on hilltop forts, a culture that was to be developed and refined after the arrival of Celtic peoples around 700 to 600 B.C. These, the first permanent settlements, were concentrated in northern Portugal – and particularly in the Minho, where excavations have revealed literally dozens of **citânias**, or fortified villages. The most impressive is at Briteiros, near Braga, with its paved streets, drainage systems and circuits of defensive walls; like many of the citânias it survived, remarkably unchanged, well into the Roman era. Settlements in neighbouring Trás-os-Montes, in contrast, reflect less of a defensive spirit – but all that remains of this more pastoral **verracos** culture are the crude granite *porcas*, stone figures venerating wild sows as objects of a primitive fertility cult.

The potential for new trading outlets – and the quest for metals, in particular tin for making bronze – attracted a succession of peoples from across the Mediterranean but the emphasis of their settlement lay on the eastern seaboard and so fell within 'Spanish' history. The **Phoenicians**, however, established an outpost at Lisbon around 900 B.C. and there were probably contacts, too, with Mycenaean Greeks. In the mid third century B.C., they were followed by **Carthaginians**, who recruited Celtic tribesmen for military aid against the Roman empire. Once again, though, their influence was predominantly on the eastern seaboard and in the south; with defeat in the Second Punic War (218–202 B.C.) they were to be replaced by a more determined colonising force.

ROMANS, SUEVI AND VISIGOTHS

Entering the peninsula in 210 B.C., the **Romans** swiftly subdued and colonised the Mediterranean coast and the south of Spain and Portugal – the areas most affected by earlier trading links. In the interior, however, they met with great resistance from the Celtiberian tribes, and in 193 B.C. the Lusitani rose up in arms. Based in central Portugal, between the rivers Tagus and Lima, they were, in the words of the Roman historian Strabo, 'the most powerful of the Iberian peoples, who resisted the armies of Rome for the longest period'. For some fifty years, in fact, they held up the Roman advance, under the leadership of **Viriatus**, a legendary Portuguese hero and masterful exponent of the feigned retreat who on several occasions brought the Romans to accept his autonomous rule. He was betrayed after a successful campaign in 139 B.C., and within two years the Lusitani had capitulated as the legions of Decimus Junius Brutus swept through the north. Nonetheless, over a century later their name was given to this most westerly of the Roman provinces, and in the northern Celtic villages Roman colonisation can scarcely have been felt.

Integration into the Roman Empire came largely under Julius Caesar, who in 60 B.C.

established a capital at Olisipo (Lisbon) and significant colonies at Ebora (Évora), Scallabis (Santarém) and Pax Julia (Beja). In 27 B.C. the Iberian provinces were further reorganised under Augustus, all but the north of Portugal being governed – as Lusitania – from the great Roman city of Merida in Spanish Extremadura. The Minho formed part of a separate province, later added to northwest Spain to create Gallaecia, with an important regional centre at Bracara Augusta (Braga). In general though it was the south where Roman influence was deepest; here they established huge agricultural estates (the infamous *Latifundia* which still survive in Alentejo) and changed the nature of the region's crops, as they introduced wheat, barley, olives and the vine to the area.

There are no great **Roman sites** in Portugal – at least nothing to compare with Spanish Merida, Tarragona or Italica – though both Évora and Conimbriga have individual monuments of interest. The mark of six centuries of Roman rule consists more in their network of roads (used well into the Middle Ages) and their bridges, many of them still in use today. There is a more basic legacy, too – the Portuguese language is very heavily derived from Latin.

The **decline of the Roman Empire** in Portugal echoes its pattern elsewhere, though perhaps with greater indifference, the territory always being something of a provincial backwater. Christianity reached Portugal's southern coast towards the end of the first century, and by the third century bishoprics were established at Braga, Évora, Faro and Lisbon. But the state was already disintegrating, and in 409 the first waves of barbarian invaders crossed the Pyrenees into Spain. Vandals, Alans, Suevi and Visigoths all passed through Portugal, though only the last two were of any real importance.

The **Suevi**, a semi-nomadic people from eastern Germany, eventually settled in the area between the Douro and Minho rivers, establishing courts at Braga and Portucale (Porto). They seem to have coexisted fairly peacefully with the Hispano-Roman nobility and were converted to Christianity by St. Martin of Dume – a saint frequently found in the dedications of northern churches. But around 585 their state disappeared, suppressed and incorporated into the **Visigothic** empire, a heavily Romanised yet independent force which for two centuries maintained a spurious unity and rule over most

of the peninsula. The Visigothic kings, however, ruled from Toledo, supported by a small and elite aristocratic warrior-caste, so in Portugal their influence was neither great nor lasting. By the end of the seventh century their divisions, exacerbated by an elective monarchy, and their intolerance (including the first Iberian persecution of the Jews), resulted in one faction appealing for aid from Muslim North Africa. In 711 a first force of **Moors** crossed the straits into Spain, and within a decade they had advanced and conquered all but the mountainous reaches of the Asturias in northern Spain.

THE MOORS . . . AND CHRISTIAN RECONQUEST

In Portugal, Aveiro probably marked the northernmost point of the **Moorish advance**. The Moors met with little resistance but the dank, green hills of the Minho seem to have had a dissuasive effect on the would-be colonisers. The area remained only sparsely populated throughout the following century. Most of the Moors were content to settle in the south: in the Tagus valley, the rich wheat belts around Évora and Beja, and above all the coastal region of the **al-Gharb**. Here they established a capital at Shelb, modern Silves, and, by the middle of the ninth century, an independent kingdom, detached from the great Muslim emirate of al-Andalus which covered most of Spain.

They were a mix of ethnic races – for the most part Berbers from Morocco, but also considerable numbers of Syrians and, around Faro, a contingent of Egyptians, some of them probably Coptic Christians. In contrast to the Visigoths, the Moors were tolerant and productive, and their rule a civilising influence. Both Jews and Christians were allowed freedom of worship and their own civil laws, while under Muslim law small landholders continued to occupy lands that they themselves cultivated. For most of these 'Moçárabes' – Christians subject to Moorish rule – life must have improved. Roman irrigation techniques were perfected and the Moors introduced the rotation of crops and cultivation of cotton, rice, oranges and lemons. Their culture and scholarship led the world – though less from al-Gharb than from Cordoba and Sevilla – and they forged important trade links, many of which were to continue centuries after their fall. Perhaps still more important, **urban life** developed, with prosperous local craft industries: Lisbon, Évora, Beja and Santarém all emerged as sizeable towns.

The Christian **'Reconquista'** – at least by tradition – began at Covadonga in 718, when one Pelayo, at the head of a small band of Visigoths, halted the advance of a Moorish expeditionary force. The battle's significance has doubtless been inflated, but from the victory a tiny kingdom of the Asturias does seem to have been established. Initially only 40 by 30 miles in extent, it expanded over the next two centuries to take in León, Galicia and the 'lands of Portucale', the latter an area roughly equivalent to the old Swabian state between the Douro and the Minho.

By the eleventh century **Portucale** had the status of a country, its governors appointed by the kings of León. In 1073 Alfonso VI came to the throne. It was to be a reign hard-pressed by a new wave of Muslim invaders – the fanatical Almoravides, who crossed over to Spain in 1086 after appeals from al-Andalus and established a new Muslim state at Sevilla. Like many kings of Portugal after him, Alfonso was forced to turn to European crusaders, many of whom would stop in at the shrine of St. James in Compostela. One of them, Raymond of Burgundy, married his eldest daughter and became heir-apparent to the throne of León; his cousin Henry, married to another daughter, Teresa, was given jurisdiction over Portucale. With Henry's death Teresa became regent for her son, **Afonso Henriques**, and began to try to forge a union with Galicia. Afonso, however, had other ideas, and having defeated his mother at the battle of São Mamede (1128), he established a capital at **Guimarães** and set about extending his domains to the south.

The reconquest of central Portugal was quickly achieved – Afonso's victory at Ourique in 1139 was a decisive blow, and by 1147 he had taken Santarém. In the same year Lisbon fell, after a siege in which passing crusaders again played a vital role – though not sailing on to the Holy Land before murderously sacking the city. Many of them were English, and some stayed on – Gilbert of Hastings became Archbishop. By now Afonso was dubbing himself the **first King of Portugal**, a title

tacitly acknowledged by Alfonso VII (the new king of León) in 1137 and officially confirmed by the Treaty of Zamora in 1143. His kingdom spread more or less to the borders of modern Portugal, though in the south Alentejo and the Algarve were still in Muslim hands.

For the next century and a half Afonso's successors struggled to dominate this last stronghold of the Moors. Sancho I (1185–1211) took their capital, Silves, in 1189, but his gains were not consolidated and almost everything south of the Tagus was recaptured the following year by al-Mansur, the last great campaigning vizier of al-Andalus. The overall pattern, though, was of steady expansion with occasional setbacks. Sancho II (1223–48) invaded the Alentejo and Eastern Algarve, while his successor **Afonso III** (1248–79) moved westwards, taking Faro and establishing the kingdom in pretty much its final shape.

THE BURGUNDIAN KINGS

The reconquest of land from the Muslims was also a process of **recolonisation**. As it fell into the king's hands, new territory was granted to such of his subjects as he felt would be able to defend it. In this way much of the country came to be divided between the church, the Holy Orders – chief among them the Knights Templar – and 100 or so powerful nobles or *riĉos homens*. The entire kingdom had a population of under half a million, the majority of them concentrated in the north. Here there was little displacement of the traditional feudal ties, but in the south the influx of Christian peasants blurred the distinction between serf and settler, dependent relationships coming to be based on the payment of rent.

Meanwhile a **political infrastructure** was growing up. The land was divided into municipalities (*concelhos*), each with their own charter (*foral*). A formalised structure of consultation began to be seen, with the first **Cortes** being held in Coimbra in 1211. At first consisting mainly of the clergy and nobility, it later came to include wealthy merchants and townsmen, a development speeded both by the need to raise taxes and by later kings' constant struggles against the growing power of the church. The capital, which Afonso Henriques had moved to Coimbra in 1139, was transferred to **Lisbon** about 1260 by Afonso III.

The Burgundian dynasty lasted, through nine kings, for 257 years. In the steady process of consolidating the new kingdom, one name stands out above all others, that of **Dom Dinis** (1279–1325). With the reconquest barely complete when he came to the throne, Dinis set about a far-sighted policy of stabilisation and of strengthening the nation to ensure its future independence. During his reign, fifty fortresses were constructed along the frontier with Castile, while at the same time negotiations were going on, leading eventually to the Treaty of Alcañices (1297) by which Spain acknowledged Portugal's frontiers. At home he established a major programme of forest planting and of agricultural reform; grain, olive oil, wine, salt, salt fish and dried fruit became staple exports to Flanders, Brittany, Catalonia and Britain. Importance, too, was attached to education and the arts: a **university**, later transferred to Coimbra, was founded at Lisbon in 1290. Dinis also helped entrench the power of the monarchy, forcing the church to accept a much larger degree of state control and in 1319 reorganising the Knights Templar – at this time being suppressed all over Europe – as the **Order of Christ**, still enormously powerful but now responsible directly to the king rather than to the pope.

Despite Dinis's precautions, fear of **Castilian domination** continued to play an important part in the reigns of his successors, largely due to consistent intermarrying between the two royal families. On the death of the last of the Burgundian kings, Fernando I, power passed to his widow Leónor, who ruled as regent. Leónor, whose only daughter had married Juan I of Castile, promised the throne to the children of that marriage. In this she had the support of most of the nobility, but the merchant and peasant classes strongly opposed a Spanish ruler, supporting instead the claim of João, Grand Master of the House of Avis and a bastard heir of the Burgundian line. A popular revolt against Leónor led to two years of war with Castile, finally settled at the **Battle of Aljubarrota** (1385), in which João, backed up by a force of English archers, wiped out the much larger Castilian army. The great abbey of **Batalha** was built to commemorate the victory. João I, first king of the House of Avis, was crowned at Coimbra in the same year, sealing relations with England through

the Treaty of Windsor (1386) – an alliance which has lasted into the twentieth century – and by his marriage to Philippa of Lancaster, daughter of John of Gaunt, the following year.

DOM MANUEL AND THE MARITIME EMPIRE

Occupying such a strategic position between the Atlantic and the Mediterranean, it was inevitable that Portuguese attention would at some stage turn to **maritime expansion**. When peace was finally made with Castile in 1411, João I was able to turn his resources towards Morocco. The outpost at Ceuta fell in 1415, but successive attempts to capture Tangier were not realised until the reign of Afonso V, in 1471.

At first such overseas adventuring was undertaken partly in a crusading spirit, partly to keep potentially troublesome nobles busy. The proximity of North Africa made it a constant feature of foreign policy, giving a welcome boost to the economy of the Algarve. The first real advances in exploration, however, came about through the activities of **Prince Henry 'the Navigator'**, third son of João and Philippa. As Grand Master of the Order of Christ, he turned that organisation's vast resources toward marine development, founding a School of Navigation on the desolate promontory of Sagres (then regarded as the end of the world) and staffing it with Europe's leading cartographers, navigators and seamen. As well as improving the art of offshore navigation, they redesigned the caravel, making it a vessel well suited to long ocean-going journeys. **Madeira** and the **Azores** were discovered in 1419 and 1427 respectively, and by Henry's death in 1460 the **Cape Verde Islands** and the **west coast of Africa** down to Sierra Leone had both been explored.

After a brief hiatus, overseas expansion received a fresh boost in the reigns of João II, Manuel I and João III. In 1487 **Bartolomeu Dias** finally made it around the southern tip of Africa, christening it 'Cabo da Boa Esperança' in the hope of things to come. Within ten years **Vasco da Gama** had sailed on past it to open up the **trade route to India**. This was the great breakthrough and the Portuguese monarchy, already doing well out of African gold, promptly became the richest in Europe, taking a fifth of the profits of all trade and controlling important monopolies on some spices. The small cargo of pepper brought back by Vasco on his first expedition was enough to pay for the trip sixty times over. Meanwhile Spain was opening up the New World, and by the **Treaty of Tordesillas** in 1494 the two Iberian nations divided the world between them along an imaginary line 370 leagues west of the Cape Verde islands. This not only gave Portugal the run of the Orient but also, when it was discovered in 1500, Brazil (though its development would have to wait nearly 200 more years). By the mid-sixteenth century Portugal dominated **world trade**; strategic posts had been established at Goa (1510), Malacca (1511), Ormuz (1515) and Macau (1557), and the revenue from dealings with the East was backed up by a large-scale **slave trade** between West Africa and Europe and Brazil.

The reign of **Manuel I** (1495–1521) marked the apogee of Portuguese wealth and strength. It found its expression at home in the extraordinary exuberance of the 'Manueline' style of architecture – an elaborately decorative genre which found its inspiration in marine motifs. Notable examples can be seen in the Convent of Christ at Tomar and the Tower of Belém in Lisbon, while the best examples of civil architecture are probably the extensions made by Manuel to the royal palace at Sintra.

Enormous wealth there may have been, but very little of it filtered down through the system and in the country at large conditions barely improved. The practice of siphoning off a hefty slice of the income into the royal coffers effectively prevented the development of an entrepreneurial class, and, as everywhere else in Europe, financial matters were left very much in the hands of the Jews, who were not allowed to take up most other professions. Although Portugal had traditionally been far more lenient than other European nations towards its **Jewish citizens** (and towards the Moorish minority who had been absorbed after the Reconquest), popular resentment of their riches, and pressure from Spain forced Manuel – who had initially welcomed refugees from the Spanish persecution – to order their **expulsion** in 1496. Although many chose the pragmatic course of remaining as 'New Christian' converts, others fled to the Netherlands.

This exodus, continued as a result of the activities of the **Inquisition** (from 1531 on),

created a vacuum which left Portugal with an extensive empire based upon commerce, but deprived of much of its commercial expertise. By the 1570s the economy was beginning to collapse: incoming wealth was insufficient to cover the growing costs of maintaining an empire against increasing competition, a situation exacerbated by foreign debts, falling prices and a decline in domestic agriculture.

SPANISH DOMINATION

In the end it was a combination of reckless imperialism and impecunity which brought to an end the dynasty of the House of Avis and with it, at least temporarily, Portuguese independence. **Dom Sebastião** (1557–78), obsessed with dreams of a new crusade against Morocco, set out at the head of a huge army to satisfy his fanatical fantasies. They were crushed at the battle of Alcacer-Quibir (1578), where the Portuguese dead numbered over 8000, including Sebastião and most of Portugal's nobility. The aged Cardinal Henrique took the throne as the closest legitimate relative, and devoted his brief reign to attempting to raise the crippling ransoms for those captured on the battlefield.

The Cardinal's death without heirs in 1580 provided Spain with the pretext to renew its claim to Portugal. **Philip II** of Spain, Sebastião's uncle, defeated his rivals at Alcantara and in 1581 was crowned Filipe I of Portugal, inaugurating a period of Habsburg rule which lasted for sixty years. In the short term, although unpopular, the union had advantages for Portugal. Spanish wheat helped alleviate the domestic shortage and Spanish seapower to protect the far-flung empire. Philip, moreover, studiously protected Portuguese autonomy, maintaining an entirely separate bureaucracy and spending long periods in Portugal in an attempt to win popular support. Not that he ever did – throughout his reign pretenders appeared claiming to be Sebastião miraculously saved from the Moroccan desert, tapping a strong vein of resentment among the people. And in the long run, Spanish control proved disastrous. Association with Spain's foreign policy (part of the Armada was prepared in Lisbon) meant the enmity of the Dutch and the British, Portugal's traditional allies, losing the country an important part of its trade which was never to be regained.

Philip's successors made no attempt at all to protect Portuguese sensibilities – cynical and uninterested, they tried to rule from Madrid while raising heavy taxes to pay for Spain's wars. The final straw was the attempt by Philip IV (Filipe III of Portugal) to conscript Portuguese troops to quell a rising in Catalonia. On December 1, 1640, a small group of conspirators stormed the palace in Lisbon and deposed the Duchess of Mantua, Governor of Portugal. By popular acclaim and despite personal reluctance, the Duke of Bragança, senior member of a family which had long been the most powerful in the country, took the throne as **João IV**.

THE HOUSE OF BRAGANÇA

At first the newly independent nation looked shaky, deprived of most of its trade routes and with the apparently imminent threat of invasion from Spain hanging over it. As it turned out, however, the Spanish were so preoccupied with wars elsewhere that they had little choice but to accept the situation, although not formally doing so until 1668 under the Treaty of Lisbon. João IV used the opportunity to rebuild old alliances, and although the Portuguese were often forced into unfavourable terms, they were at least trading again. Relations with Britain had been strained during that country's Commonwealth, with Oliver Cromwell's particular brand of Protestant commercialism, but were revived by the marriage of Charles II to Catherine of Bragança in 1661.

At home Portugal was developing an increasingly centralised administration – the **discovery of gold and diamonds in Brazil** during the reign of Pedro II (1683–1706) made the crown financially independent and did away with the need for the Cortes (or any form of popular representation) for most of the next century. It was **João V**, coming to the throne in 1706, who most benefited from the new riches, which he squandered in an orgy of lavish baroque building. His massive convent at **Mafra**, built totally without regard to expense, employed at times as many as 50,000 workmen, virtually bankrupting the state. Meanwhile nothing was being done to revive the economy, what little remained from João's grandiose schemes going mainly to pay for imports. The infamous Methuen Treaty, signed in 1703 to stimulate trade with Britain, only made matters worse – although it opened up

new markets for Portuguese wine, it helped destroy the native textile industry by letting in British cloth at preferential rates.

The accession of João's apathetic son, José I (1750–77), allowed the total concentration of power in the hands of one man, the king's chief minister. The **Marquês de Pombal** became the classic 'enlightened despot' of eighteenth-century history. It was the **Great Earthquake of 1755** that sealed his dominance over the age; while everyone else was panicking, Pombal's policy was simple – 'bury the dead and feed the living'. He saw his mission as being to modernise all Portuguese life into an efficient and secular bureaucracy, renewing the system of taxation, setting up export companies, protecting Portuguese trade, and abolishing slavery within Portugal. It was a strategy that made him many enemies among the old aristocracy and above all within the church, whose overbearing influence he fought at every turn. Opposition was ruthlessly dealt with and an assassination attempt on the king in 1758 (which some say was staged by Pombal) gave him the chance he needed to destroy his enemies. Denouncing them as responsible, Pombal executed the country's leading aristocrats and abolished the Jesuits, who had long dominated education and much of religious life in both Portugal and Brazil.

Although Pombal himself was taken to trial (and found guilty but pardoned on the grounds of old age) with the accession of María I (1777–1816), the majority of his labours survived him, most notably the reform of education along scientific lines and the completely rebuilt capital. Further development, however, was soon stymied by a new invasion.

FRENCH OCCUPATION AND THE MIGUELITE YEARS

With **Napoleon's** appearance on the international scene, Portugal once more became embroiled in the affairs of Europe. The French threatened to invade unless the Portuguese supported their naval blockade of Britain, a demand that no one expected them to obey since the British ports were the destination for most of Portugal's trade. Only the protection of the British fleet, especially after the victory at Trafalgar in 1805, kept the country's trade routes open. General Junot duly marched into Lisbon in November 1807.

On British advice the Royal Family had already gone into exile in Brazil, where they were to stay until 1821, and the war was left largely in the hands of British generals **Beresford** and **Wellington**. Having twice been driven out and twice reinvaded, the French were finally forced back into Spain in 1811 following the Battle of Buçaco (1810) and a long period of near starvation before the lines of Torres Vedras. Britain's prize for this was the right to trade freely with **Brazil**, which together with the declaration of that country as a kingdom in its own right, fatally weakened the dependent relationship that had profited the Portuguese treasury for so long. Past roles were reversed, with Portugal becoming effectively a colony of Brazil (where the Royal Family remained) and a protectorate of Britain, with General Beresford as administrator. The only active national institution was the army, many of whose officers had absorbed the constitutional ideals of revolutionary France.

In August 1820, with Beresford temporarily out of the country and king João VI still in Brazil, a group of officers called an unofficial Cortes and proceeded to draw up a new **constitution**. Inspired by the recent liberal advances in Spain, it called for an assembly – to be elected every two years by universal male suffrage – and the abolition of clerical privilege and the traditional rights of the nobility. The king, forced to choose between Portugal and Brazil, where his position looked even more precarious, came back in 1821 and accepted its terms. His queen, Carlota, and younger son **Miguel**, however, refused to take the oath of allegiance and became the dynamic behind a reactionary revival which drew considerable support in rural areas.

With João VI's death in 1826, a delegation was sent to Brazil to pronounce crown prince Pedro the new king. Unfortunately Pedro was already Emperor of Brazil – having declared independence some years earlier. He resolved to pass the crown to his infant daughter, with **Miguel** as regent, provided that he swore to accept a new **Charter**, drawn up by Pedro and somewhat less liberal than the earlier constitution. Miguel agreed, but once in power promptly tore up the agreement, abolished the charter and returned to the old, absolutist ways. This was a surprisingly popular move in Portugal, certainly in the countryside, but not

with the governments of Britain, Spain or France who backed the liberal rebels and finally put Pedro IV (who had meanwhile been deposed in Brazil) on the throne after Miguel's defeat at Évora-Monte in 1834.

THE DEATH OF THE MONARCHY

Pedro didn't survive long. The rest of the century – under the rule of his daughter María II (1834-53), and his grandsons Pedro V (1853–61) and Luís (1861–89) – saw almost constant struggle between those who supported the Charter and others favouring a return to the more liberal constitution of 1822. In 1846 the position deteriorated virtually to a state of **civil war** between María, who was fanatical in her suport of her father's charter, and the radical constitutionalists. Only a further intervention by foreign powers maintained peace, imposed at the Convention of Gramido (1847).

In the second half of the century, with relative stability and the two warring factions to some extent institutionalised into a revolving two-party system, the economy began at last to recover, with the first signs of widespread industrialisation and a major public works programme under the minister Fontes Pereira de Melo. The monarchy, however, was almost bankrupt and its public humiliation over possessions in Africa – imperial Britain and Germany simply ignored the Portuguese claim to the land between Angola and Mozambique – helped strengthen growing republican feelings.

Republicanism took root particularly easily in the army and among the urban poor, fuelled by falling standards of living, and growing anger at government ineptitude. Dom Carlos (1898–1908) attempted to rule dictatorially after 1906, alienating most sectors of the country in the process, and was assassinated, along with his eldest son, following a failed republican coup in 1908. Finally, on October 5 1910, the monarchy was overthrown once and for all by a joint revolt of the army and navy. Dom Manuell went into exile and died in Britain in 1932.

THE 'DEMOCRATIC' REPUBLIC

In the elections of 1911 republican parties won a clear majority, yet throughout the life of **the republic** politic life was in chaos and the hopes, perhaps unrealistically high, of its supporters never began to be realised. Dominant from the start was the Democratic Party under **Afonso Costa**, who proved determined to retain power by any means – manipulating elections through patronage and deriding opposition, even from fellow republicans, as 'anti-Democratic'. The overblown, inefficient bureaucracy, too, clung to power; its employees, largely survivors from the monarchist era, proved unwilling or unable to carry out many of the government's policies. In office, meanwhile, governments became increasingly dependent on the armed forces for survival; since neither president nor prime minister had the power to dissolve parliament, **military intervention** came to be the normal means of governmental change – there were 45 such 'changes' between 1910 and 1926.

The forces that had brought the republic into being had their base largely in the urban and rural poor, yet new electoral laws based on a literacy test led to a smaller electorate than under the monarchy, disenfranchising most of the republic's stongest supporters. Successive governments failed to fulfil the lowest aspirations. Anticlericalism had been a major plank of Costa's platform, but attempts to place **the church** under state control misfired badly, arousing massive hostility in the countryside. Legalising the right to strike merely gave workers a chance to voice their discontent in a massive wave of work stoppages. Further fuel was given to the reaction by Portugal's economically disastrous decision to enter **World War I** on the side of the Allies in 1916, and by the vicissitudes of the post-war recession. By 1926 not even the trade unions were prepared to stand by the republic, preferring to maintain 'proletarian neutrality' in the face of what at first seemed no more significant a military intervention than any other.

SALAZAR AND THE 'NEW STATE'

While the military may have known what they wanted to overthrow in 1926, they were at first divided as to whether to replace it with a new republican government or a restored monarchy. From the infighting a Catholic monarchist, **General Carmona**, eventually emerged as president (which he remained until his death in 1951) with the republican constitution

suspended. A pragmatic fear of popular reaction prevented Carmona from restoring the monarchy; his eventual solution was to formalise his position through elections, in 1828, in which he was the only candidate.

In the same year one **Dr. Salazar** joined the Cabinet as Finance Minister. A professor of economics at Coimbra University, he took the post only on condition that he would control the spending and revenue of all government departments. His strict monetarist line (helped by a change in the accounting system) immediately balanced the budget for the first time since 1913, and in the short term the economic situation was visibly improved. From then on he effectively controlled the country, becoming prime minister in 1932, and not relinquishing that role until 1968.

His regime was very much in keeping with the political tenor of the 1930s, and while it had few of the ideological pretensions of a **fascist** state, it had many of the trappings. Members of the National Assembly were chosen from the one permitted political association, the National Union (UN); 'workers' organisations' were set up, but run by their employers; education was strictly controlled by the state to promote Catholic values; and censorship was strictly enforced. Opposition was kept in check by the *PIDE* – a **secret police** force set up with Gestapo assistance – which used systematic torture and long-term detention in camps on the Azores to defuse most resistance. The army, too, was heavily infiltrated by *PIDE* and none of the many coups mounted against Salazar came close to success. Despite remaining formally neutral throughout the **Spanish civil war**, Salazar had openly assisted the plotters in their preparations, and later sent unofficial units of the Portuguese army to fight with Franco. Republican refugees were deported to face certain execution at Nationalist hands.

At home Salazar succeeded in producing the infrastructure of a modern economy but the results of growth were felt by only a few, and agriculture, in particular, was allowed to stagnate. Internal unrest, though, while widespread, was surprisingly muted and apparently easily controlled; the new state's downfall, when it came, was precipitated far more by external factors. Salazar was an ardent imperialist who found himself faced with growing

colonial wars – costly and bringing international disapprobation. India seized Goa and the other Portuguese possessions in 1961, and at about the same time the first serious disturbances were occurring in Angola and Mozambique. The regime was prepared to make only the slightest concessions, attempting to defuse the freedom movements by speeding economic development.

The government's reign came to an end in 1968 when Salazar's deck-chair collapsed, resulting in brain damage. Incapacitated, he lived for another two years, deposed as premier – though such was the fear of the man, no one ever dared tell him. His successor, **Marcelo Caetano**, attempted to prolong the regime by offering limited democratisation at home. However, tensions beneath the surface were fast becoming more overt, and attempts to liberalise foreign policy failed to check the growth of guerilla activity in the remaining colonies, or of **discontent in the army**.

It was in the Africa-stationed army especially that opposition crystallised. There the young conscript officers came more and more to sympathise with the freedom movements they were intended to suppress, and to resent the cost – in economic terms and in lives – of the hopeless struggle. From their numbers above all grew the revolutionary *Movimento das Forças Armadas* (MFA).

REVOLUTION

By 1974 the situation in Africa was deteriorating rapidly and at home Caetano's liberalisation had come to a dead end; morale, among the army and the people, was lower than ever. The **MFA**, formed originally as an officer's organisation to press for better conditions, then increasingly politicised, was already laying its plans for a takeover. Dismissal of two popular generals – Spinola and the defence minister, Costa Gomes – for refusing publically to support Caetano, led to a first chaotic and abortive attempt on March 16. Finally on April 25, 1974, the plans laid by **Major Otelo Saraiva de Carvalho** for the MFA were complete and their virtually bloodless **coup** went without a hitch, no serious attempt being made to defend the government.

The next two years were perhaps the most extraordinary in Portugal's history, a period of continual **revolution**, massive politicisation,

and virtual anarchy, during which decisions of enormous importance were nevertheless taken – above all the granting of independence to all of the overseas territories. At first there was little clear idea of any programme beyond the fact that the army wanted out of Africa. Though the *MFA* leadership was clearly to the left, and at first associated with the *PCP* (Portuguese Communist Party), the bulk of the officers were less political, and **General Spínola**, whom they had been forced to accept as a figurehead, was only marginally to the left of Caetano and strongly opposed total independence for the colonies. Spínola's dream was clearly to 'do a De Gaulle' in Portugal, while the army were above all determined not to replace one dictator with another.

In the event their hands were forced by the massive popular response, and especially by huge demonstrations on May Day. It was clear that whatever the leadership might decide, the people, especially in the cities, demanded a rapid **move to the left**. From the start every party was striving to project itself as the true defender of the 'ideals of April 25'. Provisional governments came and went but real power rested, where it had begun, with the *MFA*, now dominated by Saraiva de Carvalho and Vasco Gonçalves. While politicians argued around them, the army claimed to speak directly to the people, leading the country steadily left. It was a period of extraordinary contradictions, with the *PCP*, hoping to consolidate their position as the 'true' revolutionary party, opposing liberalisation and condemning strikes as counter-revolutionary, while ultraconservative peasants were happily seizing their land from its owners.

Sudden **independence** and the withdrawal of Portuguese forces from the **former colonies** – while generally greeted in Portugal with relief – did not always work so well for the countries involved. Guiné-Bissau and Mozambique, the first to go, experienced relatively peaceful transitions, but **Angola** came to be a serious point of division between Spínola and the *MFA*. When independence finally came, after Spínola's resignation, the country was already in the midst of a full-scale civil war. The situation was even worse in **East Timor**, where more than 10 percent of the population was massacred by invading Indonesian forces following Portuguese withdrawal. In Portugal itself the arrival of over half a million colonial refugees – many of them destitute, most bitter – came to be a major problem for the regime, though their eventual integration proved one of its major triumphs.

At home, the first **crisis** came in September 1974, when Spínola, with Gonçalves and Saraiva de Carvalho virtual prisoners in Lisbon's Belém Palace, moved army units to take over key positions. The *MFA*, however, proved too strong and Spínola was forced to resign, General Costa Gomes replacing him as President. By the summer of 1975 more general reaction was setting in and even the *MFA* began to show signs of disunity; the country was increasingly split, supporting the revolution in the south, deeply conservative in the north. The Archbishop of Braga summed up the north's traditional views, declaring that the struggle against Communism should be seen 'not in terms of man against man, but Christ against Satan'. Nevertheless the revolution continued to advance; a coup attempt in March failed when the troops involved turned against their officers. The Council of the Revolution was formed, promptly nationalising banking and private insurance; widespread land seizures went ahead in the Alentejo, and **elections** in the summer resulted in an impressive victory for Mário Soares' Socialist Party (*PS*).

On November 25, 1975, elements of the army opposed to the rightward shift in the government moved for yet another **coup**, taking over major air bases across the country. Otelo Saraiva de Carvalho, however, declined to bring his Lisbon command to their aid; nor did the hoped-for mass mobilisation of the people take place. Government troops under Coronel Ramalho Eanes moved in to force their surrender and – again virtually without bloodshed – the revolution had ended.

DEMOCRACY AND EUROPE: THE 1980s

The period since November 1975 has been one of slow, and sometimes shaky **retrenchment**. The Socialist Party was still in power at the end of the year, and won further ground in the elections that followed, helping to shape the post-revolutionary constitution – a mildly socialist document, though providing for a fairly

powerful president. Early fears of a rightist coup led by Spínola failed to materialise, helped by the election of **General Eanes**, a man whom the army trusted, as president. Saraiva de Carvalho came a close second, despite the fact that no major party supported him – a token of the degree of popular following enjoyed by the MFA during the revolution.

Although parties of the right and centre have consistently polled higher votes, the Socialists had effective control until 1980 when Dr. Sá Carneiro managed to create the **Democratic Alliance**, uniting the larger groupings on the right. But within a few months he died in a plane crash. His successor as prime minister, Francisco Pinto Balsemão, barely managed to maintain the coalition for the two years of the term remaining, and then only because the rightist parties were united in their determination to amend the constitution 'to eliminate clauses which were appropriate in the post-revolutionary atmosphere of 1976 but not to today's needs'.

The most enigmatic figure throughout this period remained **President Eanes**, a career soldier who supported the *MFA* in its early days, later led the forces who ended the revolution, and is now accused by the right of being a 'Marxist sympathiser'. He above all seemed to be the figure of stability, with enormous popular support though (at least until recently) apparently little ambition, being happy to concentrate on developing Portugal's links with the Third World, and overseeing a gradual normalisation process.

In elections held on the ninth anniversary of the revolution, April 25, 1983, **Mário Soares's Socialist Party** again became the largest single party in the national assembly, though requiring the support of the Social Democrats to maintain a coalition government. Soares's premiership was dogged by the unpopularity of his **economic austerity measures** (in part insisted on by the *IMF*) and by constant delays and breakdowns in the talks over Portuguese and Spanish **entry into the European Community**. These problems (now resolved) did at least have one positive result, namely closer relations with the traditionally hostile government in Madrid. But the government's economic problems led eventually to the withdrawal of Social Democratic support and to the collapse of the coalition.

New elections in October 1985 were barely conclusive: the leftist vote split three ways, and the Socialists lost their position as largest party to the **Social Democrats**, whose flamboyant leader, **Dr. Amíbal Cavaco Silva**, became Prime Minister. But the main feature of the election was disillusionment with the government and the choices on offer to the electorate. There was massive and countrywide abstention, and in rural districts (worried by the effects of EC membership) attacks on polling booths. In the months that followed, the revolutionary hero Colonel Otelo Saraiva de Carvalho was arrested and tried in Lisbon, accused of being the leader of 73 suspected terrorists in the *FP25* urban guerilla group.

President Eanes, meanwhile, the other great figure of the revolution, had been forced to resign the presidency on completion of his second term in January 1986. His political life, however, looks far from over; in the previous parliamentary elections he had established the **Democratic Renewal Party**, which emerged as a third force behind the Social Democrats and Socialists. He remains a highly popular, respected and influential figure in Portuguese politics. Eanes' place as president was taken by Mário Soares, who, with the reluctant support of the Communists, narrowly defeated the candidate of the centre-right.

In effect the government's overall political balance was little altered. However the elections did signal a significant change in voting patterns, with people turning toward the major parties. And, Eanes aside, the party leaders are now identifiably a **post-revolution generation**: the Socialists' **Vítor Constâncio**, and the Social Democrats' **Amíbal Cavaco Silva**. The gap between right and left, at least in these two mainstream parties, has also considerably narrowed. Both Constâncio and Cavaco Silva are trained economists, and the quest for some kind of economic stability dominates any particular social or political ideology of their parties.

The main concern – and the overriding economic factor – has, of course, been Portugal's gradual move towards full **membership of the EC**, a process due for dramatic completion in 1992, when the community removes all remaining trade and employment barriers. Many Portuguese are deeply pessimistic about the effects, particularly on the traditional transatlantic trade ties. But it is has to be said that such ties were not sufficient to support the ecomomy prior to EC entry. The trade deficit stood at 2 billion pounds (it is now, just about, in credit), there was severe inflation and heavy unemployment, and economic stagnation had reached a point where many companies failed to pay their workers regularly.

Coincidentally, Portugal itself, the weakest of the community states, will inherit the EC presidency in 1992. It hopes by then to be in some position to compete, especially in light industry, and in particular with its textiles base. This, with new trade fairs established in Lisbon and Porto, and a number of progressive companies, is a bright spot on the economic front. However, there seems to be some climate of recovery in Portuguese industry as a whole, and the Lisbon stock market has lately experienced a boom, though one accompanied, worryingly for the government, by spiralling wages and inflation. Agriculture, which still plays an enormously significant role (especially in the north), is more problematic, though EC policies of loans to small farmers have helped to cushion the effects of membership.

The big test for the government in managing the **post-1992 economy** is going to be in maintaining a balance between attracting foreign investors – who already dominate much of the commercial scene – and preventing Portugal's own markets from being flooded by other European goods. It also needs to hang on to its tourist trade in a period of decreasing prices on flights to more exotic destinations.

MONUMENTAL CHRONOLOGY

2000 B.C.– 1500 B.C.	**Neolithic** settlements in the north – **Verracos Culture** in Trás-os-Montes.	*Porcas* (stone boars) of Bragança, Murça, etc.
700 B.C.– 600 B.C.	**Castro Culture** of fortified hill-towns, or *citânias*, concentrated in the Minho; refined by the **Celtic** Iron Age invasions.	**Citânia de Briteiros** (near Braga) and other sites; best collection of artifacts in Sarmento Museum, Guimarães.
210 B.C.	**Romans** enter peninsula and begin colonisation; northern Portugal not finally pacified until 19 B.C.	**Conímbriga**, 4th-c. Celtic town near Coimbra, adapted to Roman occupation (survives until 5th c. A.D.).
60 B.C.	Julius Caesar establishes a capital at Lisbon and towns at Beja, Évora, Santarém, etc.	Walls and other remains at Idanha, in Beira Baixa; temple and aqueducts of Évora; bridges at Chaves, Ponte de Lima, Leiria and elsewhere.
A.D. 4th c.	Bishoprics founded at Braga, Évora, Faro and Lisbon.	
409–411	**Barbarian** invasions: Suevi settle in the north.	
585	**Visigoths** incorporate Suevian state into their Iberian empire.	Isolated churches, mainly in the north, include 7th-c. São Pedro de Balsemão (near Lamego) and São Frutuoso at Braga.
711	**Moors** from North Africa invade and conquer peninsula within seven years.	Fortresses/walls survive at Silves, Lisbon, Sintra, Elvas, Mértola, Alcácez do Sal, etc.
9th c.	**Al-Gharb** (Algarve) becomes an independent Moorish kingdom, governed from Silves.	Moorish legacy also includes *azulejos* (ceramic tiles), later designed by Muslim (Mudejar) craftsmen for royal palace at Sintra, etc.
868	Porto reconquered by Christian kings of Asturias-León.	
11th c.	Country of **Portucale** emerges and (1097) is given to Henry of Burgundy.	Cluniac monks, administering pilgrimage route to Santiago, bring Romanesque architecture from France. 12th-c. churches at Bravães, Tomar, etc. Council chamber at Bragança.
1143	**Afonso Henriques** recognised as first king of Portucale at the Treaty of Zamora.	Guimarães Castle
1147	Afonso takes Lisbon and Santarém from the Moors; followed in 1162 by Beja and Évora, and in 1189 (temporarily) Silves.	Fortress-like **Romanesque cathedrals** of Lisbon, Coimbra, Évora, Braga and Porto.
1212	First assembly of the Cortes (parliament) at Coimbra.	1153: Cistercians found abbey of **Alcobaça**: in this and other Cistercian churches, notably at Coimbra, Gothic architecture enters Portugal.
1249	Afonso III completes reconquest of the Algarve.	

1279–1325	Reign of **Dom Dinis**. 1297: Castile recognises Portuguese borders.	Over fifty castles built along Spanish border, including Beja and Estremoz. Pinhal Real forest planted. Coimbra University (1308).
1385	Battle of Aljubarrota: João I defeats Castilians to become first king of **House of Avis.**	Abbey of **Batalha**, the great triumph of mature Portuguese Gothic, built in celebration of victory. Paço Real built at Sintra.
1415	Henry the Navigator (d. 1460) sets up School of Navigation at Sagres. 1419: Madeira discovered. 1427: Azores discovered. 1457: Cape Verde Islands discovered.	Forts at Sagres and Lagos. Painters: Flemish-influenced 'Portuguese Primitives' include Nuno Gonçalves (fl. 1450–71: see Arte Antiga museum, Lisbon).
1495–1521	Reign of **Dom Manuel I** ('The Fortunate'). 1497: Vasco da Gama opens up sea route to India. 1500: Cabral discovers Brazil. 1513: Portuguese reach China.	Late Gothic **Manueline style** develops, with strong marine motifs and flamboyance anticipating art nouveau. Greatest examples at Tomar, Batalha, Lisbon (Belém) and Sintra. By 1530s Renaissance forms are introduced and merged.
1521–57	Reign of João III.	Painters include Grão Vasco (fl. 1506–42: see "Viseu").
1557–78	Reign of Dom Sebastião. 1578: Disastrous expedition to Morocco, loss of king and mass slaughter of nobility at Alcacer-Quibir.	Important sculptural school at **Coimbra** (1520–70) centred on French Renaissance sculptors Nicolas Chanterence, Filipe Hodart and Jean de Rouen.
1581–1640	Philip II brings **Spanish** (Habsburg) rule.	
1640	João IV, Duke of **Bragança**, restores independence.	Severe late Renaissance style: São Vicente, Lisbon (designed by Felipe Terzi), etc.
1706–50	Reign of Dom João. Gold and diamonds discovered in Brazil, reaching a peak of wealth and exploitation in the 1740s.	Baroque palace-monastery of **Mafra** (1717–35). Decoration of Coimbra University Library. High Baroque carved, all-gilt church interiors (Lagos, etc.). Simpler, more rustic Baroque style of plaster/ granite: best at Lamego and **Bom Jesus**. Rococo Palace of Queluz (1752).
1755	**Great Earthquake** destroys Lisbon, and parts of the Alentejo and Algarve.	'Pombaline' neoclassical rebuilding of Lisbon (Baixa).
1843–53	Half-mad Queen María holds throne with German consort.	Wholly mad **Pena Palace** built on the crags of Sintra.
1910	Exile of Manuel II ('The Unfortunate') and end of Portuguese monarchy.	Dissolution of monasteries. Cubist painter Amadeu de Sousa Cardoso (d. 1918); museum devoted to him at Amarante.
1910–26	'Democratic' Republic.	
1932–68	**Salazar** dictatorship.	
1974	April 25 **revolution**.	
1986	Entry to European Community.	Permanent gallery of modern Portuguese artists at Lisbon's **Gulbenkian Foundation**.

BOOKS

Portugal has been covered very sparsely by British writers and publishers. Much of the material available on the country is old and out of print. However, there are a few classics around in libraries, and some recent translations of modern fiction.

TRAVEL

Rose Macaulay *They Went to Portugal* (Penguin, £5.95). The book covers British travellers to Portugal from the Crusaders to Byron, weaving an anecdotal history of the country in the process. A serious study if you take it as such; a good read if you just feel like dipping into the stories.

William Beckford *Recollections of an Excursion to the Monasteries of Alcobaça and Batalha, Travels in Spain and Portugal (1778-88)* (o/p; but in many libraries). Mad and enormously rich, Beckford lived for some time at Sintra and travelled widely in Estremadura. His accounts, told with a fine eye for the absurd, are fun (see the *Estremadura and Ribatejo* chapter and "Sintra" in *Lisbon and Around*).

Almeida Garrett, *Travels in My Homeland* (Peter Owen, £12.95). A classic Portuguese writer, Garrett was exiled to Europe in the 1820s, came into contact with the Romantics, and later returned to play a part in the liberal government of the 1830s. This is a witty, discursive narrative ramble around the country.

Byron *Selected Letters and Journals* (Penguin, £4.95). Only a few days of Portuguese travel but memorable ones – beginning with romantic enthusiasm, ending in outright abuse.

Hans Christian Andersen, *A Visit to Portugal* (Peter Owen, £11.95). Mildly interesting rtecord of the Scandinavian writer's stay in Portugal in the 1860s.

HISTORY AND POLITICS

Harold Livermore *A New History of Portugal* (Cambridge University Press, 1976, o/p). The best single-volume coverage; thorough if not exactly inspiring, and revised a little too soon after the 1974 revolution.

António de Figueiredo *Portugal: Fifty Years of Dictatorship* (Pelican, o/p). Much more illuminating – if you can get hold of a copy – this takes as its starting-point the 1926 military coup that brought the fascist Salazar to power and goes through to the popular revolutionary coup of 1974.

Robert Harvey *Portugal: Birth of a Democracy* (Macmillan, o/p). Similar coverage to the above, though with three more years' update on the Revolution.

Lawrence S. Graham and Harry M. Makler, eds. *Contemporary Portugal: The Revolution and Its Antecedents* (University of Texas Press, US, 1979); **Lawrence S. Graham and Douglas L. Wheeler, eds.** *In Search of Modern Portugal: The Revolution and Its Consequences* (University of Wisconsin Press, US, 1983); **Phil Mailer** *Portugal: The Impossible Revolution* (Black Rose Books [dist. U. of Toronto Press], Canada, 1977). A trio of more academic works on the 1974 revolution and beyond.

ART AND ARCHITECTURE

Sacheverell Sitwell *Portugal and Madeira* (Batsford, o/p). Mix of art history/observation and rather pompous upper-class travelogue. Sitwell's big enthusiasm is Portuguese Baroque.

Robert C. Smith *The Arts of Portugal 1500-1800* (Meredith Press, 1968, o/p). Weighty, heavily illustrated academic tome.

PORTUGUESE FICTION

Eça de Queiroz *The Sin of Father Amaro* (Black Swan, £3.95); *The Maias* (Dent, £4.95). Queiroz is *the* great Portuguese novelist, responsible for a string of classic nineteenth-century narratives. These are the only ones in print and form an entertaining introduction. Check out others in libraries; most have been translated.

José Saramago, *Baltasar and Blimunda* (Cape, £11.95). Saramago is one of Portugal's major contemporary novelists. This, his first work to be translated into English, is a black comedy set in the reign of Dom João V. It brings alive the era of the inquisition, the building of Mafra, and the climate of times before the Great Earthquake.

António Lobo Antunes *South of Nowhere* (Chatto p/b, o/p). First-person narrative about Portugal's colonial war in Angola, its themes focussed by the scene of the telling as the narrator attempts seduction but drinks himself into a stupor in a Lisbon bar. Recommended.

José Cardoso Pires, *Ballad of Dog's Beach* (Dent, £4.50). Ostensibly a detective thriller but the murder described actually took place during the last years of Salazar's dictatorship, and Pires' research draws upon the original secret-police files. Compelling, highly original and with acute psychological insights, it was awarded Portugal's highest literary prize and is currently being made into a film.

María Isabel Barreno, María Teresa Horta and **María Velho da Costa** *New Portuguese Letters: The Three Marías* (Paladin, o/p). Published (and prosecuted in Portugal) in 1972, this collage of stories, letters and poems is a modern feminist parable based on the seventeenth-century 'Letters of a Portuguese Nun'. Well worth a trip to the library.

POETRY

Luís de Camões *The Lusiads* (Penguin, £6.95). Portugal's national epic, celebrating the ten-month voyage of Vasco da Gama which opened the sea route to India. This is a good prose translation.

Fernando Pessoa *Selected Poems* (Penguin, £3.95). Pessoa, who died in 1933, wrote startling, lyrical verse in four quite different personas. Virtuoso stuff – and remarkable in the way he produces very simple poems from highly complex themes.

FOOD AND WINE

Edite Viera, *The Taste of Portugal* (Robinson, £5.99). A delight to read, let alone cook from, Vierira combines snippets of history and passages from Portuguese writers (very well translated) to illustrate her dishes. Highly recommended.

Jan Read, *The Wines of Portugal* (Faber, £5.95). Very full descriptions of every region and particularly of soon to be internationally recognised wines. Clear explanations, too, of why each region has its own flavour, and much interesting social and historical background.

MUSIC

Portugal has a rich musical culture, with roots harking back to Provençal troubadours, continuing through ballads and the unique 'blues' of the *fado*, and encompassing, more recently, the rhythms of the country's former West African colonies.

Each of these elements has a currency in the sounds that you hear today – from the French Provençal strain in the folk music played at northern festivals, to the cosmopolitan rock and jazz of the larger cities. An additional element is added by the wealth of singer-songwriters, most of them from the highly political 'New Song' movement fostered by the dramatic events of the 1970s, as the country threw off the thirty-year dictatorship of Salazar, and was forced to withdraw from its colonies.

INSTRUMENTS, VOICES AND RHYTHMS

There is a startling variety of Portuguese **folk instruments**: bagpipes, harmonicas, accordions, flutes, assorted drums (*caixas, bombos, adufes, pandeiros, sarroncas*) and countless percussion instruments (*reco-reco, ferrinhos, genebres, trancanholas*).

But the country's pride and glory are its **strings**, which include violins, the classic twelve-stringed 'Portuguese guitar', and six varieties of '**viola-guitars**', unknown elsewhere in Europe. Each of these has a character, tuning and design of its own. Best known is the little, four-stringed *cavaquinho*. Others range through elaborate combinations of single, double and triple strings.

One of the most common combinations of instruments is the **zés-pereira**, made up of a large *bombo*, a *caixa*, and a bagpipe or fife (depending on whether you're in the Minho or Beiras region), and often used to announce grand occasions. Another traditional combination popular throughout the country is the **rancho**, made up of violins, guitars, clarinets, harmonicas and *ferrinhos*, with the later addition of the accordion.

If the folk traditions are rich in instruments, its **singers** are unrivalled. In every town and district there is an amateur choir. After a good meal someone will always start an **acappella** song, followed intuitively by the other guests. It is not at all unusual, if you go to a **fado** performance, to find the entire staff of the establishment taking part, from the owner to the cloakroom attendant. To listen to a vocal ensemble of three women from Manhouce, or a rural male choir from **Alentejo**. is to hear genuinely popular roots music. Alentejo is home also to the *saia*, sung by women accompanying themselves on the *pandeireta*.

Since Portugal is a rural society, still relatively unaffected by industrialisation, there are a great many **songs** reflecting the cycles of nature, such as *natal, reis* and *janeiras* – lullabies, tilling, sowing and harvest songs.

Equally authentic, if less harmonious, are the **singing contests** in which rival performers exchange improvisations on a theme, or the *fandango*, a dance where two men match their footwork. Among other popular **traditional dances** are *modas, despiques, chulas, rusgas, corridinhos, viras,* waltzes, and the ritual steps of the *pauliteiros* (stick-dancers) of Miranda in the Douro region.

FADO

The *fado* is Portugal's most famous – though perhaps also its least accessible – music. Lyrical and sentimental, it is thought to have origins in African slave songs, though the influence of Portugal's own maritime and colonial past is equally apparent. After the 1974 revolution, when the empire disintegrated, it went through something of a crisis. Today, it has come to be identified with a general sense of frustration and, some would have it, with an endemic and peculiarly Portuguese fatalism.

There are two versions of the *fado*. That of the humble **Alfama and Mouraria districts of Lisbon** (performed mainly in the Bairro Alto clubs, these days) is highly personal and full of feeling. The more academic strand from **Coimbra** reflects that city's ancient university traditions, and is still performed mainly by students. In both the theme is usually love, though *fados* have been composed on all kinds of subjects.

By far the most famous of the *fado* singers, and arguably its greatest performer, is **Amália Rodrigues**. She can be seen at prestige clubs and concerts in Lisbon, though bear in mind that in recent years she has strayed into other genres, even variety. If you're buying one of her records, make sure that it is all *fado*.

Other big traditional names include Florêncio Carvalho, Alberto Prado and Castro Rodrigo. Recent performers have adapted the form to a more modern rhythm, including, most recently, Manuel Osório and (a name to look out for in the clubs) **Carlos do Carmo**. The 'singer-songwriters', too, have looked towards *fado*. Following the lead of José Afonso (see below), nearly all the stars have produced one or two of their own interpretations of the form.

THE BALLAD

It was an attempt to update the Coimbra *fado* that resulted in the modern Portuguese ballad, and which in turn, in the last few years of the dictatorship, gave way to the 'New Song'. This, from the revolution of 25 April 1974 onwards, became a genuine political song movement, broadening in recent years to a movement known as *Música Popular* – essentially contemporary folk music, composed and performed by an impressive roster of 'singer-songwriters'.

The **lyrics** generated by this movement were – and are – as significant as the music. Many artists turned to modern poetry that dealt with contemporary social and cultural issues. They also drew on music rooted in popular tradition, both rural and urban, that reflected influences of various kinds – colonial, French, English or Spanish – but avoided the easy rhythms of commercial pop.

One of the forerunners of the genre was the 1956 LP *Canções Heróicas – Canções Regionais Portuguesas* (Heroic Songs – Portuguese Regional Songs), arranged by Fernando Lopes Graça and performed by the Choir of the Amateur Musicians' Academy. Although the harmonisations are a long way from the New Song, two basic elements are already present: committed lyrics and respect for genuine **regional music**.

Another LP, *Fados of Coimbra* by José Afonso and Luís Gois, appeared in May of the same year. The *fado* was out of favour in radical circles at the time. It had become just another branch of 'national song', with overtones of vulgar soap-opera.

José Afonso gradually abandoned the Portuguese guitar for the Spanish, which allows for more freedom in the accompaniment. His first solo records came out in 1960, including *Balada do Outono* (Autumn Ballad), which gave its name to the new genre and made it respectable. He was soon joined by Adriano Correia de Oliveira and the **poets** Manuel Alegre, Ary dos Santos and Manuel Correia, whose work provided the text for numerous songs.

After the onset of the **colonial wars** censorship began to wreak havoc. *Menino do Bairro Negro* (Black Slum Kid) and *Os Vampiros* (The Vampires), both by José Afonso, were withdrawn from the market and only instrumental versions allowed to be sold. Some singers chose to go into exile. Luís Cília released several records in Paris under the general title of *A Poesia Portuguesa de Hoje e de Sempre* (Portuguese Poetry of Today and All Times), on which he sung his own arrangements of poems by Camões, Pessoa, Saramago and others.

The release in 1968 of José Afonso's *Cantares do Andarilho* (Songs of the Road) marked the coming of age of the ballad. By now Adriano was making his first LPs, as were Manuel Freire, José Jorge Letria, José Mario Branco, Father Fanhais, and soon afterwards Fausto, Pedro Barroso and the Angolan Rui Mingas. At the same time, the **social climate** was becoming increasingly suffocating. These singers were banned from TV and hardly ever heard on the radio. With very few venues and permits granted only sparingly, they had to take other jobs to make a living.

NEW SONG

José Afonso's *Cantigas de Maio* (Songs of May), José Mario Branco's *Mudam-se os Tempos, Mudam-se as Vontades* (Changing Times, Changing Wishes), and Adriano Correia de Oliveira's *Gente d'Aqui e de Agora* (People Here and Now) show an improvement in the quality of the material. The lyrics went further in their reflections on living conditions and were more open in their **protest**. The music explored new forms, rhythms and means of expression. José Mário Branco made a key contribution as an arranger and producer. Preproduction **censorship**, however, continued to be strictly imposed and some singers stopped recording to avoid it. Others, like José Afonso, resorted to ever more cryptic lyrics.

This was how things stood on the night of **April 24 1974**. At 10.55pm João Paulo Dinis of the 'Associates of Lisbon' radio programme played *E Depois do Adeus* (After the Goodbyes), Paulo de Caravalho's Eurovision Song Contest entry for the year. At midnight came the final signal, Leite Vasconcelos played *Grândola Vila Morena* on Radio Renascença's 'Limite' programme. The army captains went into action and on the following day the coup was a reality: Portugal was returning to democracy.

There began an uncertain period during which it was unclear who held power. Singers like Sérgio Godinho, Luís Cília, José Mário Branco and Father Fanhais returned from exile. Now that censorship had been lifted New Song gave way to **political song**. Everyone had slogans, analyses and solutions to offer in the process of clarification which followed.

Singers were suddenly in constant demand for the political and cultural events being improvised with a minimum of technical resources all over the country, giving performances in factories, cooperatives, squatters' settlements, etc. They set up various groups according to their political leanings: Free Song (*Canto Livre*), the October Group (*Grupo Outubro*), and the Group for Cultural Action — Voices for the Cause (*Grupo de Acção Cultural Vozes na Luta*, or *GAC*). The latter, in mixing traditional songs with sloganeering political ones, set an unconscious pattern for future developments. Other artists slowly branched out into work with the numerous theatre groups of the time and on soundtracks for films. Some singers and musicians also formed cooperatives, such as *Eranova* (New Age) and *Cantarabril* (Song of April).

FOLK GROUPS

As time passed and things returned to normal, **traditional music** enjoyed a revival, bringing with it the first commercial folk groups.

In the 1960s, much work had been done in studying and recording traditional Portuguese music, most notably by Fernando Lopes Graça and Michel Giacometti, who produced a five-volume *Antologia de Música Regional Portuguesa*. Over the last decade, the group **Almanaque** of Lisbon has followed in their footsteps, producing a series of records from the oral tradition, as well as reworking the traditional themes in a slightly more modern form.

The **Brigada Victor Jara** of Coimbra also began by collecting folk tunes but soon turned to new directions, adapting the work of other folk writers. Although none of its original members are still in the lineup, this group is one of Portugal's best, producing well-crafted work based on sound ideas. Other active folk groups, adopting similar approaches, include *Raízes* (Roots) from Vila Verde (Braga); the *Grupo Etnográfico de Cantares e Trajes* (Ethnographic Song and Costume Group) from Manhouce; *Terra a Terra* (Land, Land); *Vai de Roda*, an ethnic arts cooperative from Oporto; *Trigo Limpo* (Clean Wheat) from Alentejo; and *Ronda dos Quatro Caminhos* (Crossroads) from Lisbon.

A more **contemporary** and ambitious folk music has also emerged over the last decade. **Trovante**, which was formed in 1975, is highly acclaimed in Portugal and has worked extensively with José Afonso and Fausto. Its work is full of uneven swayings and sudden changes of direction. Of interest, too, though generally less successful, are *Charanga*, *Pedra d'Hera*, *Construção*, *Disto e Daquilo* and *Rosa dos Ventos*.

Música Popular — as more recent folk has become known — owes much of its renewed popularity, however, to the work of some singer-songwriters who have dedicated themselves exclusively to it, and to musicians who have made records devoted to individual folk instruments.

PORTUGUESE FOLK: THE KEY FIGURES

JOSÉ AFONSO The 'father of modern Portuguese popular music' made a key contribution to song from the 1950s onwards and won fame far beyond his country's borders. He was born in Aveiro, and as the son of a civil servant visited several colonies as a child, but it was not until later, when he made a trip to Angola as a student, that he became aware of the colonial realities.

His first records were collections of *fado* made with Luís Gois in 1956. In the 1960s he began to write songs on social issues. His records were censored and he was persecuted by the secret police but nothing would deter him. His whole life was dedicated to song and his personal crusade against fascism.

After the revolution, he continued to work prolifically, and to consistently high standards, composing music for films and the theatre as well as producing nearly twenty LPs. His work was constantly evolving, yet his first compositions are still fresh today. With their careful attention to music, lyrics, arrangement and voice, any of his records is a miniature work of art. He lived modestly and died after a long illness in 1987.

FAUSTO The work of this singer combines the most diverse influences – modern and traditional, Portuguese and African – with a marked urban slant and a lyrical delivery. His skill lies in the subtlety with which he links African rhythms to Portuguese melodies and instruments, and the delicacy of his singing.

His early songs provide a poetic analysis of the uncertain post-revolutionary period. Later ones use tales of the deeds of *conquistadores*, sailors and other Portuguese heroes to reflect on the country's history.

SÉRGIO GODINHO Born in Porto, Godinho went into exile as an economics student to avoid military service in the colonial war. He travelled in France, Switzerland and Canada, working at one time as an interpreter for the musical *Hair*, and at another as a member of *Living Theatre*.

Due to these influences he is one of the more modern, cosmopolitan singers of his generation. His songs are usually narrative and he has a particular knack for affectionate character sketches. When dealing more directly with political issues he employs a fine sense of humour. His music is both loud and cheerful, intimate and sophisticated.

LUÍS CILIA Of the new songwriters, Luís Cilia is the one who has devoted most attention to setting his poems to music. His work is rigorous and serious, showing a pronounced French influence. He is good at capturing the essence and general atmosphere of a given political moment in his lyrics. Musically, he has worked in two apparently contrasting fields: traditional song, and experimental work with synthesizers from which he has produced a solo album.

JOSÉ MÁRIO BRANCO Another native of Porto, Mário Branco's chief contribution has been as an arranger and producer of records, though he has made important records himself, both individually and as a member of the *Grupo de Acção Cultural*. His skill in the studio has given an added dimension to the records of Portuguese singers.

VITORINO The songs of Vitorino are inextricably linked with the Alentejo region and its farming cooperatives and rural communities, though recently he has made more contact with the city. His early records were uneven in their development, a mixture of Alentejo folk songs, revolutionary anthems and love songs. It is with the latter genre that he has had most success in his recent work.

JANITA SALOMÉ Brother of Vitorino, he also has links with Alentejo, though he has concentrated increasingly on the Arab heritage there and in the Algarve. His music, full of percussion and gentle touches, also betrays the influence of José Afonso, with whom he worked closely in the last years of his life.

Among **instrumentalists**, perhaps the most outstanding figure is the guitarist **Carlos Paredes**. He explores both the folk and the classical sides of the Portuguese guitar, with surprising results; his records are a rare treat. Another excellent instrumentalist is **Júlio Pereira**, who began as a songwriter but became interested in traditional stringed instruments and has recently experimented to great effect in combining them with synthesisers, rhythm boxes and samplers in compositions inspired by folk tradition.

ROCK, JAZZ, AND AFRICAN

Though Portuguese rock and jazz cannot even begin to match the maturity of its songwriting tradition, there have been some interesting recent developments. Two names to watch out for are the blues singer **Rui Veloso** and the pop singer **Mafalda Veiga**. Among groups, the most established include **GNR**, **Heróis do Mar**, **Madredeus**, **Chutos e Pontapés**, **Radio Macau** and **Sétima Legião**.

An intriguing figure, midway between jazz and 'New Age', is the saxophonist **Rão Kyao**. As for jazz proper, there is the great vocalist **María João**, the **Lisbon Jazz Sextet**, the experimental trio **Shish** and the pianist **António Pinho Vargas**.

On the contemporary Portuguese rock scene, however, by far the most exciting development is the appearance of groups from the former colonies of **Angola, Moçambique, Cabo Verde, Guiné Bissau** and **São Tomé Príncipe**. Many musicians, particularly from Cabo Verde (Cape Verde Islands), settled in Lisbon during the very hard years following the colonial wars and independence. Others spend part of the year based in Portugal, recording, and touring Europe, drawn by the comparatively high fees to be made.

Staying in Lisbon, you're most likely to get a chance to see Cabo Verde groups, which include among their styles *morna*, similar to the Portuguese *fado*, and the more danceable *moradeira*.

From **Guiné Bissau** the sounds are an unusual mix of African and Latin, akin to zouk. Big groups to look out for include **Justinio Delgado**, **Super Mama Diombo**, **Manecas**, **Africa Libre** and **Jetu Katem**.

Finally, if you get a chance to see them, two outstanding southern African groups are **Guem** from **Angola** and **Fernando Luís** from **Mozambique**.

Manuel Dominguez

RECORDS

Records in Portugal are excellent value; the following is a personal selection of the most interesting.

Folk
Almanaque *Desafiando Cantigas; Sementes.*
Brigada Victor Jara *Marcha dos Foliões.*
Ronda do Quatro Caminhos *Fados Velhos.*
Vai de Roda *Vai de Roda.*

Fado
Amália Rodrigues *O Melhor.*
Carlos do Carmo *Um Homem na Cidade; Um Homem no País.*

Portuguese Guitar
Carlos Paredes *Guitarra Portuguesa; Movimento Perpétuo; Concerto em Frankfurt; Espelho de Sons.*
Pedro Caldeira Cabral *Encontros; A Guitarra Portuguesa nos Salões dos sec. XVIII.*

Singer-Songwriters
Adriano Correia de Oliveira *Memória de Adriano.*
Fausto *Madrugada dos Trapeiros; Por Este Rio Acima; Despertar dos Alquimistas.*
Janita Salomé *Lavrar em teu Peito; Olho de Fogo.*
José Afonso *Cantigas do Maio; Venham Mais Cinco; Coro do Tribunais; Com as Minhas Tamanquinhas; Fura Fura; Fados de Coimbra e Outras Canções; Como se Fora Seu Filho; Galinhas do Mato.*

José Mário Branco *Ser Solidário.*
Júlio Pereira *Cavaquinho; Braguesa; Cadoi; Os Sete Instrumentos; Miradouro.*
Luís Cilia *Cancioneiro; Penumbra.*
Sérgio Godinho *De Pequeninho se Torce o Destinho; Coincidências; Na Vida Real.*
Vitorino *Romances; Negro Fado.; Erol de la Mar.*

Rock/Pop
G.N.R. *Os Homeus não se Querem Bonitos.*
Heróis do Mar *Mãe.*
Madredeus *Os Dias da Madredeus.*
Rádio Macau *Rádio Macau.*
Sétima Legião *Mar d'Outubro.*
Trovante *Terra Firme.*

Jazz
António Pinho Vargas *Variações.*
María João *Conversa.*
Rão Kyao *Fado Bailado; Dancas de Rua.*
Sexteto de Jazz de Lisboa *Sexteto.*

African
Caba Mane *Chefo Mae Mae* (Guiné Bissau).
Guem *Dans Voyage* (Angola).
Fernando Luís *Bassopa* (Mozambique).

ONWARD FROM PORTUGAL

SPAIN

The simplest, most obvious onward move from Portugal is into Spain. If you're travelling by road or rail you have no choice anyway but to cover vast tracts of it – though even if you're exclusively based in Portugal, a few quick forays are worth considering.

From the north the most obvious destinations are the great pilgrimage city of **Santiago de Compostela** in Galicia, or **León**, with its tremendous Gothic cathedral; either can be reached within a day by train or bus.

From central Portugal, **Salamanca**, a university city and possibly the most elegant in Spain, is within easy striking distance; from here, too, you could also continue to **Madrid and Toledo**. Heading by train from Lisbon to Madrid, it's well worth breaking your journey in the medieval conquistador town of **Cáceres**.

The Algarve borders Spanish **Andalucía**; **Sevilla** is only a few hours' drive while **Cordoba** and **Granada**, with their spectacular Moorish monuments, can be combined in a few days' circuit.

All of these cities – and a great deal more besides – are fully covered in the *Rough Guide to Spain*.

MOROCCO

If you have time, even just a few days, try and take in at least a glimpse of Morocco. From the Algarve you can now catch a passenger **ferry direct to Tangier from Faro** – a service which may be expanded in future years to call at Portimão and other Algarve ports. The boat runs throughout the year, leaving Faro, currently on Mondays, Thursdays and Saturdays at noon, arriving Tangier 9pm. For details and tickets, contact the Lisbon agency, *ACP Viages*, Rua Rosa Araugo 49a, 1200 Lisboa (☎01/527-858, 01/560-382).

Alternatives are to take a bus or train to Sevilla and from there to **Algeciras** (easiest reached by bus via Cadiz). Tangier is under three hours across by boat from Algeciras or just half an hour on the hydrofoil from Tarifa.

Arrival: Tangier can be a slightly tricky place to get acclimatised. More than anywhere in Morocco – with the possible exception of Tetouan, the first Moroccan town after Ceuta (the other port served by Algeciras ferries) – it is rampant with 'guides' and hustlers, all out to exploit your initial innocence. Don't take one. Just head straight for a hotel (turn left along the waterfront for a good selection) or – if you don't feel like any hassle – get a train straight out.

Trains: Tangier is the beginning of the railway line, with connections to Fes, Meknes and Marrakesh (the great imperial cities), and to Casablanca, Rabat and the coastal resort of Asilah. Asilah and Rabat are perhaps the easiest places in which to get used to the country.

Buses: There are departures on most main routes on *CTM* buses (run by the state) and, much more erratically, on private local lines. A good alternative, and only slightly more expensive, is to travel by *grand taxi* – big, collective taxis which cram in six passengers on a straight fee basis.

Costs: Hotels and basic café meals are inexpensive – and among the few things you don't need to bargain for. There is always a choice between getting accommodation in the *Medina* (the 'old town') and *Ville Nouvelle* (usually built during the years of French colonisation); the former is cheaper but often lacking such modern conveniences as running water.

Currency: *Dirhams* are the standard and run at about 16 to £1. You sometimes hear them subdivided into *francs* (100 to the dirham).

Highlights: The cities of Fes and Marrakesh, the High Atlas mountains, and the southern 'desert routes'. All easily accessible by normal local transport.

Language: French is very widely spoken throughout Morocco – and will get you by without problems. If you don't know any French get yourself a phrase book. Moroccan Arabic, very different from the 'Classical' Arabic of Egypt or the Gulf, is the main language, though in the mountains most communities speak one of three Berber dialects.

Guide: Without the slightest hint of bias, we would unreservedly recommend *The Rough Guide to Morocco* (Harrap-Columbus, £5.95).

MADEIRA AND THE AZORES

There are no longer any boats sailing from Portugal to Madeira or the Azores, but you can fly to either from Lisbon. The cheapest way is probably to get a week or two's package deal from there.

MADEIRA, a dramatically beautiful, though beachless, volcanic island, has an almost perfect climate year round. But it's more expensive than the mainland, there are large concrete hotels almost everywhere, and tourism is very evidently a major industry.

It costs more to get to **THE AZORES**, but it's likely to prove far more rewarding. The fickleness of the Atlantic climate has kept away most package tourists, and the little group of islands are still a fascinating mirror of rural Portugal in the midst of the ocean. If you can get a flight-only deal there are cheap places to stay in all the islands' main towns, and small boats regularly ply between them.

LANGUAGE

If you have some knowledge of Spanish and/or French you won't have much problem reading Portuguese. Understanding it when it's spoken, though, is not so straightforward: pronunciation is entirely different and at first even the easiest words are hard to distinguish – the sound is more like that of an East European language than of the Romance tongues it has its roots in. If you're stuck, most people will understand Spanish (albeit reluctantly) and in the cities and tourist areas French and English are also widely spoken. Even so, it's well worth the effort to master at least the rudiments, and once you've started to figure out the words it gets a lot easier very quickly.

PRONUNCIATION

The chief difficulty with **pronunciation** is its lack of clarity – consonants tend to be slurred, vowels nasal and often ignored altogether.

The **consonants** are, at least, consistent:

C is soft before E and I, hard otherwise unless it has a cedilla – *açucar* (sugar) is pronounced 'assookar'.

CH is somewhat softer than in English; *Chá* (tea) sounds like Shah.

J is pronounced like the 's' in pleasure, as is **G** except when it comes before a 'hard' vowel (A, O, and U).

LH sounds like 'lyur' (Batalha).

Q is always pronounced as a 'k'.

S before a consonant or at the end of a word becomes 'sh', otherwise it's as in English – Cascais is pronounced 'Kashkaish', Sagres is 'Sahgresh'.

X has the same sound as S – *caixa* (cash desk) is pronounced 'kaisha'.

Vowels are worse – flat and truncated, they're often difficult for English-speaking tongues to get around. The only way to learn is to listen. **Accents**, ã, ô, or é, turn them into longer, more familiar sounds.

When two vowels come together they continue to be enunciated separately except in the case of **EI** and **OU** – which sounds like a and long o respectively.

E at the end of a word is silent unless it has an accent, so that *carne* (meat) is pronounced 'karn', while *café* is much as you'd expect.

The **tilde over Ã or Õ** renders the pronunciation much like the French -an and -on endings only more nasal.

More common is **ÃO** (as in *pão*, bread – *são*, saint – *limão*, lemon), which sounds something like a strangled yelp of 'Ow!' cut off in midstream.

Even if you speak no Portuguese at all there are **a few key words** which can help you out in an enormous number of situations. *Há* (the H is silent) means 'there is' or 'is there?' and can be used for just about anything. Thus: '*Há uma pensão aqui?* (Is there a pension here?), '*Há uma camioneta para . . .?* (Is there a bus to . . .?), or even '*Há um quarto?* (Do you have a room?). More polite, and better in shops or restaurants are '*tem . . .?* (do you have . . .?) or '*queria . . .* (I'd like . . .). And of course there are the old standards 'Do you speak English?' (*Fala Inglês?*) and 'I don't understand' (*Não comprendo*).

LANGUAGE LEARNING MATERIALS

Discovering Portuguese (BBC Books; accompanies the TV series; tapes also available). The best introduction to the language, explaining much about the country and people along the way – the food, phones, emigration, attitudes to the revolution and everyday life. Invaluable as a point of reference.

Harrap's Portuguese Phrasebook (Harrap, £1.65). Again, the best of its kind – straightforward and accurate, with clear phonetic spelling of phrases and a good dictionary section.

PORTUGUESE WORDS AND PHRASES

sim; não	yes; no	agora; mais tarde	now; later
olá; bom dia	hello; good morning	mais; menos	more; less
boa tarde/noite	good afternoon/night	grande; pequeno	big; little
adeus, até logo	goodbye, see you later	aberto; fechado	open; closed
hoje; amanhã	today; tomorrow	senhoras; homens	women; men
por favour/se faz favour	please	lavabo/quarto de banho	restroom (w.c)
está bem	it's all right/OK	banco; câmbio	bank; change
obrigado/a*	thank you	correios	post office
onde; que	where; what	bilhete (para)	ticket (to)
quando; porquê	when; why	ida e volta	round trip
como; quanto	how; how much	(dois) selos	(two) stamps
não sei	I don't know	chave	key
sabe . . .?	do you know . . .?	domingo	Sunday
pode . . .?	could you . . .?	segunda-feira	Monday
desculpe	sorry/excuse me	terça-feira	Tuesday
aqui; ali	here; there	quarta-feira	Wednesday
perto; longe	near; far	quinta-feira	Thursday
este/a; esse/a	this; that	sexta-feira	Friday
		sábado	Saturday

* Obrigado agrees with the sex of the person speaking – a woman says obrigada, a man obrigado.

para ir a . . .?	How do I get to . . .?	queria um quarto	I'd like a room
esquerda, direita, sempre em frente	left, right, straight ahead	é para uma noite (semana)	It's for one night (week)
onde é o estação de camionetas?	Where is the bus station?	é para uma pessoa (duas pessoas)	It's for one person (two people)
a paragem de autocarro para. . .	the bus stop for . . .	posso ver?	May I see/look round?
o estação de comboios	the railway station	está bem, fico com ele	OK, I'll take it
donde parte o autocarro para. . .?	where does the bus to . . . leave from?	quanto custa?	How much is it?
é este o comboio para Coimbra?	Is this the train for Coimbra?	é caro, não o quero	It's expensive, I don't want it
a que horas parte? (chega a)	What time does it leave? (arrive at)	posso/podemos deixar os sacos aqui até . . ?	Can I/we leave the bags here until . . ?
qual é a estrada para. . .?	Which is the road to . . .?	há um quarto mais barato?	Is there a cheaper room?
vou a (para onde vai?)	I'm going to (Where are you going?)	com duche (quente/frio)	With a shower (hot/cold)
está bem, muito obri-gado/a	That's great, thanks a lot	pode-se acampar aqui?	Can we camp here?
pare aqui por favour	Stop here please	o que é isso? quanto e?	What's that? How much is it?
há uma pensão aqui perto?	Is there a pension near here?	como se chama (chamo–me . . .)	What's your name? (my name is . . .)
		sou Ingles/a	I am English
		como se diz isto em Português?	What's this called in Portuguese?

1	um	8	oito	15	quinze	30	trinta	100	cem
2	dois	9	nove	16	dezasseis	40	quarenta	101	cento e um
3	três	10	dez	17	dezassete	50	cinquenta	200	duzentos
4	quatro	11	onze	18	dezoito	60	sessenta	500	quinhentos
5	cinco	12	doze	19	dezanove	70	setenta	1000	mil
6	seis	13	treze	20	vinte	80	oitenta	2000	dois mil
7	sete	14	catorze	21	vinte e um	90	noventa	1,000,000	um milhão

PORTUGUESE TERMS: A GLOSSARY

AFONSINO of the reign of Dom Afonso Henriques, first king of Portugal.

ALAMEDA promenade (also called ESPLANADA along a seafront).

ALBUFEIRA reservoir.

ALDEIA village.

AZULEJO glazed and painted tiles; originally used as geometric decoration around the base of doorways of a church or mansion; by the late sixteenth century whole pictorial blocks were created. From the late seventeenth until the mid-eighteenth century – the main period – tiles were exclusively blue and white.

BAIRRO quarter (of a town); ALTO is upper, BAIXO lower.

BAIXA commercial, shopping centre of town.

CÂMARA MUNICIPAL town hall (also PAÇOS DE CONCELHO).

CAPELA chapel; CAPELA-MOR is a chancel or sanctuary.

CENTRO COMERCIAL large shopping centre, where you can find almost anything.

CHAFARIZ public fountain (also FONTE).

CIDADE city.

CITÂNIA prehistoric/Celtic hill settlement (see *The Minho* chapter).

CLAUSTRO cloister.

CORO central, often enclosed, part of church built for choir.

CORREIO post and telephone office, abbreviated **CTT**.

DOM, DONA courtesy titles (sir, madam) usually applied to kings and queens; INFANTE is prince, INFANTA princess.

ELÉCTRICO tramcar, found in Lisbon and Porto.

ELEVADOR lift or funicular, the most famous of which is in Lisbon – the *Elevador de Santa Justa* designed by Eiffel.

ERMIDA remote chapel – not necessarily a hermitage.

ESTAÇÃO station; . . . DE COMBOIOS railway station; . . . DE AUTOCARROS bus station.

ESTRADA road; ESTRADA NACIONAL is a main road, designated EN on maps.

FEIRA weekly or monthly fair or market.

FESTA festival or carnival, as in Spanish *fiesta*.

GRUTAS caves

HORÁRIO timetable for trains or buses.

IGREJA church; IGREJA MATRIZ parish church.

LAGO lake.

LARGO square.

MANUELINO flamboyant, marine-influenced style of late Gothic architecture developed in the reign of Manuel I (1495–1521).

MERCADO market, often in covered buildings or an enclosure.

MIRADOURO belvedere or viewpoint of any sort.

MOÇÁRABE Moorish-Arabic (usually of architecture or a design).

MOSTEIRO not always a monastery, often an old church (can be CONVENTO instead); most orders were suppressed in 1834–38.

MUDÉJAR Moorish-style architecture and decoration.

NOSSA SENHORA (N.S.) Our Lady – the Virgin Mary.

PAÇO/PALÁCIO palace or country house, not necessarily royal (REAL).

PARQUE NACIONAL National Park – there are several, the most famous of which is Gerês in the north.

PASTELARIA bakery selling *pasteis* (pastry or cakes).

PELOURINHO stone pillory, seen in almost every northern village.

POUSADA luxury state-run hotel, sometimes converted from a castle or monastery; you're free to walk in and look around the main parts.

PRAÇA square (also LARGO and CAMPO); **PRAÇA DE TOUROS** bullring.

PRAIA beach.

QUINTA country estate, or its main house.

RETÁBULO altarpiece – usually large, carved and heavily gilt.

ROMARIA pilgrimage-festival.

SALA DO CAPÍTULO chapter house.

SÉ cathedral.

SENHOR Sir, man, or Mr.; SENHORA woman or Mrs. (MENINA means Miss).

SOLAR manor house or important town mansion.

TORRE DE MENAGEM keep of a castle.

INDEX

HELP US UPDATE

We've gone to a lot of effort to ensure that this new edition of *The Rough Guide To Portugal* is completely up-to-date and accurate. However, things do change – places get 'discovered', opening hours are notoriously fickle – and any suggestions, comments, or corrections would be much appreciated.

We'll credit all contributions, and send a copy of the next edition (or any other Rough Guide if you prefer) for the best letters. Please write to:

Mark Ellingham and John Fisher, The Rough Guides, 149 Kennington Lane, London SE11 4EZ.

Our thanks go to all those who have responded to past appeals to Help us Update,
a list by now far too long to include in its entirety.
So all of you who have been mentioned in the past, thanks once again.
For this latest edition the roll of honour includes, in no particular order:

Steve Avery, Dixon Adams, Tania McLean and Mike Sanders, Bernie Milward, Clare Staines, Mark Sellin, Dick Sharples, Pete Radcliffe and Anne Thompson, Andrew Bell, Odd Karsten Krogh, John Dawson and Brigid Casey, Fiona Hodgkins, Frank and Margaret Connolly, Andy Warren, Christopher Fox, Paul Lee and Dori Rosenblum, James Salmon, Dave Hill and Janet Kirby, Michael Walters, Andrea Robinson, Barbara Smith, Simon Cooper, Nick Maslen and Anne Burrows, Rod Lipscombe, Dr Barrie Jones, Jennifer Wallace, Andrew Hewett, Maria Jose Andrade, Valerie Bailey, Martine Pearcey, Yvonne Furley and Karen Paine, Chris Esmond, Bridget Fin-Klaire, Carole Ball, Cathy Bradley, Ian Jones, Aixa Gaitskell and Andy Kendrick, Nick Stephen, Rose Williams, John Brownlow, Nicola Stephenson, Andrea Fullalore and Nick Bradley, Gail Whitney, Angela Thompson and Jenny Moore, Michael Teesdale, Celia Goldsmith, Wendy Brady, Sylvia Welyczko, Stephen Webster, Caroline Price, Lesley Dewhurst, Donna Sleeman, Janna Letts and Cathy Myers, James Robinson, Nick Goss, A.J. Cragg, Caroline Halston, Noel Yarwood, Judith Burgin, Paul Wrigley, Rob Hale and Lesley Andrews, Mike Alfred, June Higgins, Ann Lamb, Carola Scupham, H.T. Uitermark, Herbert Morel, Paul Farrow, Mike Duley and Tina Randall, Corry Roessingh, Jo Hanson, Andrew Curry, Len Cueston and Hilary White, Magne Høyberget, David Clark, A.R.L. Chivers, Steve Pottinger and Karen Emmanuel, Ian Roberts, Tim Nisbet, Louise Capstick, Jack Causton, Chris Storrs and Anne-Marie Gartland, Tessa vd Schoot, Martin Leaver, Jonathan Spector and Helene Ryding, Monique Nort, Ian Christoplos, Jennie Burrows, Fiona Gosling and Francis Haysom, Mrs I Davies, Peter Sanders, Rodney Paul, Mrs B Colyer, Les Parsons, Marjorie and Tom Freer, Erica Allin, Andrew Neather, Paul Simmons, John Hicks, John Peel, Peter Lewis and Dave Collins, Jennifer Wallace, Nigel Buckle, Vic Smith, Sally Wilton, John Dower, Diana Musgrave, Malcolm James, Chris Richardson and Richard McCance, Michael Frost, Jennifer and Phil Jenkins, Charles Taylor, Nigel Taylor, Geoff Wallis, R.B. Vickery, Mark Smulian, Mrs P Stone, Cathie McTaggart, Mark Azavedo, Pete Smith, S. Cowan, Bill Godby, Lorna Frost, C.A. Linton, B.J. Blackwell, Brian Kingsmill, Dr J Edge, Chris Carnie, Marilyn Jones, Charles Lielbling, Jordan Jarrett, Bruce Pearson, Tim Fuller, Gary Brooks, Tania McLean and Mike Sanders, J.H. Van der Plas, Bente Simonsen, Darren Green and Ruth Lewis, and many more whose signatures we couldn't read or whose names have simply gone missing.